X-FACTOR

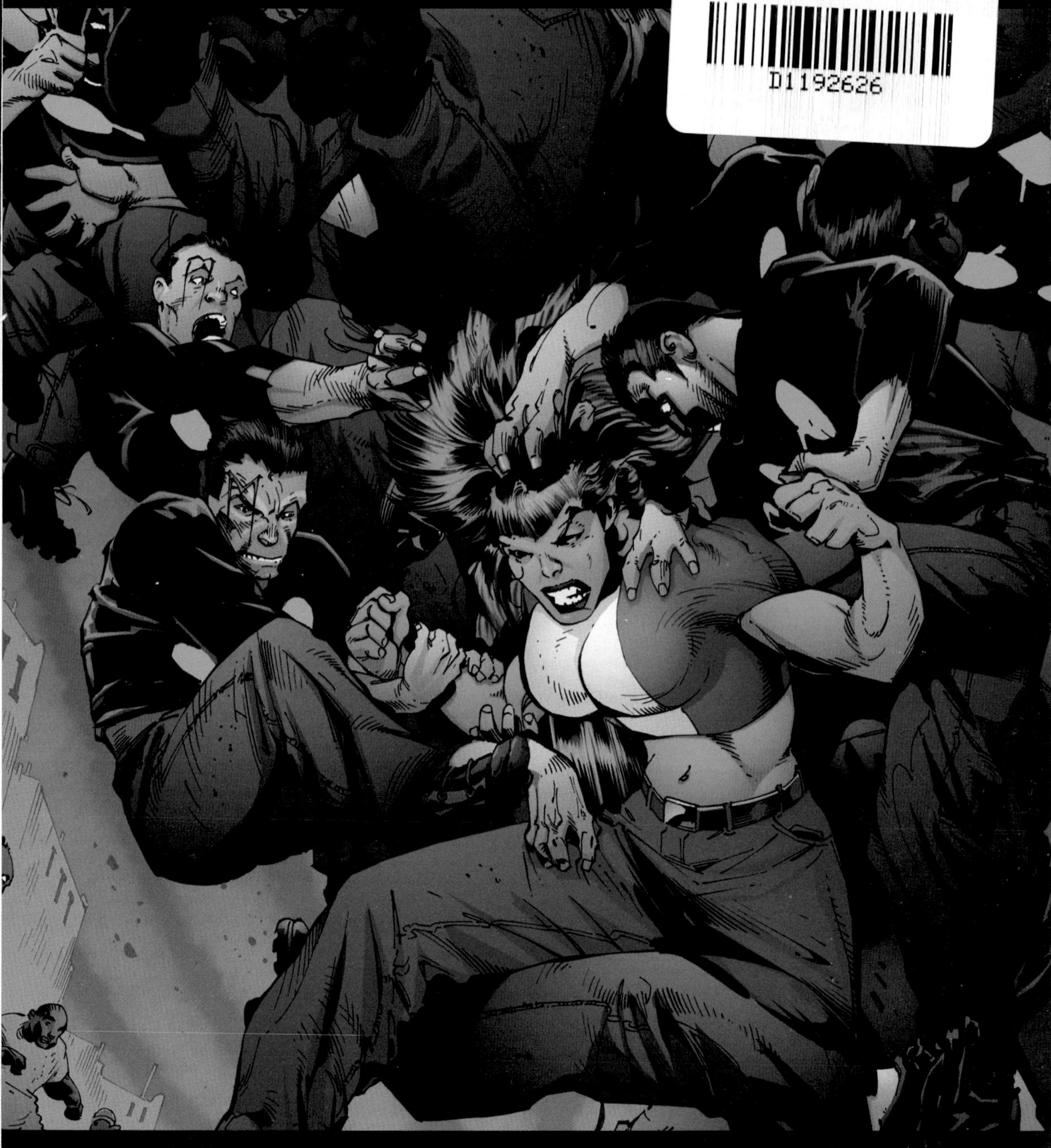

SECRET INVASION

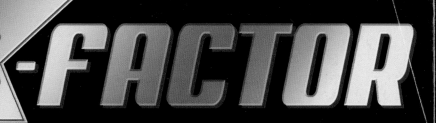

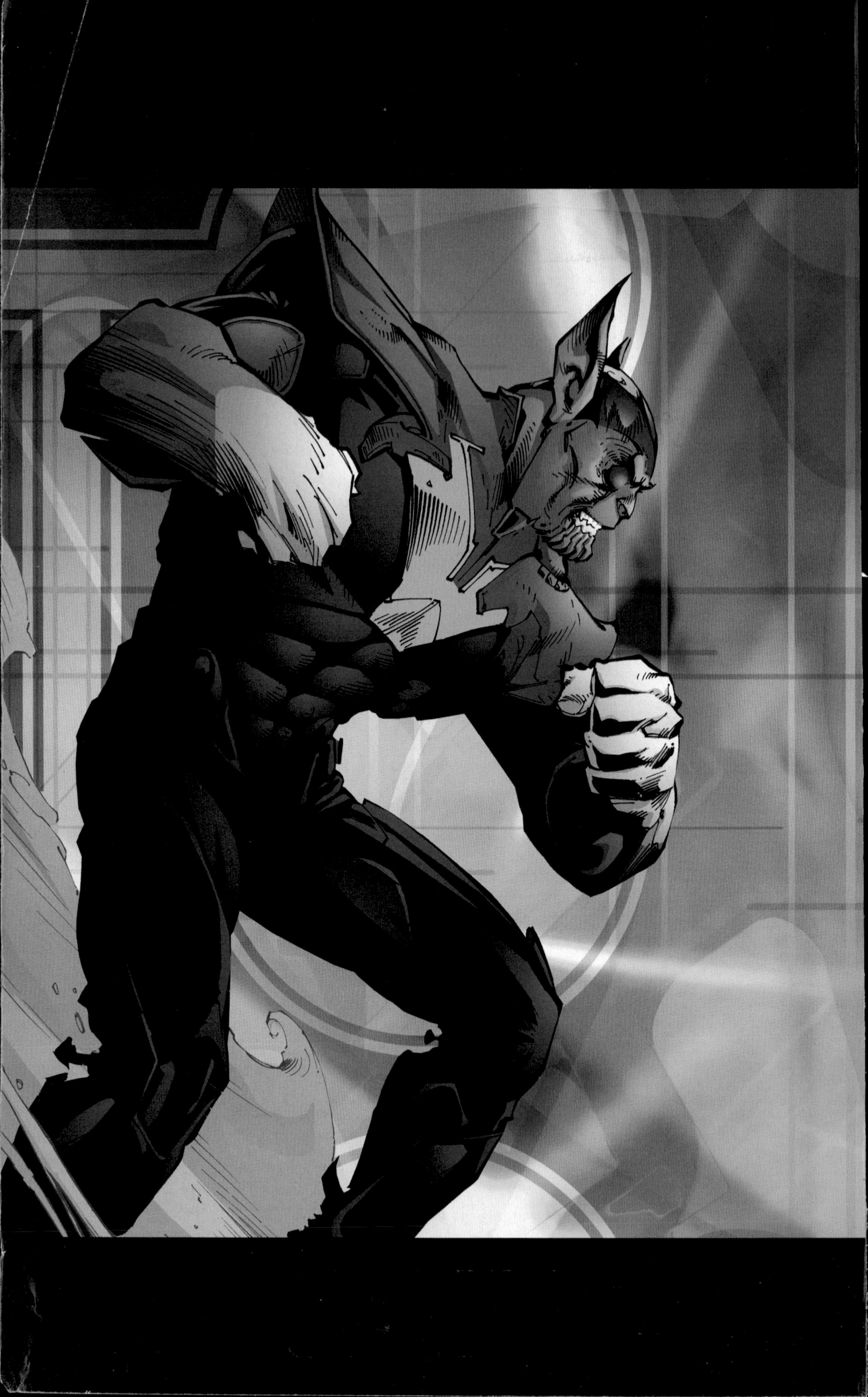

X-FACTOR

SECRET INVASION

Writer: PETER DAVID

X-Factor #33-36:
Penciler: LARRY STROMAN
Inker: JON SIBAL

X-Factor #37:
Penciler: VALENTINE DE LANDRO
Inker: CRAIG YEUNG

X-Factor #38
Penciler: NELSON WITH LARRY STROMAN (PAGES 1-4)
Inker: NELSON WITH JON SIBAL (PAGES 1-4)

Colorist: JEROMY COX WITH ROB SCHWAGER (ISSUE #38)
Letterer: VIRTUAL CALLIGRAPHY'S CORY PETIT
Cover Art: BOO COOK WITH MIKE MAYHEW & ANDY TROY (ISSUE #38)
Assistant Editor: MICHAEL HORWITZ
Editors: WILL PANZO, AUBREY SITTERSON & JOHN BARBER

Collection Editor: JENNIFER GRÜNWALD
Editorial Assistant: ALEX STARBUCK
Assistant Editors: CORY LEVINE & JOHN DENNING
Editor, Special Projects: MARK D. BEAZLEY
Senior Editor, Special Projects: JEFF YOUNGQUIST
Senior Vice President of Sales: DAVID GABRIEL
Vice President of Creative: TOM MARVELLI

Editor in Chief: JOE QUESADA
Publisher: DAN BUCKLEY
Executive Producer: ALAN FINE

She-Hulk #31
Penciler: VINCENZO CUCCA
Inker: VINCENZO ACUNZO
Colorist: BARBARA CIARDO
Team Coordinator: GIULIANO MONNI
Letterer: DAVE SHARPE
Cover Art: MIKE DEODATO & RAIN BEREDO
Assistant Editor: LAUREN SANKOVITCH
Editor: BILL ROSEMANN

WITHDRAWN

Fitchburg Public Library
5530 Lacy Road
Fitchburg, WI 53711

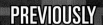

PREVIOUSLY

Having left Mutant Town behind as a smoldering wreck, X-Factor has relocated to Detroit, promptly lowering the property value of Larry Stroman's house. Calling themselves XF Investigations, they have quickly developed a reputation for being the go-to agency for cases that are somewhat unusual. Meanwhile, the team is convinced that they have left the threats of Val Cooper and the O*N*E behind, unaware that Val knows exactly where they are and has been insisting on Madrox's cooperation lest she make XF's life extremely difficult.

#33

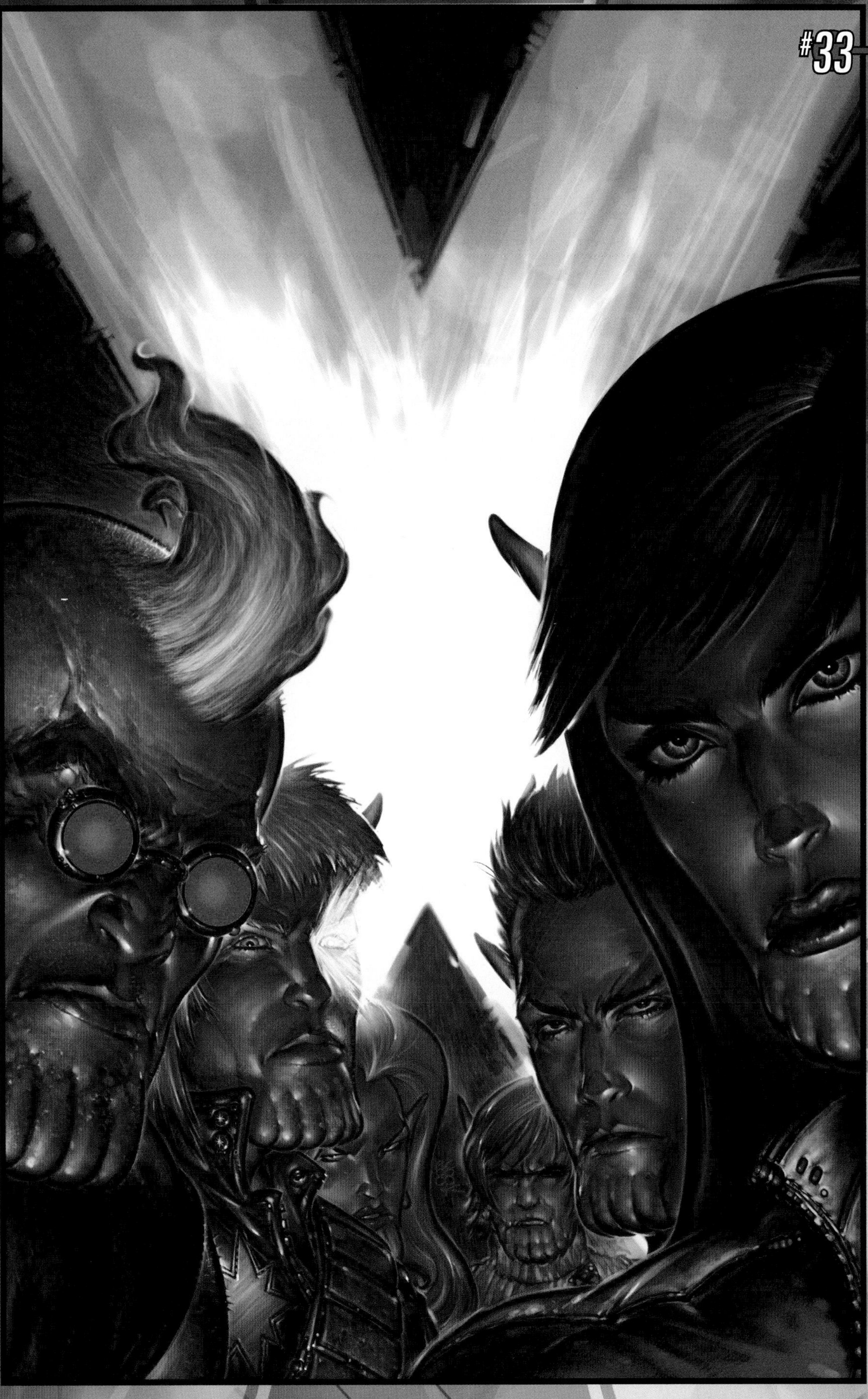

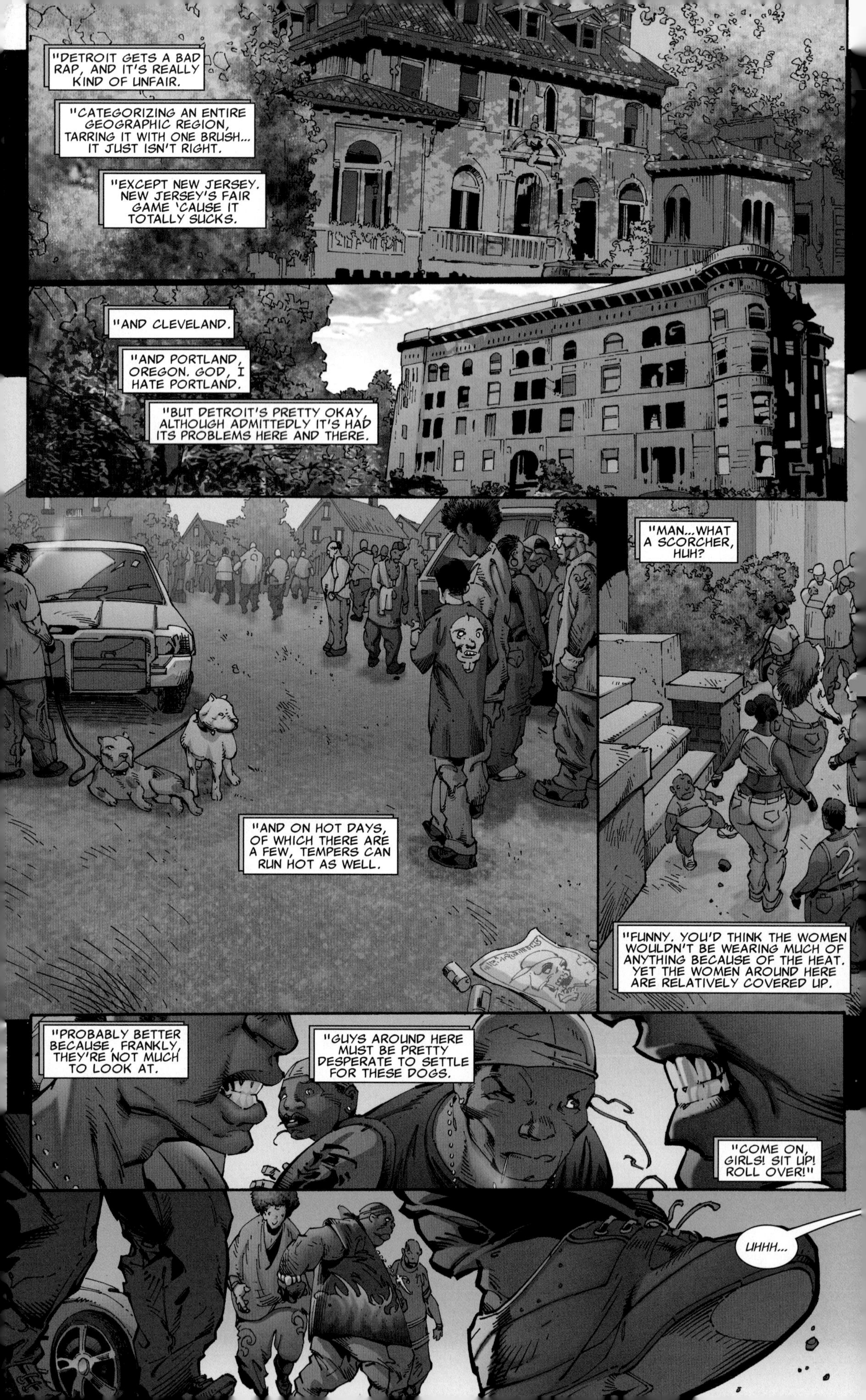
"DETROIT GETS A BAD RAP, AND IT'S REALLY KIND OF UNFAIR.
"CATEGORIZING AN ENTIRE GEOGRAPHIC REGION, TARRING IT WITH ONE BRUSH... IT JUST ISN'T RIGHT.
"EXCEPT NEW JERSEY. NEW JERSEY'S FAIR GAME 'CAUSE IT TOTALLY SUCKS.
"AND CLEVELAND.
"AND PORTLAND, OREGON. GOD, I HATE PORTLAND.
"BUT DETROIT'S PRETTY OKAY, ALTHOUGH ADMITTEDLY IT'S HAD ITS PROBLEMS HERE AND THERE.
"AND ON HOT DAYS, OF WHICH THERE ARE A FEW, TEMPERS CAN RUN HOT AS WELL.
"MAN...WHAT A SCORCHER, HUH?
"FUNNY. YOU'D THINK THE WOMEN WOULDN'T BE WEARING MUCH OF ANYTHING BECAUSE OF THE HEAT. YET THE WOMEN AROUND HERE ARE RELATIVELY COVERED UP.
"PROBABLY BETTER BECAUSE, FRANKLY, THEY'RE NOT MUCH TO LOOK AT.
"GUYS AROUND HERE MUST BE PRETTY DESPERATE TO SETTLE FOR THESE DOGS.
"COME ON, GIRLS! SIT UP! ROLL OVER!"
UHHH...

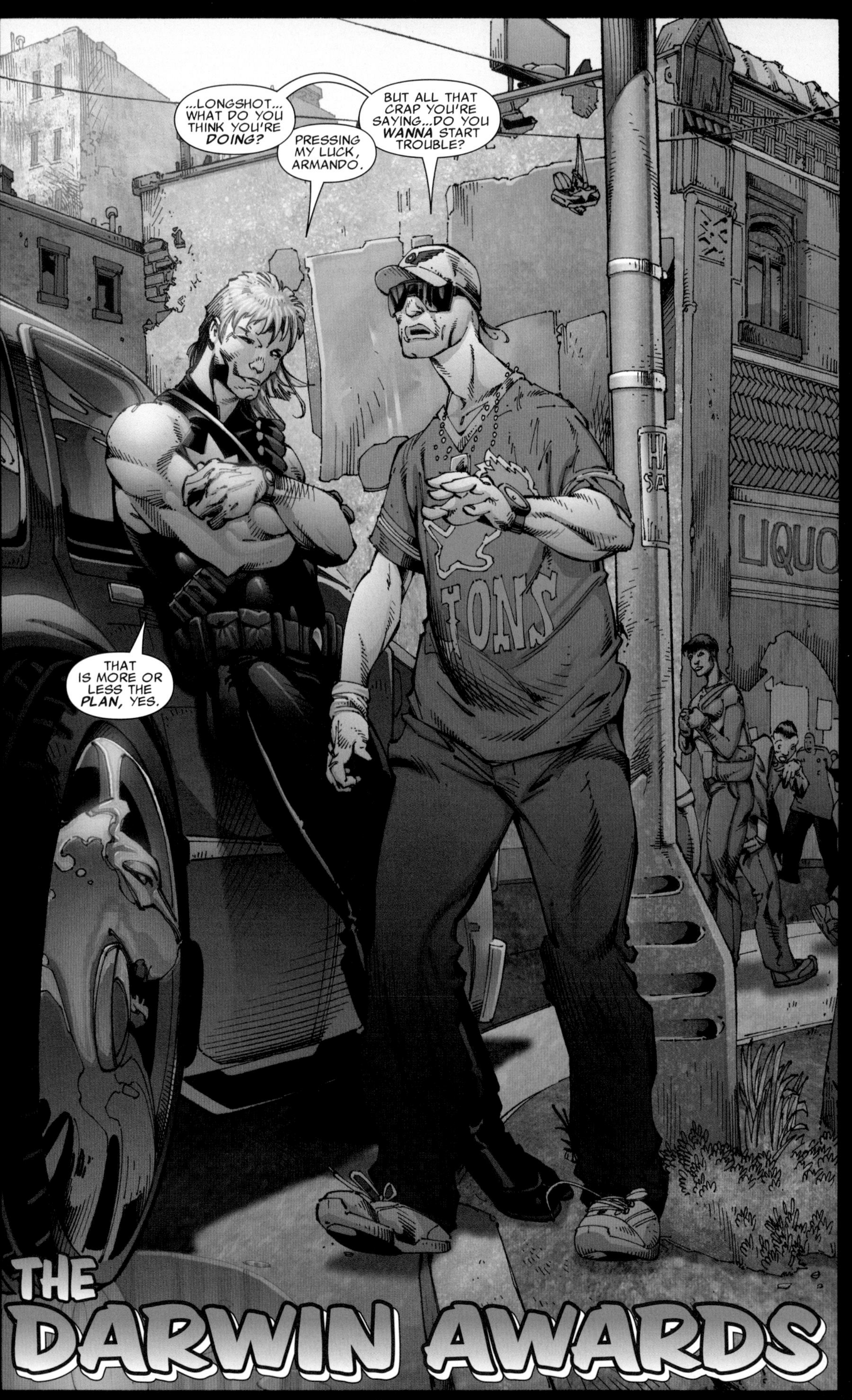
...LONGSHOT... WHAT DO YOU THINK YOU'RE DOING?
BUT ALL THAT CRAP YOU'RE SAYING...DO YOU WANNA START TROUBLE?
PRESSING MY LUCK, ARMANDO.
THAT IS MORE OR LESS THE PLAN, YES.
LIQUO
THE DARWIN AWARDS

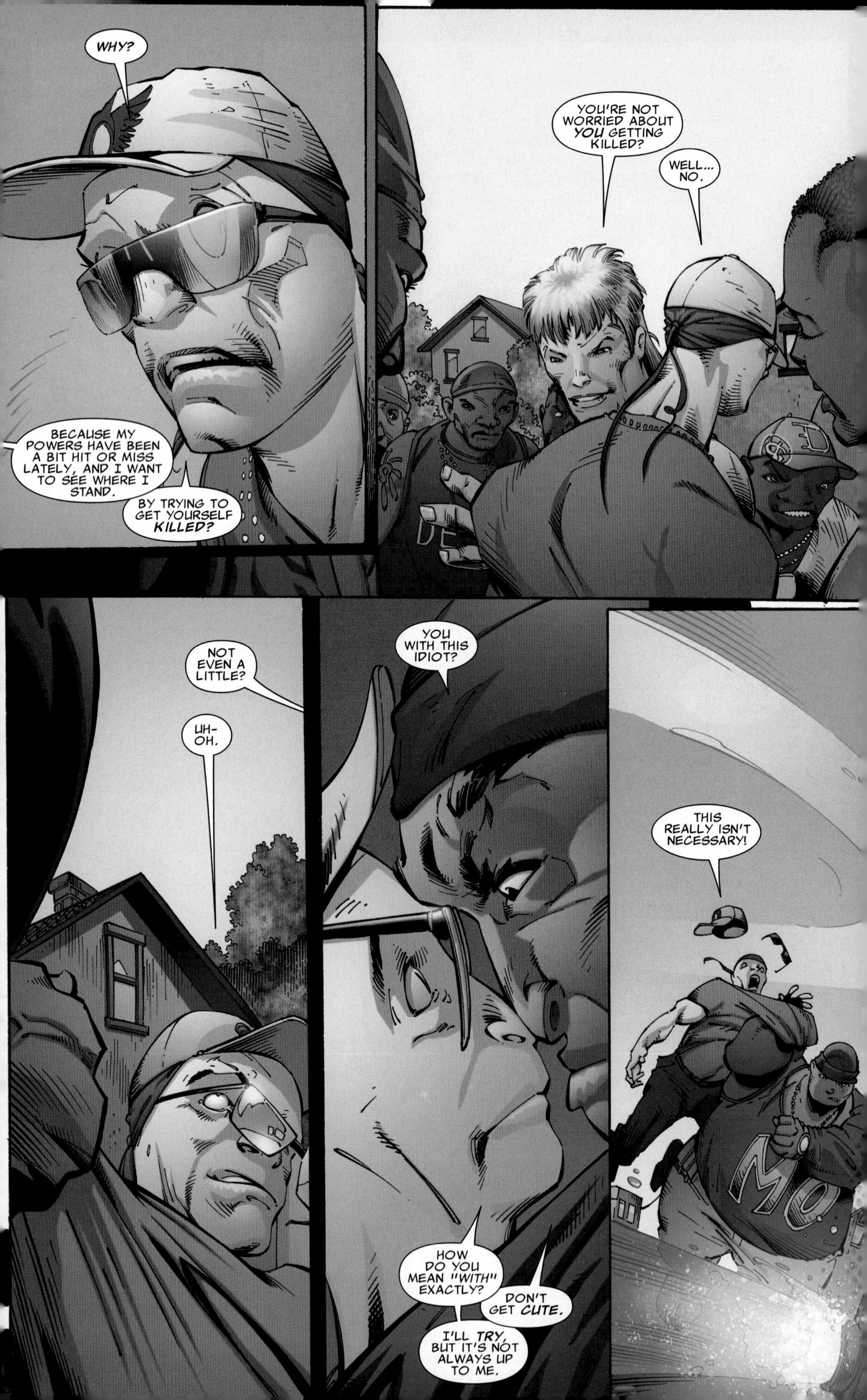
WHY?
BECAUSE MY POWERS HAVE BEEN A BIT HIT OR MISS LATELY, AND I WANT TO SEE WHERE I STAND.
BY TRYING TO GET YOURSELF KILLED?
YOU'RE NOT WORRIED ABOUT YOU GETTING KILLED?
WELL... NO.
NOT EVEN A LITTLE?
UH-OH.
YOU WITH THIS IDIOT?
HOW DO YOU MEAN "WITH" EXACTLY?
DON'T GET CUTE.
I'LL TRY, BUT IT'S NOT ALWAYS UP TO ME.
THIS REALLY ISN'T NECESSARY!

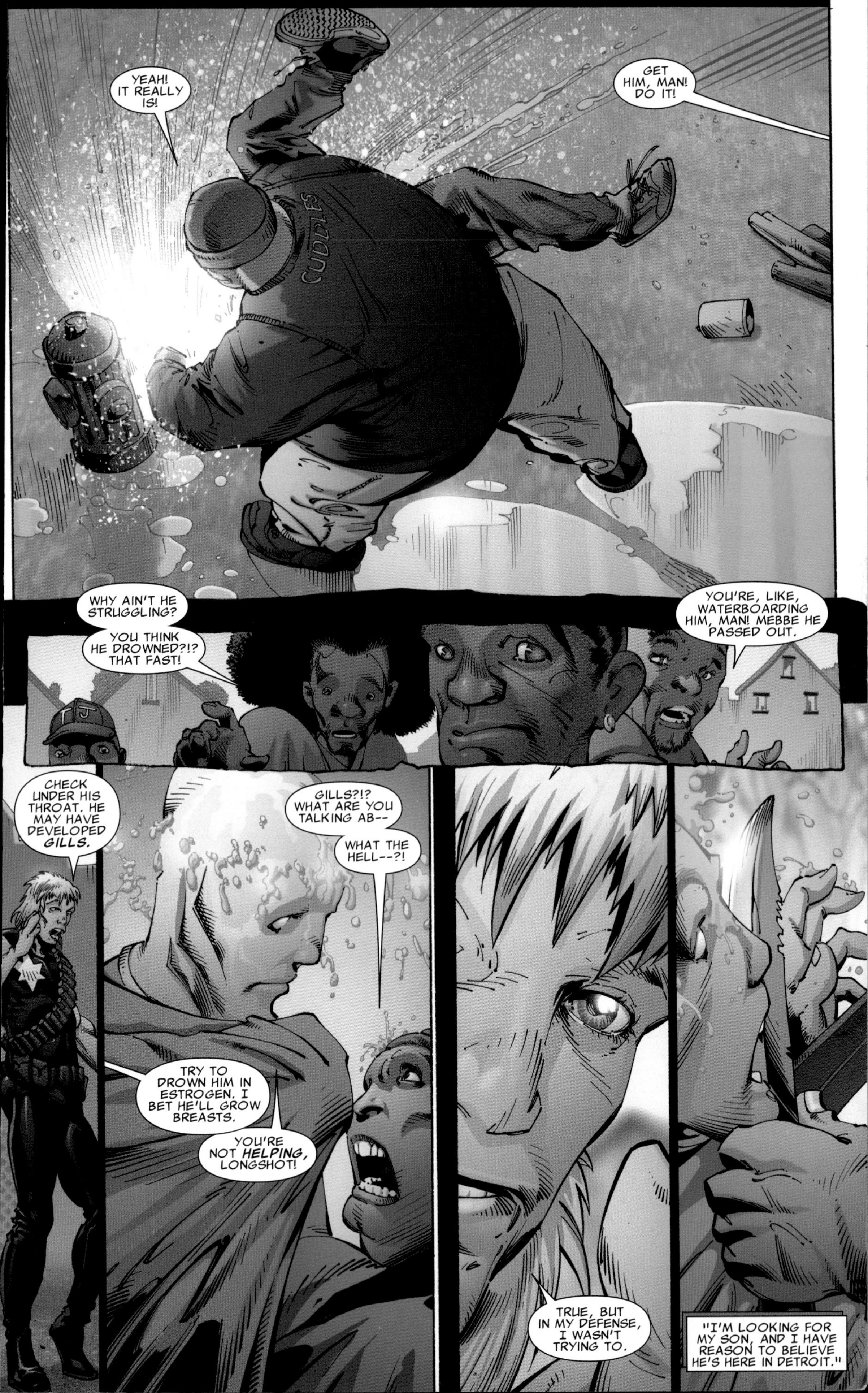
YEAH! IT REALLY IS!
GET HIM, MAN! DO IT!
CUDDLES
WHY AIN'T HE STRUGGLING?
YOU THINK HE DROWNED?!? THAT FAST!
YOU'RE, LIKE, WATERBOARDING HIM, MAN! MEBBE HE PASSED OUT.
TJ
CHECK UNDER HIS THROAT. HE MAY HAVE DEVELOPED *GILLS.*
GILLS?!? WHAT ARE YOU TALKING AB--
WHAT THE HELL--?!
TRY TO DROWN HIM IN ESTROGEN. I BET HE'LL GROW BREASTS.
YOU'RE NOT *HELPING,* LONGSHOT!
TRUE, BUT IN MY DEFENSE, I WASN'T TRYING TO.
"I'M LOOKING FOR MY SON, AND I HAVE REASON TO BELIEVE HE'S HERE IN DETROIT."

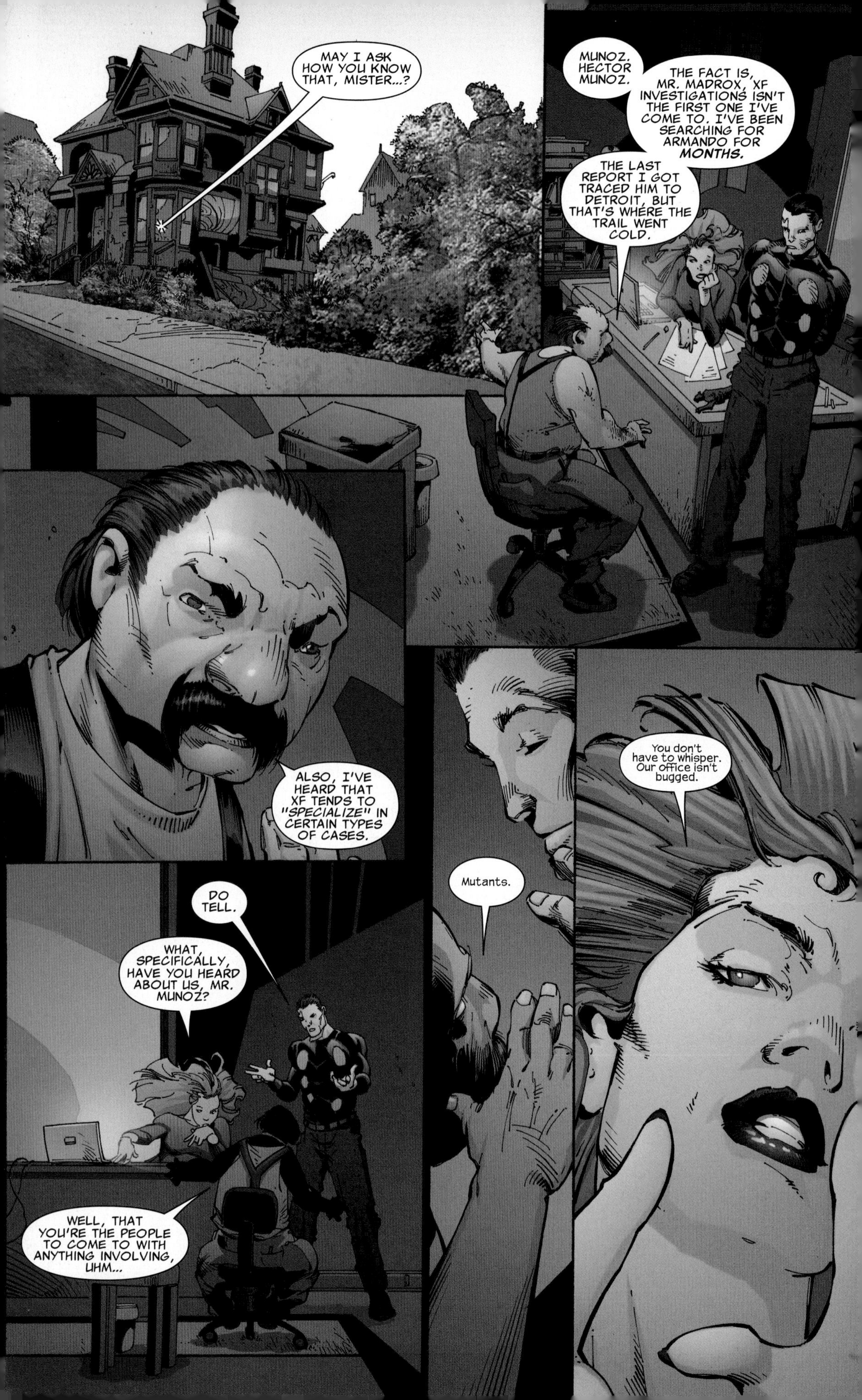
MAY I ASK HOW YOU KNOW THAT, MISTER...?
MUNOZ. HECTOR MUNOZ.
THE FACT IS, MR. MADROX, XF INVESTIGATIONS ISN'T THE FIRST ONE I'VE COME TO. I'VE BEEN SEARCHING FOR ARMANDO FOR MONTHS.
THE LAST REPORT I GOT TRACED HIM TO DETROIT, BUT THAT'S WHERE THE TRAIL WENT COLD.
ALSO, I'VE HEARD THAT XF TENDS TO "SPECIALIZE" IN CERTAIN TYPES OF CASES.
DO TELL.
WHAT, SPECIFICALLY, HAVE YOU HEARD ABOUT US, MR. MUNOZ?
WELL, THAT YOU'RE THE PEOPLE TO COME TO WITH ANYTHING INVOLVING, UHM...
Mutants.
You don't have to whisper. Our office isn't bugged.

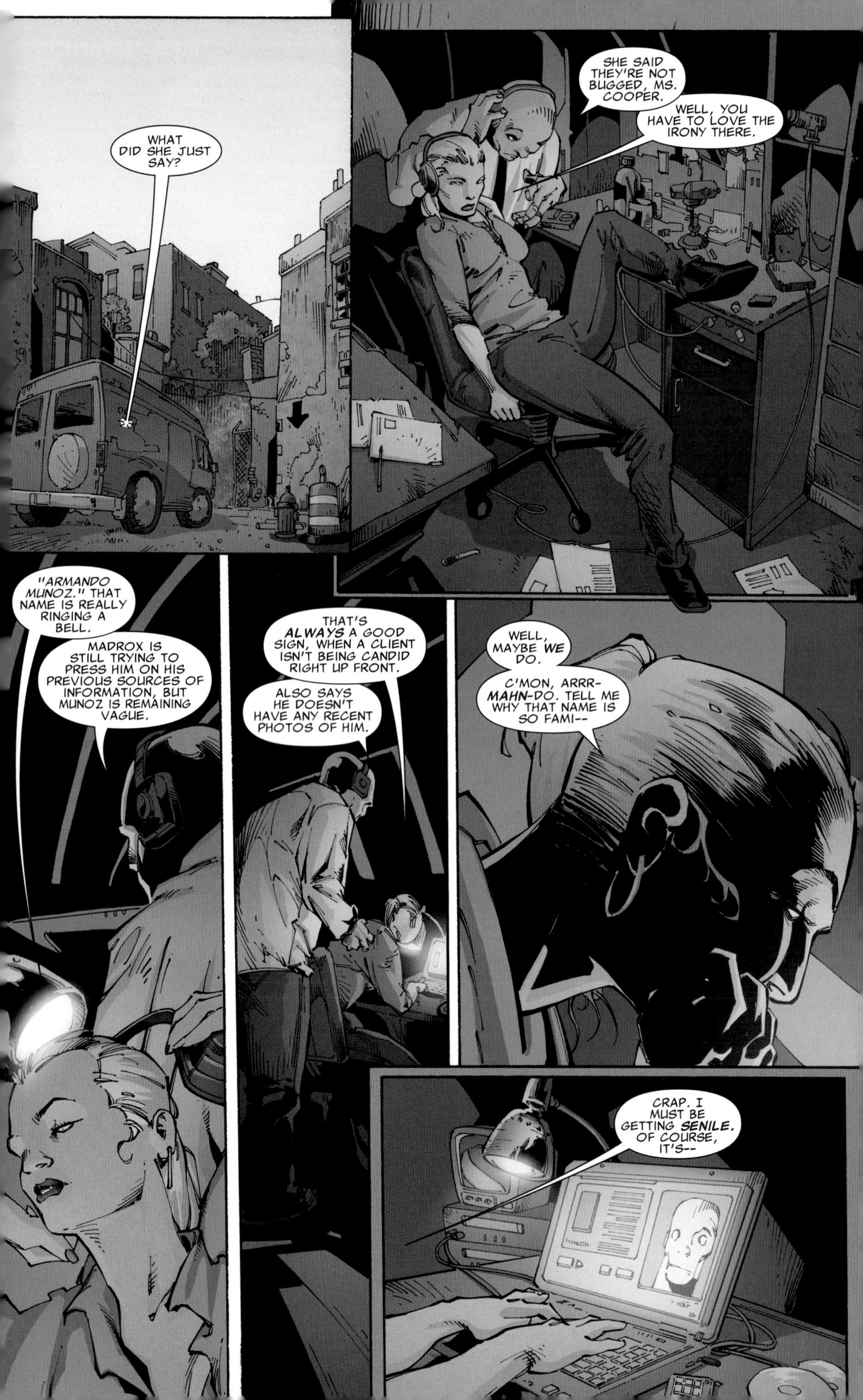
WHAT DID SHE JUST SAY?
SHE SAID THEY'RE NOT BUGGED, MS. COOPER.
WELL, YOU HAVE TO LOVE THE IRONY THERE.
"ARMANDO MUNOZ." THAT NAME IS REALLY RINGING A BELL.
MADROX IS STILL TRYING TO PRESS HIM ON HIS PREVIOUS SOURCES OF INFORMATION, BUT MUNOZ IS REMAINING VAGUE.
THAT'S ALWAYS A GOOD SIGN, WHEN A CLIENT ISN'T BEING CANDID RIGHT UP FRONT.
ALSO SAYS HE DOESN'T HAVE ANY RECENT PHOTOS OF HIM.
WELL, MAYBE WE DO.
C'MON, ARRR-MAHN-DO. TELL ME WHY THAT NAME IS SO FAMI--
CRAP. I MUST BE GETTING SENILE. OF COURSE, IT'S--

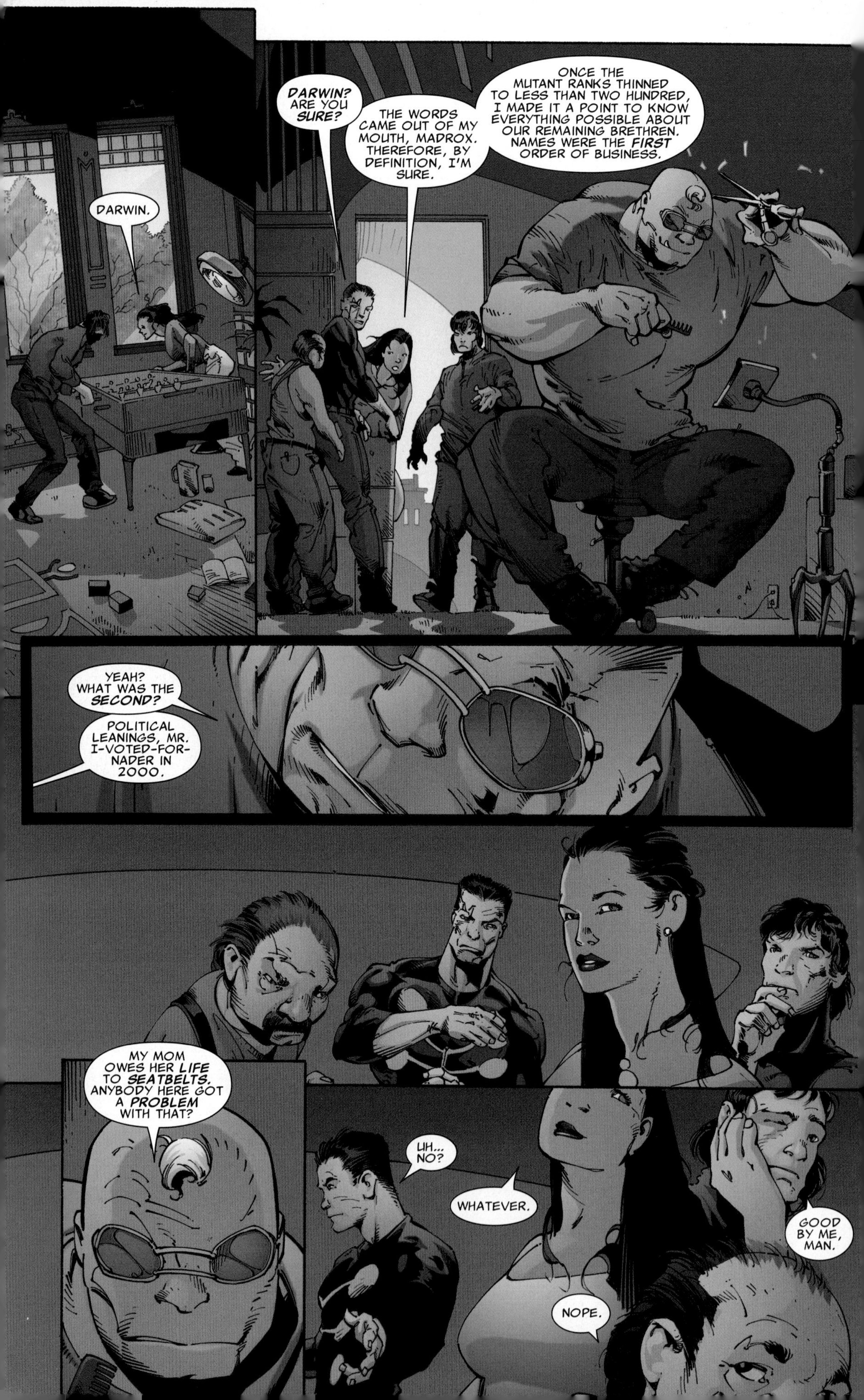

DARWIN.
DARWIN? ARE YOU SURE?
THE WORDS CAME OUT OF MY MOUTH, MADROX. THEREFORE, BY DEFINITION, I'M SURE.
ONCE THE MUTANT RANKS THINNED TO LESS THAN TWO HUNDRED, I MADE IT A POINT TO KNOW EVERYTHING POSSIBLE ABOUT OUR REMAINING BRETHREN. NAMES WERE THE FIRST ORDER OF BUSINESS.
YEAH? WHAT WAS THE SECOND?
POLITICAL LEANINGS, MR. I-VOTED-FOR-NADER IN 2000.
MY MOM OWES HER LIFE TO SEATBELTS. ANYBODY HERE GOT A PROBLEM WITH THAT?
UH... NO?
WHATEVER.
GOOD BY ME, MAN.
NOPE.

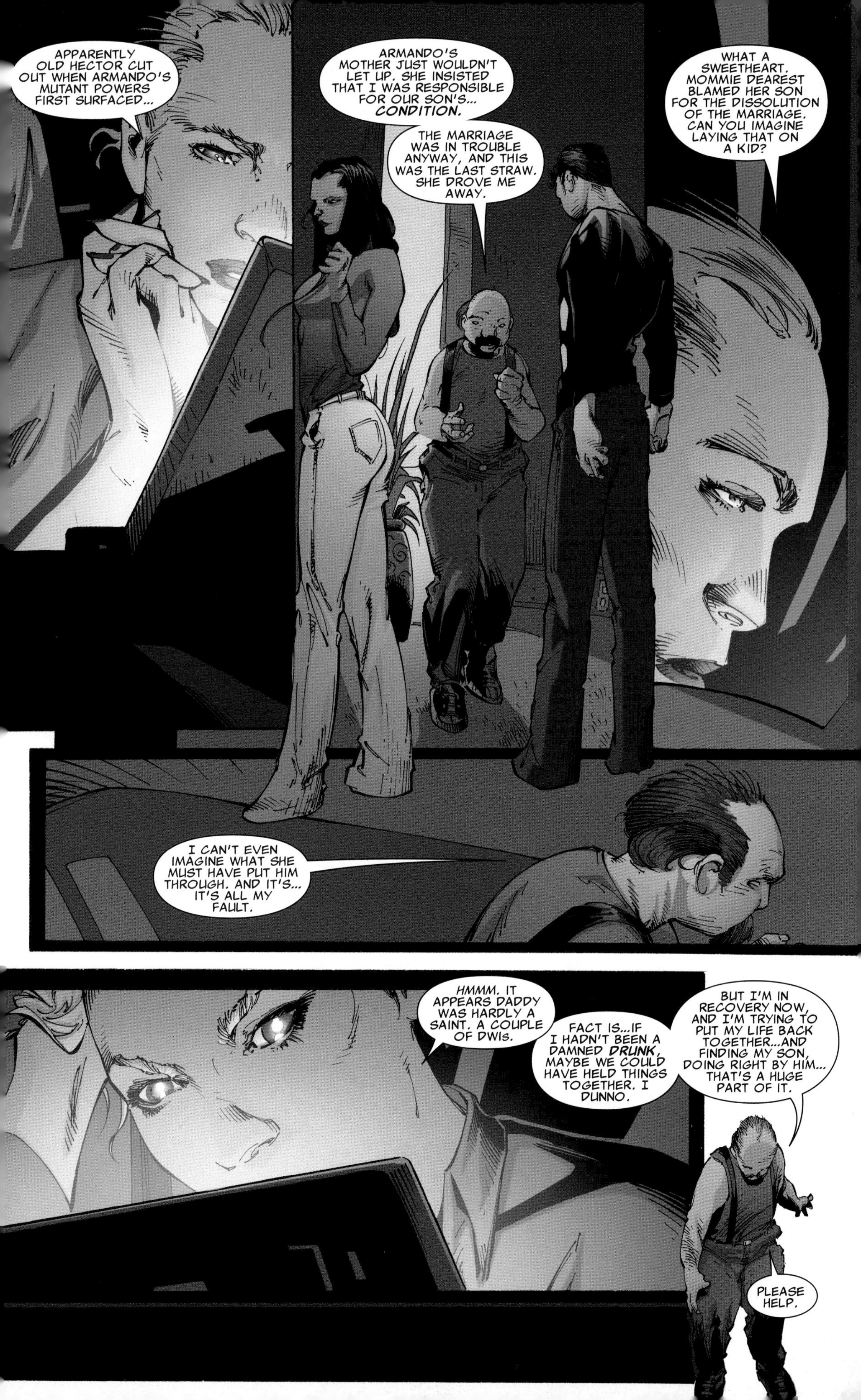
APPARENTLY OLD HECTOR CUT OUT WHEN ARMANDO'S MUTANT POWERS FIRST SURFACED...
ARMANDO'S MOTHER JUST WOULDN'T LET UP. SHE INSISTED THAT I WAS RESPONSIBLE FOR OUR SON'S... CONDITION.
THE MARRIAGE WAS IN TROUBLE ANYWAY, AND THIS WAS THE LAST STRAW. SHE DROVE ME AWAY.
WHAT A SWEETHEART. MOMMIE DEAREST BLAMED HER SON FOR THE DISSOLUTION OF THE MARRIAGE. CAN YOU IMAGINE LAYING THAT ON A KID?
I CAN'T EVEN IMAGINE WHAT SHE MUST HAVE PUT HIM THROUGH. AND IT'S... IT'S ALL MY FAULT.
HMMM. IT APPEARS DADDY WAS HARDLY A SAINT. A COUPLE OF DWIs.
FACT IS...IF I HADN'T BEEN A DAMNED DRUNK, MAYBE WE COULD HAVE HELD THINGS TOGETHER. I DUNNO.
BUT I'M IN RECOVERY NOW, AND I'M TRYING TO PUT MY LIFE BACK TOGETHER...AND FINDING MY SON, DOING RIGHT BY HIM... THAT'S A HUGE PART OF IT.
PLEASE HELP.

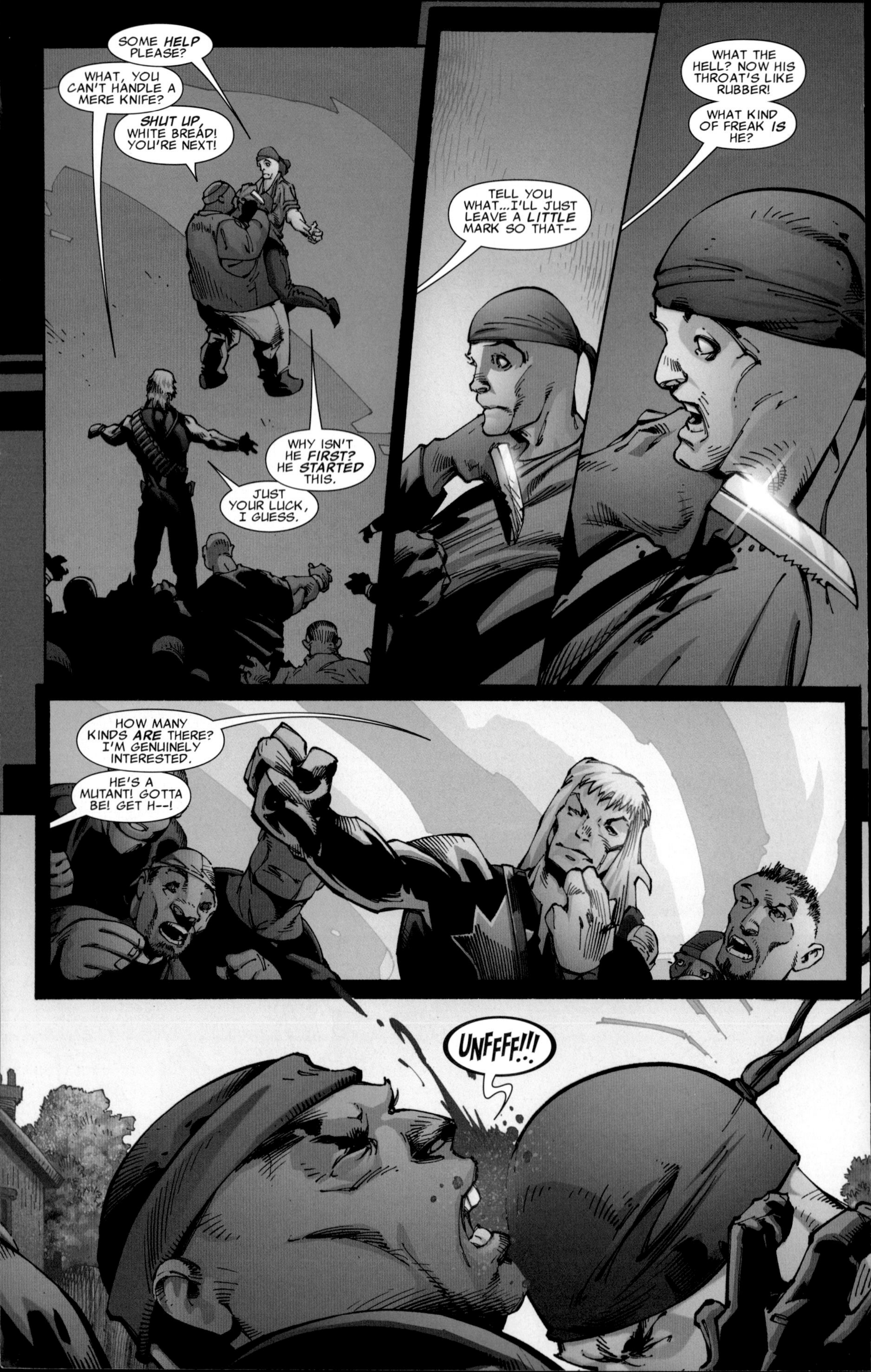
SOME HELP PLEASE?
WHAT, YOU CAN'T HANDLE A MERE KNIFE?
SHUT UP, WHITE BREAD! YOU'RE NEXT!
WHY ISN'T HE FIRST? HE STARTED THIS.
JUST YOUR LUCK, I GUESS.
TELL YOU WHAT...I'LL JUST LEAVE A LITTLE MARK SO THAT--
WHAT THE HELL? NOW HIS THROAT'S LIKE RUBBER!
WHAT KIND OF FREAK IS HE?
HOW MANY KINDS ARE THERE? I'M GENUINELY INTERESTED.
HE'S A MUTANT! GOTTA BE! GET H--!
UNFFFF!!!

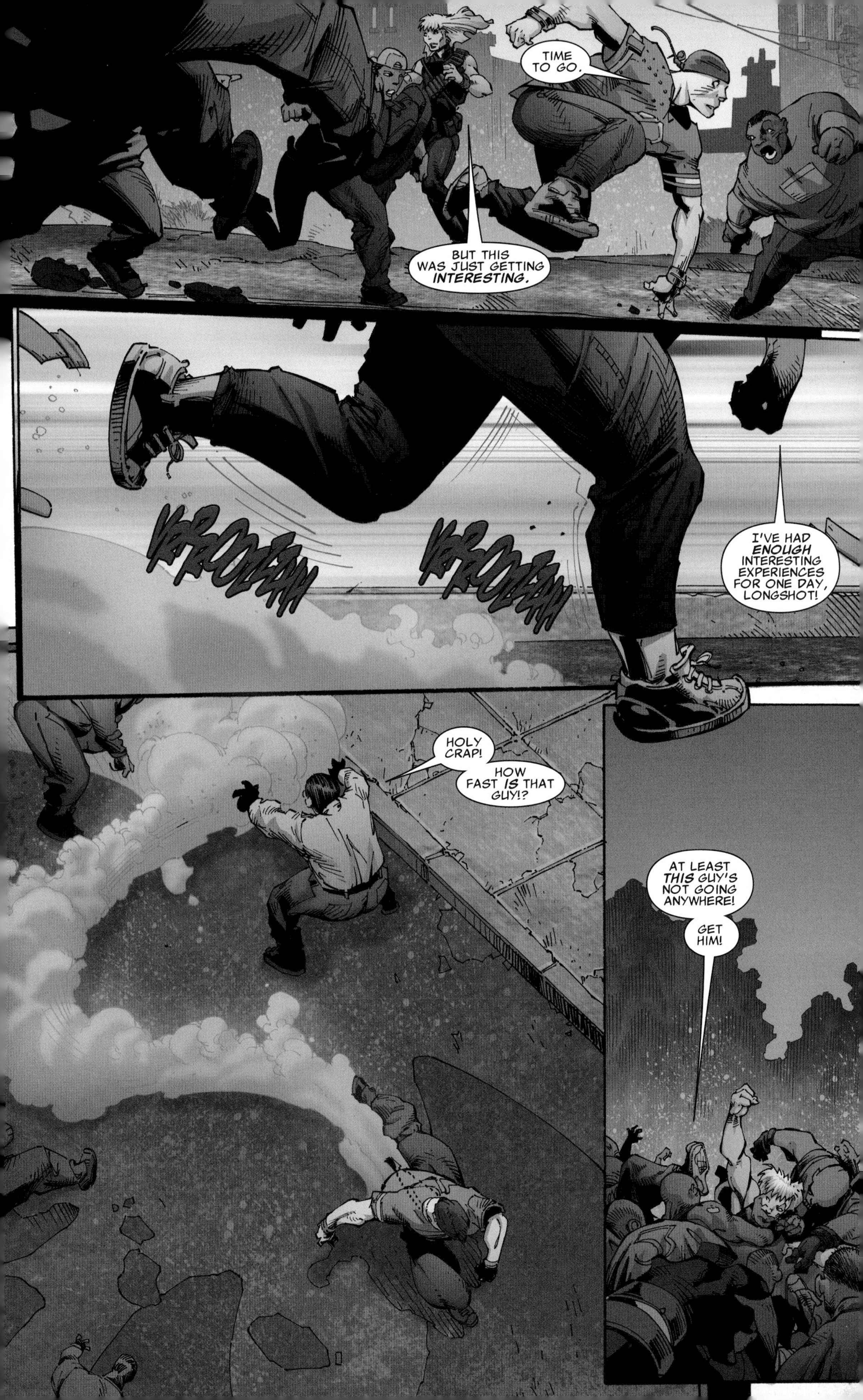
TIME TO GO.
BUT THIS WAS JUST GETTING INTERESTING.
VRROOOM
VRROOOM
I'VE HAD ENOUGH INTERESTING EXPERIENCES FOR ONE DAY, LONGSHOT!
HOLY CRAP!
HOW FAST IS THAT GUY!?
AT LEAST THIS GUY'S NOT GOING ANYWHERE!
GET HIM!

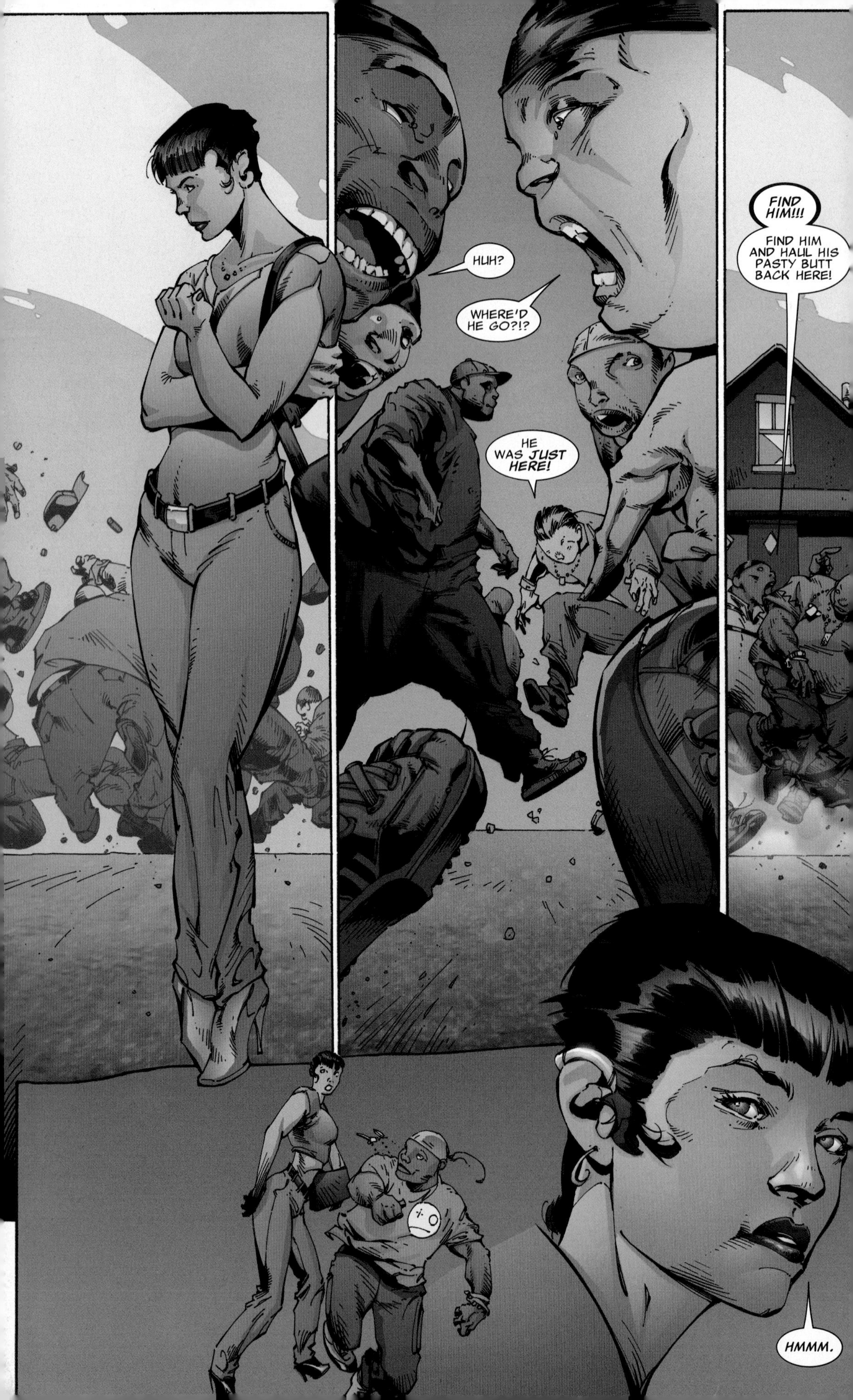
HUH?
WHERE'D HE GO?!?
HE WAS JUST HERE!
FIND HIM!!!
FIND HIM AND HAUL HIS PASTY BUTT BACK HERE!
HMMM.

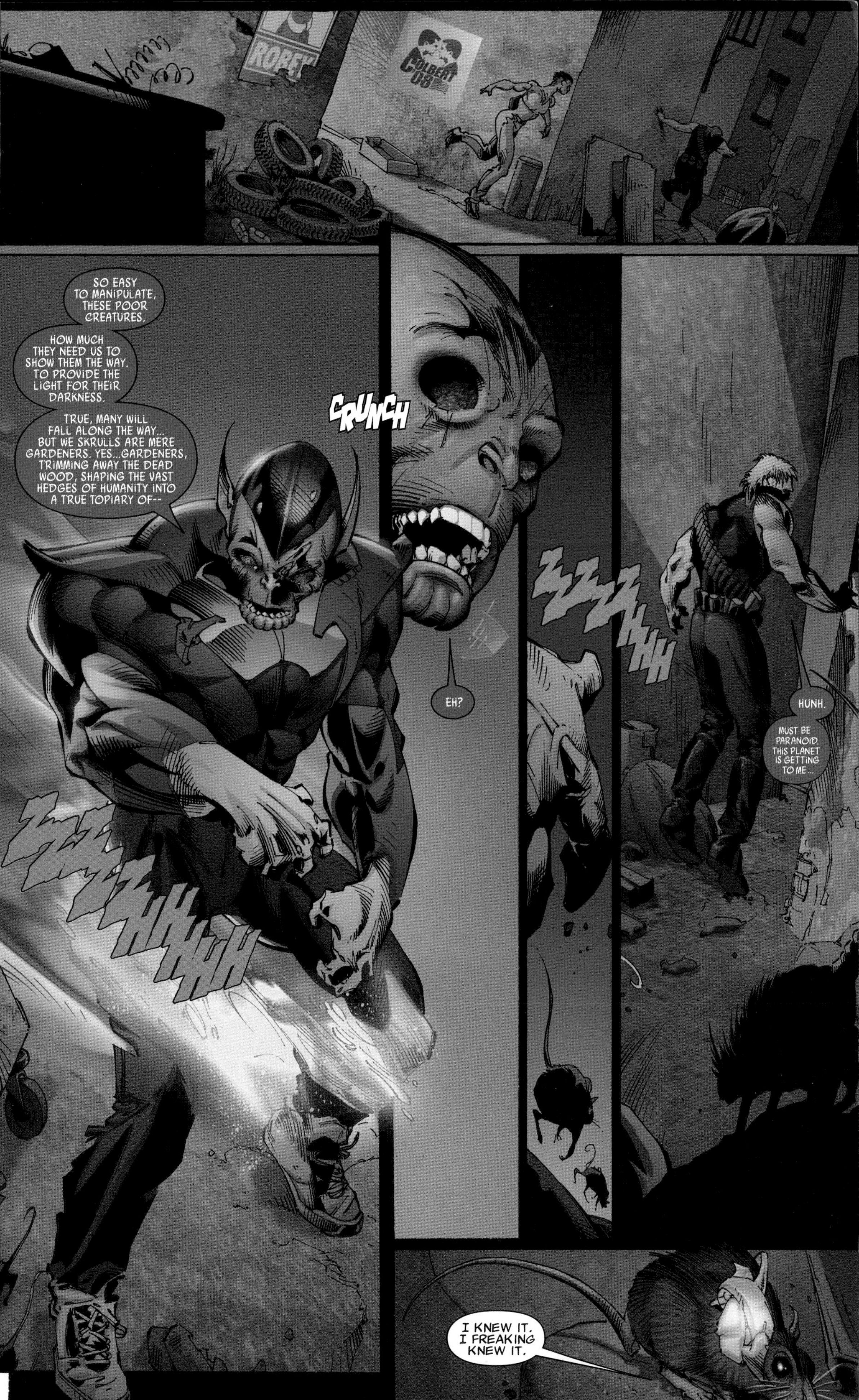
ROBEY
COLBERT '08
SO EASY TO MANIPULATE, THESE POOR CREATURES.
HOW MUCH THEY NEED US TO SHOW THEM THE WAY. TO PROVIDE THE LIGHT FOR THEIR DARKNESS.
TRUE, MANY WILL FALL ALONG THE WAY... BUT WE SKRULLS ARE MERE GARDENERS. YES...GARDENERS, TRIMMING AWAY THE DEAD WOOD, SHAPING THE VAST HEDGES OF HUMANITY INTO A TRUE TOPIARY OF--
CRUNCH
ZZZZHHHHH
EH?
ZZZZHHH
HUNH.
MUST BE PARANOID. THIS PLANET IS GETTING TO ME...
I KNEW IT. I FREAKING KNEW IT.

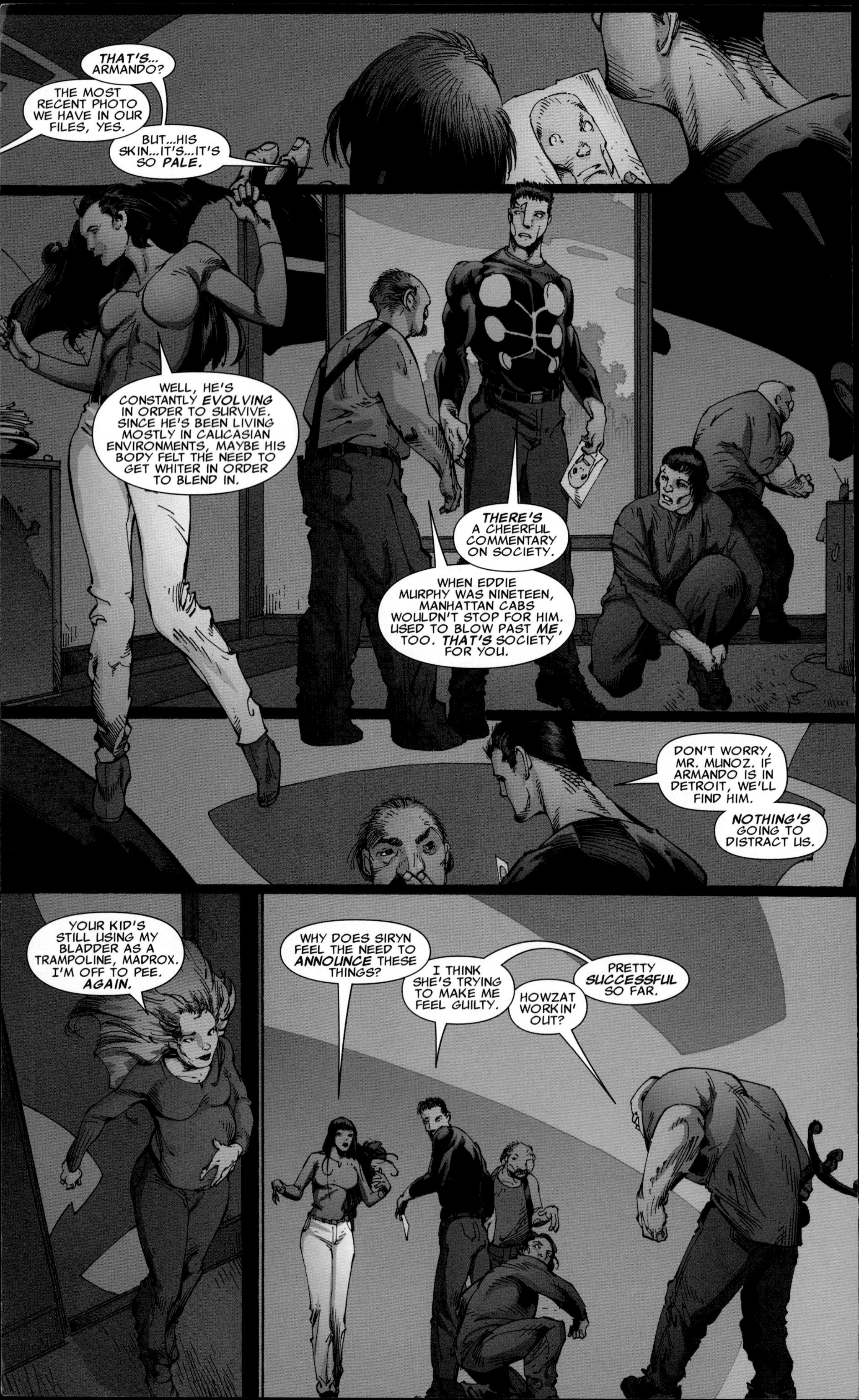
THAT'S... ARMANDO?
THE MOST RECENT PHOTO WE HAVE IN OUR FILES, YES.
BUT...HIS SKIN...IT'S...IT'S SO PALE.
WELL, HE'S CONSTANTLY EVOLVING IN ORDER TO SURVIVE. SINCE HE'S BEEN LIVING MOSTLY IN CAUCASIAN ENVIRONMENTS, MAYBE HIS BODY FELT THE NEED TO GET WHITER IN ORDER TO BLEND IN.
THERE'S A CHEERFUL COMMENTARY ON SOCIETY.
WHEN EDDIE MURPHY WAS NINETEEN, MANHATTAN CABS WOULDN'T STOP FOR HIM. USED TO BLOW PAST ME, TOO. THAT'S SOCIETY FOR YOU.
DON'T WORRY, MR. MUNOZ. IF ARMANDO IS IN DETROIT, WE'LL FIND HIM.
NOTHING'S GOING TO DISTRACT US.
YOUR KID'S STILL USING MY BLADDER AS A TRAMPOLINE, MADROX. I'M OFF TO PEE. AGAIN.
WHY DOES SIRYN FEEL THE NEED TO ANNOUNCE THESE THINGS?
I THINK SHE'S TRYING TO MAKE ME FEEL GUILTY.
HOWZAT WORKIN' OUT?
PRETTY SUCCESSFUL SO FAR.

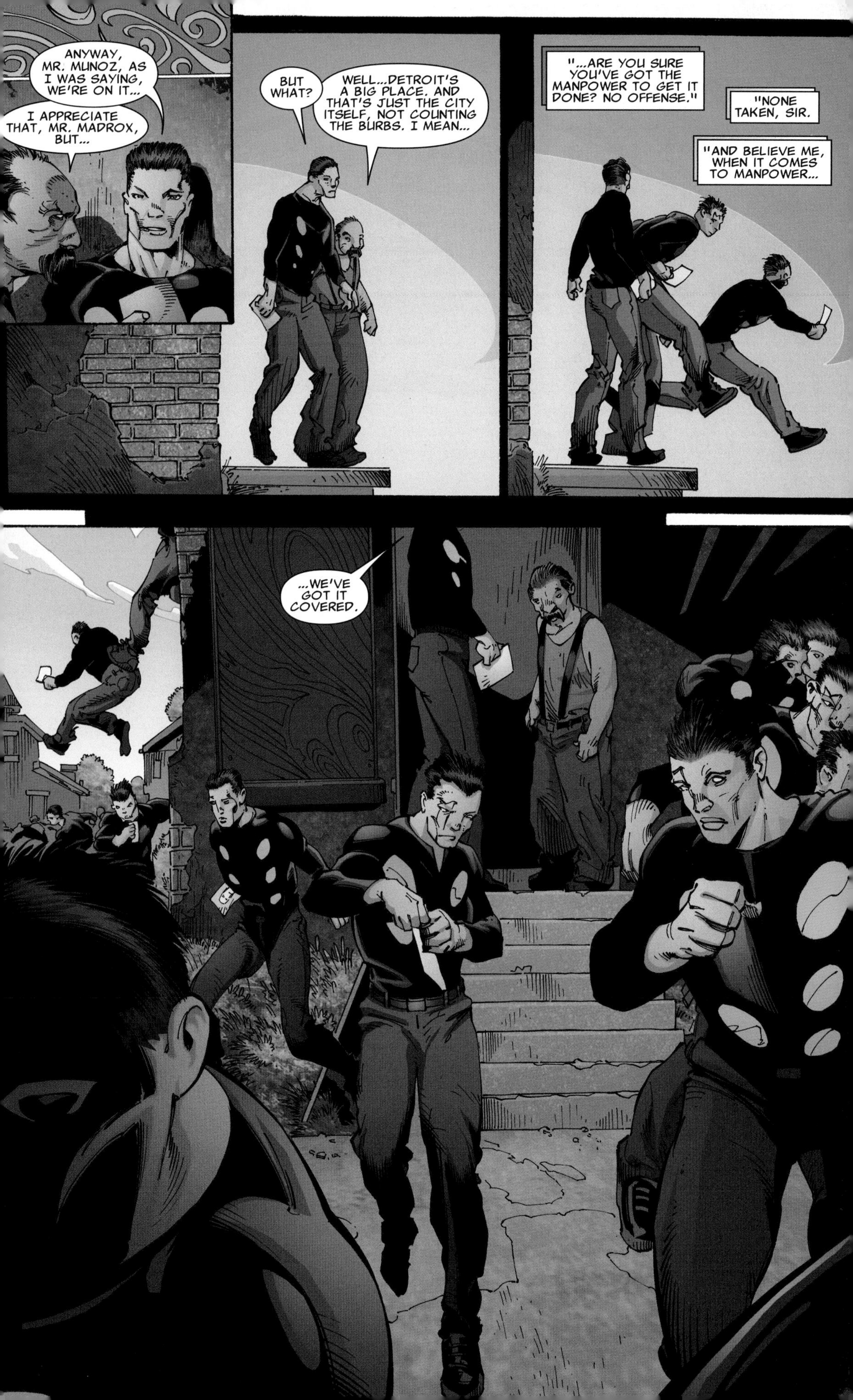
ANYWAY, MR. MUNOZ, AS I WAS SAYING, WE'RE ON IT...
I APPRECIATE THAT, MR. MADROX, BUT...
BUT WHAT?
WELL...DETROIT'S A BIG PLACE. AND THAT'S JUST THE CITY ITSELF, NOT COUNTING THE BURBS. I MEAN...
"...ARE YOU SURE YOU'VE GOT THE MANPOWER TO GET IT DONE? NO OFFENSE."
"NONE TAKEN, SIR.
"AND BELIEVE ME, WHEN IT COMES TO MANPOWER...
...WE'VE GOT IT COVERED.

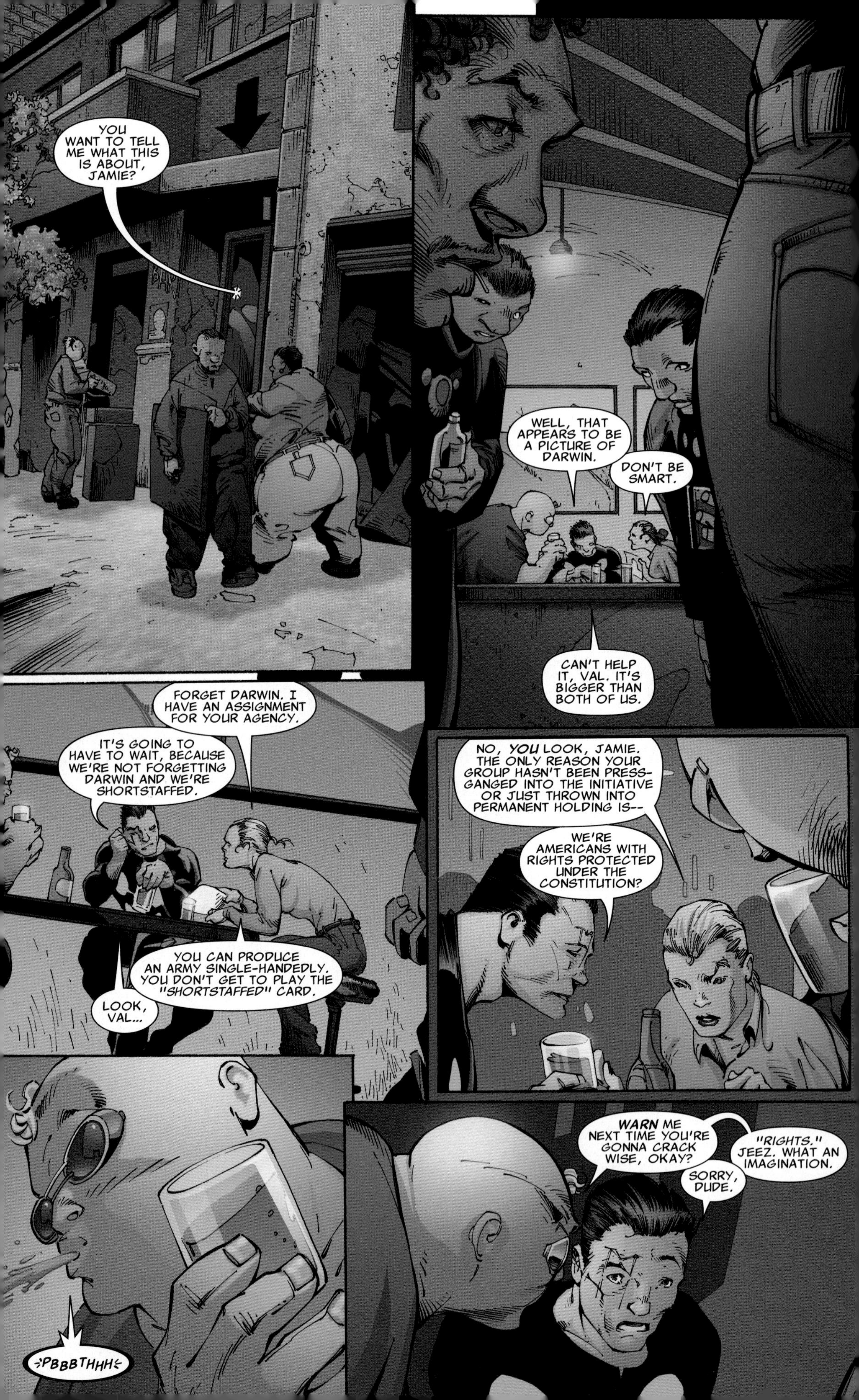
YOU WANT TO TELL ME WHAT THIS IS ABOUT, JAMIE?
WELL, THAT APPEARS TO BE A PICTURE OF DARWIN.
DON'T BE SMART.
CAN'T HELP IT, VAL. IT'S BIGGER THAN BOTH OF US.
FORGET DARWIN. I HAVE AN ASSIGNMENT FOR YOUR AGENCY.
IT'S GOING TO HAVE TO WAIT, BECAUSE WE'RE NOT FORGETTING DARWIN AND WE'RE SHORTSTAFFED.
LOOK, VAL...
YOU CAN PRODUCE AN ARMY SINGLE-HANDEDLY. YOU DON'T GET TO PLAY THE "SHORTSTAFFED" CARD.
NO, YOU LOOK, JAMIE. THE ONLY REASON YOUR GROUP HASN'T BEEN PRESS-GANGED INTO THE INITIATIVE OR JUST THROWN INTO PERMANENT HOLDING IS--
WE'RE AMERICANS WITH RIGHTS PROTECTED UNDER THE CONSTITUTION?
PBBBTHHH
WARN ME NEXT TIME YOU'RE GONNA CRACK WISE, OKAY?
SORRY, DUDE.
"RIGHTS." JEEZ. WHAT AN IMAGINATION.

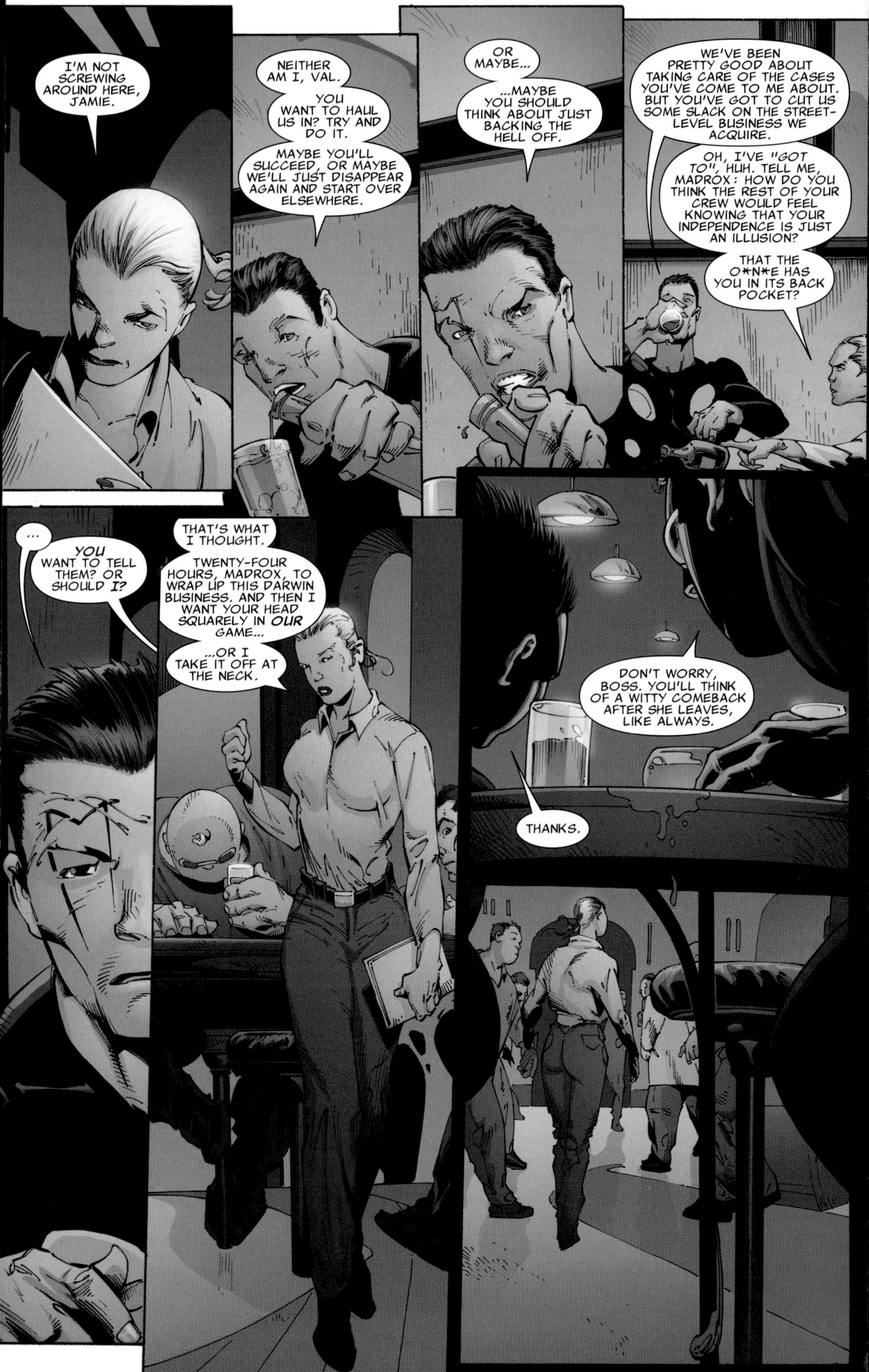
I'M NOT SCREWING AROUND HERE, JAMIE.
NEITHER AM I, VAL.
YOU WANT TO HAUL US IN? TRY AND DO IT.
MAYBE YOU'LL SUCCEED, OR MAYBE WE'LL JUST DISAPPEAR AGAIN AND START OVER ELSEWHERE.
OR MAYBE...
...MAYBE YOU SHOULD THINK ABOUT JUST BACKING THE HELL OFF.
WE'VE BEEN PRETTY GOOD ABOUT TAKING CARE OF THE CASES YOU'VE COME TO ME ABOUT. BUT YOU'VE GOT TO CUT US SOME SLACK ON THE STREET-LEVEL BUSINESS WE ACQUIRE.
OH, I'VE "GOT TO", HUH. TELL ME, MADROX: HOW DO YOU THINK THE REST OF YOUR CREW WOULD FEEL KNOWING THAT YOUR INDEPENDENCE IS JUST AN ILLUSION?
THAT THE O*N*E HAS YOU IN ITS BACK POCKET?
...
YOU WANT TO TELL THEM? OR SHOULD *I*?
THAT'S WHAT I THOUGHT.
TWENTY-FOUR HOURS, MADROX, TO WRAP UP THIS DARWIN BUSINESS. AND THEN I WANT YOUR HEAD SQUARELY IN *OUR* GAME...
...OR I TAKE IT OFF AT THE NECK.
DON'T WORRY, BOSS. YOU'LL THINK OF A WITTY COMEBACK AFTER SHE LEAVES, LIKE ALWAYS.
THANKS.

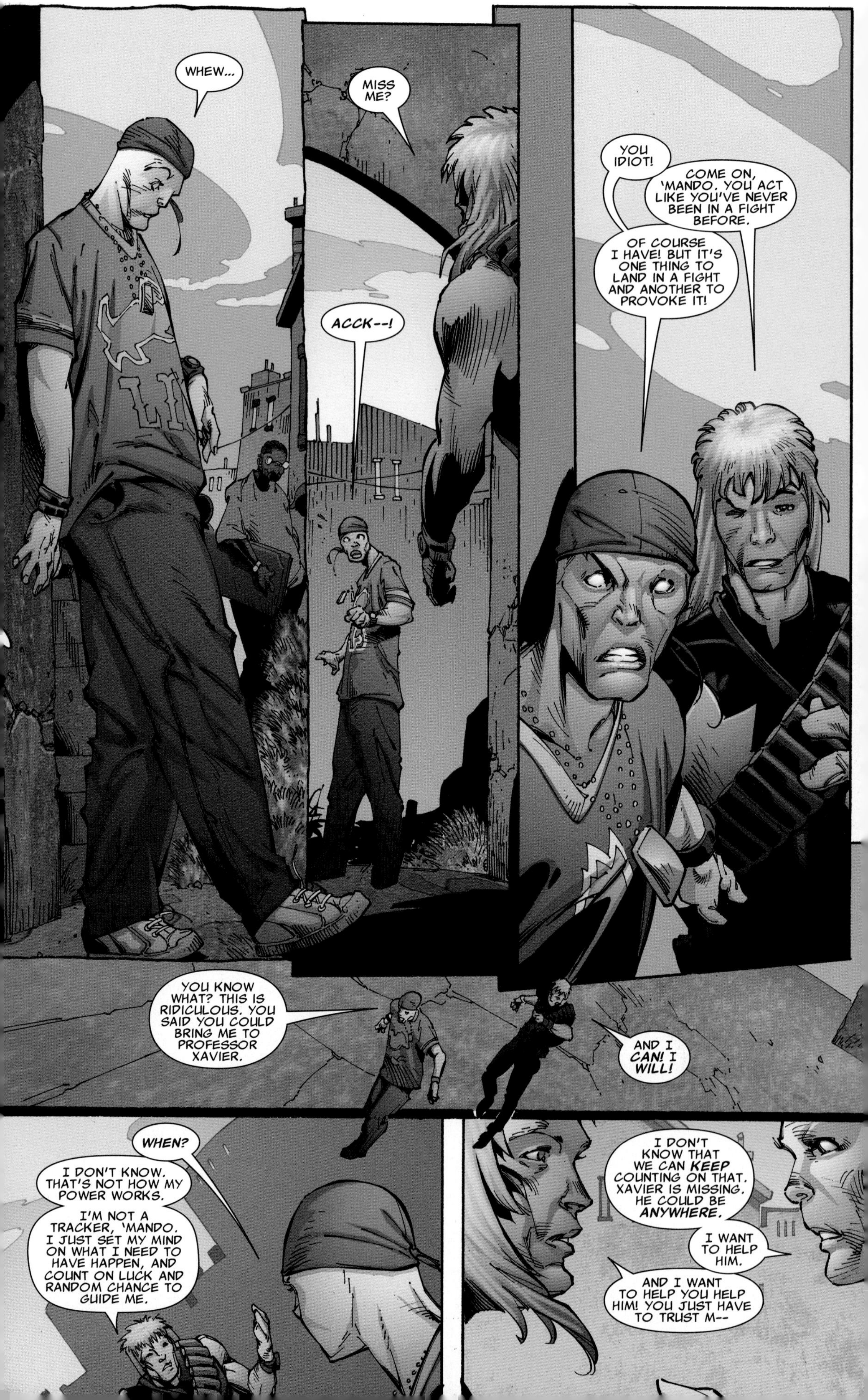
WHEW...
MISS ME?
ACCK--!
YOU IDIOT!
COME ON, 'MANDO. YOU ACT LIKE YOU'VE NEVER BEEN IN A FIGHT BEFORE.
OF COURSE I HAVE! BUT IT'S ONE THING TO LAND IN A FIGHT AND ANOTHER TO PROVOKE IT!
YOU KNOW WHAT? THIS IS RIDICULOUS. YOU SAID YOU COULD BRING ME TO PROFESSOR XAVIER.
AND I CAN! I WILL!
WHEN?
I DON'T KNOW. THAT'S NOT HOW MY POWER WORKS.
I'M NOT A TRACKER, 'MANDO. I JUST SET MY MIND ON WHAT I NEED TO HAVE HAPPEN, AND COUNT ON LUCK AND RANDOM CHANCE TO GUIDE ME.
I DON'T KNOW THAT WE CAN KEEP COUNTING ON THAT. XAVIER IS MISSING. HE COULD BE ANYWHERE.
I WANT TO HELP HIM.
AND I WANT TO HELP YOU HELP HIM! YOU JUST HAVE TO TRUST M--

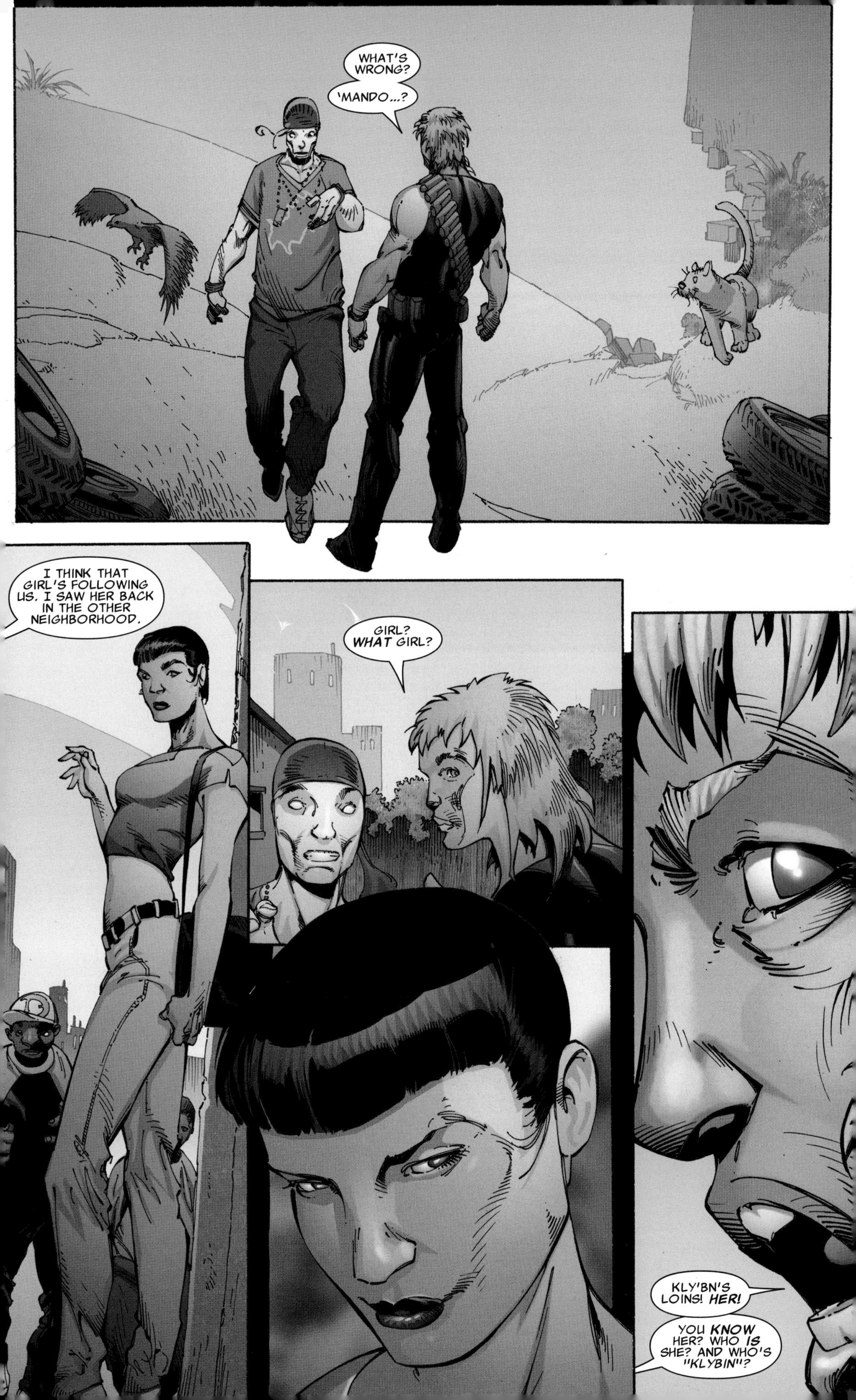
WHAT'S WRONG?
'MANDO...?
I THINK THAT GIRL'S FOLLOWING US. I SAW HER BACK IN THE OTHER NEIGHBORHOOD.
GIRL? WHAT GIRL?
KLY'BN'S LOINS! HER!
YOU KNOW HER? WHO IS SHE? AND WHO'S "KLYBIN"?

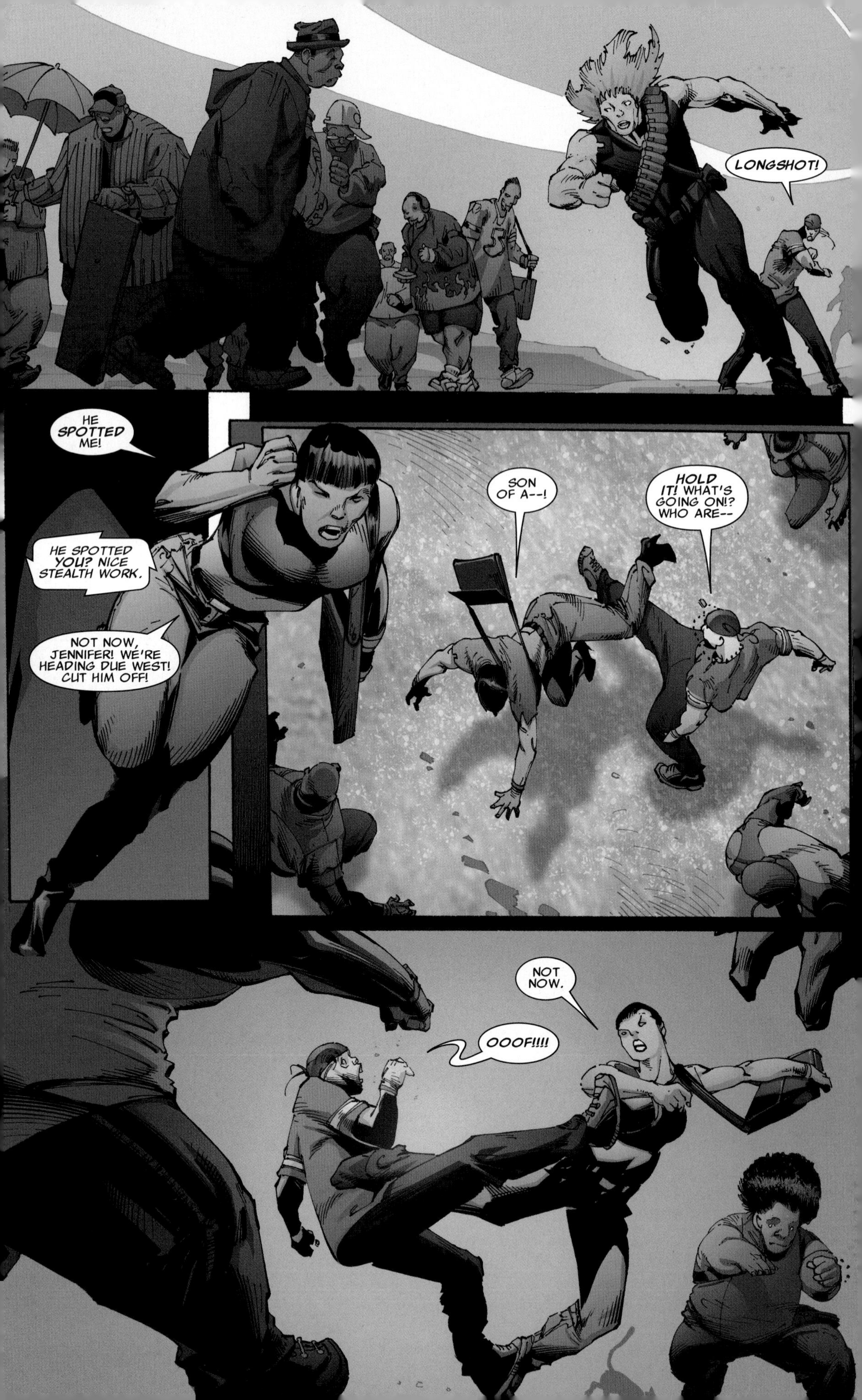
LONGSHOT!
HE SPOTTED ME!
HE SPOTTED YOU? NICE STEALTH WORK.
NOT NOW, JENNIFER! WE'RE HEADING DUE WEST! CUT HIM OFF!
SON OF A--!
HOLD IT! WHAT'S GOING ON!? WHO ARE--
NOT NOW.
OOOF!!!!

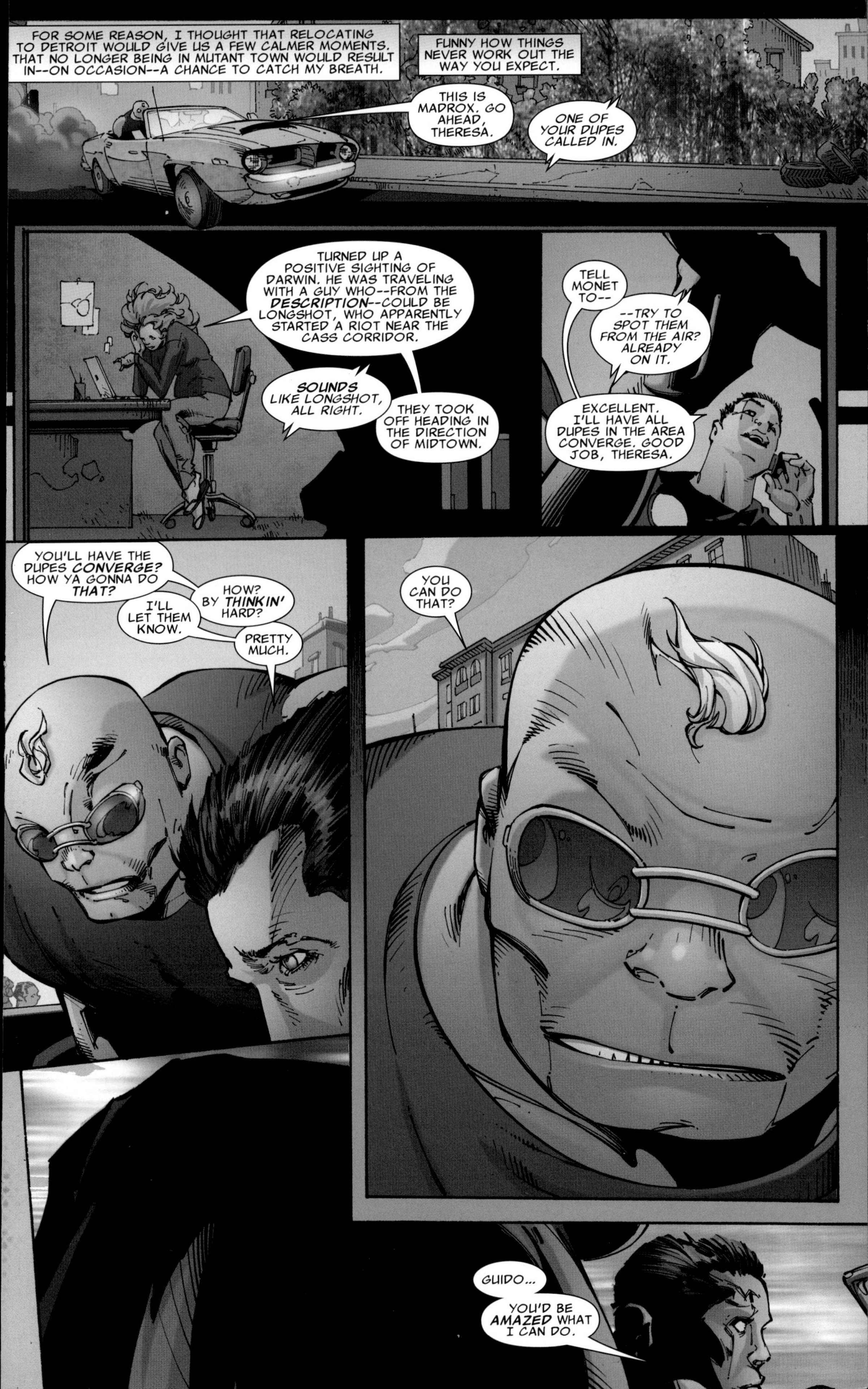

FOR SOME REASON, I THOUGHT THAT RELOCATING TO DETROIT WOULD GIVE US A FEW CALMER MOMENTS. THAT NO LONGER BEING IN MUTANT TOWN WOULD RESULT IN--ON OCCASION--A CHANCE TO CATCH MY BREATH.
FUNNY HOW THINGS NEVER WORK OUT THE WAY YOU EXPECT.
THIS IS MADROX. GO AHEAD, THERESA.
ONE OF YOUR DUPES CALLED IN.
TURNED UP A POSITIVE SIGHTING OF DARWIN. HE WAS TRAVELING WITH A GUY WHO--FROM THE DESCRIPTION--COULD BE LONGSHOT, WHO APPARENTLY STARTED A RIOT NEAR THE CASS CORRIDOR.
SOUNDS LIKE LONGSHOT, ALL RIGHT.
THEY TOOK OFF HEADING IN THE DIRECTION OF MIDTOWN.
TELL MONET TO--
--TRY TO SPOT THEM FROM THE AIR? ALREADY ON IT.
EXCELLENT. I'LL HAVE ALL DUPES IN THE AREA CONVERGE. GOOD JOB, THERESA.
YOU'LL HAVE THE DUPES CONVERGE? HOW YA GONNA DO THAT?
I'LL LET THEM KNOW.
HOW? BY THINKIN' HARD?
PRETTY MUCH.
YOU CAN DO THAT?
GUIDO...
YOU'D BE AMAZED WHAT I CAN DO.

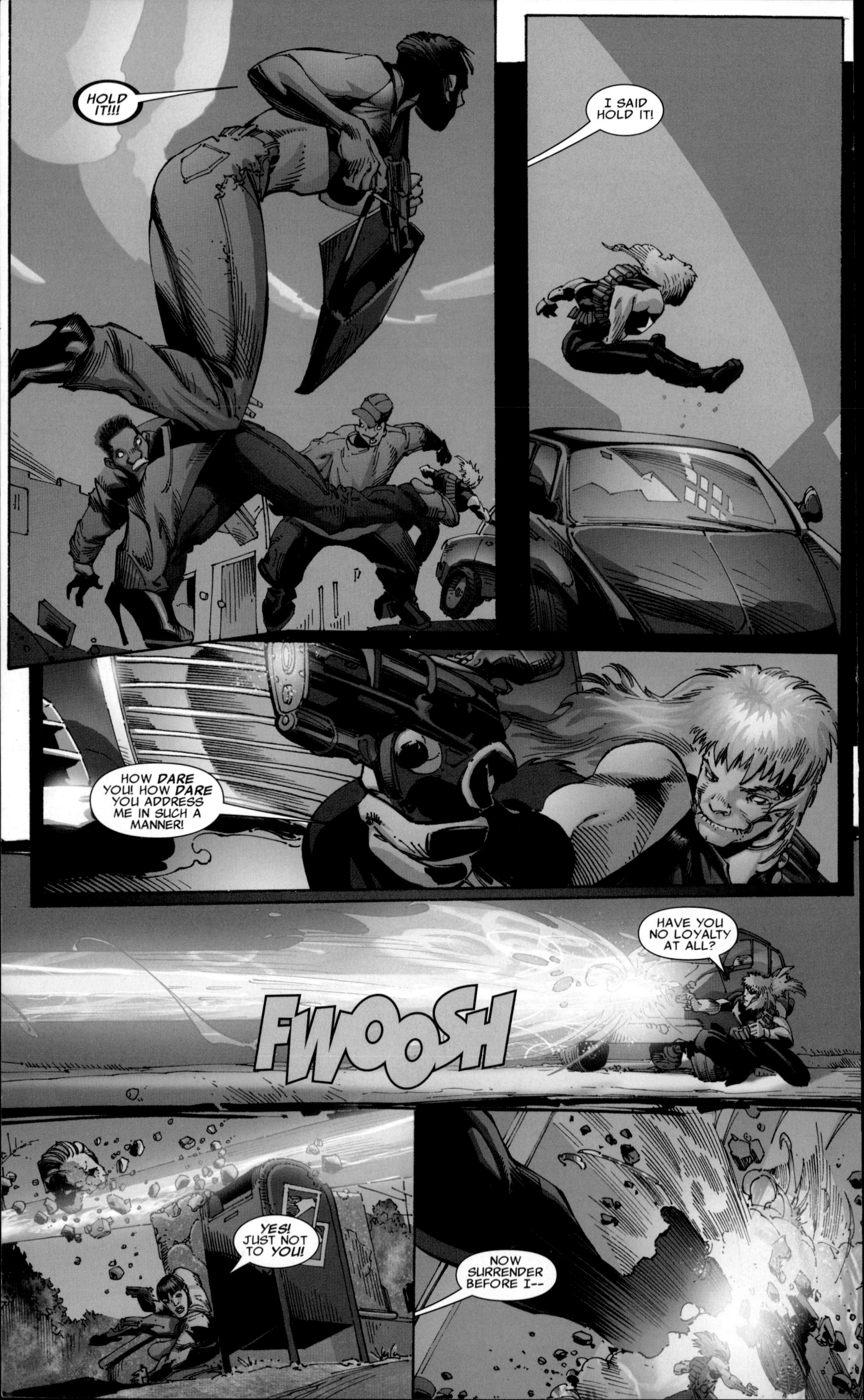
HOLD IT!!!
I SAID HOLD IT!
HOW DARE YOU! HOW DARE YOU ADDRESS ME IN SUCH A MANNER!
HAVE YOU NO LOYALTY AT ALL?
FWOOSH
YES! JUST NOT TO YOU!
NOW SURRENDER BEFORE I--

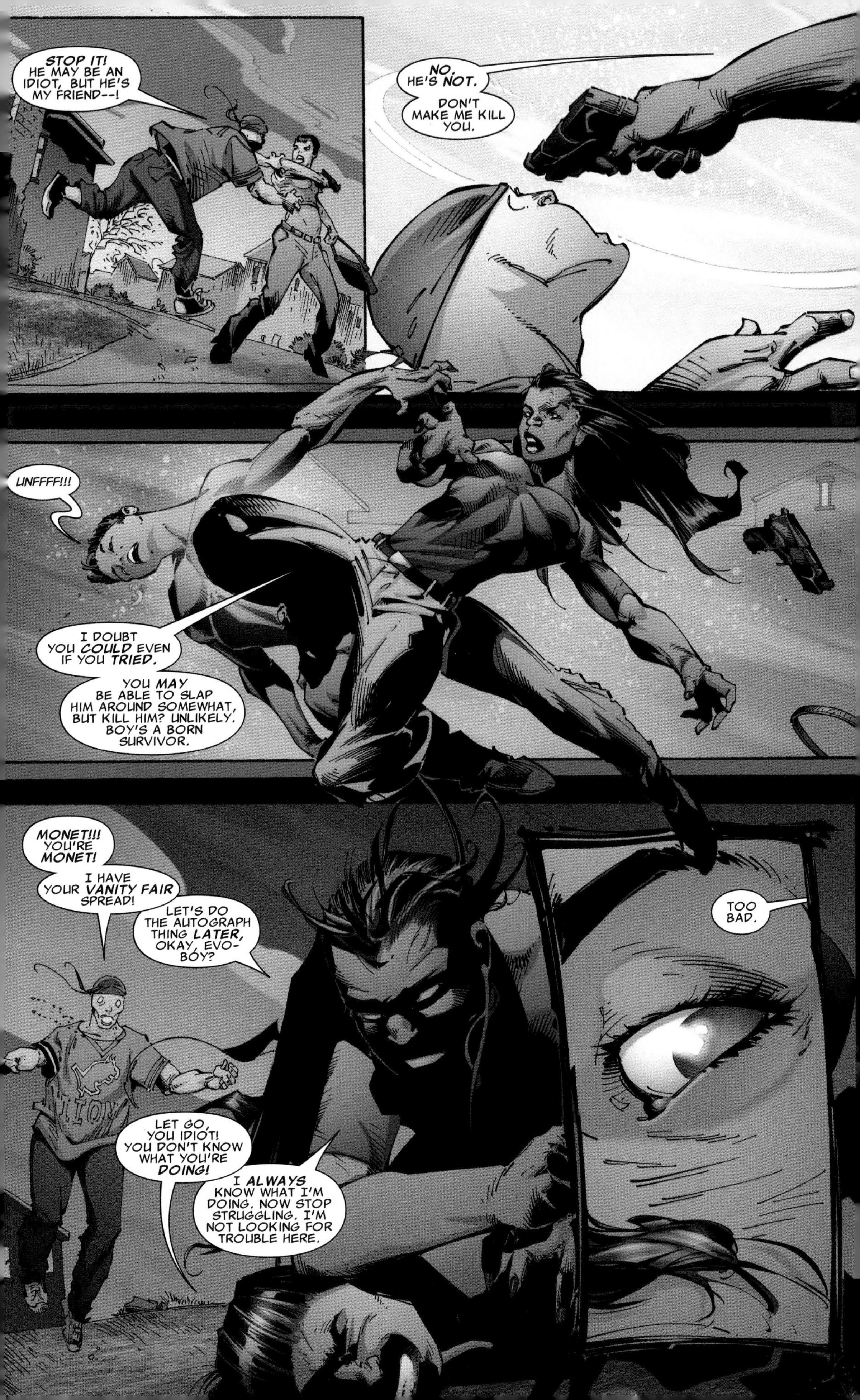
STOP IT! HE MAY BE AN IDIOT, BUT HE'S MY FRIEND--!
NO, HE'S NOT.
DON'T MAKE ME KILL YOU.
UNFFFF!!!
I DOUBT YOU COULD EVEN IF YOU TRIED.
YOU MAY BE ABLE TO SLAP HIM AROUND SOMEWHAT, BUT KILL HIM? UNLIKELY. BOY'S A BORN SURVIVOR.
MONET!!! YOU'RE MONET!
I HAVE YOUR VANITY FAIR SPREAD!
LET'S DO THE AUTOGRAPH THING LATER, OKAY, EVO-BOY?
TOO BAD.
LET GO, YOU IDIOT! YOU DON'T KNOW WHAT YOU'RE DOING!
I ALWAYS KNOW WHAT I'M DOING. NOW STOP STRUGGLING. I'M NOT LOOKING FOR TROUBLE HERE.

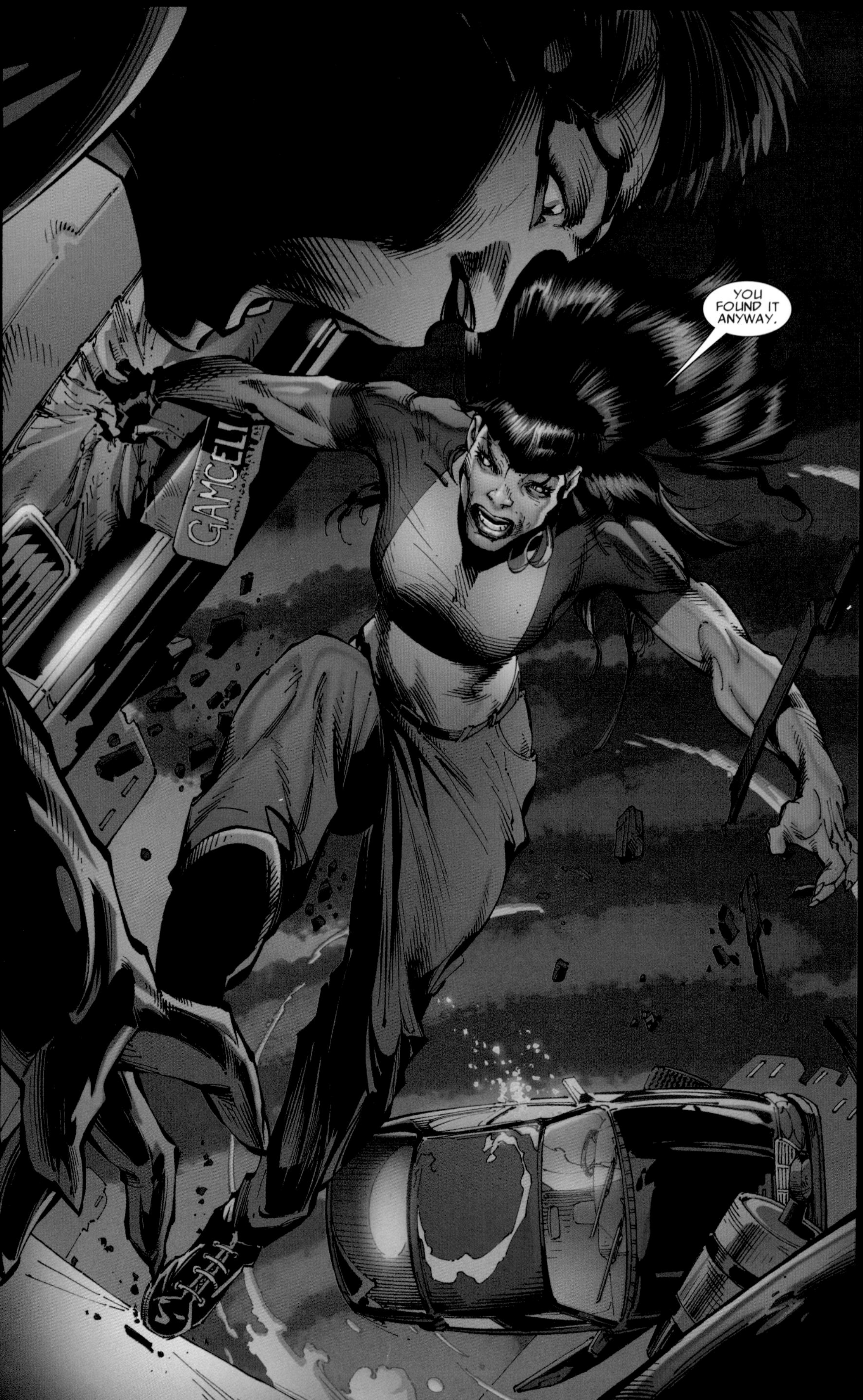
YOU FOUND IT ANYWAY.
GAMCELLI

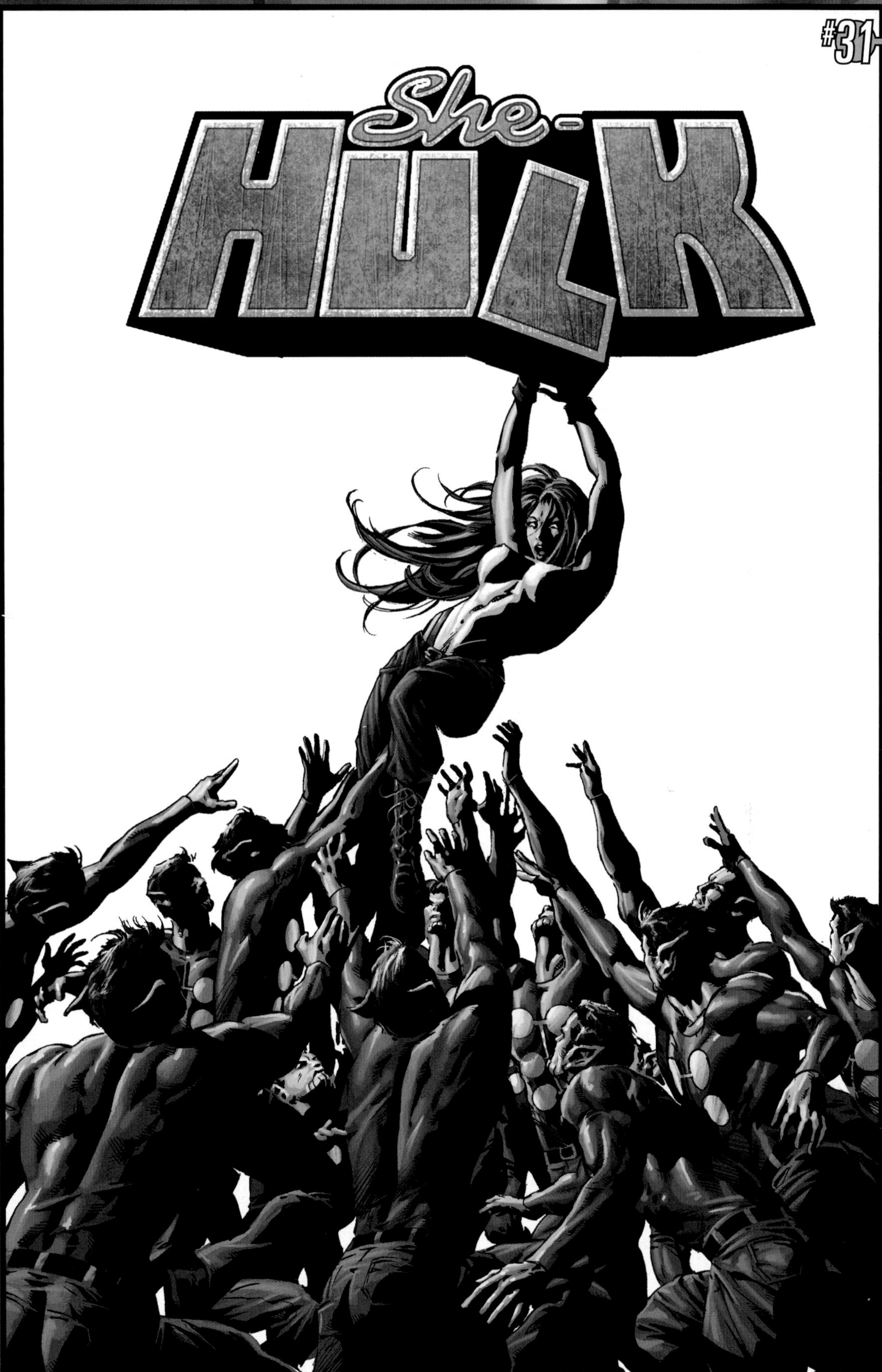
#31
She-
HULK

MUTANTS.
WHY DID IT HAVE TO BE MUTANTS? ESPECIALLY THESE MUTANTS.
X-FACTOR, THE MUTANT DETECTIVE AGENCY. I THOUGHT THEY WERE HEADQUARTERED IN NEW YORK. WHAT THE HELL ARE THEY DOING IN DETROIT?
AND WHY ARE THEY GETTING BETWEEN ME AND MY BOUNTY?
YOU KNOW WHAT? SCREW IT. I DON'T HAVE THE TIME FOR THIS. I DON'T HAVE THE PATIENCE FOR THIS.
AND I CERTAINLY DON'T NEED THE HASSLE OF DEALING WITH THE LEGENDARILY INSUFFERABLE MONET ST. CROIX.
P
THE DARWIN AWARDS PART 2

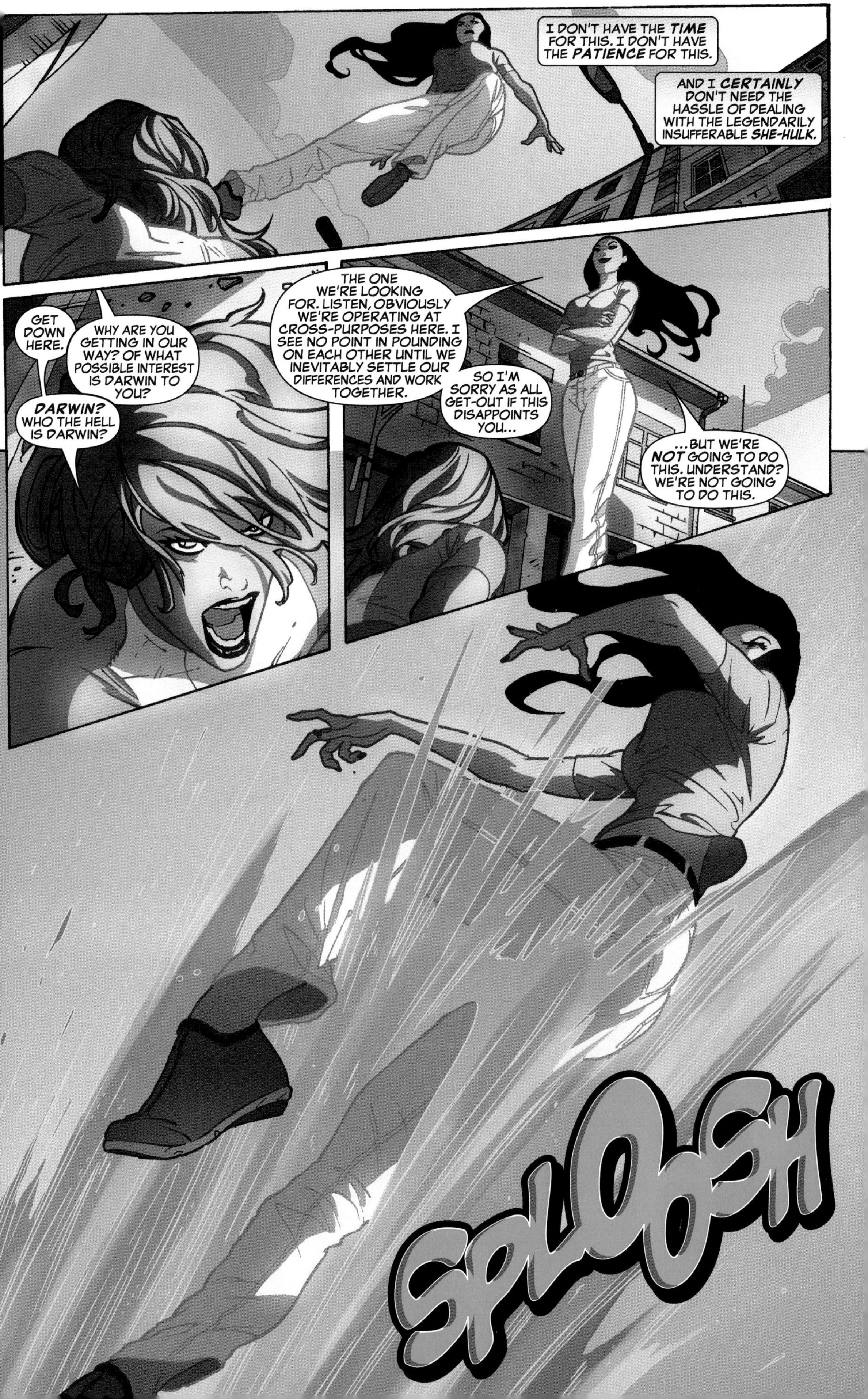

I DON'T HAVE THE TIME FOR THIS. I DON'T HAVE THE PATIENCE FOR THIS.
AND I CERTAINLY DON'T NEED THE HASSLE OF DEALING WITH THE LEGENDARILY INSUFFERABLE SHE-HULK.
GET DOWN HERE.
WHY ARE YOU GETTING IN OUR WAY? OF WHAT POSSIBLE INTEREST IS DARWIN TO YOU?
DARWIN? WHO THE HELL IS DARWIN?
THE ONE WE'RE LOOKING FOR. LISTEN, OBVIOUSLY WE'RE OPERATING AT CROSS-PURPOSES HERE. I SEE NO POINT IN POUNDING ON EACH OTHER UNTIL WE INEVITABLY SETTLE OUR DIFFERENCES AND WORK TOGETHER.
SO I'M SORRY AS ALL GET-OUT IF THIS DISAPPOINTS YOU...
...BUT WE'RE NOT GOING TO DO THIS. UNDERSTAND? WE'RE NOT GOING TO DO THIS.
SPLOOSH

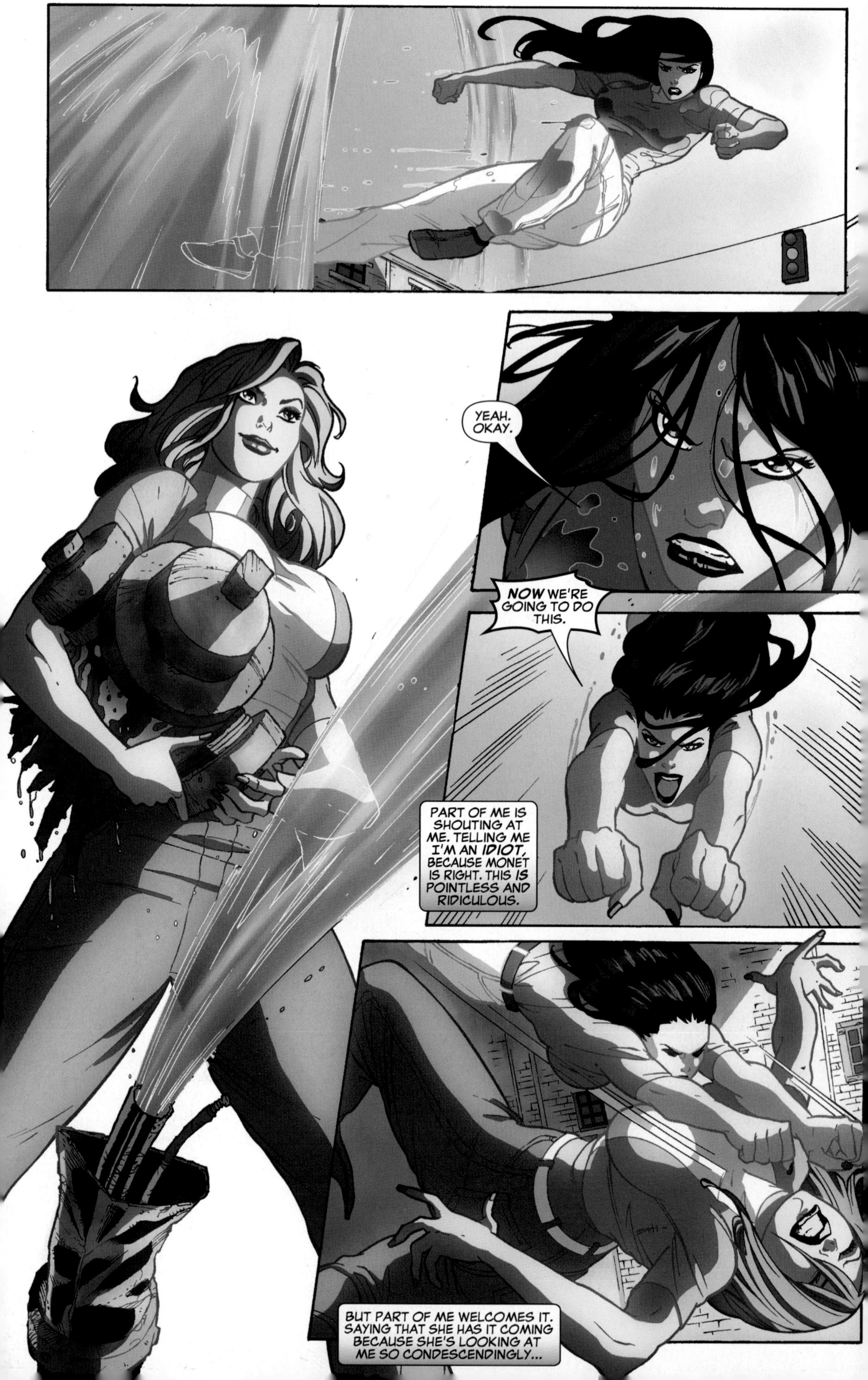
YEAH. OKAY.
NOW WE'RE GOING TO DO THIS.
PART OF ME IS SHOUTING AT ME. TELLING ME I'M AN IDIOT, BECAUSE MONET IS RIGHT. THIS IS POINTLESS AND RIDICULOUS.
BUT PART OF ME WELCOMES IT. SAYING THAT SHE HAS IT COMING BECAUSE SHE'S LOOKING AT ME SO CONDESCENDINGLY...

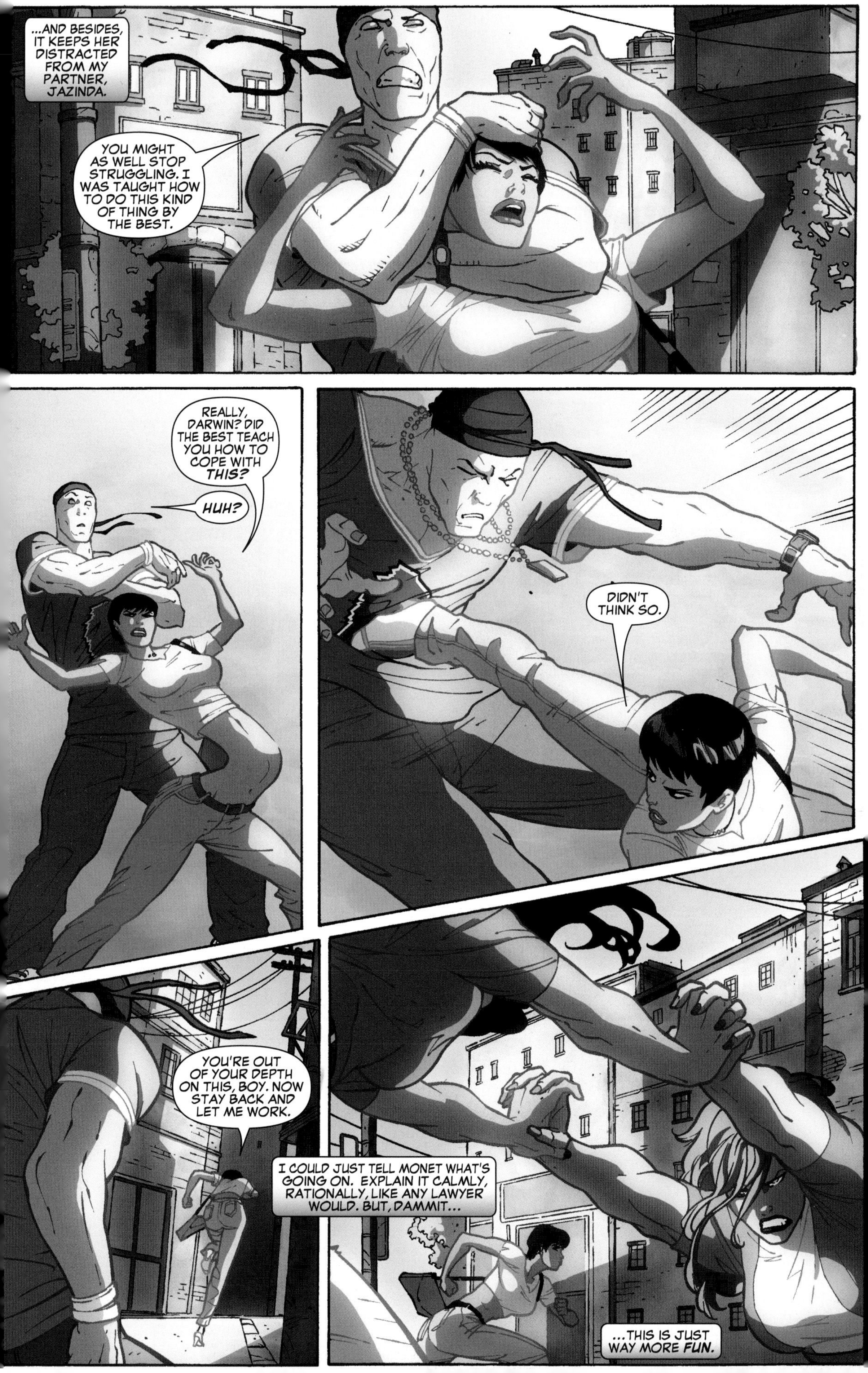
...AND BESIDES, IT KEEPS HER DISTRACTED FROM MY PARTNER, JAZINDA.
YOU MIGHT AS WELL STOP STRUGGLING. I WAS TAUGHT HOW TO DO THIS KIND OF THING BY THE BEST.
REALLY, DARWIN? DID THE BEST TEACH YOU HOW TO COPE WITH THIS?
HUH?
DIDN'T THINK SO.
YOU'RE OUT OF YOUR DEPTH ON THIS, BOY. NOW STAY BACK AND LET ME WORK.
I COULD JUST TELL MONET WHAT'S GOING ON. EXPLAIN IT CALMLY, RATIONALLY, LIKE ANY LAWYER WOULD. BUT, DAMMIT...
...THIS IS JUST WAY MORE FUN.

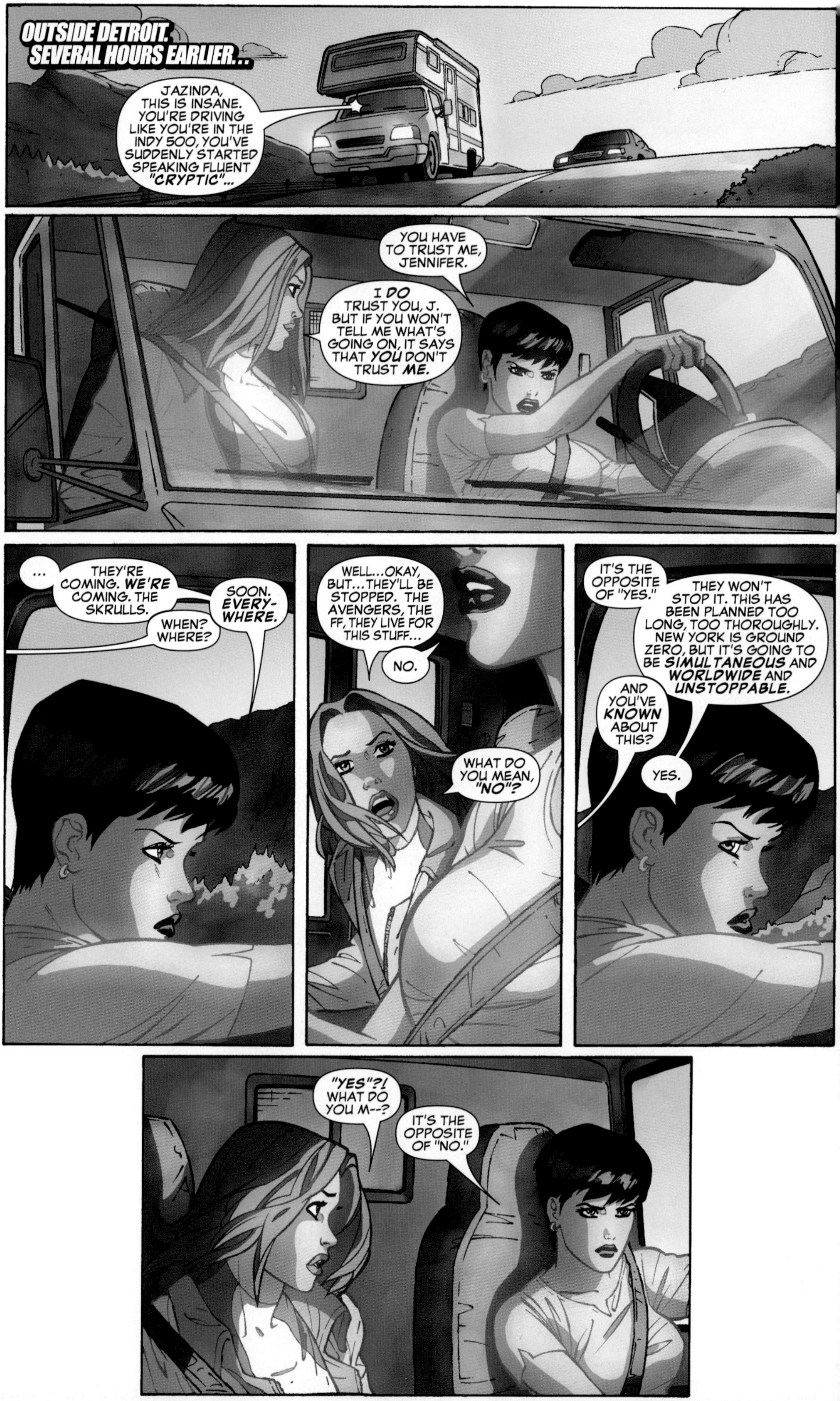
OUTSIDE DETROIT. SEVERAL HOURS EARLIER...
JAZINDA, THIS IS INSANE. YOU'RE DRIVING LIKE YOU'RE IN THE INDY 500, YOU'VE SUDDENLY STARTED SPEAKING FLUENT "CRYPTIC"...
YOU HAVE TO TRUST ME, JENNIFER.
I DO TRUST YOU, J. BUT IF YOU WON'T TELL ME WHAT'S GOING ON, IT SAYS THAT YOU DON'T TRUST ME.
...
THEY'RE COMING. WE'RE COMING. THE SKRULLS.
SOON. EVERY-WHERE.
WHEN? WHERE?
WELL...OKAY, BUT...THEY'LL BE STOPPED. THE AVENGERS, THE FF, THEY LIVE FOR THIS STUFF...
NO.
WHAT DO YOU MEAN, "NO"?
IT'S THE OPPOSITE OF "YES."
THEY WON'T STOP IT. THIS HAS BEEN PLANNED TOO LONG, TOO THOROUGHLY. NEW YORK IS GROUND ZERO, BUT IT'S GOING TO BE SIMULTANEOUS AND WORLDWIDE AND UNSTOPPABLE.
AND YOU'VE KNOWN ABOUT THIS?
YES.
"YES"?! WHAT DO YOU M--?
IT'S THE OPPOSITE OF "NO."

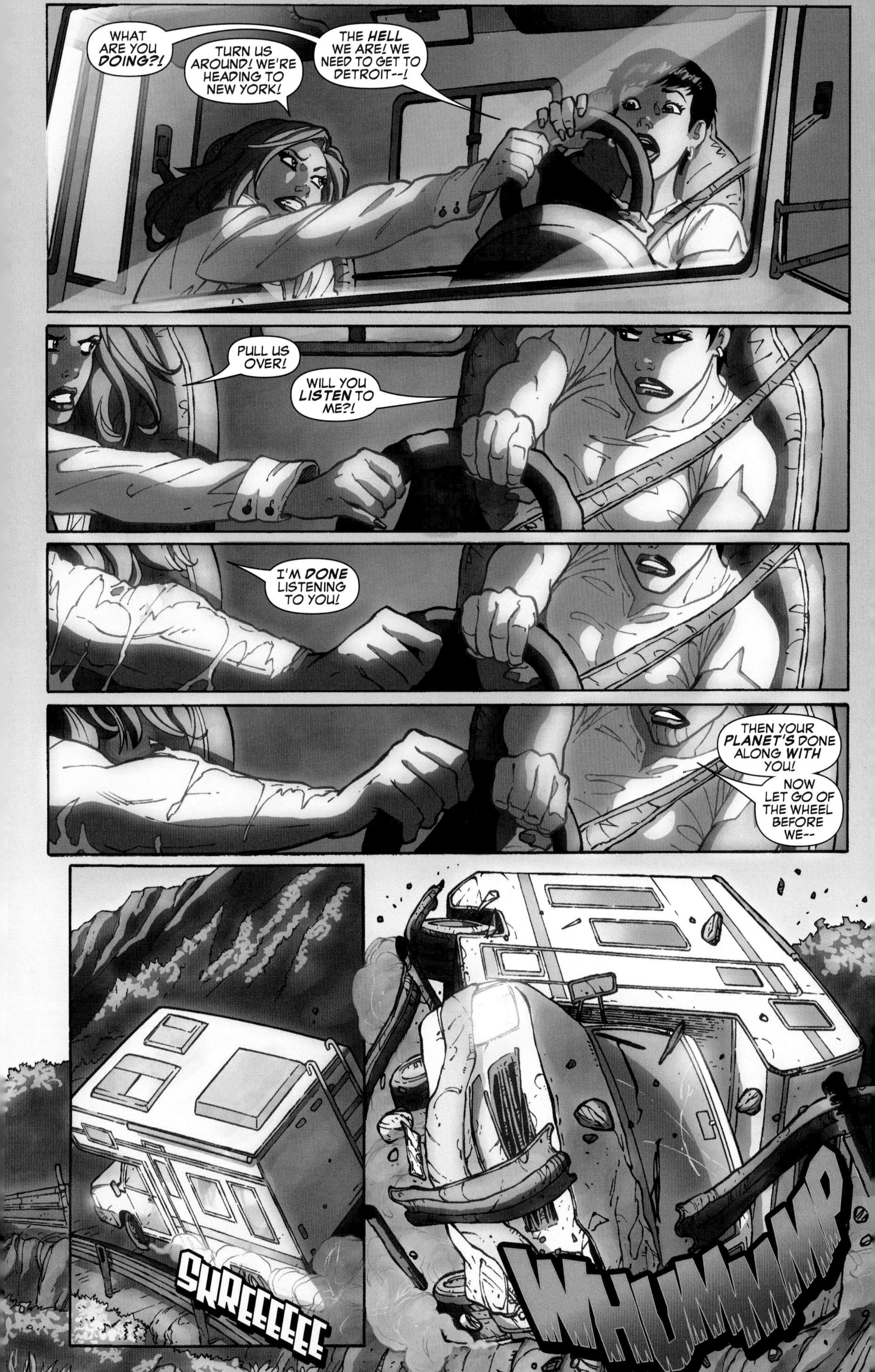
WHAT ARE YOU DOING?!
TURN US AROUND! WE'RE HEADING TO NEW YORK!
THE HELL WE ARE! WE NEED TO GET TO DETROIT--!
PULL US OVER!
WILL YOU LISTEN TO ME?!
I'M DONE LISTENING TO YOU!
THEN YOUR PLANET'S DONE ALONG WITH YOU!
NOW LET GO OF THE WHEEL BEFORE WE--
SHREEEEEEE
WHUMMMP

TERRIFIC. I HOPE YOU'RE *HAPPY*, JENNI--

OOOOOOOF!

I *AM* YOUR FRIEND, YOU IDIOT.

YEAH? OKAY, HERE'S A COUPLE OF GUIDELINES TO BEING A *FRIEND*...

HOW DARE YOU!

YOU ACT LIKE MY *FRIEND* AND THEN YOU *KEEP THIS* FROM ME!

ONE: FRIENDS DON'T LET OTHER FRIENDS DRIVE DRUNK.

TWO: FRIENDS GIVE YOU A HEADS UP WHEN *ALIENS* ARE ABOUT TO TURN YOUR PLANET INTO A REAL-LIFE VERSION OF "SPACE INVADERS"!

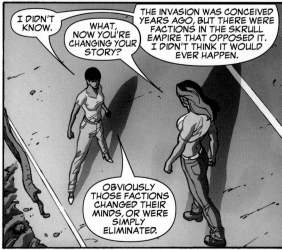

I DIDN'T KNOW.

WHAT, NOW YOU'RE CHANGING YOUR STORY?

THE INVASION WAS CONCEIVED YEARS AGO, BUT THERE WERE FACTIONS IN THE SKRULL EMPIRE THAT OPPOSED IT. I DIDN'T THINK IT WOULD EVER HAPPEN.

OBVIOUSLY THOSE FACTIONS CHANGED THEIR MINDS, OR WERE SIMPLY ELIMINATED.

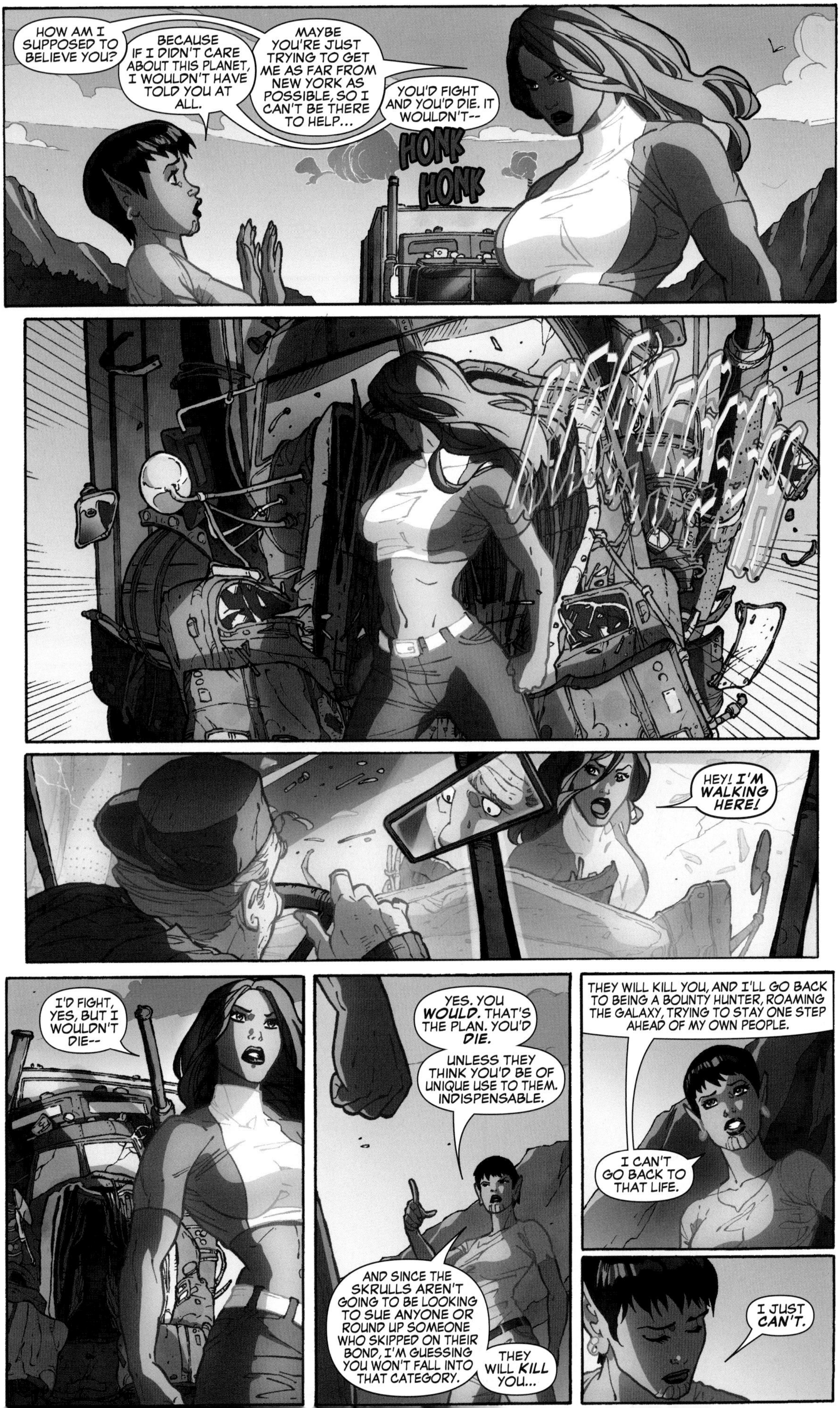
HOW AM I SUPPOSED TO BELIEVE YOU?
BECAUSE IF I DIDN'T CARE ABOUT THIS PLANET, I WOULDN'T HAVE TOLD YOU AT ALL.
MAYBE YOU'RE JUST TRYING TO GET ME AS FAR FROM NEW YORK AS POSSIBLE, SO I CAN'T BE THERE TO HELP...
YOU'D FIGHT AND YOU'D DIE. IT WOULDN'T--
HONK
HONK
HEY! I'M WALKING HERE!
I'D FIGHT, YES, BUT I WOULDN'T DIE--
YES. YOU WOULD. THAT'S THE PLAN. YOU'D DIE.
UNLESS THEY THINK YOU'D BE OF UNIQUE USE TO THEM. INDISPENSABLE.
AND SINCE THE SKRULLS AREN'T GOING TO BE LOOKING TO SUE ANYONE OR ROUND UP SOMEONE WHO SKIPPED ON THEIR BOND, I'M GUESSING YOU WON'T FALL INTO THAT CATEGORY.
THEY WILL KILL YOU...
THEY WILL KILL YOU, AND I'LL GO BACK TO BEING A BOUNTY HUNTER, ROAMING THE GALAXY, TRYING TO STAY ONE STEP AHEAD OF MY OWN PEOPLE.
I CAN'T GO BACK TO THAT LIFE.
I JUST CAN'T.

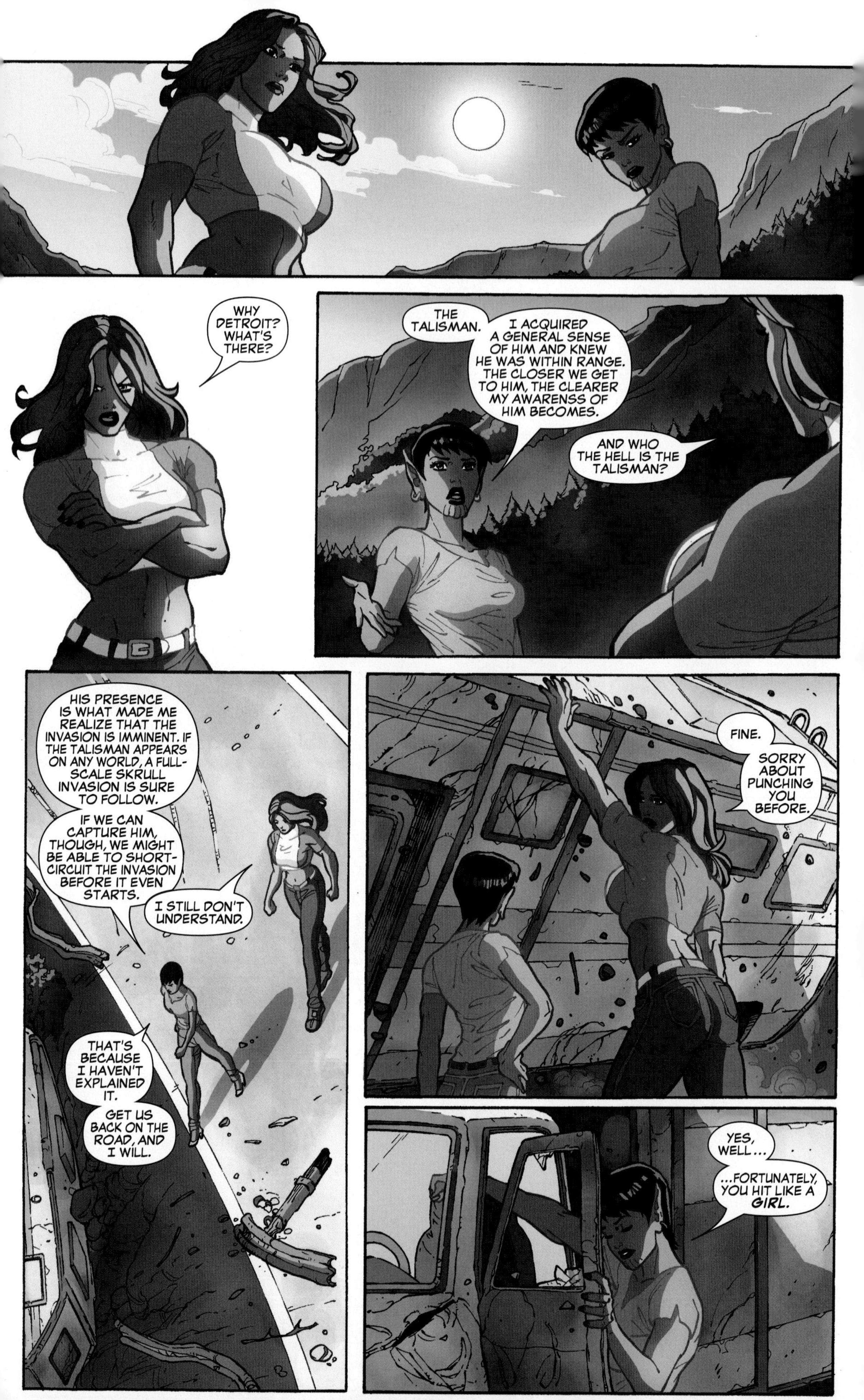
WHY DETROIT? WHAT'S THERE?
THE TALISMAN.
I ACQUIRED A GENERAL SENSE OF HIM AND KNEW HE WAS WITHIN RANGE. THE CLOSER WE GET TO HIM, THE CLEARER MY AWARENSS OF HIM BECOMES.
AND WHO THE HELL IS THE TALISMAN?
HIS PRESENCE IS WHAT MADE ME REALIZE THAT THE INVASION IS IMMINENT. IF THE TALISMAN APPEARS ON ANY WORLD, A FULL-SCALE SKRULL INVASION IS SURE TO FOLLOW.
IF WE CAN CAPTURE HIM, THOUGH, WE MIGHT BE ABLE TO SHORT-CIRCUIT THE INVASION BEFORE IT EVEN STARTS.
I STILL DON'T UNDERSTAND.
THAT'S BECAUSE I HAVEN'T EXPLAINED IT.
GET US BACK ON THE ROAD, AND I WILL.
FINE.
SORRY ABOUT PUNCHING YOU BEFORE.
YES, WELL...
...FORTUNATELY, YOU HIT LIKE A **GIRL.**

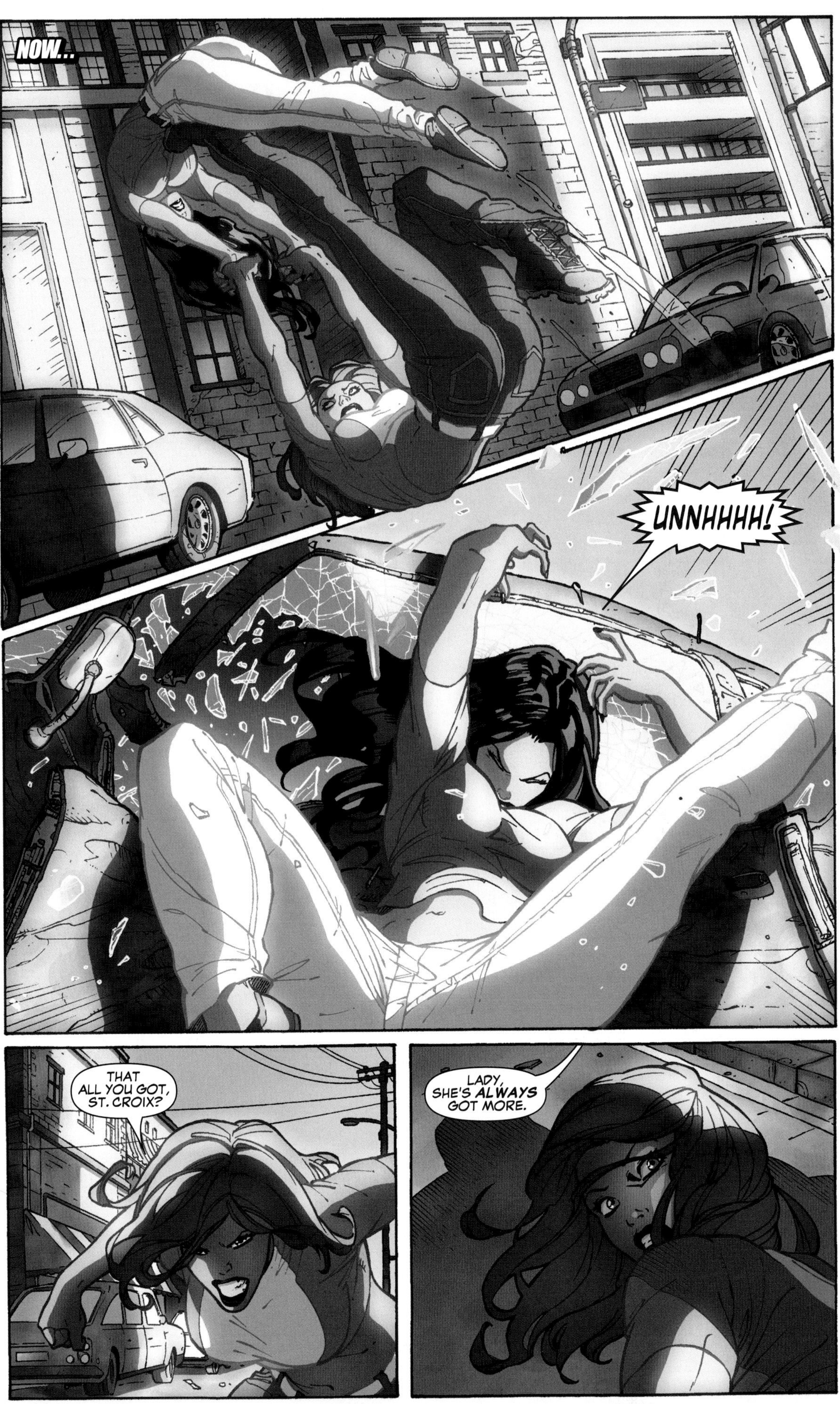
NOW...
UNNHHHH!
THAT ALL YOU GOT, ST. CROIX?
LADY, SHE'S ALWAYS GOT MORE.

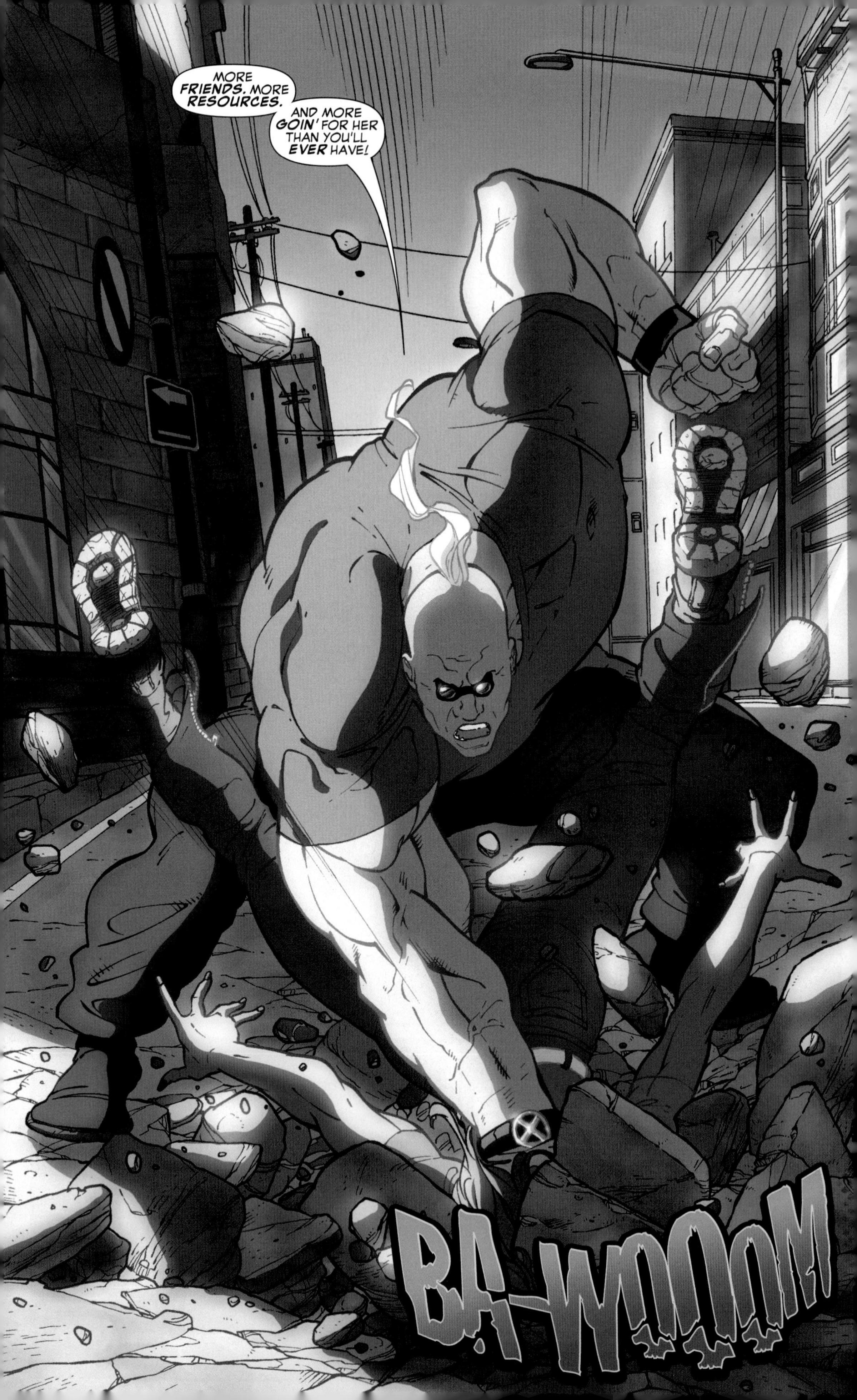
MORE FRIENDS. MORE RESOURCES.
AND MORE GOIN' FOR HER THAN YOU'LL EVER HAVE!
BA-WOOOOM

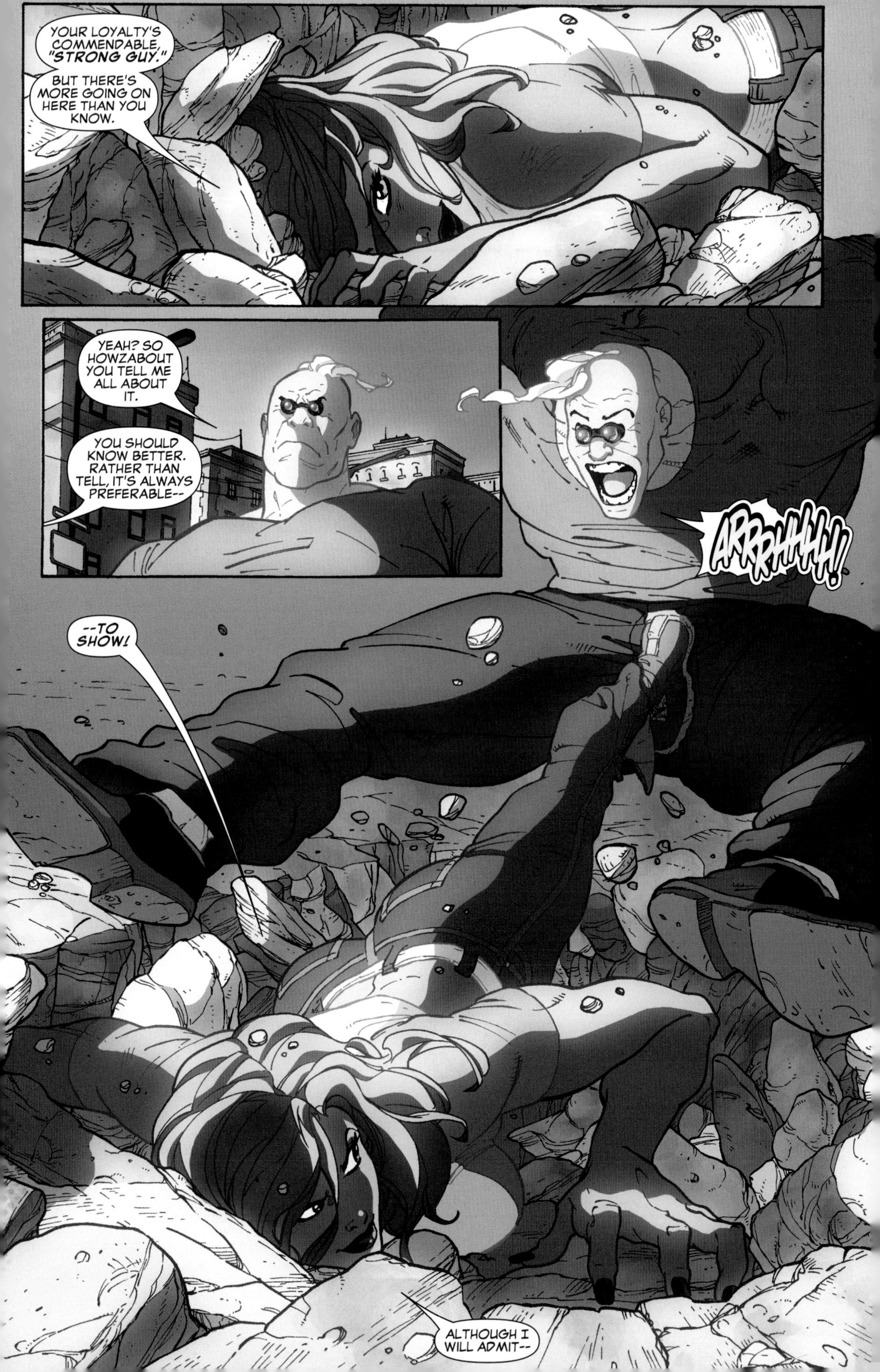
YOUR LOYALTY'S COMMENDABLE, "STRONG GUY."
BUT THERE'S MORE GOING ON HERE THAN YOU KNOW.
YEAH? SO HOWZABOUT YOU TELL ME ALL ABOUT IT.
YOU SHOULD KNOW BETTER. RATHER THAN TELL, IT'S ALWAYS PREFERABLE--
ARRRHHHH!!
--TO SHOW!
ALTHOUGH I WILL ADMIT--

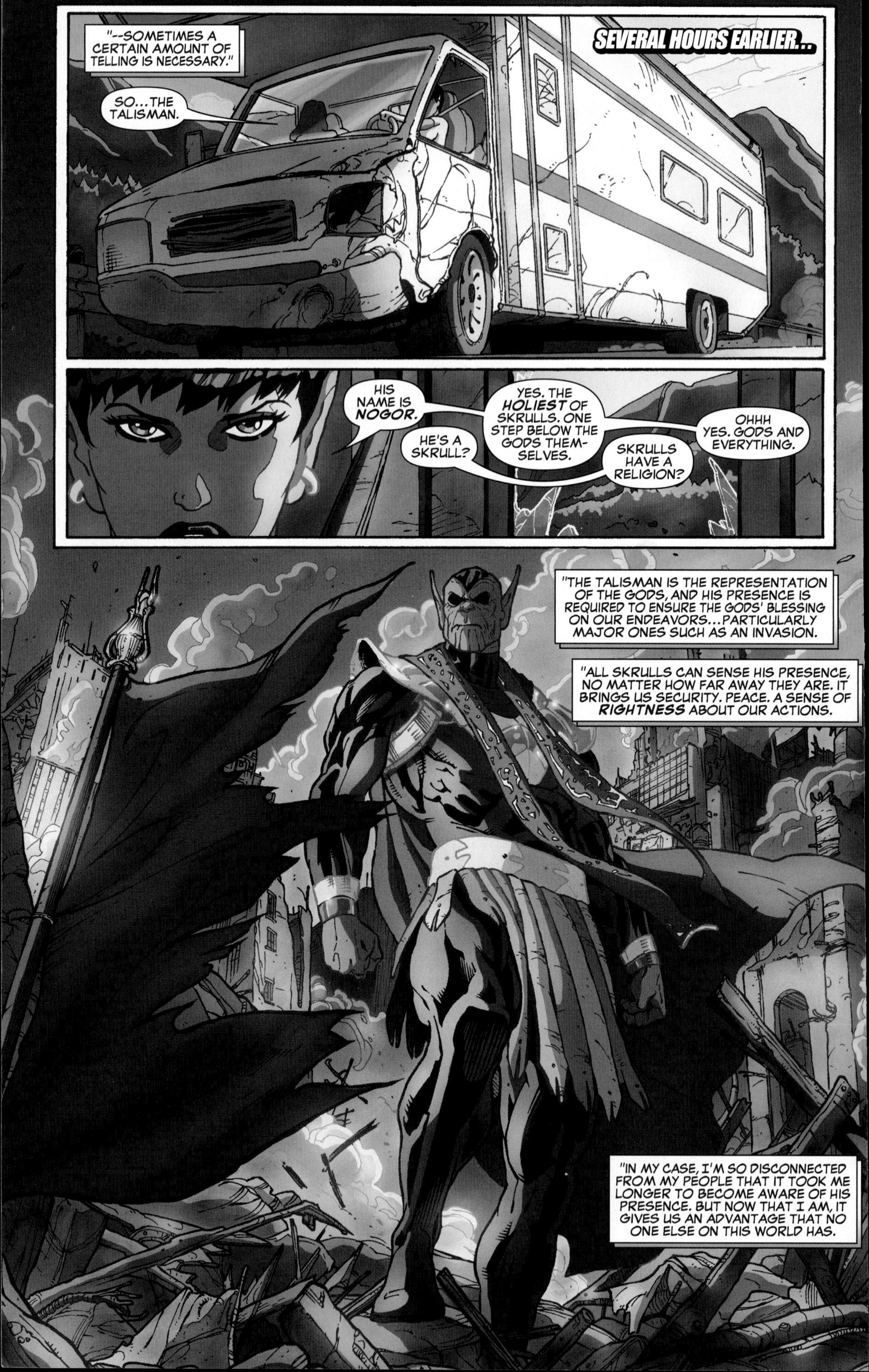
"--SOMETIMES A CERTAIN AMOUNT OF TELLING IS NECESSARY."
SEVERAL HOURS EARLIER...
SO...THE TALISMAN.
HIS NAME IS NOGOR.
HE'S A SKRULL?
YES. THE HOLIEST OF SKRULLS. ONE STEP BELOW THE GODS THEM-SELVES.
SKRULLS HAVE A RELIGION?
OHHH YES. GODS AND EVERYTHING.
"THE TALISMAN IS THE REPRESENTATION OF THE GODS, AND HIS PRESENCE IS REQUIRED TO ENSURE THE GODS' BLESSING ON OUR ENDEAVORS...PARTICULARLY MAJOR ONES SUCH AS AN INVASION.
"ALL SKRULLS CAN SENSE HIS PRESENCE, NO MATTER HOW FAR AWAY THEY ARE. IT BRINGS US SECURITY. PEACE. A SENSE OF RIGHTNESS ABOUT OUR ACTIONS.
"IN MY CASE, I'M SO DISCONNECTED FROM MY PEOPLE THAT IT TOOK ME LONGER TO BECOME AWARE OF HIS PRESENCE. BUT NOW THAT I AM, IT GIVES US AN ADVANTAGE THAT NO ONE ELSE ON THIS WORLD HAS.

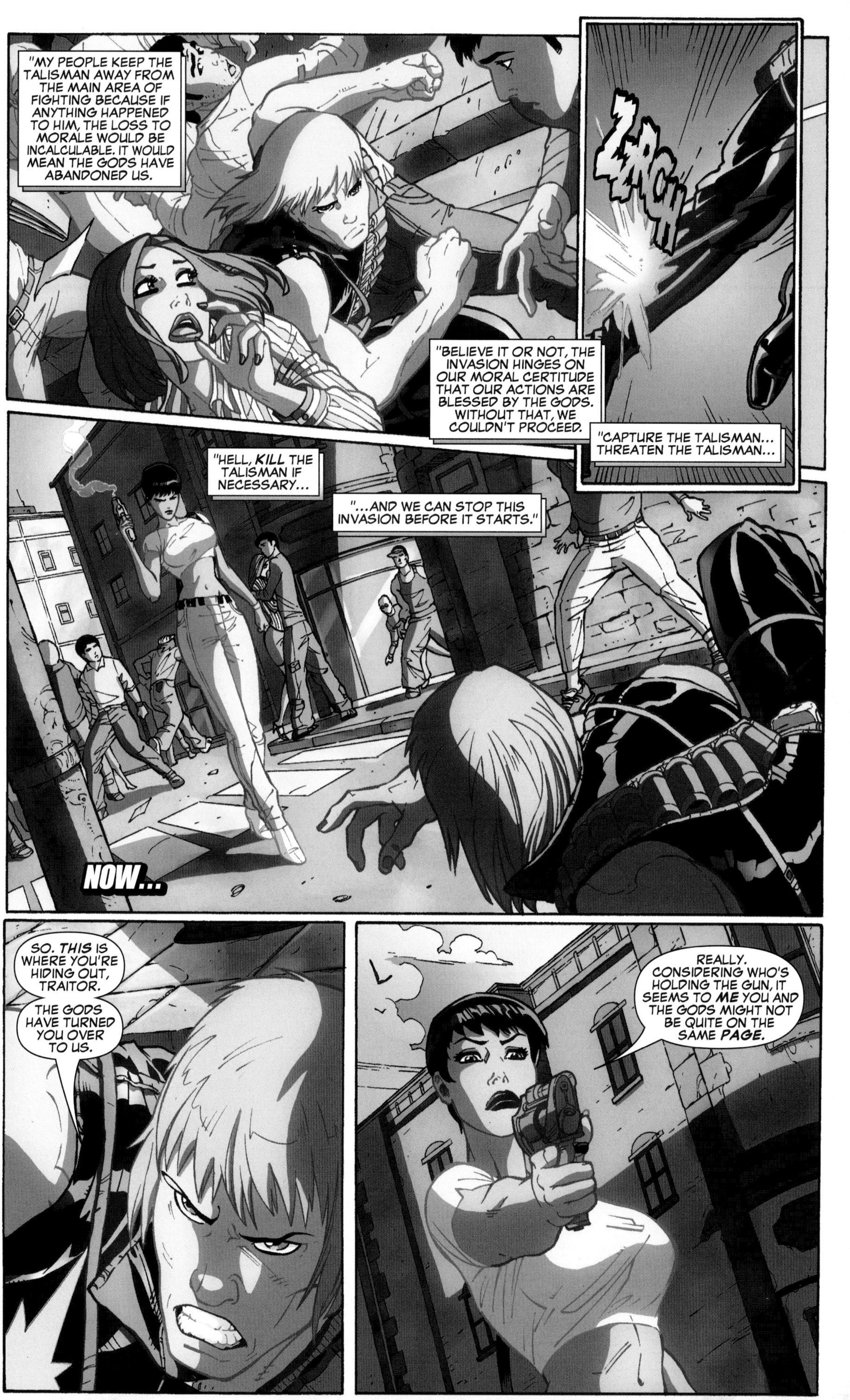
"MY PEOPLE KEEP THE TALISMAN AWAY FROM THE MAIN AREA OF FIGHTING BECAUSE IF ANYTHING HAPPENED TO HIM, THE LOSS TO MORALE WOULD BE INCALCULABLE. IT WOULD MEAN THE GODS HAVE ABANDONED US.
ZRCH
"BELIEVE IT OR NOT, THE INVASION HINGES ON OUR MORAL CERTITUDE THAT OUR ACTIONS ARE BLESSED BY THE GODS. WITHOUT THAT, WE COULDN'T PROCEED.
"CAPTURE THE TALISMAN... THREATEN THE TALISMAN...
"HELL, KILL THE TALISMAN IF NECESSARY...
"...AND WE CAN STOP THIS INVASION BEFORE IT STARTS."
NOW...
SO. THIS IS WHERE YOU'RE HIDING OUT, TRAITOR.
THE GODS HAVE TURNED YOU OVER TO US.
REALLY. CONSIDERING WHO'S HOLDING THE GUN, IT SEEMS TO ME YOU AND THE GODS MIGHT NOT BE QUITE ON THE SAME PAGE.

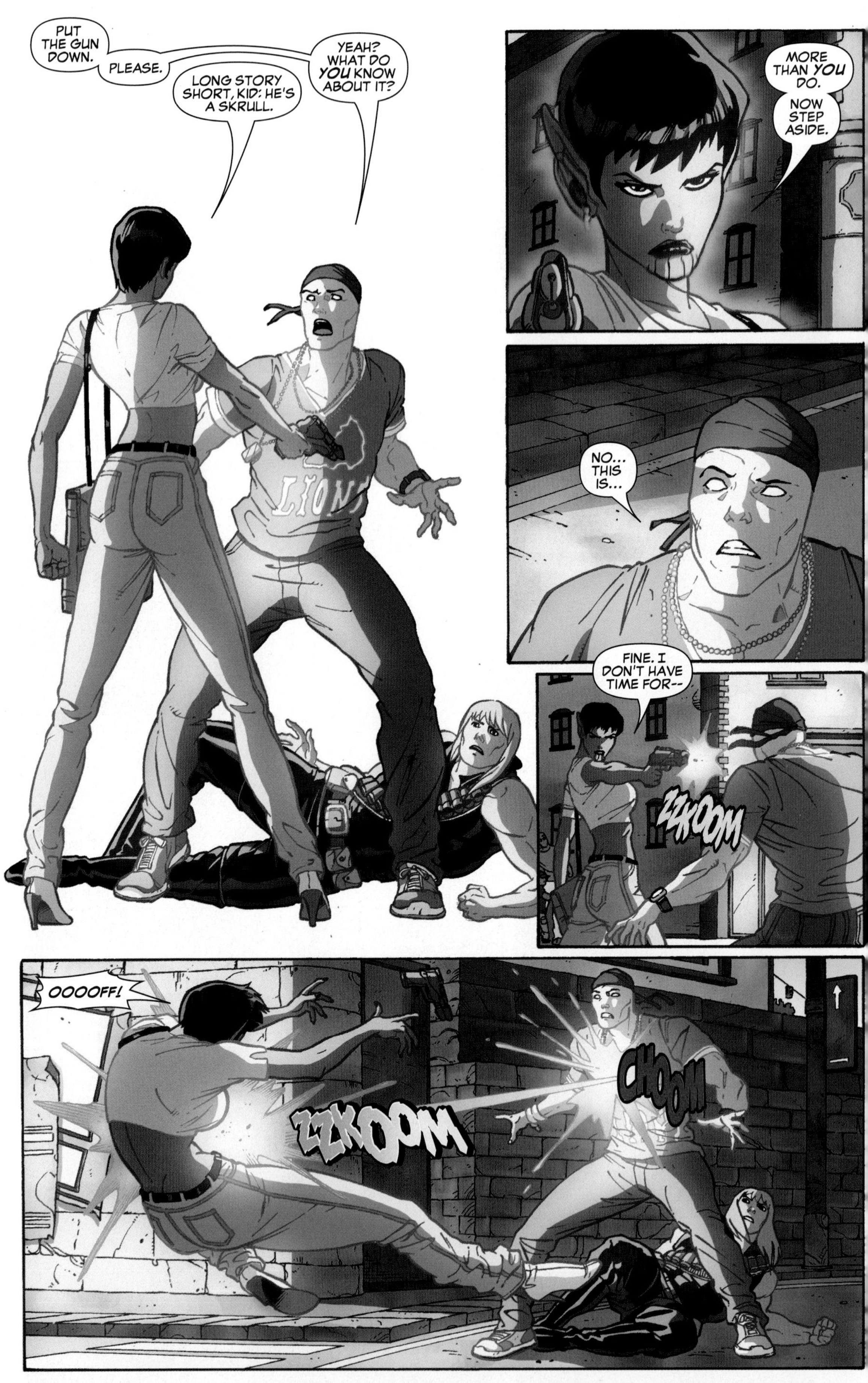
PUT THE GUN DOWN.
PLEASE.
LONG STORY SHORT, KID: HE'S A SKRULL.
YEAH? WHAT DO *YOU* KNOW ABOUT IT?
MORE THAN *YOU* DO.
NOW STEP ASIDE.
NO... THIS IS...
FINE. I DON'T HAVE TIME FOR--
ZZKOOM
OOOOFF!
CHOOM
ZZKOOM

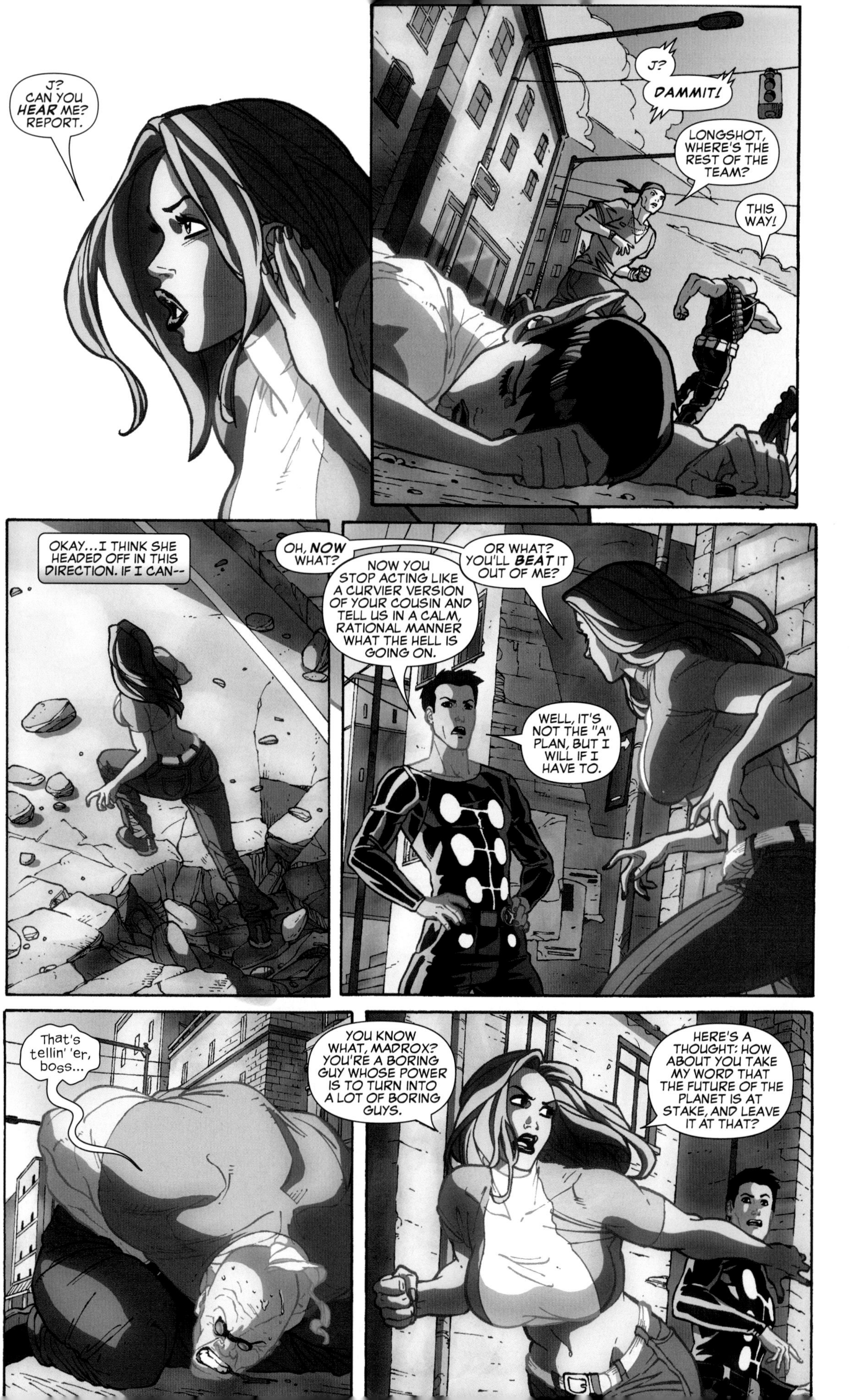
J? CAN YOU HEAR ME? REPORT.
J?
DAMMIT!
LONGSHOT, WHERE'S THE REST OF THE TEAM?
THIS WAY!
OKAY...I THINK SHE HEADED OFF IN THIS DIRECTION. IF I CAN--
OH, NOW WHAT?
OR WHAT? YOU'LL BEAT IT OUT OF ME?
NOW YOU STOP ACTING LIKE A CURVIER VERSION OF YOUR COUSIN AND TELL US IN A CALM, RATIONAL MANNER WHAT THE HELL IS GOING ON.
WELL, IT'S NOT THE "A" PLAN, BUT I WILL IF I HAVE TO.
That's tellin' 'er, boss...
YOU KNOW WHAT, MADROX? YOU'RE A BORING GUY WHOSE POWER IS TO TURN INTO A LOT OF BORING GUYS.
HERE'S A THOUGHT: HOW ABOUT YOU TAKE MY WORD THAT THE FUTURE OF THE PLANET IS AT STAKE, AND LEAVE IT AT THAT?

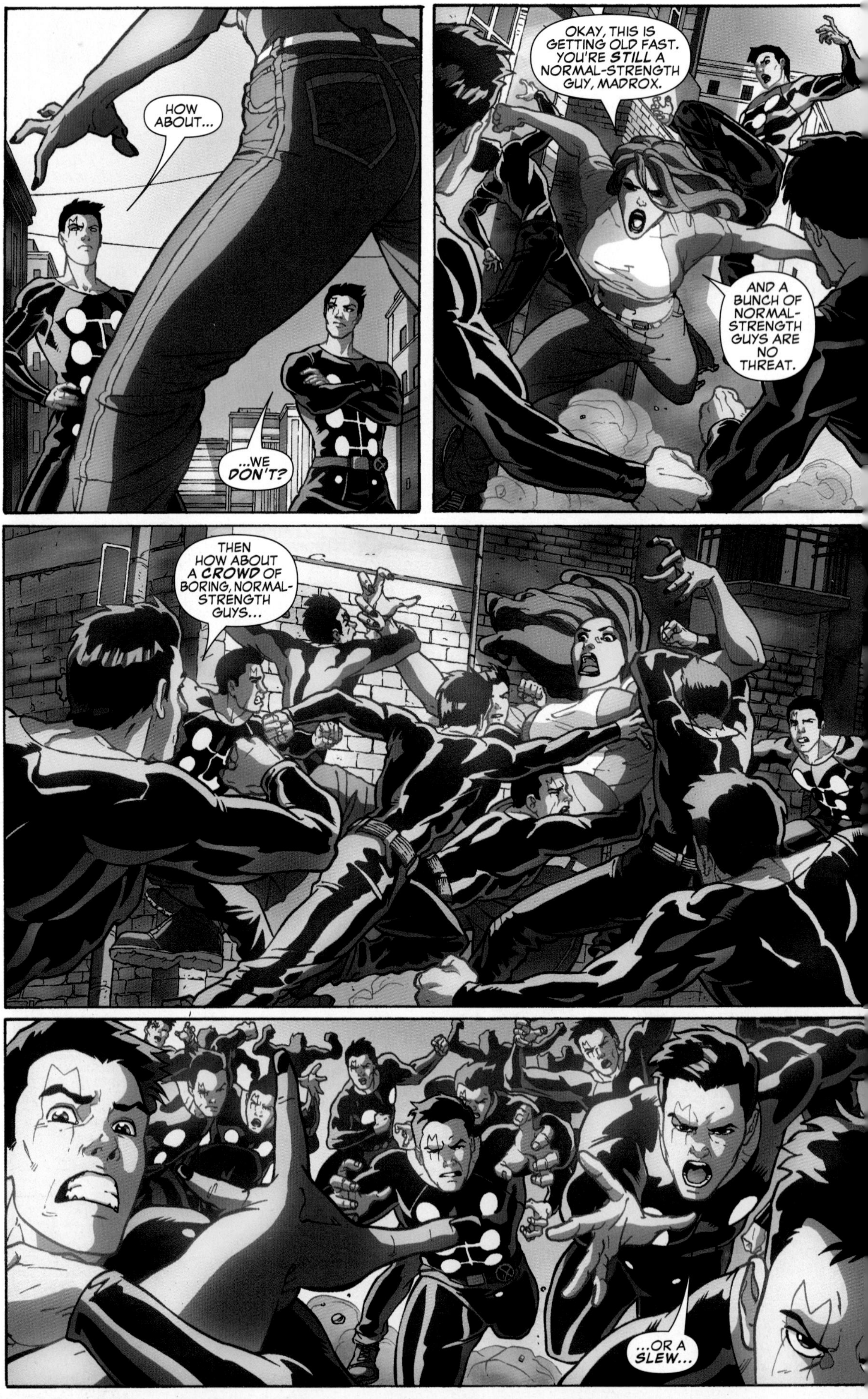
HOW ABOUT...
...WE DON'T?
OKAY, THIS IS GETTING OLD FAST. YOU'RE STILL A NORMAL-STRENGTH GUY, MADROX.
AND A BUNCH OF NORMAL-STRENGTH GUYS ARE NO THREAT.
THEN HOW ABOUT A CROWD OF BORING, NORMAL-STRENGTH GUYS...
...OR A SLEW...

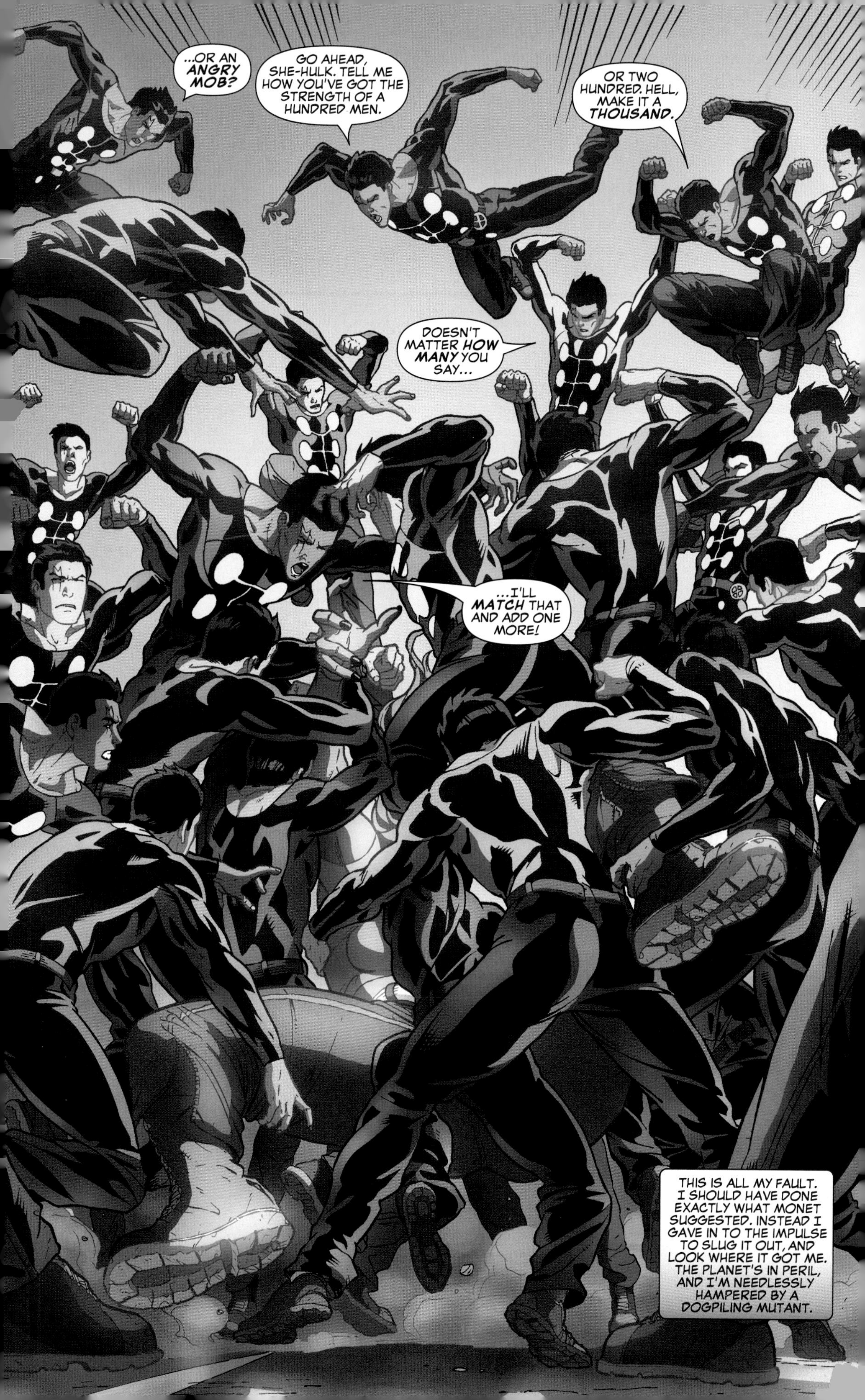
...OR AN ANGRY MOB?
GO AHEAD, SHE-HULK. TELL ME HOW YOU'VE GOT THE STRENGTH OF A HUNDRED MEN.
OR TWO HUNDRED. HELL, MAKE IT A THOUSAND.
DOESN'T MATTER HOW MANY YOU SAY...
...I'LL MATCH THAT AND ADD ONE MORE!
THIS IS ALL MY FAULT. I SHOULD HAVE DONE EXACTLY WHAT MONET SUGGESTED. INSTEAD I GAVE IN TO THE IMPULSE TO SLUG IT OUT, AND LOOK WHERE IT GOT ME. THE PLANET'S IN PERIL, AND I'M NEEDLESSLY HAMPERED BY A DOGPILING MUTANT.

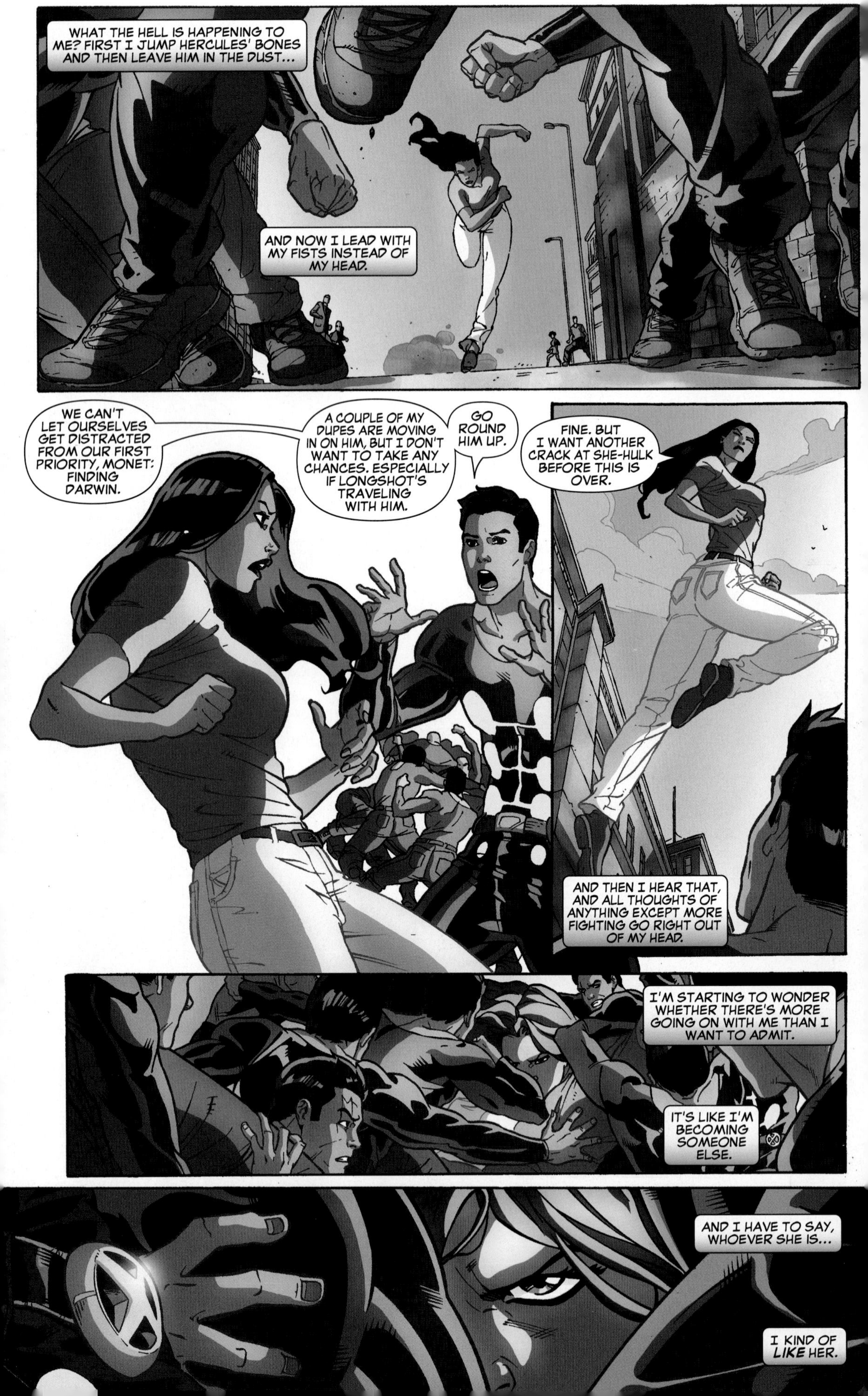
WHAT THE HELL IS HAPPENING TO ME? FIRST I JUMP HERCULES' BONES AND THEN LEAVE HIM IN THE DUST...
AND NOW I LEAD WITH MY FISTS INSTEAD OF MY HEAD.
WE CAN'T LET OURSELVES GET DISTRACTED FROM OUR FIRST PRIORITY, MONET: FINDING DARWIN.
A COUPLE OF MY DUPES ARE MOVING IN ON HIM, BUT I DON'T WANT TO TAKE ANY CHANCES. ESPECIALLY IF LONGSHOT'S TRAVELING WITH HIM.
GO ROUND HIM UP.
FINE. BUT I WANT ANOTHER CRACK AT SHE-HULK BEFORE THIS IS OVER.
AND THEN I HEAR THAT, AND ALL THOUGHTS OF ANYTHING EXCEPT MORE FIGHTING GO RIGHT OUT OF MY HEAD.
I'M STARTING TO WONDER WHETHER THERE'S MORE GOING ON WITH ME THAN I WANT TO ADMIT.
IT'S LIKE I'M BECOMING SOMEONE ELSE.
AND I HAVE TO SAY, WHOEVER SHE IS...
I KIND OF *LIKE* HER.

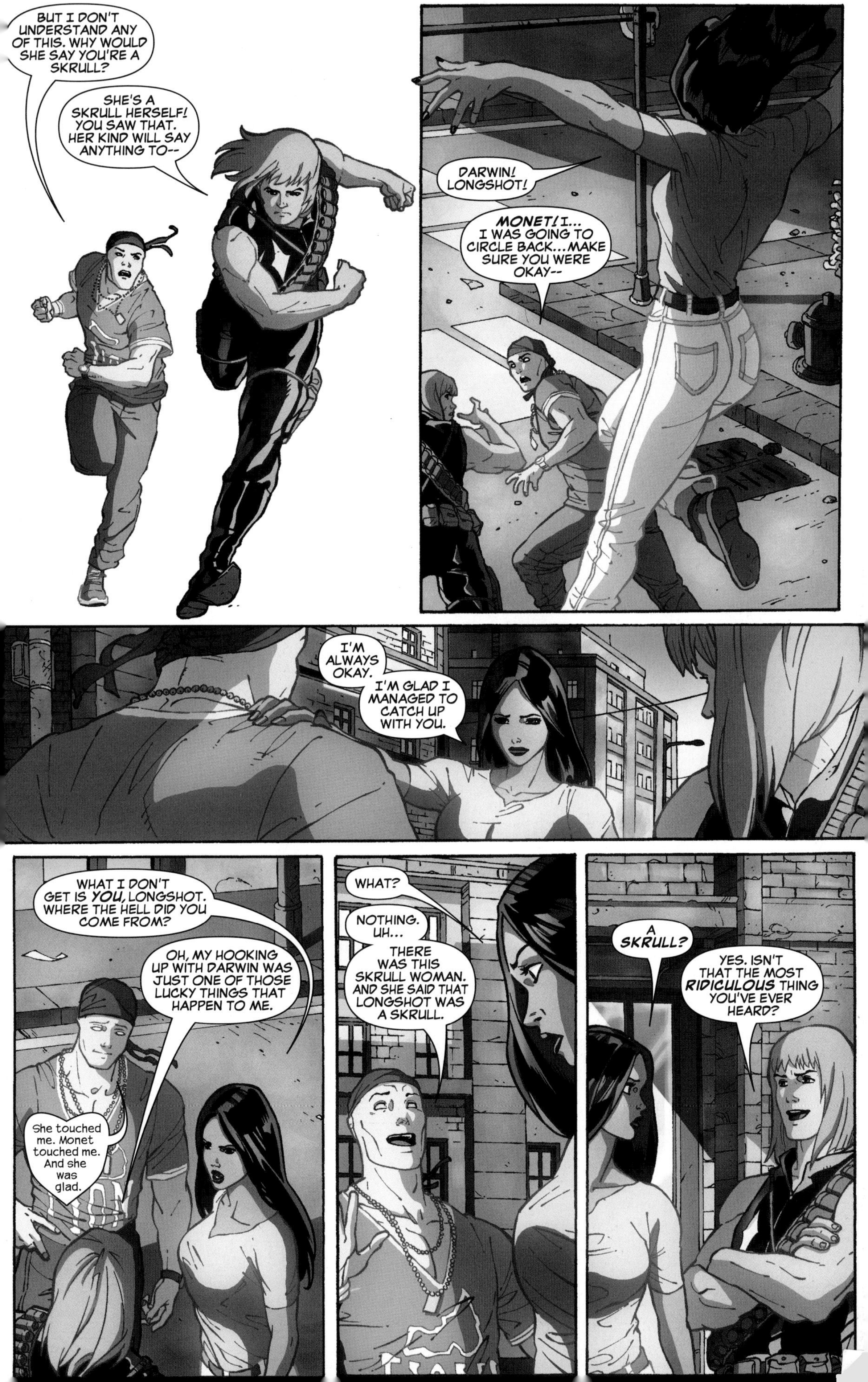
BUT I DON'T UNDERSTAND ANY OF THIS. WHY WOULD SHE SAY YOU'RE A SKRULL?
SHE'S A SKRULL HERSELF! YOU SAW THAT. HER KIND WILL SAY ANYTHING TO--
DARWIN! LONGSHOT!
MONET! I... I WAS GOING TO CIRCLE BACK... MAKE SURE YOU WERE OKAY--
I'M ALWAYS OKAY.
I'M GLAD I MANAGED TO CATCH UP WITH YOU.
WHAT I DON'T GET IS YOU, LONGSHOT. WHERE THE HELL DID YOU COME FROM?
OH, MY HOOKING UP WITH DARWIN WAS JUST ONE OF THOSE LUCKY THINGS THAT HAPPEN TO ME.
She touched me. Monet touched me. And she was glad.
WHAT?
NOTHING. UH...
THERE WAS THIS SKRULL WOMAN. AND SHE SAID THAT LONGSHOT WAS A SKRULL.
A SKRULL?
YES. ISN'T THAT THE MOST RIDICULOUS THING YOU'VE EVER HEARD?

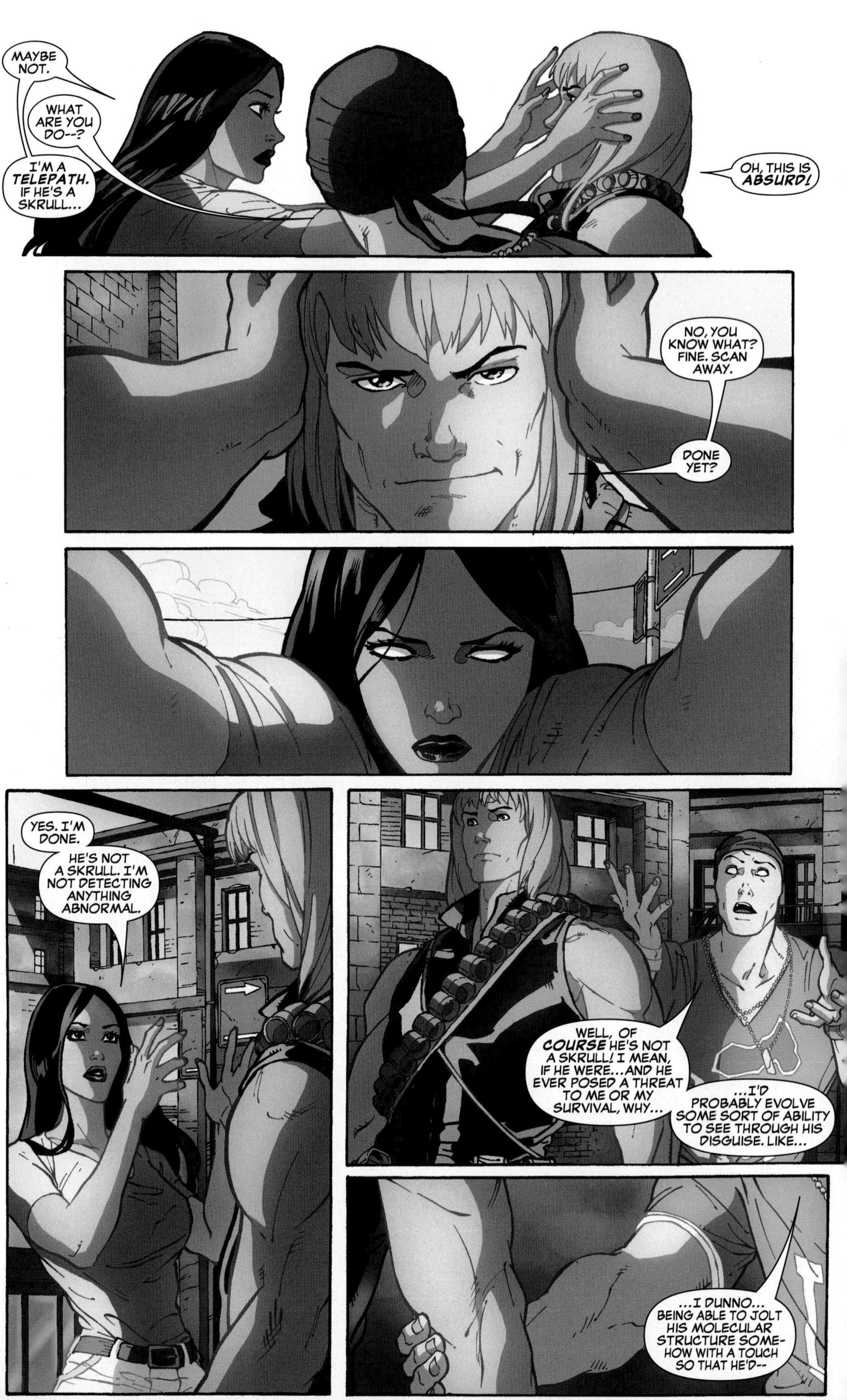

MAYBE NOT.
WHAT ARE YOU DO--?
I'M A TELEPATH. IF HE'S A SKRULL...
OH, THIS IS ABSURD!
NO, YOU KNOW WHAT? FINE. SCAN AWAY.
DONE YET?
YES. I'M DONE.
HE'S NOT A SKRULL. I'M NOT DETECTING ANYTHING ABNORMAL.
WELL, OF COURSE HE'S NOT A SKRULL! I MEAN, IF HE WERE...AND HE EVER POSED A THREAT TO ME OR MY SURVIVAL, WHY...
...I'D PROBABLY EVOLVE SOME SORT OF ABILITY TO SEE THROUGH HIS DISGUISE. LIKE...
...I DUNNO... BEING ABLE TO JOLT HIS MOLECULAR STRUCTURE SOME-HOW WITH A TOUCH SO THAT HE'D--

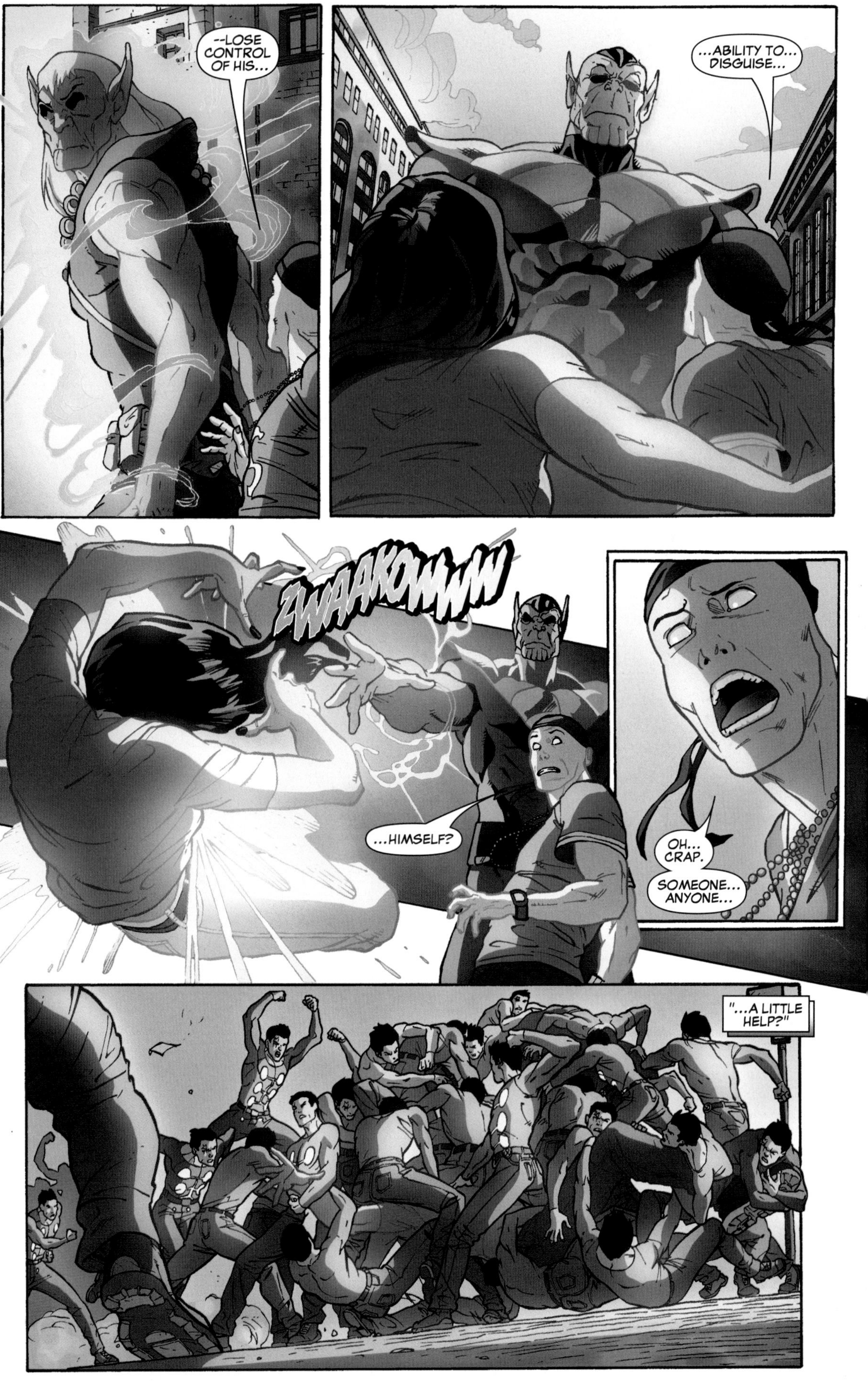
--LOSE CONTROL OF HIS...
...ABILITY TO... DISGUISE...
ZWAAKOWWW
...HIMSELF?
OH... CRAP.
SOMEONE... ANYONE...
"...A LITTLE HELP?"

#34

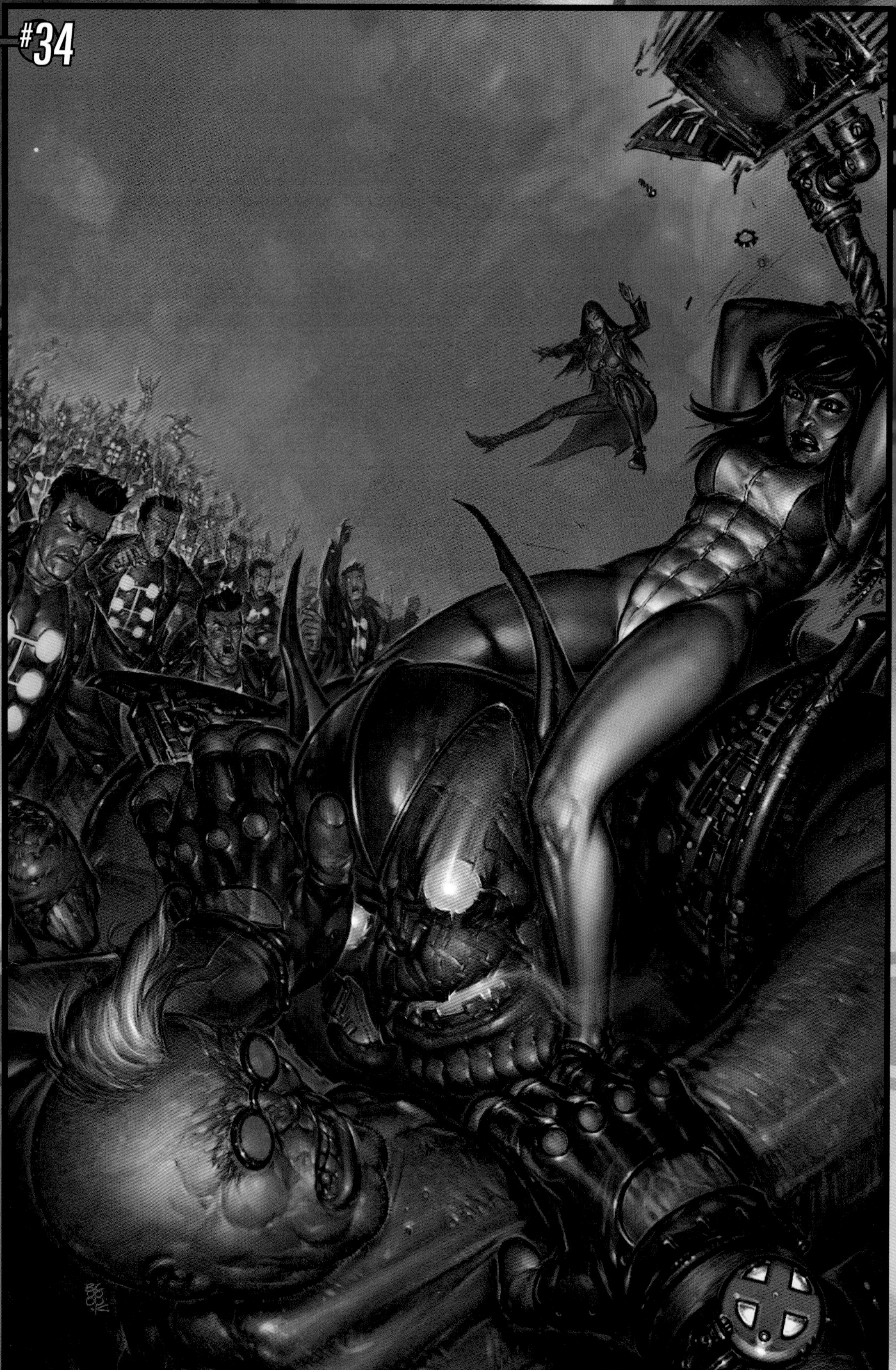

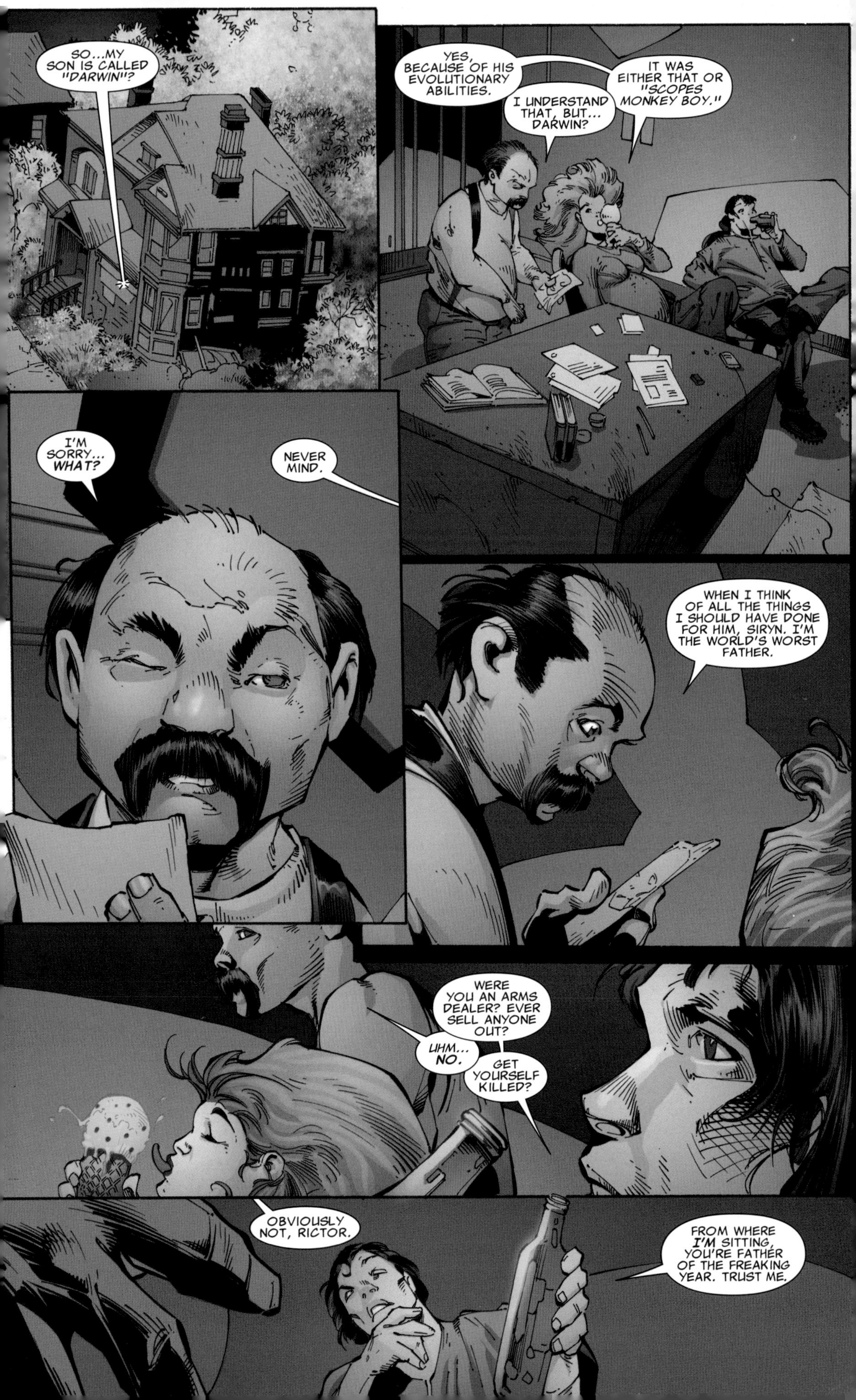
SO...MY SON IS CALLED "DARWIN"?
YES, BECAUSE OF HIS EVOLUTIONARY ABILITIES.
I UNDERSTAND THAT, BUT... DARWIN?
IT WAS EITHER THAT OR "SCOPES MONKEY BOY."
I'M SORRY... WHAT?
NEVER MIND.
WHEN I THINK OF ALL THE THINGS I SHOULD HAVE DONE FOR HIM, SIRYN. I'M THE WORLD'S WORST FATHER.
WERE YOU AN ARMS DEALER? EVER SELL ANYONE OUT?
UHM... NO.
GET YOURSELF KILLED?
OBVIOUSLY NOT, RICTOR.
FROM WHERE I'M SITTING, YOU'RE FATHER OF THE FREAKING YEAR. TRUST ME.

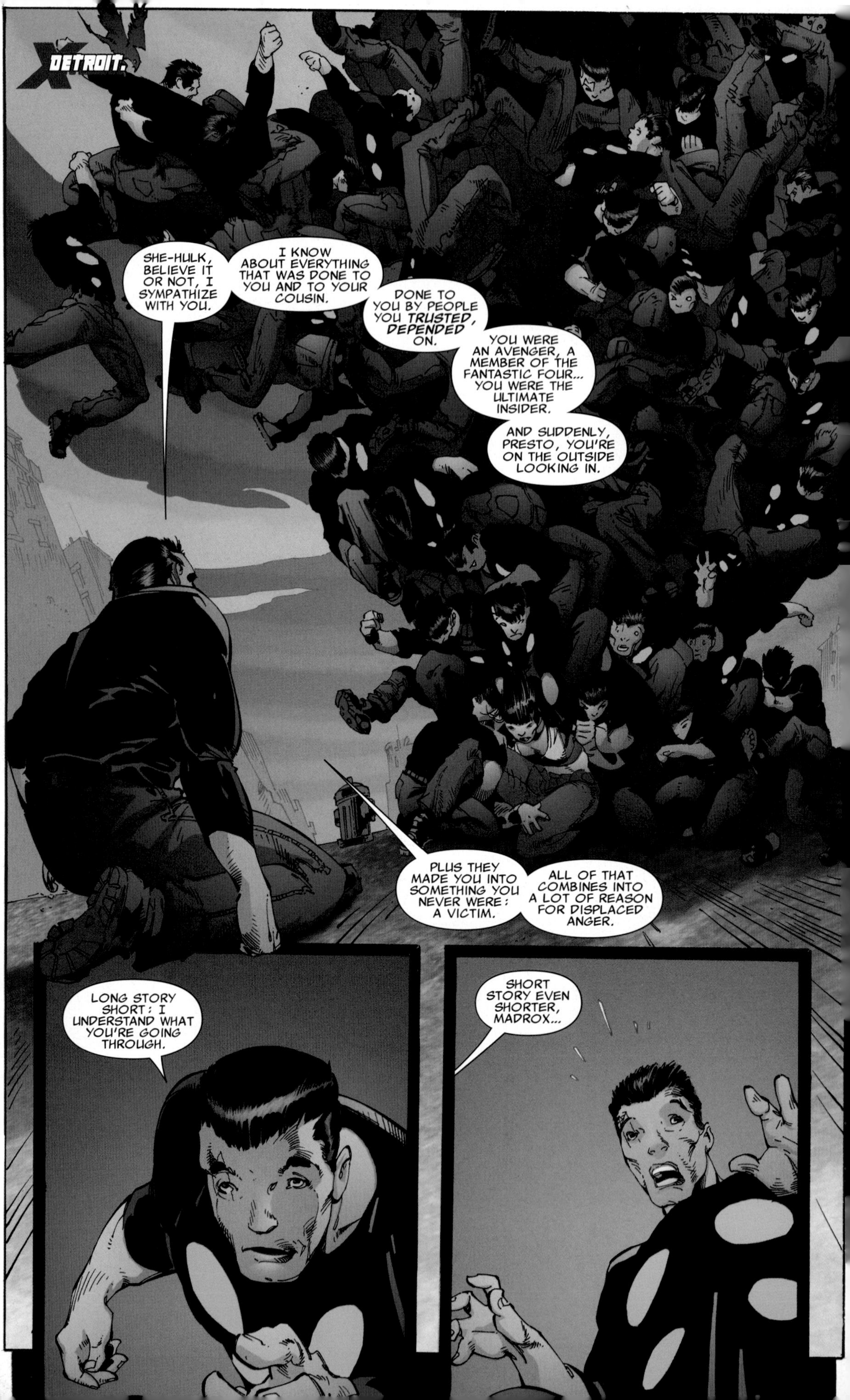
DETROIT.
SHE-HULK, BELIEVE IT OR NOT, I SYMPATHIZE WITH YOU.
I KNOW ABOUT EVERYTHING THAT WAS DONE TO YOU AND TO YOUR COUSIN.
DONE TO YOU BY PEOPLE YOU TRUSTED, DEPENDED ON.
YOU WERE AN AVENGER, A MEMBER OF THE FANTASTIC FOUR... YOU WERE THE ULTIMATE INSIDER.
AND SUDDENLY, PRESTO, YOU'RE ON THE OUTSIDE LOOKING IN.
PLUS THEY MADE YOU INTO SOMETHING YOU NEVER WERE: A VICTIM.
ALL OF THAT COMBINES INTO A LOT OF REASON FOR DISPLACED ANGER.
LONG STORY SHORT: I UNDERSTAND WHAT YOU'RE GOING THROUGH.
SHORT STORY EVEN SHORTER, MADROX...

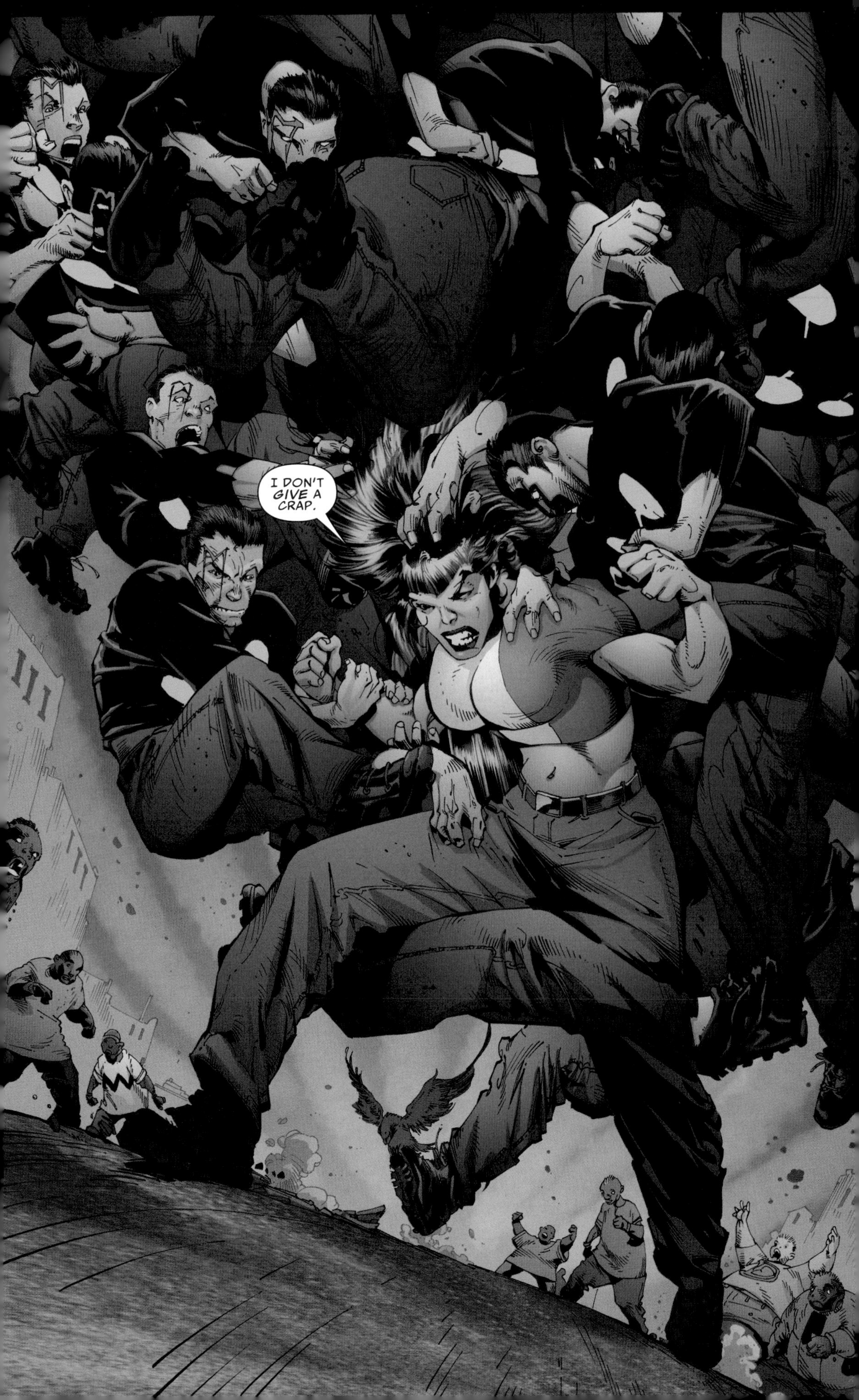
I DON'T GIVE A CRAP.

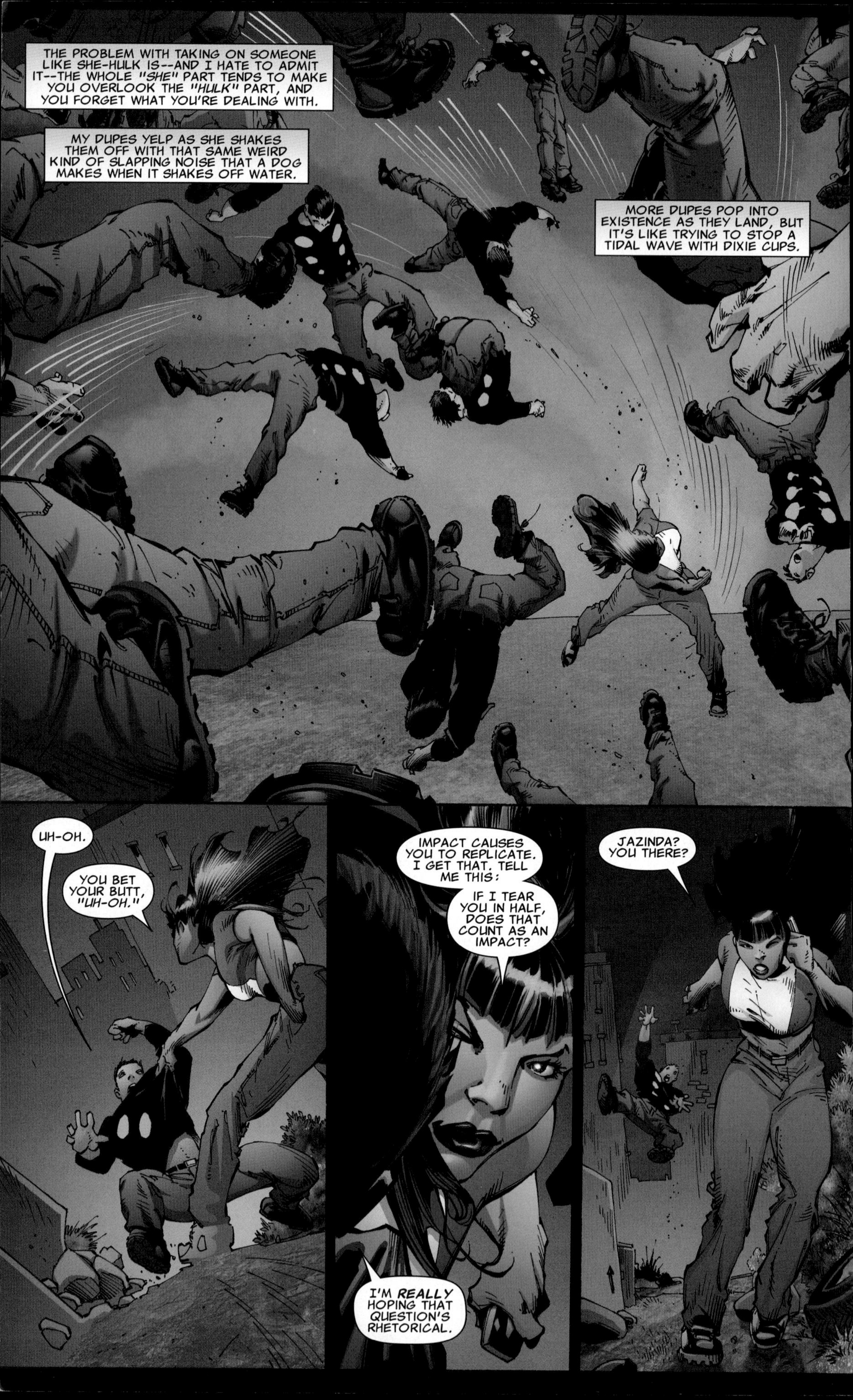

THE PROBLEM WITH TAKING ON SOMEONE LIKE SHE-HULK IS--AND I HATE TO ADMIT IT--THE WHOLE "SHE" PART TENDS TO MAKE YOU OVERLOOK THE "HULK" PART, AND YOU FORGET WHAT YOU'RE DEALING WITH.
MY DUPES YELP AS SHE SHAKES THEM OFF WITH THAT SAME WEIRD KIND OF SLAPPING NOISE THAT A DOG MAKES WHEN IT SHAKES OFF WATER.
MORE DUPES POP INTO EXISTENCE AS THEY LAND, BUT IT'S LIKE TRYING TO STOP A TIDAL WAVE WITH DIXIE CUPS.
UH-OH.
YOU BET YOUR BUTT, "UH-OH."
IMPACT CAUSES YOU TO REPLICATE. I GET THAT. TELL ME THIS:
IF I TEAR YOU IN HALF, DOES THAT COUNT AS AN IMPACT?
I'M REALLY HOPING THAT QUESTION'S RHETORICAL.
JAZINDA? YOU THERE?

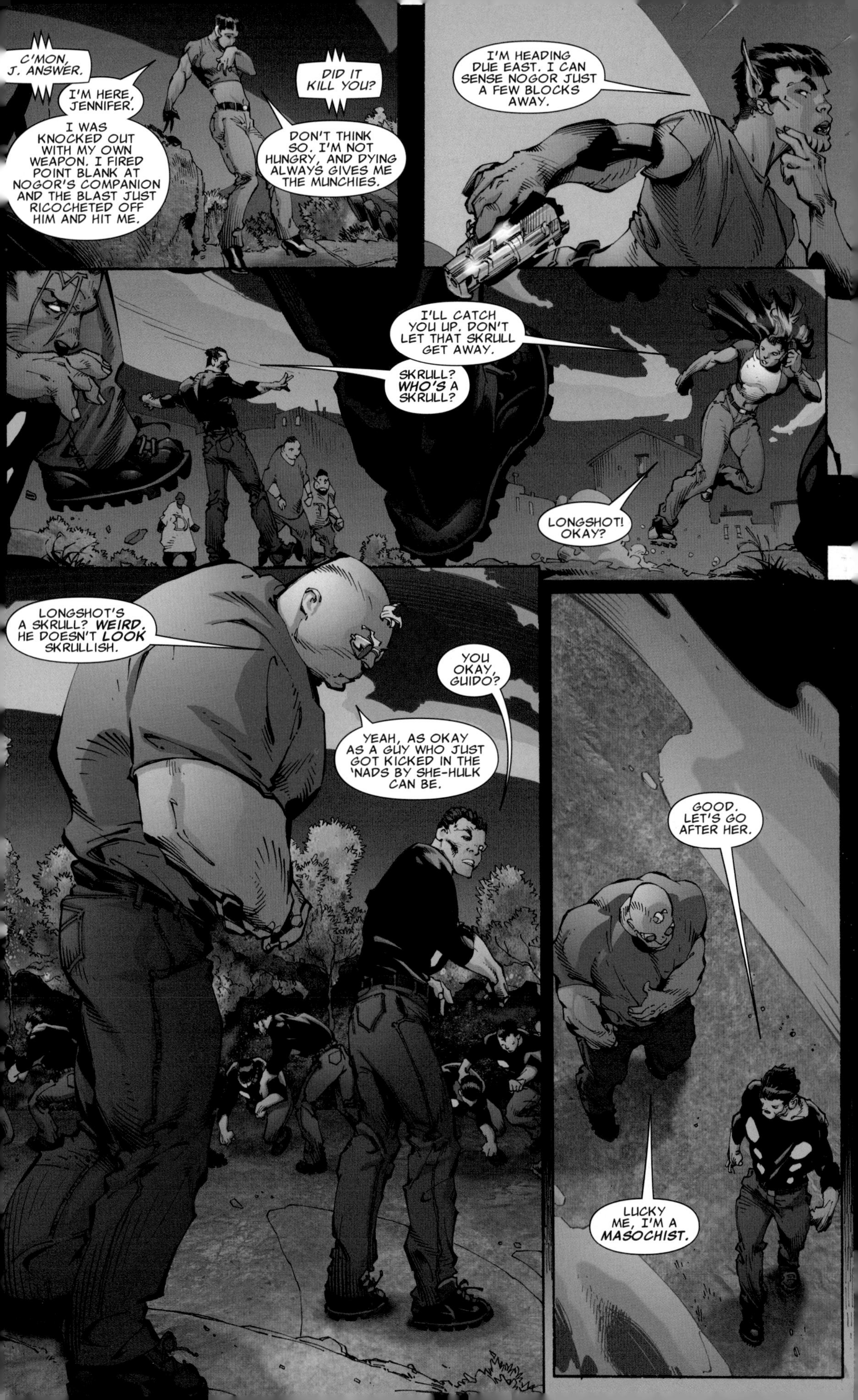
C'MON, J. ANSWER.
I'M HERE, JENNIFER.
I WAS KNOCKED OUT WITH MY OWN WEAPON. I FIRED POINT BLANK AT NOGOR'S COMPANION AND THE BLAST JUST RICOCHETED OFF HIM AND HIT ME.
DID IT KILL YOU?
DON'T THINK SO. I'M NOT HUNGRY, AND DYING ALWAYS GIVES ME THE MUNCHIES.
I'M HEADING DUE EAST. I CAN SENSE NOGOR JUST A FEW BLOCKS AWAY.
I'LL CATCH YOU UP. DON'T LET THAT SKRULL GET AWAY.
SKRULL? *WHO'S* A SKRULL?
LONGSHOT! OKAY?
LONGSHOT'S A SKRULL? **WEIRD.** HE DOESN'T **LOOK** SKRULLISH.
YOU OKAY, GUIDO?
YEAH, AS OKAY AS A GUY WHO JUST GOT KICKED IN THE 'NADS BY SHE-HULK CAN BE.
GOOD. LET'S GO AFTER HER.
LUCKY ME, I'M A **MASOCHIST.**

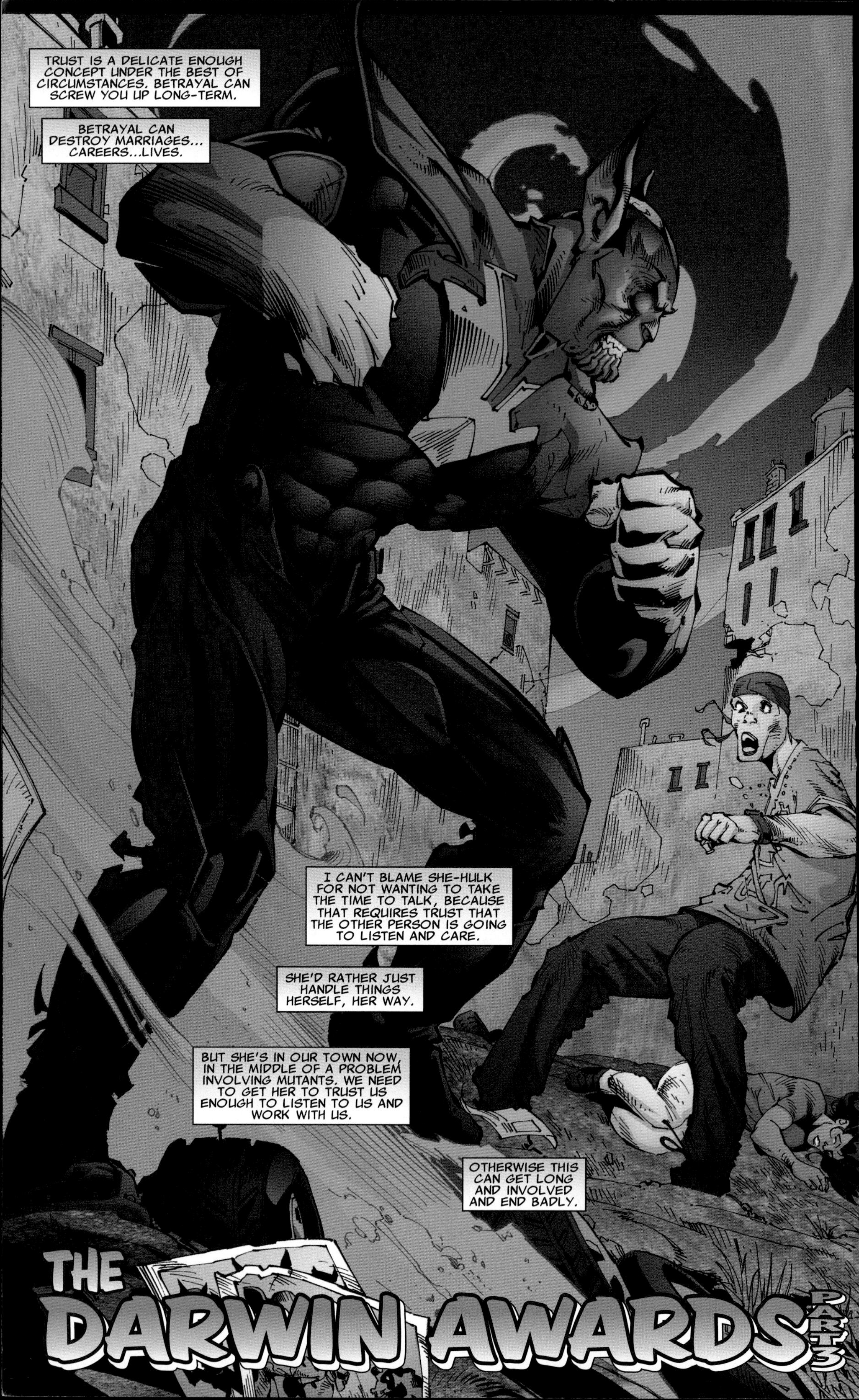
TRUST IS A DELICATE ENOUGH CONCEPT UNDER THE BEST OF CIRCUMSTANCES. BETRAYAL CAN SCREW YOU UP LONG-TERM.
BETRAYAL CAN DESTROY MARRIAGES... CAREERS...LIVES.
I CAN'T BLAME SHE-HULK FOR NOT WANTING TO TAKE THE TIME TO TALK, BECAUSE THAT REQUIRES TRUST THAT THE OTHER PERSON IS GOING TO LISTEN AND CARE.
SHE'D RATHER JUST HANDLE THINGS HERSELF, HER WAY.
BUT SHE'S IN OUR TOWN NOW, IN THE MIDDLE OF A PROBLEM INVOLVING MUTANTS. WE NEED TO GET HER TO TRUST US ENOUGH TO LISTEN TO US AND WORK WITH US.
OTHERWISE THIS CAN GET LONG AND INVOLVED AND END BADLY.
THE DARWIN AWARDS PART 3

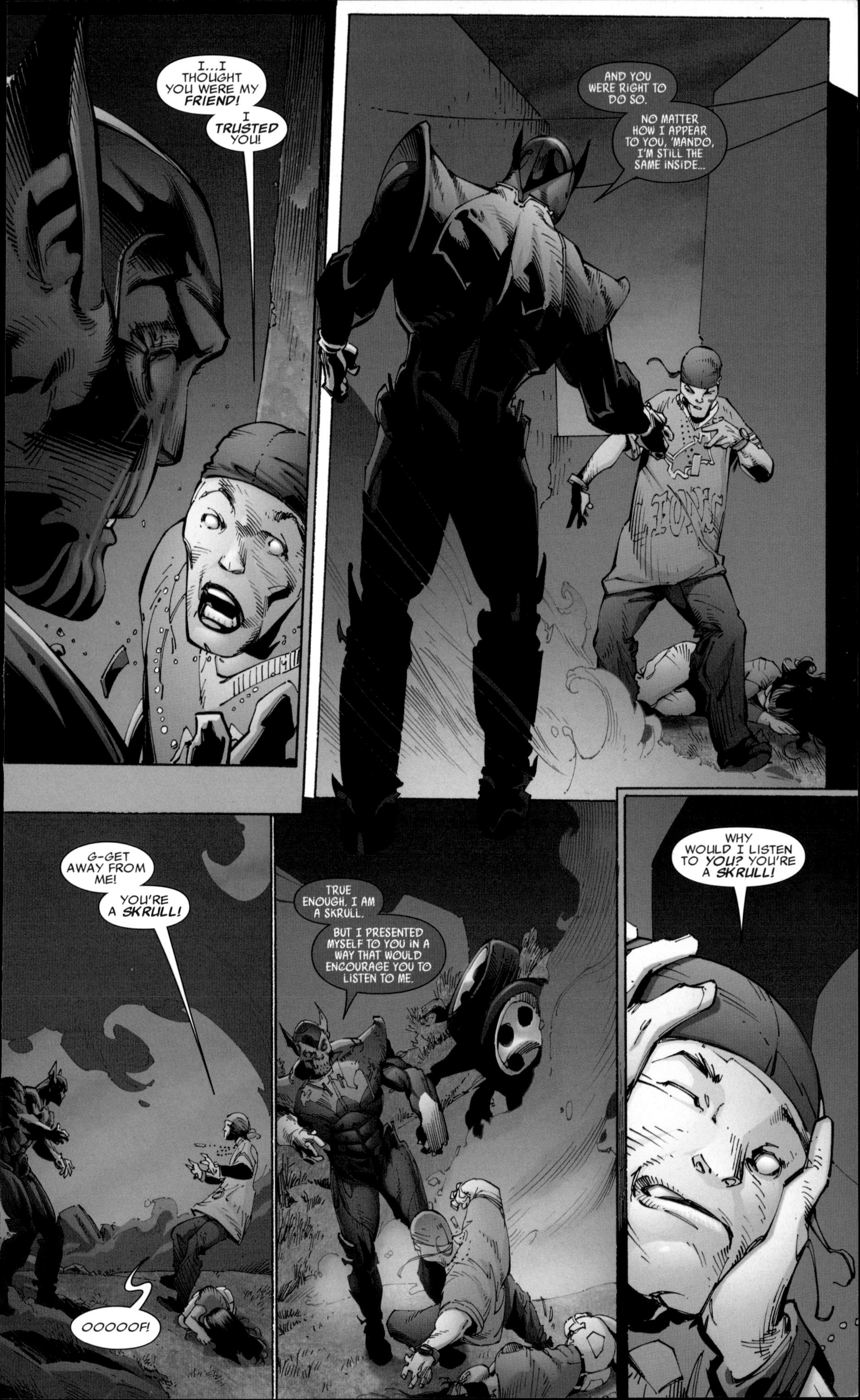
I...I THOUGHT YOU WERE MY FRIEND!
I TRUSTED YOU!
AND YOU WERE RIGHT TO DO SO.
NO MATTER HOW I APPEAR TO YOU, 'MANDO, I'M STILL THE SAME INSIDE...
G-GET AWAY FROM ME!
YOU'RE A SKRULL!
OOOOOF!
TRUE ENOUGH. I AM A SKRULL.
BUT I PRESENTED MYSELF TO YOU IN A WAY THAT WOULD ENCOURAGE YOU TO LISTEN TO ME.
WHY WOULD I LISTEN TO YOU? YOU'RE A SKRULL!

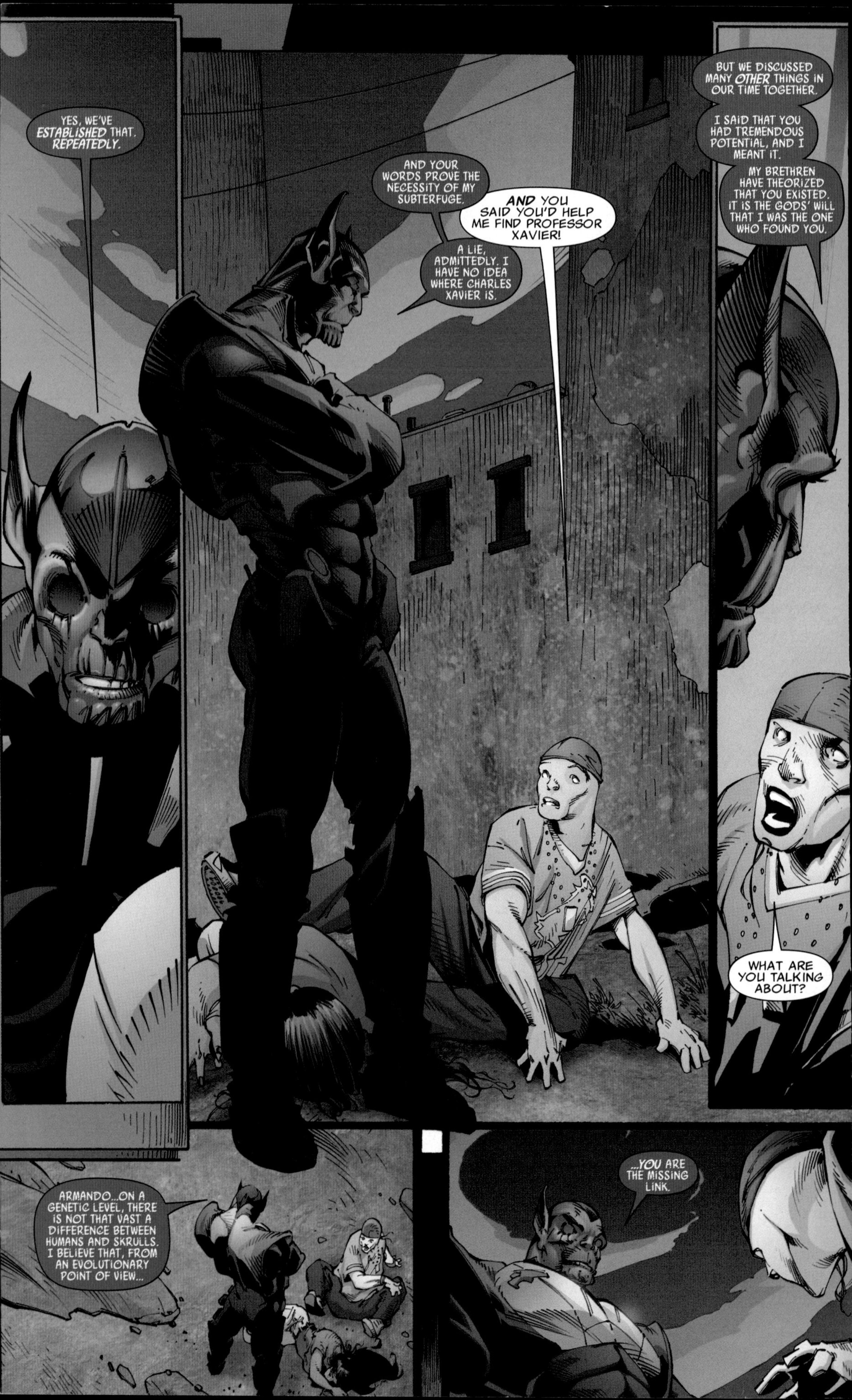
YES, WE'VE *ESTABLISHED* THAT. *REPEATEDLY.*
AND YOUR WORDS PROVE THE NECESSITY OF MY SUBTERFUGE.
A LIE, ADMITTEDLY. I HAVE NO IDEA WHERE CHARLES XAVIER IS.
AND YOU SAID YOU'D HELP ME FIND PROFESSOR XAVIER!
BUT WE DISCUSSED MANY *OTHER* THINGS IN OUR TIME TOGETHER.
I SAID THAT YOU HAD TREMENDOUS POTENTIAL, AND I MEANT IT.
MY BRETHREN HAVE THEORIZED THAT YOU EXISTED. IT IS THE GODS' WILL THAT I WAS THE ONE WHO FOUND YOU.
WHAT ARE YOU TALKING ABOUT?
ARMANDO...ON A GENETIC LEVEL, THERE IS NOT THAT VAST A DIFFERENCE BETWEEN HUMANS AND SKRULLS. I BELIEVE THAT, FROM AN EVOLUTIONARY POINT OF VIEW...
...*YOU* ARE THE MISSING LINK.

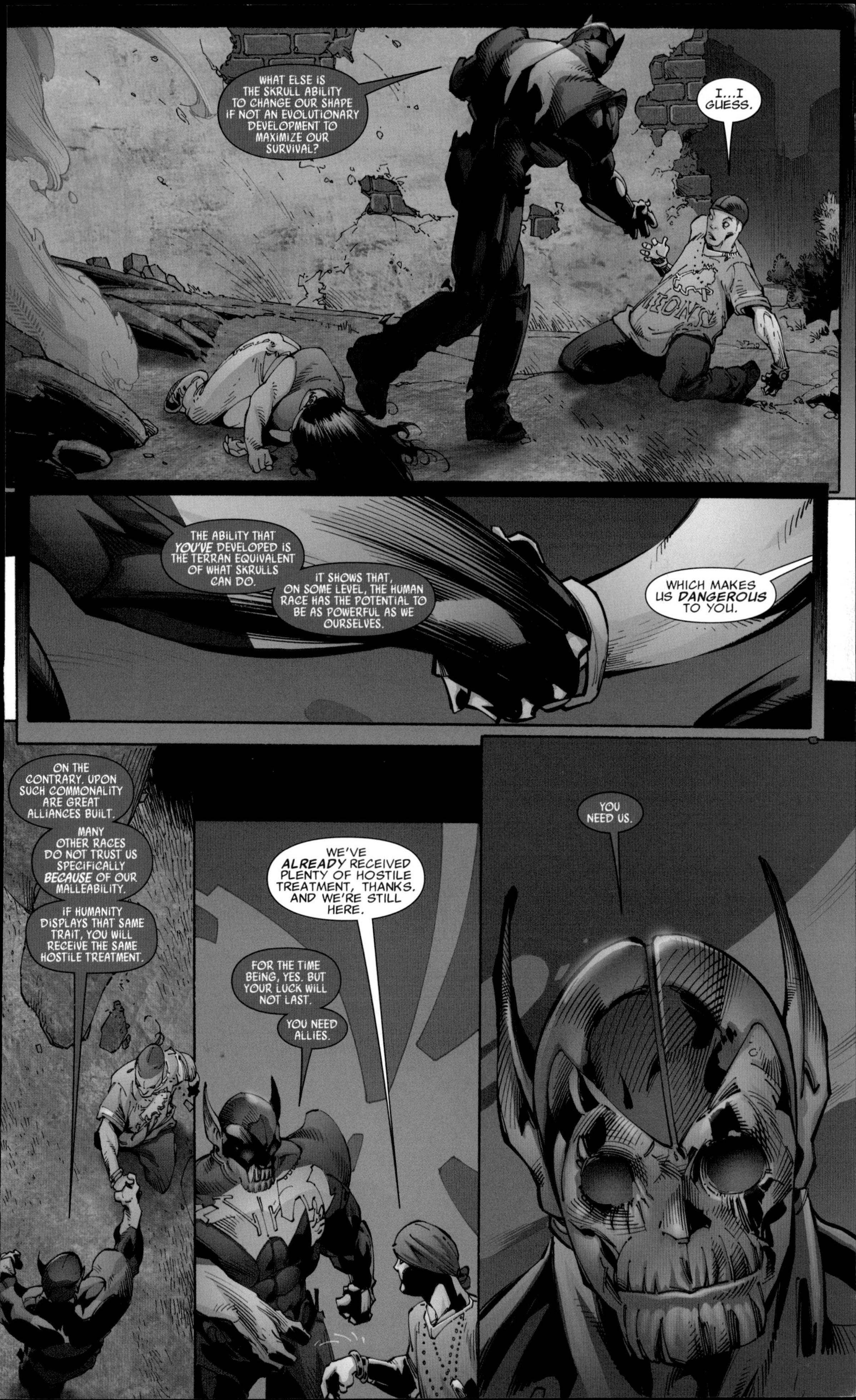
WHAT ELSE IS THE SKRULL ABILITY TO CHANGE OUR SHAPE IF NOT AN EVOLUTIONARY DEVELOPMENT TO MAXIMIZE OUR SURVIVAL?
I...I GUESS.
THE ABILITY THAT YOU'VE DEVELOPED IS THE TERRAN EQUIVALENT OF WHAT SKRULLS CAN DO.
IT SHOWS THAT, ON SOME LEVEL, THE HUMAN RACE HAS THE POTENTIAL TO BE AS POWERFUL AS WE OURSELVES.
WHICH MAKES US DANGEROUS TO YOU.
ON THE CONTRARY. UPON SUCH COMMONALITY ARE GREAT ALLIANCES BUILT.
MANY OTHER RACES DO NOT TRUST US SPECIFICALLY BECAUSE OF OUR MALLEABILITY.
IF HUMANITY DISPLAYS THAT SAME TRAIT, YOU WILL RECEIVE THE SAME HOSTILE TREATMENT.
WE'VE ALREADY RECEIVED PLENTY OF HOSTILE TREATMENT, THANKS, AND WE'RE STILL HERE.
FOR THE TIME BEING, YES. BUT YOUR LUCK WILL NOT LAST.
YOU NEED ALLIES.
YOU NEED US.

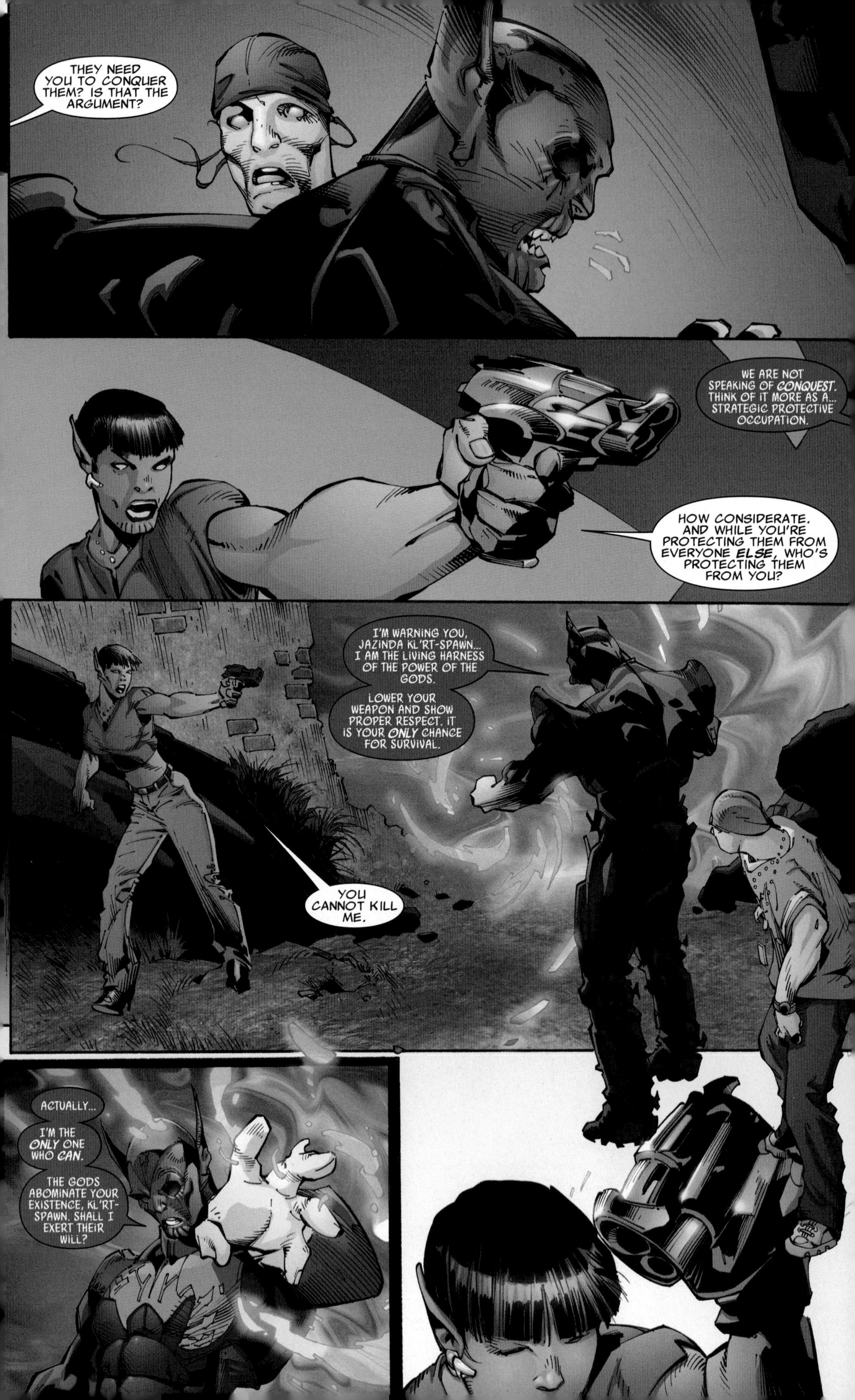
THEY NEED YOU TO CONQUER THEM? IS THAT THE ARGUMENT?
WE ARE NOT SPEAKING OF CONQUEST. THINK OF IT MORE AS A... STRATEGIC PROTECTIVE OCCUPATION.
HOW CONSIDERATE. AND WHILE YOU'RE PROTECTING THEM FROM EVERYONE ELSE, WHO'S PROTECTING THEM FROM YOU?
I'M WARNING YOU, JAZINDA KL'RT-SPAWN... I AM THE LIVING HARNESS OF THE POWER OF THE GODS.
LOWER YOUR WEAPON AND SHOW PROPER RESPECT. IT IS YOUR ONLY CHANCE FOR SURVIVAL.
YOU CANNOT KILL ME.
ACTUALLY...
I'M THE ONLY ONE WHO CAN.
THE GODS ABOMINATE YOUR EXISTENCE, KL'RT-SPAWN. SHALL I EXERT THEIR WILL?

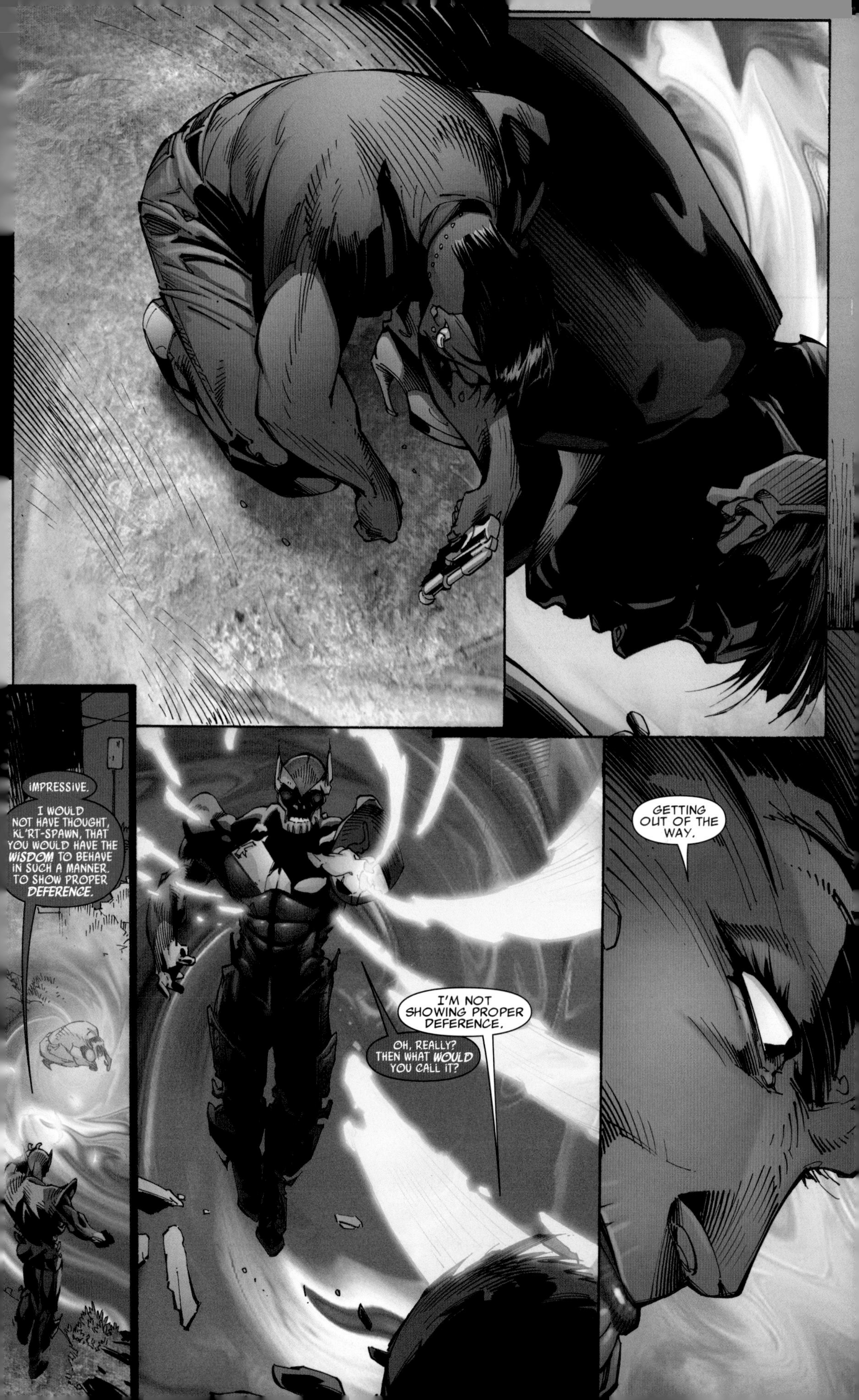
IMPRESSIVE.
I WOULD NOT HAVE THOUGHT, KL'RT-SPAWN, THAT YOU WOULD HAVE THE WISDOM TO BEHAVE IN SUCH A MANNER. TO SHOW PROPER DEFERENCE.
I'M NOT SHOWING PROPER DEFERENCE.
OH, REALLY? THEN WHAT WOULD YOU CALL IT?
GETTING OUT OF THE WAY.

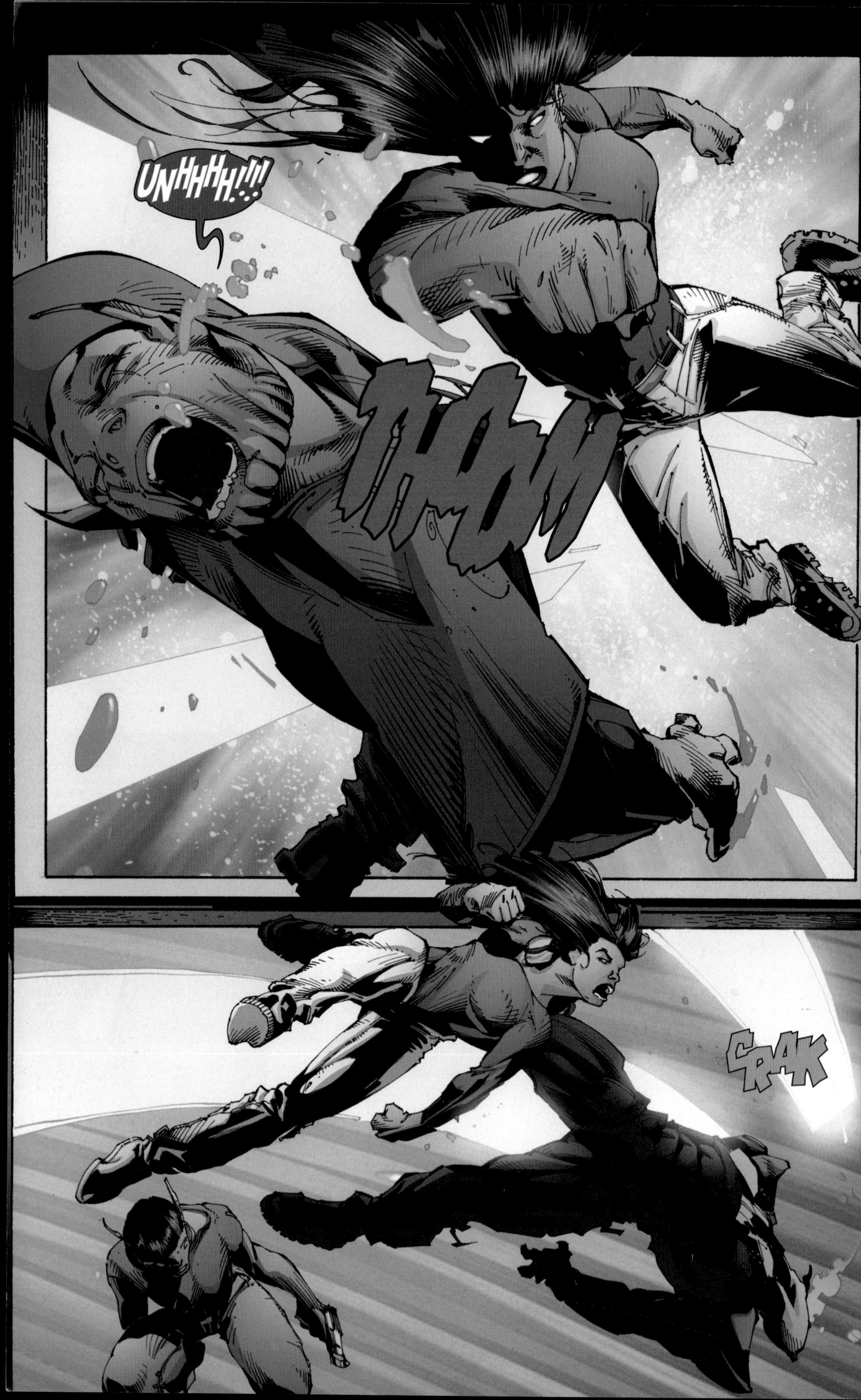
UNHHHH!!!!
THOOM
CRAK

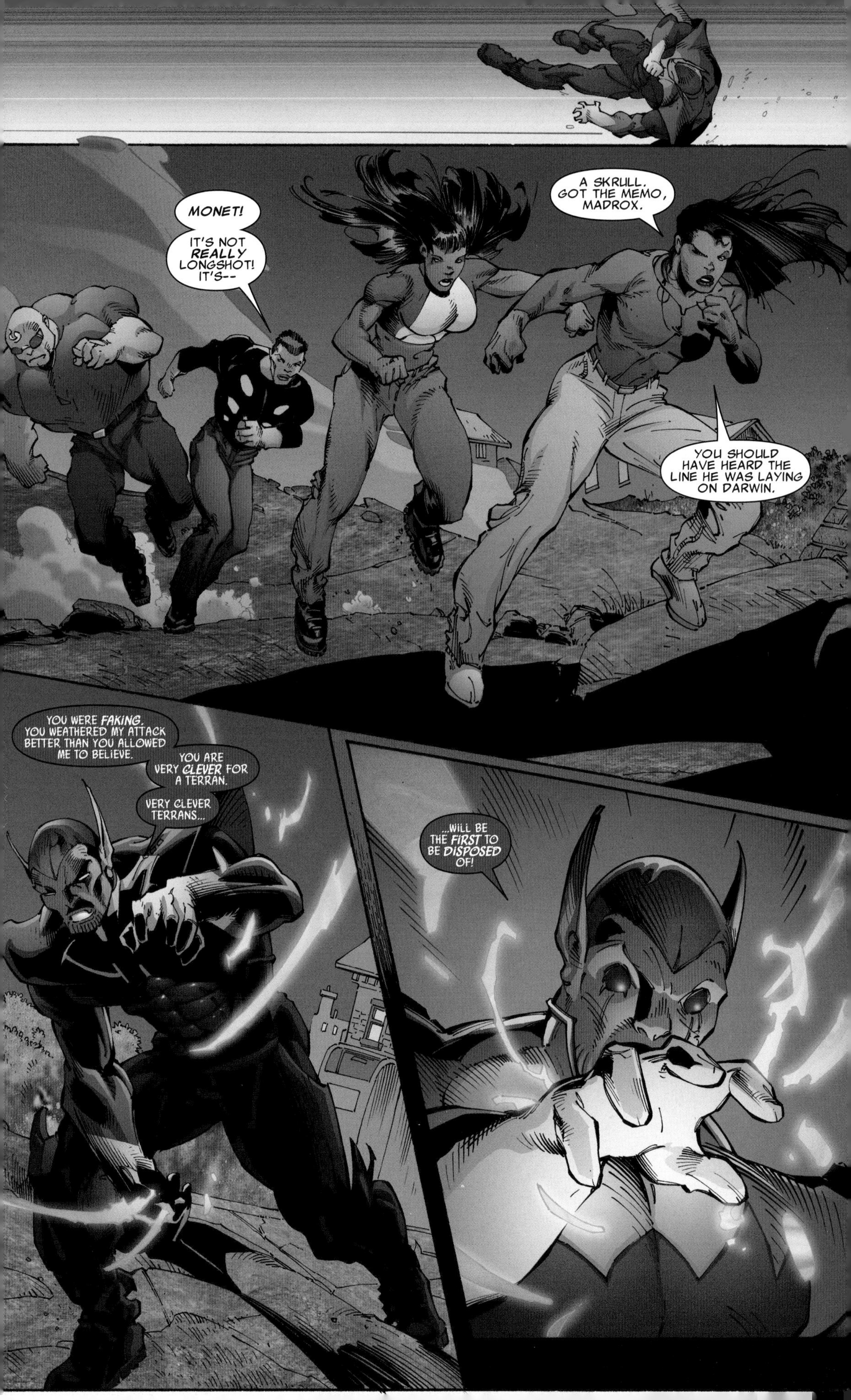
MONET!
IT'S NOT REALLY LONGSHOT! IT'S--
A SKRULL. GOT THE MEMO, MADROX.
YOU SHOULD HAVE HEARD THE LINE HE WAS LAYING ON DARWIN.
YOU WERE FAKING. YOU WEATHERED MY ATTACK BETTER THAN YOU ALLOWED ME TO BELIEVE.
YOU ARE VERY CLEVER FOR A TERRAN.
VERY CLEVER TERRANS...
...WILL BE THE FIRST TO BE DISPOSED OF!

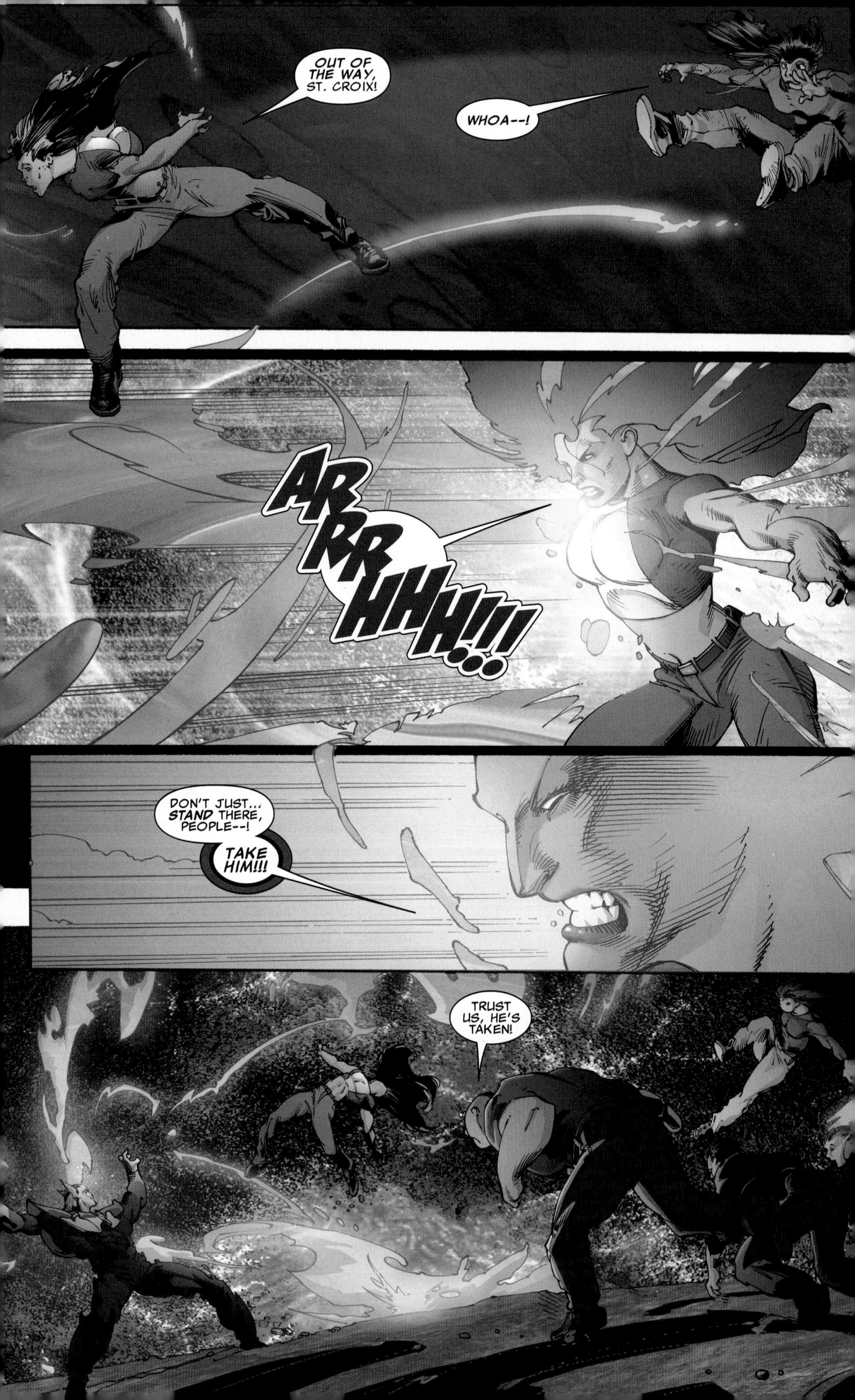
OUT OF THE WAY, ST. CROIX!
WHOA--!
ARRRHHH!!!
DON'T JUST... **STAND** THERE, PEOPLE--!
TAKE HIM!!!
TRUST US, HE'S TAKEN!

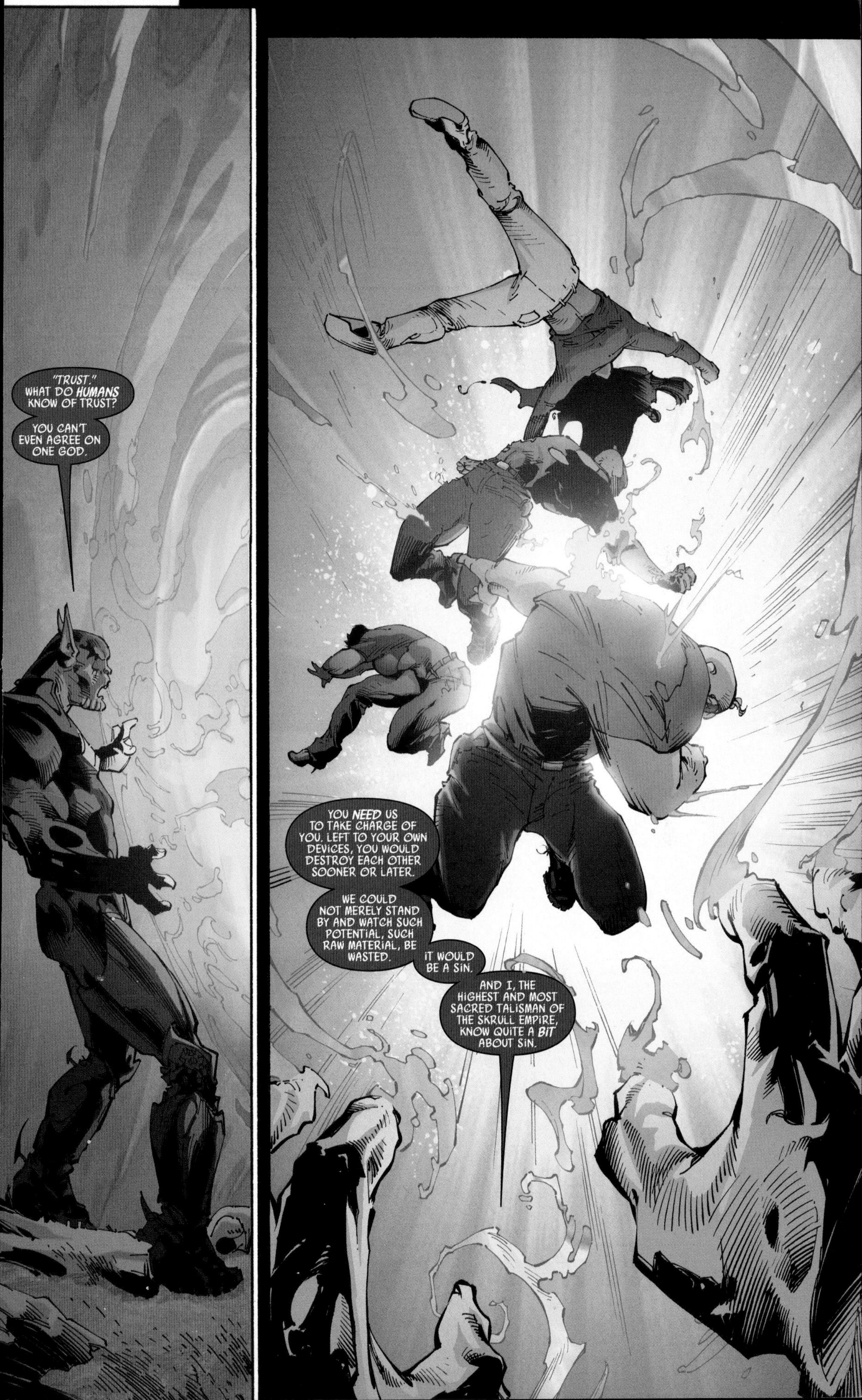
"TRUST." WHAT DO HUMANS KNOW OF TRUST?
YOU CAN'T EVEN AGREE ON ONE GOD.
YOU NEED US TO TAKE CHARGE OF YOU. LEFT TO YOUR OWN DEVICES, YOU WOULD DESTROY EACH OTHER SOONER OR LATER.
WE COULD NOT MERELY STAND BY AND WATCH SUCH POTENTIAL, SUCH RAW MATERIAL, BE WASTED.
IT WOULD BE A SIN.
AND I, THE HIGHEST AND MOST SACRED TALISMAN OF THE SKRULL EMPIRE, KNOW QUITE A BIT ABOUT SIN.

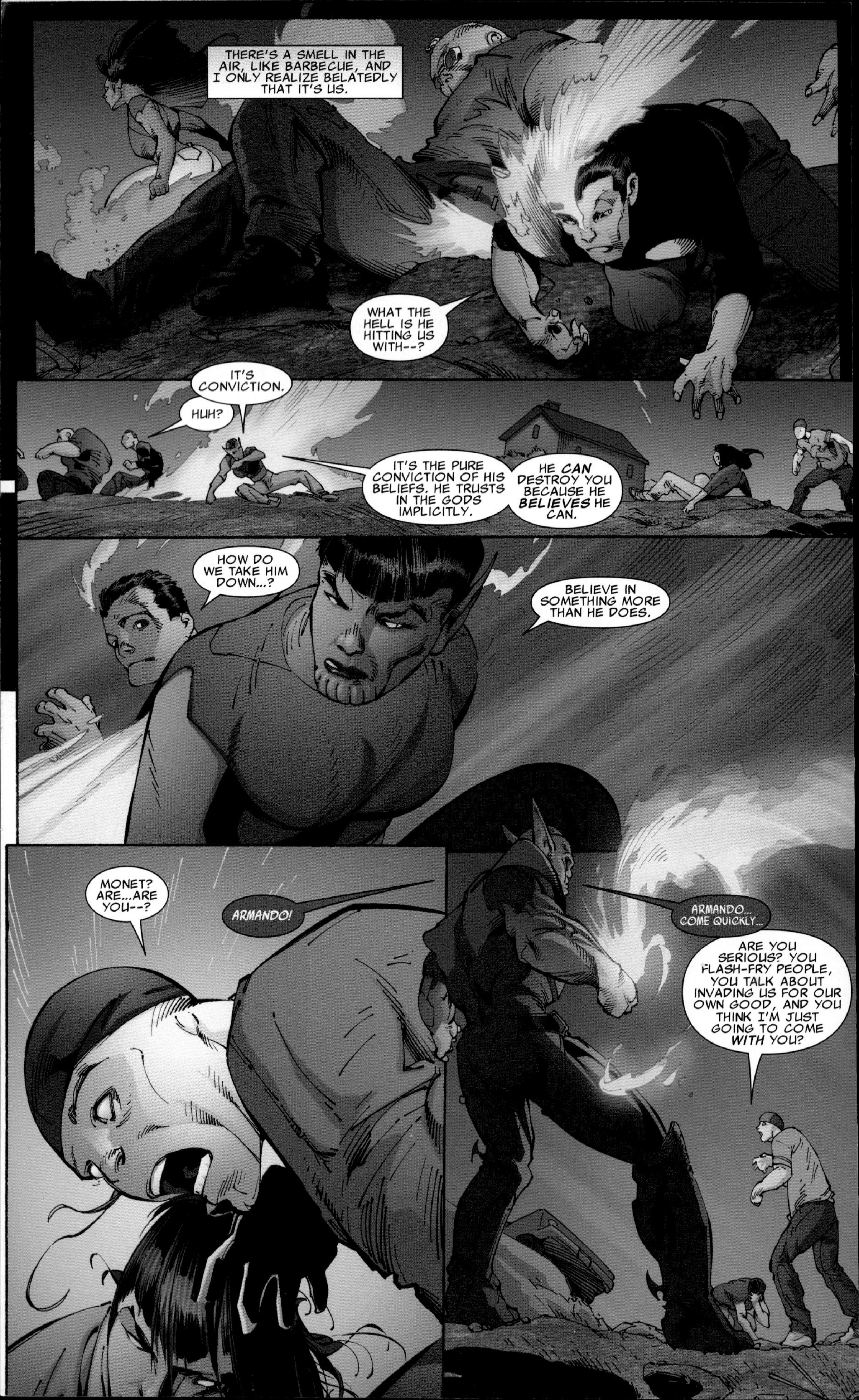
THERE'S A SMELL IN THE AIR, LIKE BARBECUE, AND I ONLY REALIZE BELATEDLY THAT IT'S US.
WHAT THE HELL IS HE HITTING US WITH--?
IT'S CONVICTION.
HUH?
IT'S THE PURE CONVICTION OF HIS BELIEFS. HE TRUSTS IN THE GODS IMPLICITLY.
HE CAN DESTROY YOU BECAUSE HE BELIEVES HE CAN.
HOW DO WE TAKE HIM DOWN...?
BELIEVE IN SOMETHING MORE THAN HE DOES.
MONET? ARE...ARE YOU--?
ARMANDO!
ARMANDO... COME QUICKLY...
ARE YOU SERIOUS? YOU FLASH-FRY PEOPLE, YOU TALK ABOUT INVADING US FOR OUR OWN GOOD, AND YOU THINK I'M JUST GOING TO COME WITH YOU?

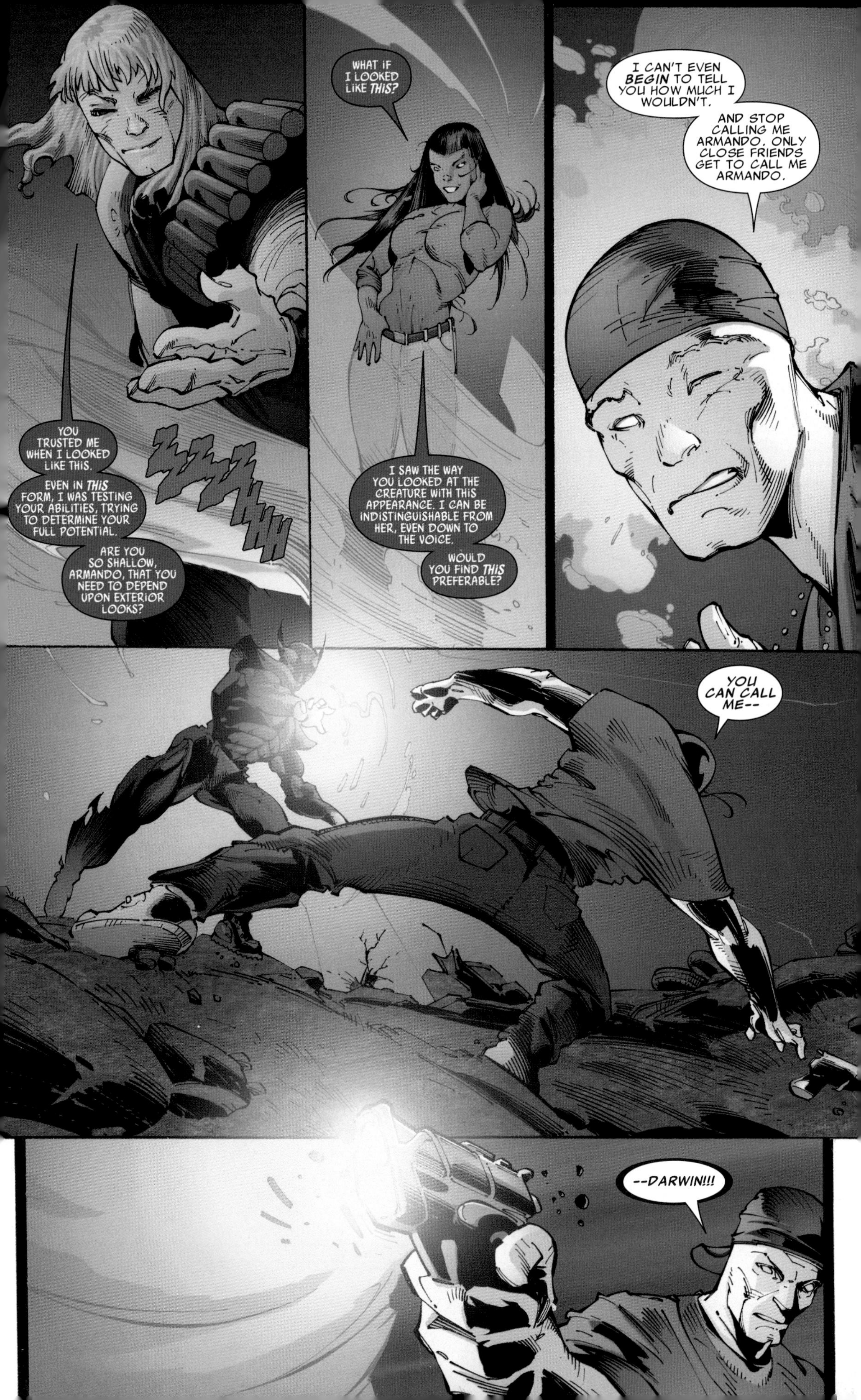

YOU TRUSTED ME WHEN I LOOKED LIKE THIS.
EVEN IN THIS FORM, I WAS TESTING YOUR ABILITIES, TRYING TO DETERMINE YOUR FULL POTENTIAL.
ARE YOU SO SHALLOW, ARMANDO, THAT YOU NEED TO DEPEND UPON EXTERIOR LOOKS?
ZZZZZHHH
WHAT IF I LOOKED LIKE THIS?
I SAW THE WAY YOU LOOKED AT THE CREATURE WITH THIS APPEARANCE. I CAN BE INDISTINGUISHABLE FROM HER, EVEN DOWN TO THE VOICE.
WOULD YOU FIND THIS PREFERABLE?
I CAN'T EVEN BEGIN TO TELL YOU HOW MUCH I WOULDN'T.
AND STOP CALLING ME ARMANDO. ONLY CLOSE FRIENDS GET TO CALL ME ARMANDO.
YOU CAN CALL ME--
--DARWIN!!!

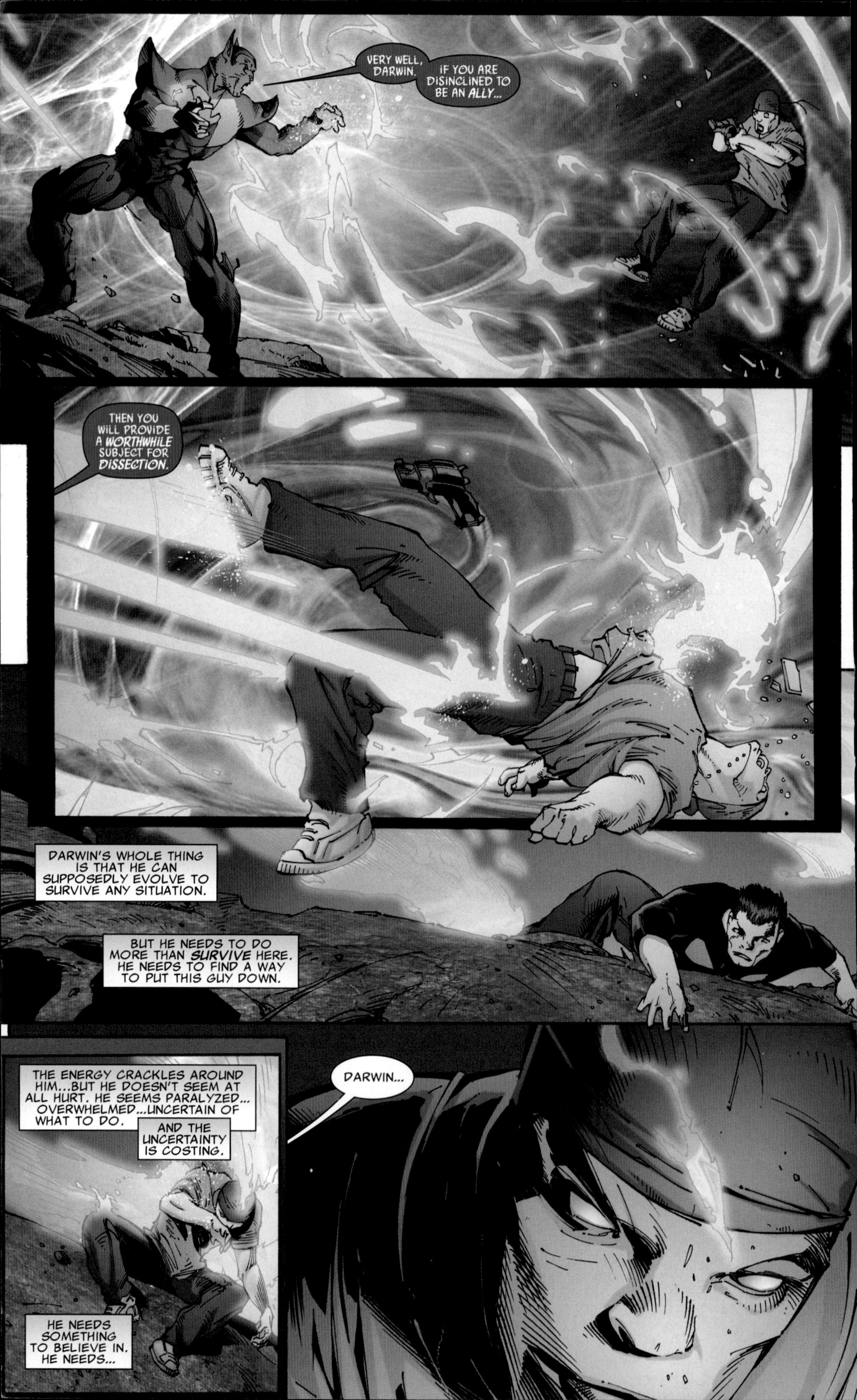
VERY WELL, DARWIN.
IF YOU ARE DISINCLINED TO BE AN ALLY...
THEN YOU WILL PROVIDE A WORTHWHILE SUBJECT FOR DISSECTION.
DARWIN'S WHOLE THING IS THAT HE CAN SUPPOSEDLY EVOLVE TO SURVIVE ANY SITUATION.
BUT HE NEEDS TO DO MORE THAN SURVIVE HERE. HE NEEDS TO FIND A WAY TO PUT THIS GUY DOWN.
THE ENERGY CRACKLES AROUND HIM...BUT HE DOESN'T SEEM AT ALL HURT. HE SEEMS PARALYZED... OVERWHELMED...UNCERTAIN OF WHAT TO DO.
AND THE UNCERTAINTY IS COSTING.
DARWIN...
HE NEEDS SOMETHING TO BELIEVE IN. HE NEEDS...

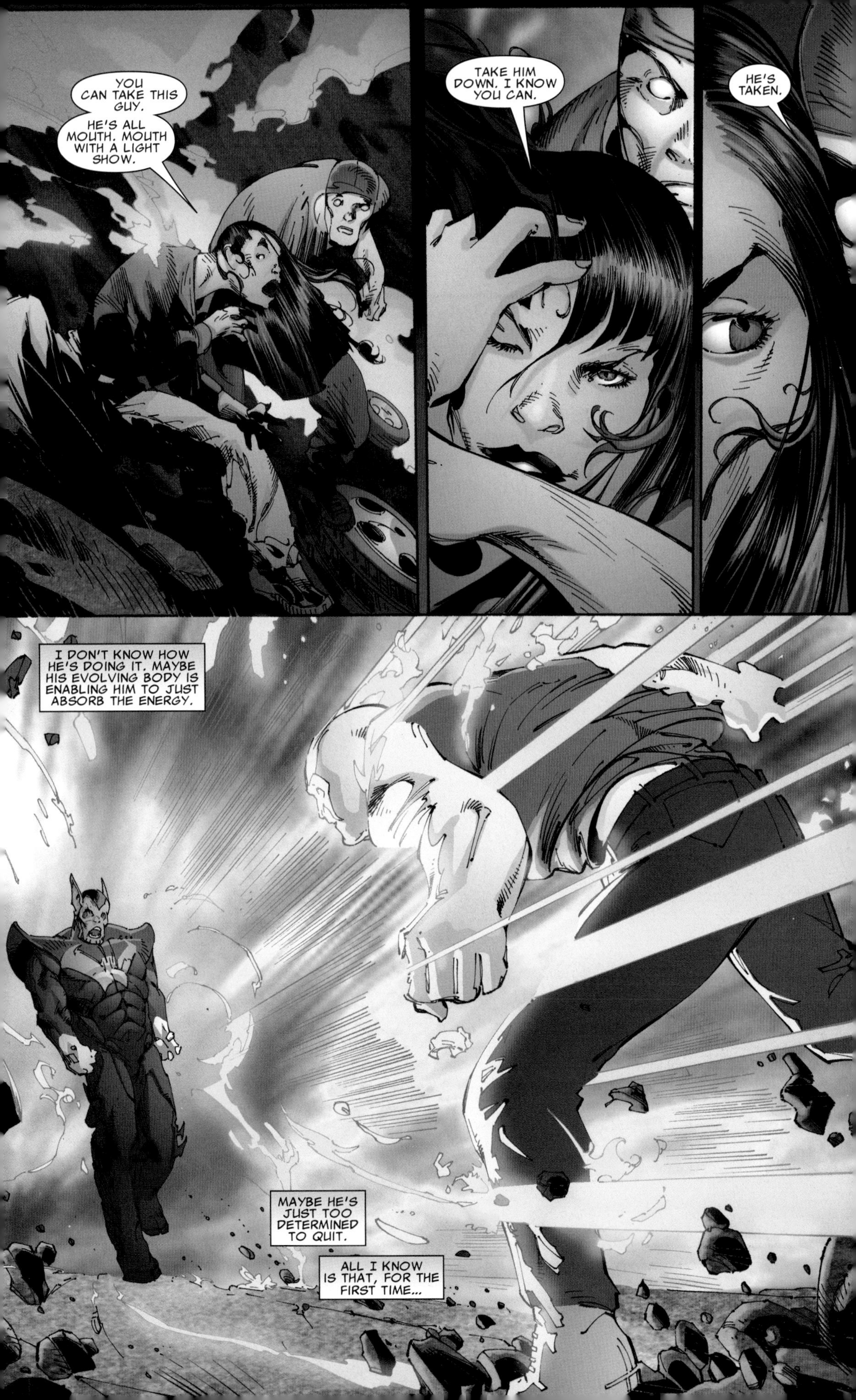
YOU CAN TAKE THIS GUY.
HE'S ALL MOUTH. MOUTH WITH A LIGHT SHOW.
TAKE HIM DOWN. I KNOW YOU CAN.
HE'S TAKEN.
I DON'T KNOW HOW HE'S DOING IT. MAYBE HIS EVOLVING BODY IS ENABLING HIM TO JUST ABSORB THE ENERGY.
MAYBE HE'S JUST TOO DETERMINED TO QUIT.
ALL I KNOW IS THAT, FOR THE FIRST TIME...

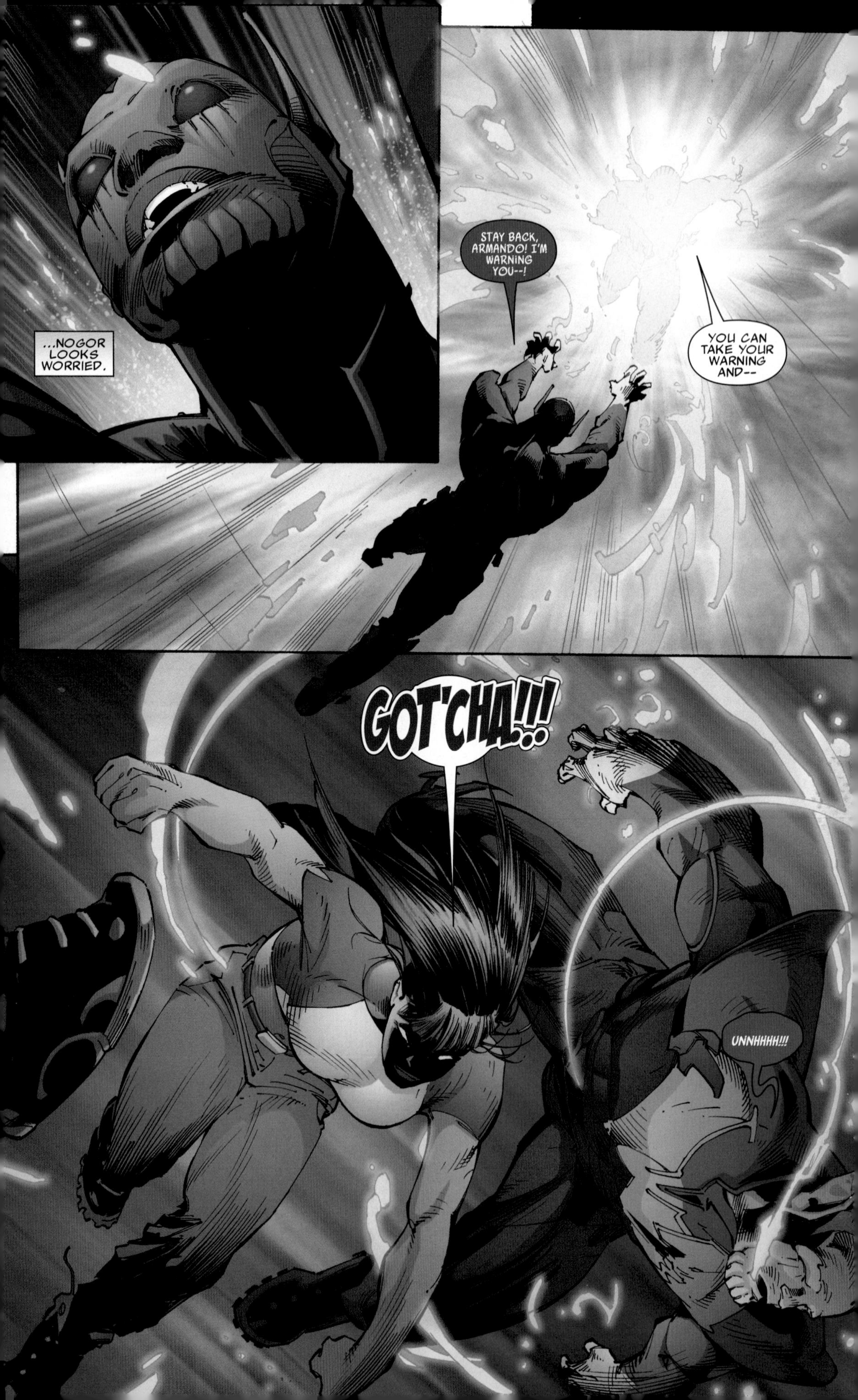
...NOGOR LOOKS WORRIED.
STAY BACK, ARMANDO! I'M WARNING YOU--!
YOU CAN TAKE YOUR WARNING AND--
GOT'CHA!!!
UNNHHHH!!!

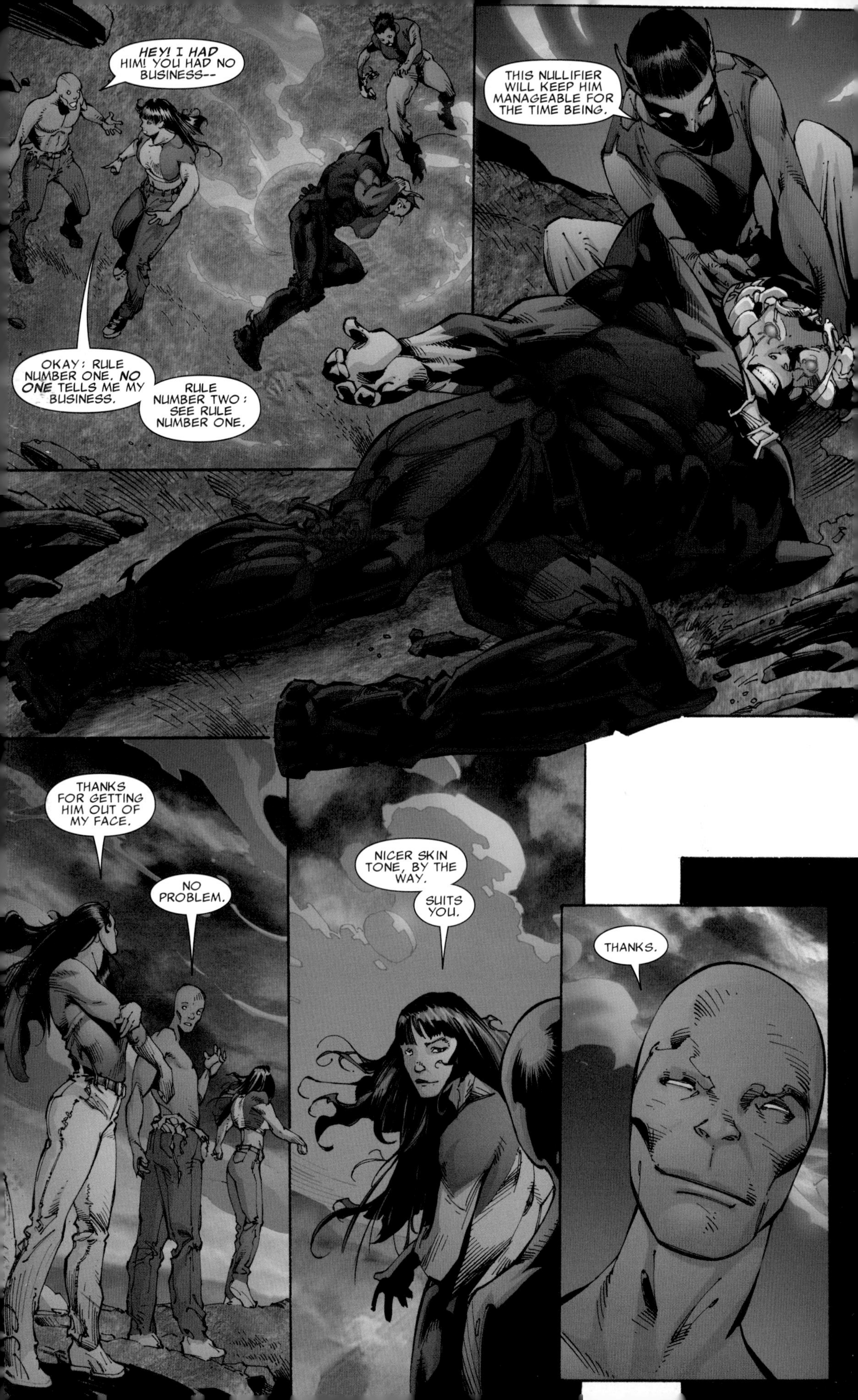
HEY! I HAD HIM! YOU HAD NO BUSINESS--
OKAY: RULE NUMBER ONE. NO ONE TELLS ME MY BUSINESS.
RULE NUMBER TWO: SEE RULE NUMBER ONE.
THIS NULLIFIER WILL KEEP HIM MANAGEABLE FOR THE TIME BEING.
THANKS FOR GETTING HIM OUT OF MY FACE.
NO PROBLEM.
NICER SKIN TONE, BY THE WAY.
SUITS YOU.
THANKS.

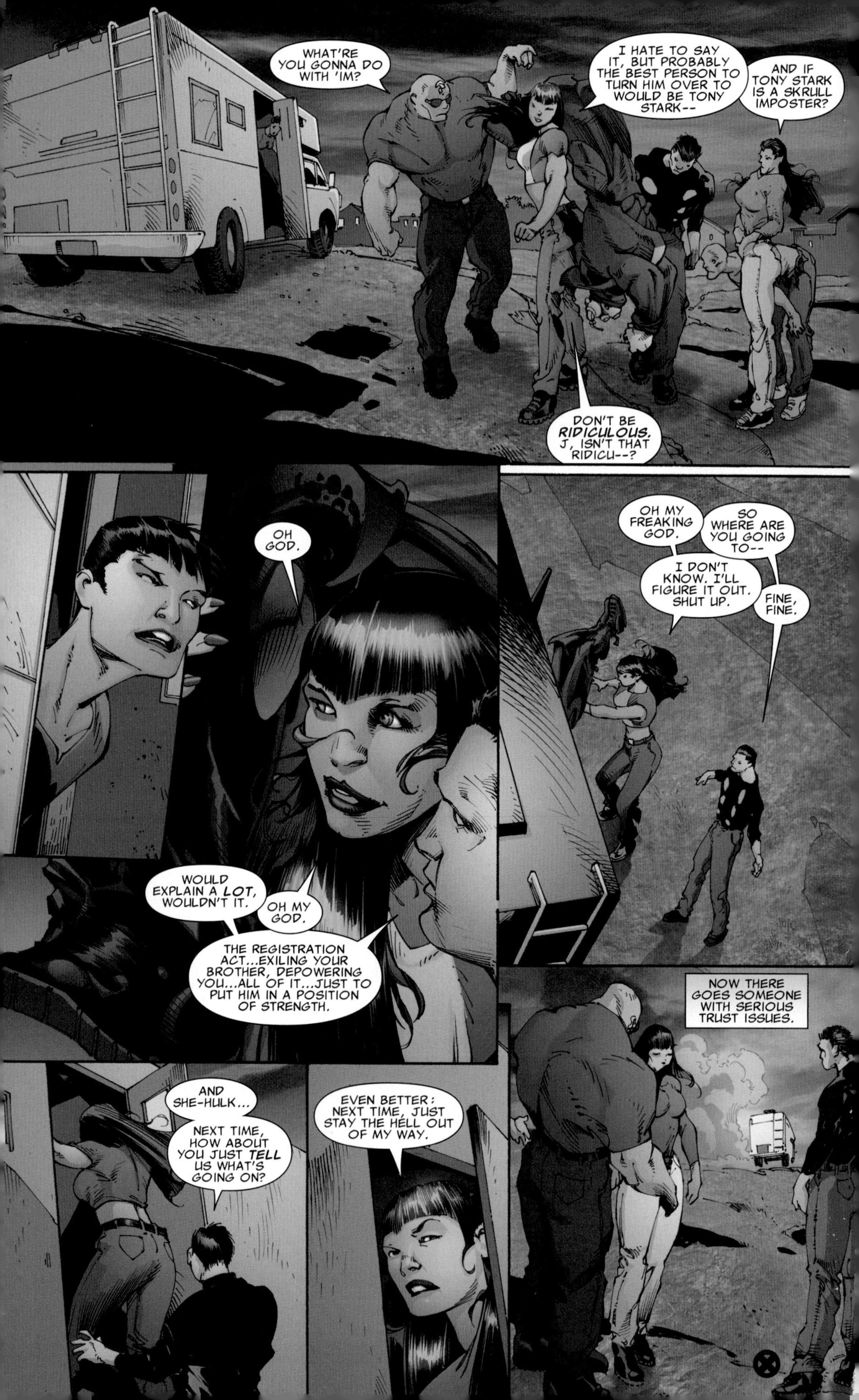
WHAT'RE YOU GONNA DO WITH 'IM?
I HATE TO SAY IT, BUT PROBABLY THE BEST PERSON TO TURN HIM OVER TO WOULD BE TONY STARK--
AND IF TONY STARK IS A SKRULL IMPOSTER?
DON'T BE RIDICULOUS. J, ISN'T THAT RIDICU--?
OH GOD.
WOULD EXPLAIN A LOT, WOULDN'T IT.
OH MY GOD.
THE REGISTRATION ACT...EXILING YOUR BROTHER, DEPOWERING YOU...ALL OF IT...JUST TO PUT HIM IN A POSITION OF STRENGTH.
OH MY FREAKING GOD.
SO WHERE ARE YOU GOING TO--
I DON'T KNOW. I'LL FIGURE IT OUT. SHUT UP.
FINE, FINE.
AND SHE-HULK...
NEXT TIME, HOW ABOUT YOU JUST TELL US WHAT'S GOING ON?
EVEN BETTER: NEXT TIME, JUST STAY THE HELL OUT OF MY WAY.
NOW THERE GOES SOMEONE WITH SERIOUS TRUST ISSUES.

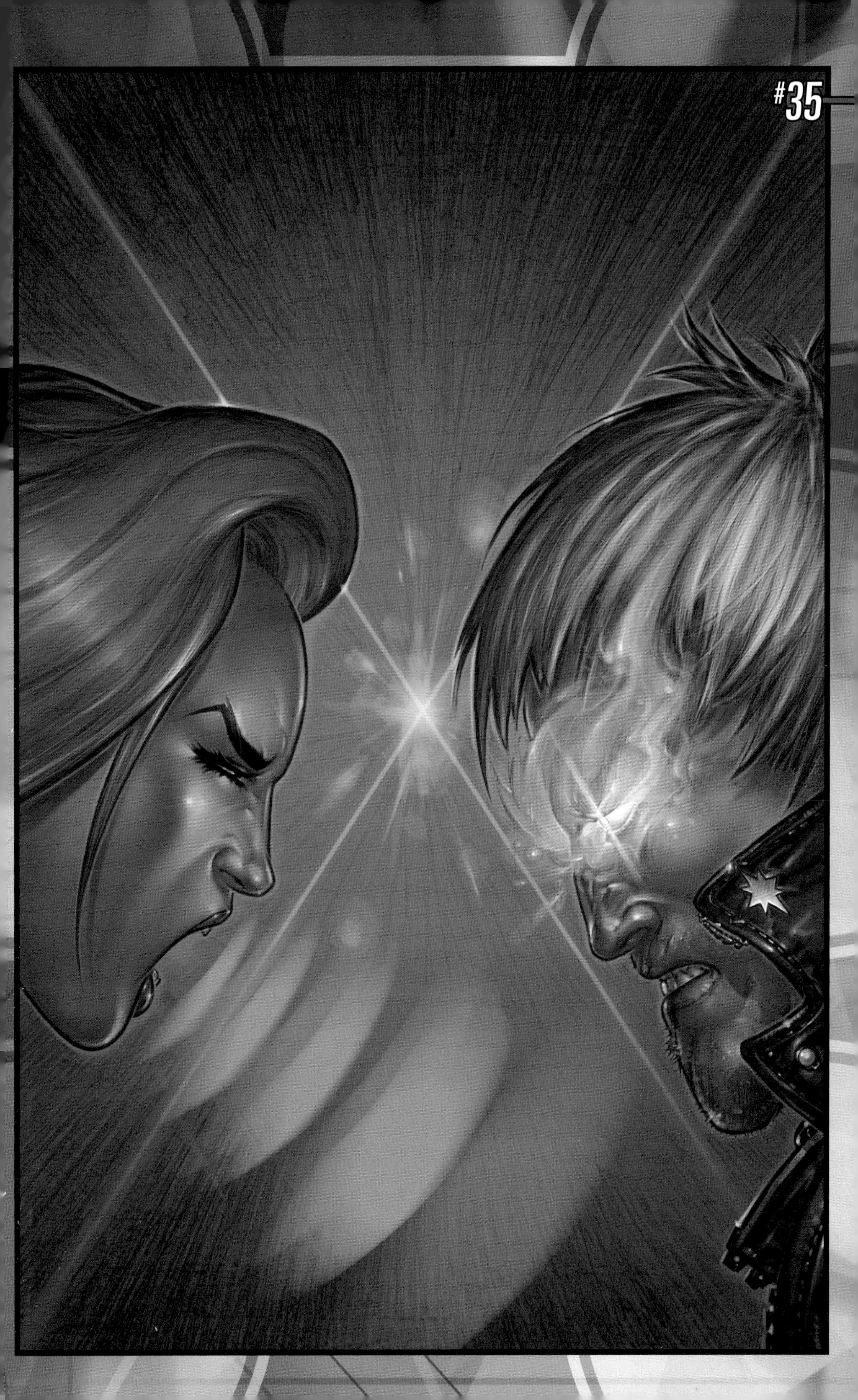
#35

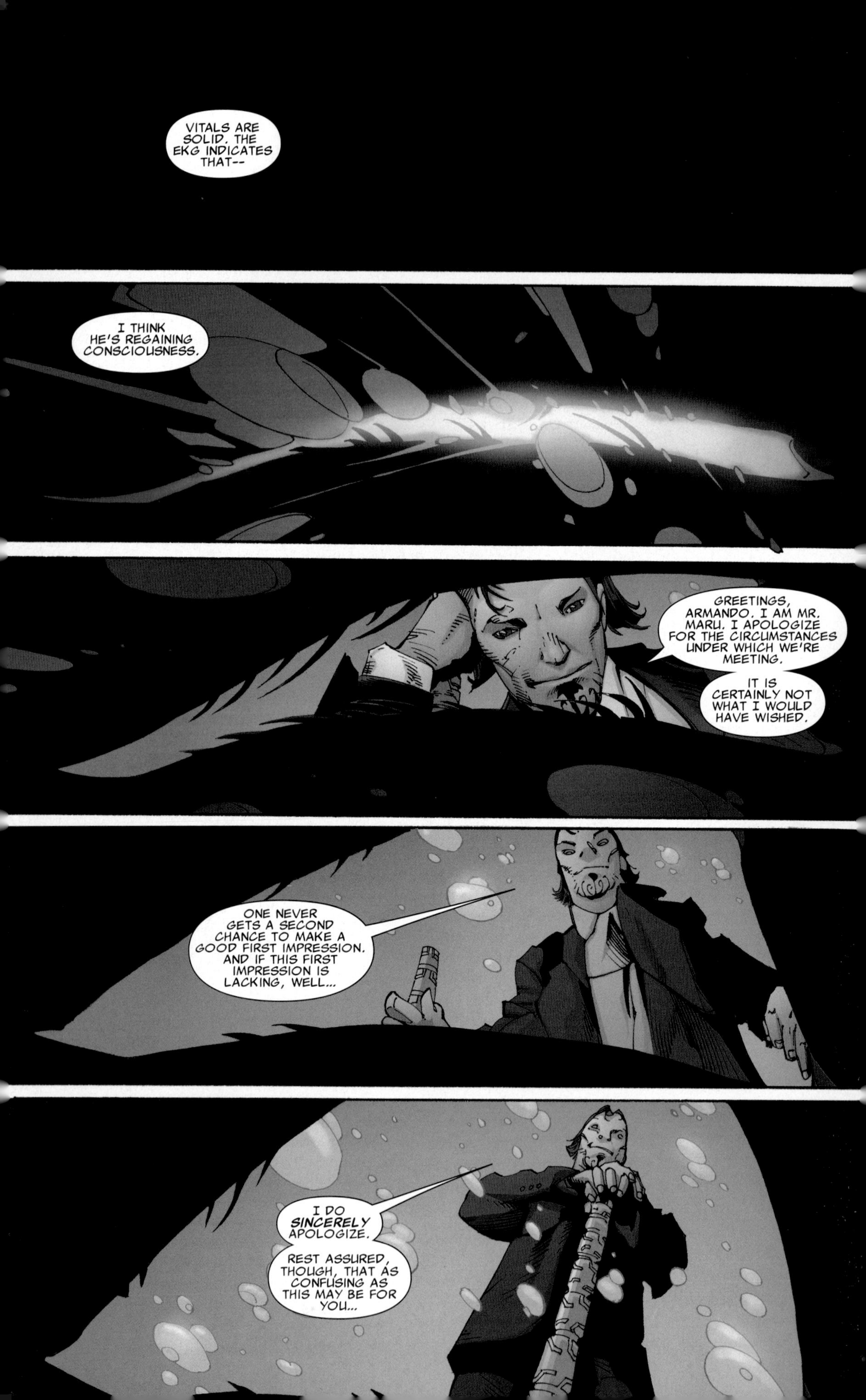
VITALS ARE SOLID. THE EKG INDICATES THAT--
I THINK HE'S REGAINING CONSCIOUSNESS.
GREETINGS, ARMANDO. I AM MR. MARU. I APOLOGIZE FOR THE CIRCUMSTANCES UNDER WHICH WE'RE MEETING.
IT IS CERTAINLY NOT WHAT I WOULD HAVE WISHED.
ONE NEVER GETS A SECOND CHANCE TO MAKE A GOOD FIRST IMPRESSION. AND IF THIS FIRST IMPRESSION IS LACKING, WELL...
I DO SINCERELY APOLOGIZE.
REST ASSURED, THOUGH, THAT AS CONFUSING AS THIS MAY BE FOR YOU...

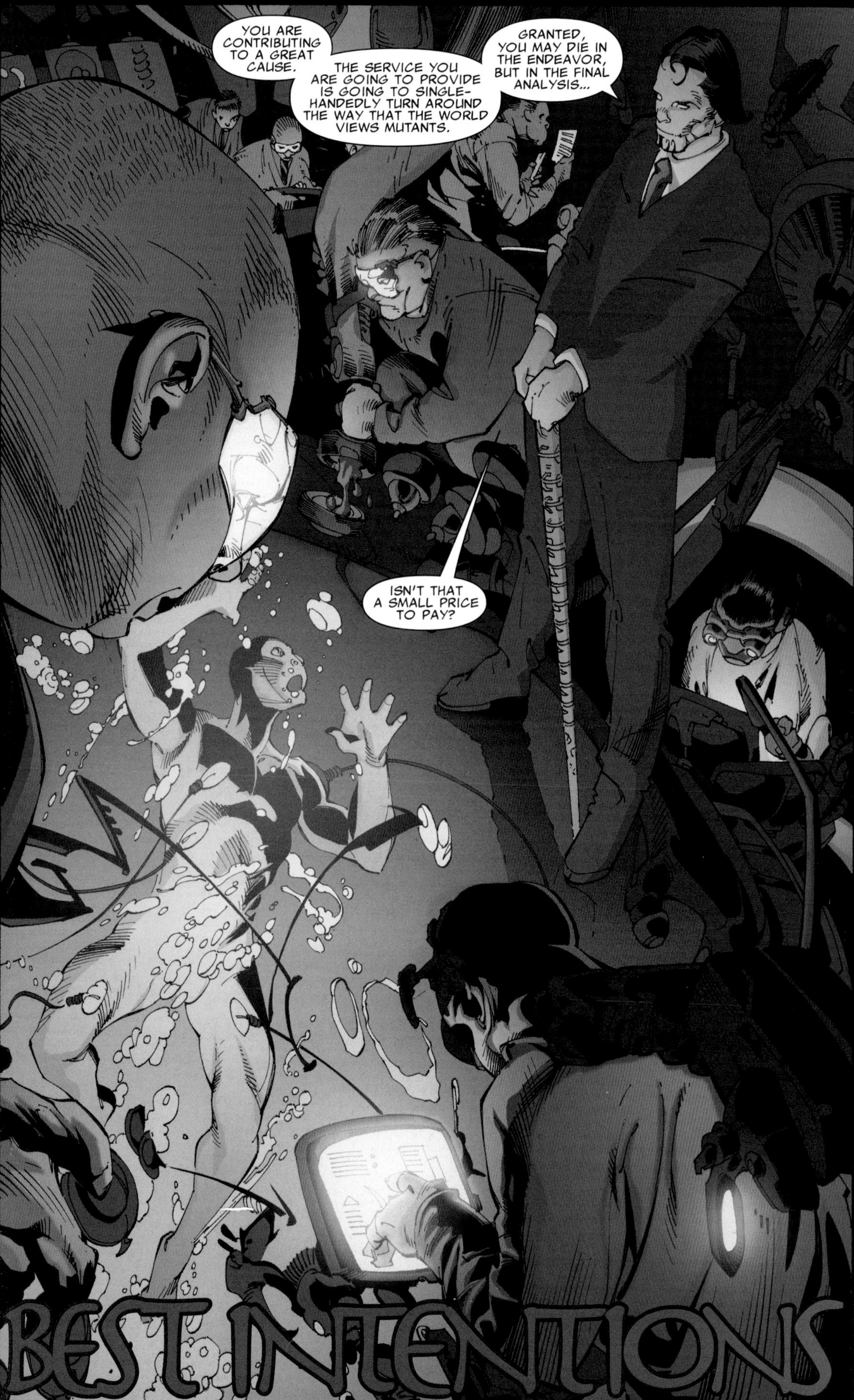
YOU ARE CONTRIBUTING TO A GREAT CAUSE.
THE SERVICE YOU ARE GOING TO PROVIDE IS GOING TO SINGLE-HANDEDLY TURN AROUND THE WAY THAT THE WORLD VIEWS MUTANTS.
GRANTED, YOU MAY DIE IN THE ENDEAVOR, BUT IN THE FINAL ANALYSIS...
ISN'T THAT A SMALL PRICE TO PAY?
BEST INTENTIONS

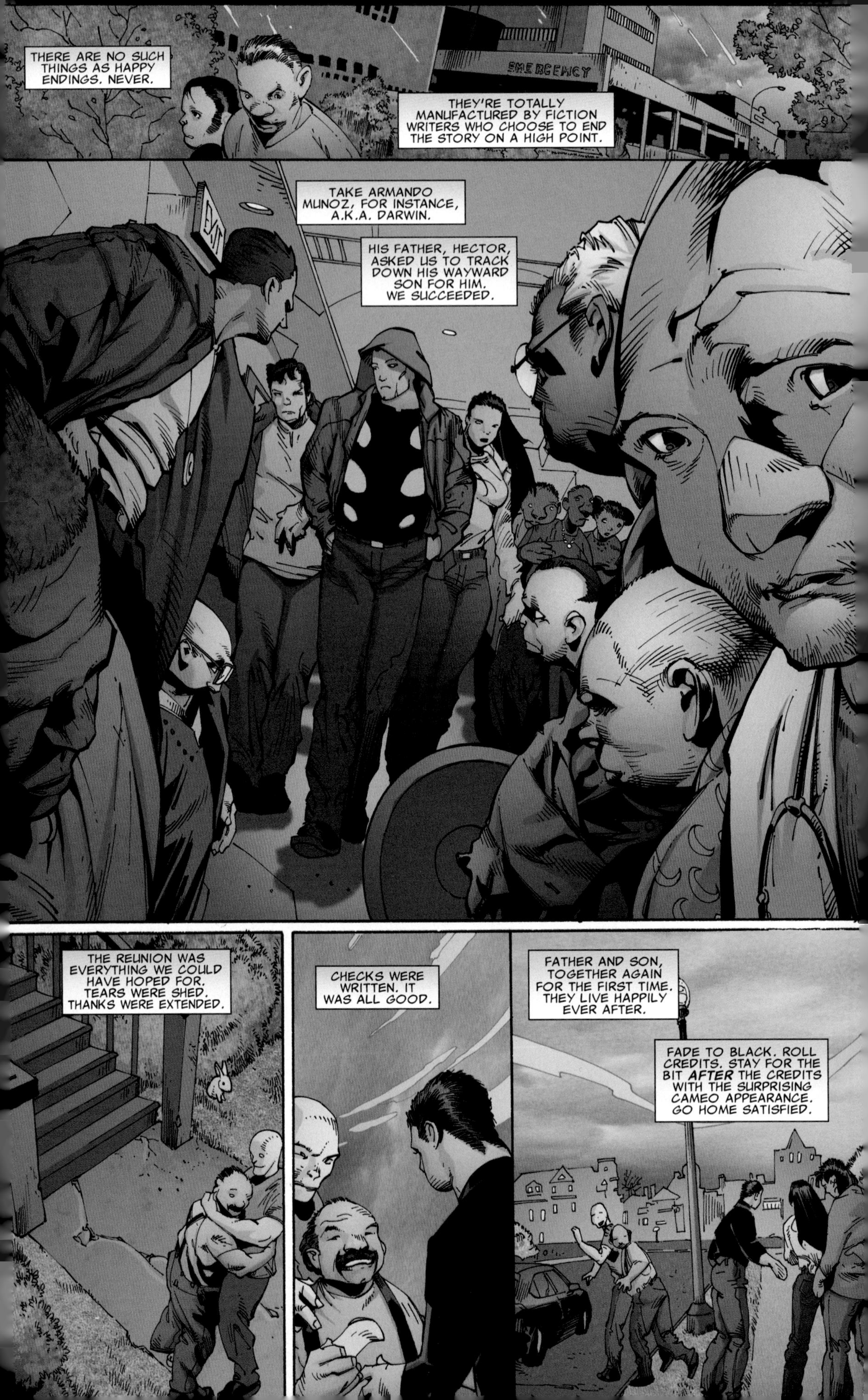
THERE ARE NO SUCH THINGS AS HAPPY ENDINGS. NEVER.
EMERGENCY
THEY'RE TOTALLY MANUFACTURED BY FICTION WRITERS WHO CHOOSE TO END THE STORY ON A HIGH POINT.
TAKE ARMANDO MUNOZ, FOR INSTANCE, A.K.A. DARWIN.
HIS FATHER, HECTOR, ASKED US TO TRACK DOWN HIS WAYWARD SON FOR HIM. WE SUCCEEDED.
EXIT
THE REUNION WAS EVERYTHING WE COULD HAVE HOPED FOR. TEARS WERE SHED. THANKS WERE EXTENDED.
CHECKS WERE WRITTEN. IT WAS ALL GOOD.
FATHER AND SON, TOGETHER AGAIN FOR THE FIRST TIME. THEY LIVE HAPPILY EVER AFTER.
FADE TO BLACK. ROLL CREDITS. STAY FOR THE BIT *AFTER* THE CREDITS WITH THE SURPRISING CAMEO APPEARANCE. GO HOME SATISFIED.

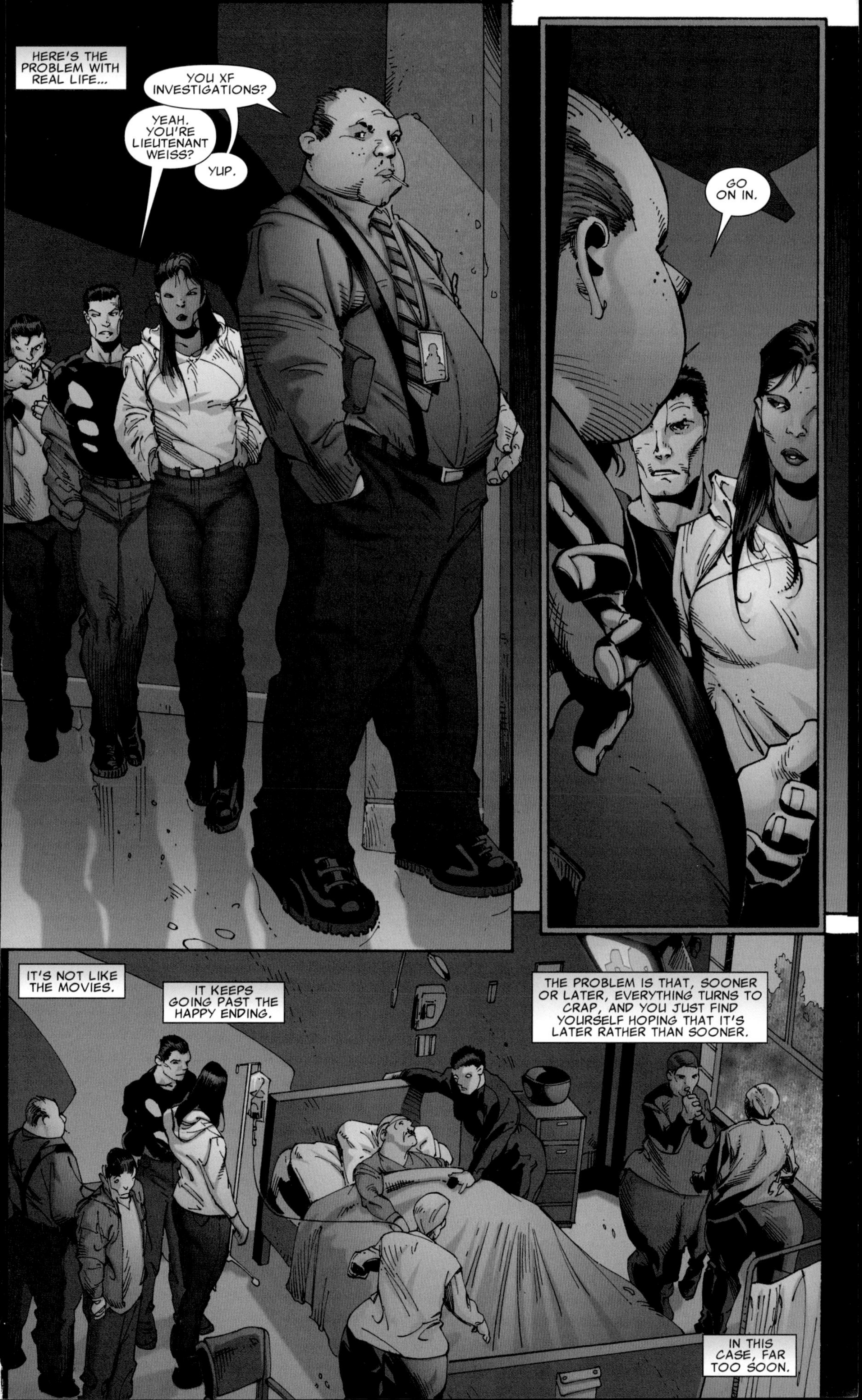
HERE'S THE PROBLEM WITH REAL LIFE...
YOU XF INVESTIGATIONS?
YEAH. YOU'RE LIEUTENANT WEISS?
YUP.
GO ON IN.
IT'S NOT LIKE THE MOVIES.
IT KEEPS GOING PAST THE HAPPY ENDING.
THE PROBLEM IS THAT, SOONER OR LATER, EVERYTHING TURNS TO CRAP, AND YOU JUST FIND YOURSELF HOPING THAT IT'S LATER RATHER THAN SOONER.
IN THIS CASE, FAR TOO SOON.

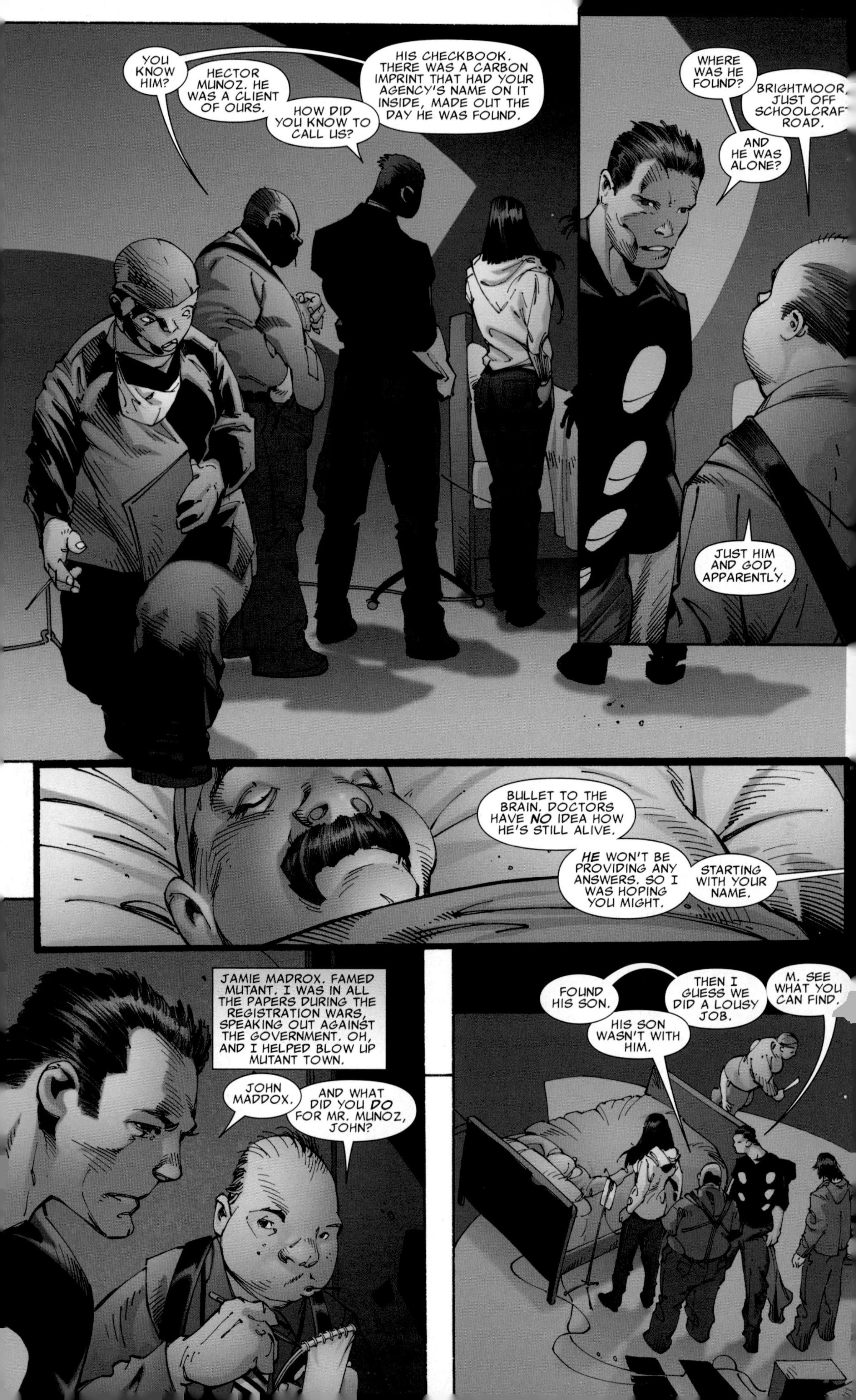
YOU KNOW HIM?
HECTOR MUNOZ. HE WAS A CLIENT OF OURS.
HOW DID YOU KNOW TO CALL US?
HIS CHECKBOOK. THERE WAS A CARBON IMPRINT THAT HAD YOUR AGENCY'S NAME ON IT INSIDE, MADE OUT THE DAY HE WAS FOUND.
WHERE WAS HE FOUND?
BRIGHTMOOR, JUST OFF SCHOOLCRAFT ROAD.
AND HE WAS ALONE?
JUST HIM AND GOD, APPARENTLY.
BULLET TO THE BRAIN. DOCTORS HAVE NO IDEA HOW HE'S STILL ALIVE.
HE WON'T BE PROVIDING ANY ANSWERS. SO I WAS HOPING YOU MIGHT.
STARTING WITH YOUR NAME.
JAMIE MADROX. FAMED MUTANT. I WAS IN ALL THE PAPERS DURING THE REGISTRATION WARS, SPEAKING OUT AGAINST THE GOVERNMENT. OH, AND I HELPED BLOW UP MUTANT TOWN.
JOHN MADDOX.
AND WHAT DID YOU DO FOR MR. MUNOZ, JOHN?
FOUND HIS SON.
HIS SON WASN'T WITH HIM.
THEN I GUESS WE DID A LOUSY JOB.
M. SEE WHAT YOU CAN FIND.

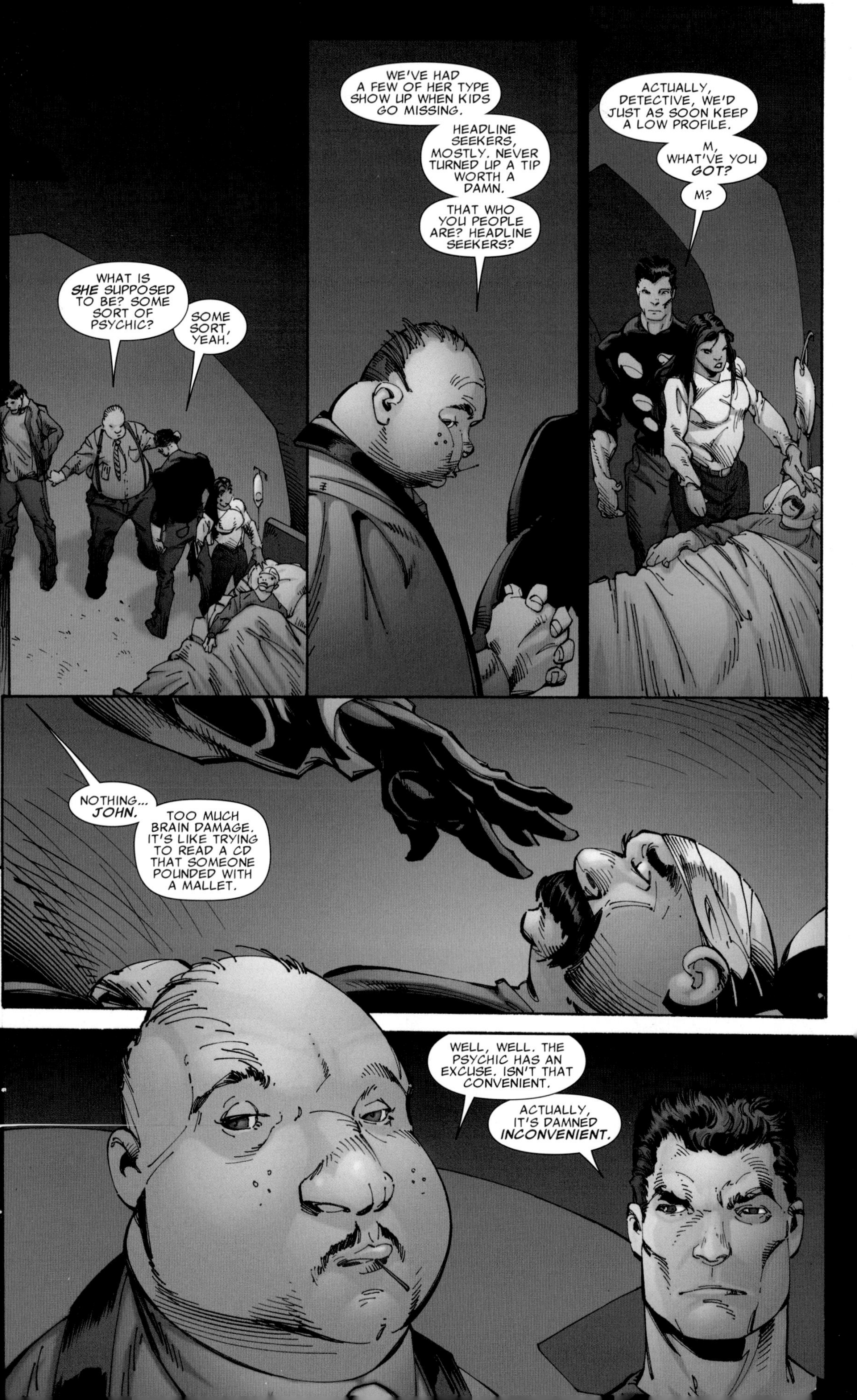
WHAT IS SHE SUPPOSED TO BE? SOME SORT OF PSYCHIC?
SOME SORT, YEAH.
WE'VE HAD A FEW OF HER TYPE SHOW UP WHEN KIDS GO MISSING.
HEADLINE SEEKERS, MOSTLY. NEVER TURNED UP A TIP WORTH A DAMN.
THAT WHO YOU PEOPLE ARE? HEADLINE SEEKERS?
ACTUALLY, DETECTIVE, WE'D JUST AS SOON KEEP A LOW PROFILE.
M, WHAT'VE YOU GOT?
M?
NOTHING... JOHN.
TOO MUCH BRAIN DAMAGE. IT'S LIKE TRYING TO READ A CD THAT SOMEONE POUNDED WITH A MALLET.
WELL, WELL. THE PSYCHIC HAS AN EXCUSE. ISN'T THAT CONVENIENT.
ACTUALLY, IT'S DAMNED INCONVENIENT.

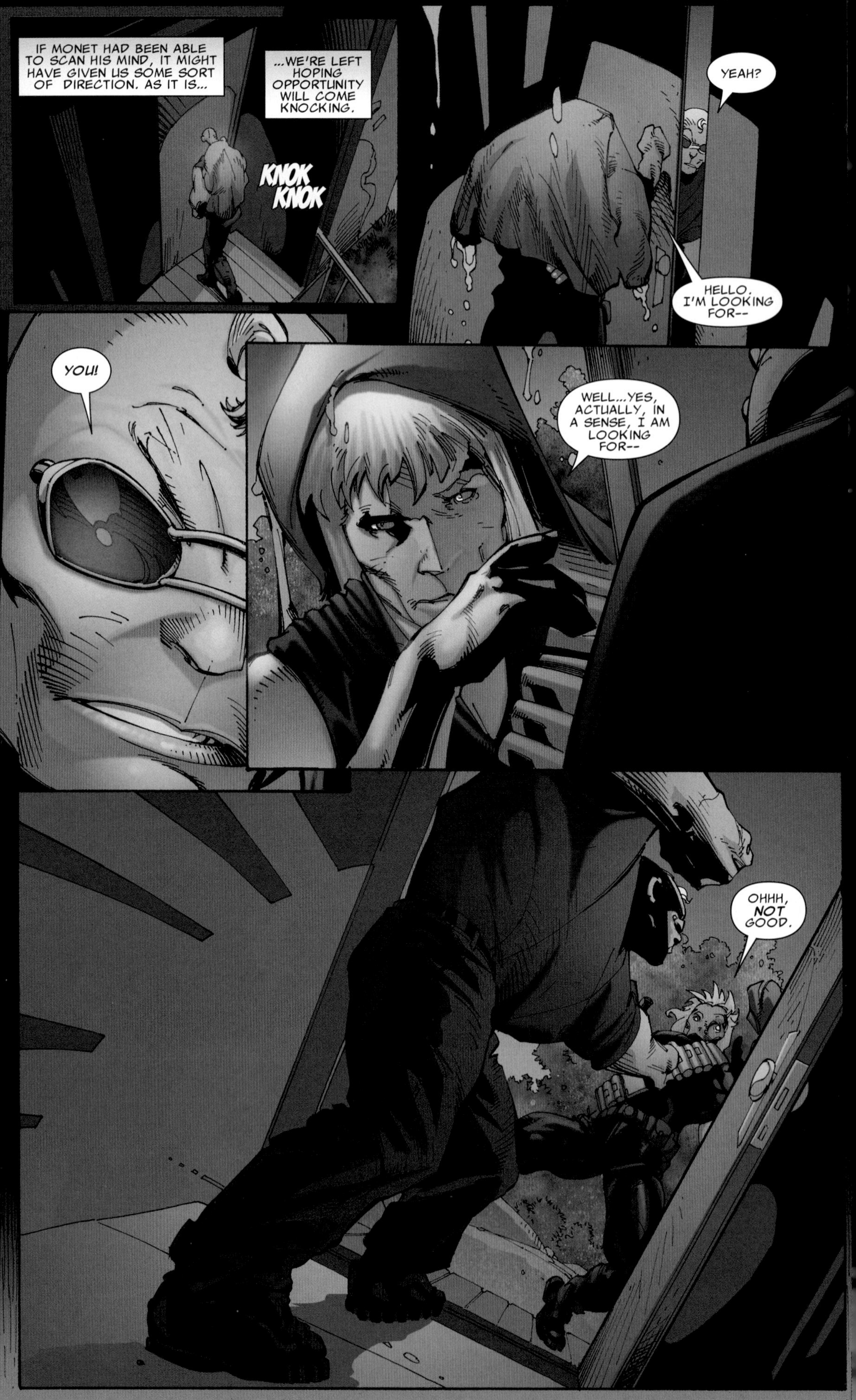
IF MONET HAD BEEN ABLE TO SCAN HIS MIND, IT MIGHT HAVE GIVEN US SOME SORT OF DIRECTION. AS IT IS...
...WE'RE LEFT HOPING OPPORTUNITY WILL COME KNOCKING.
KNOK KNOK
YEAH?
HELLO. I'M LOOKING FOR--
YOU!
WELL...YES, ACTUALLY, IN A SENSE, I AM LOOKING FOR--
OHHH, NOT GOOD.

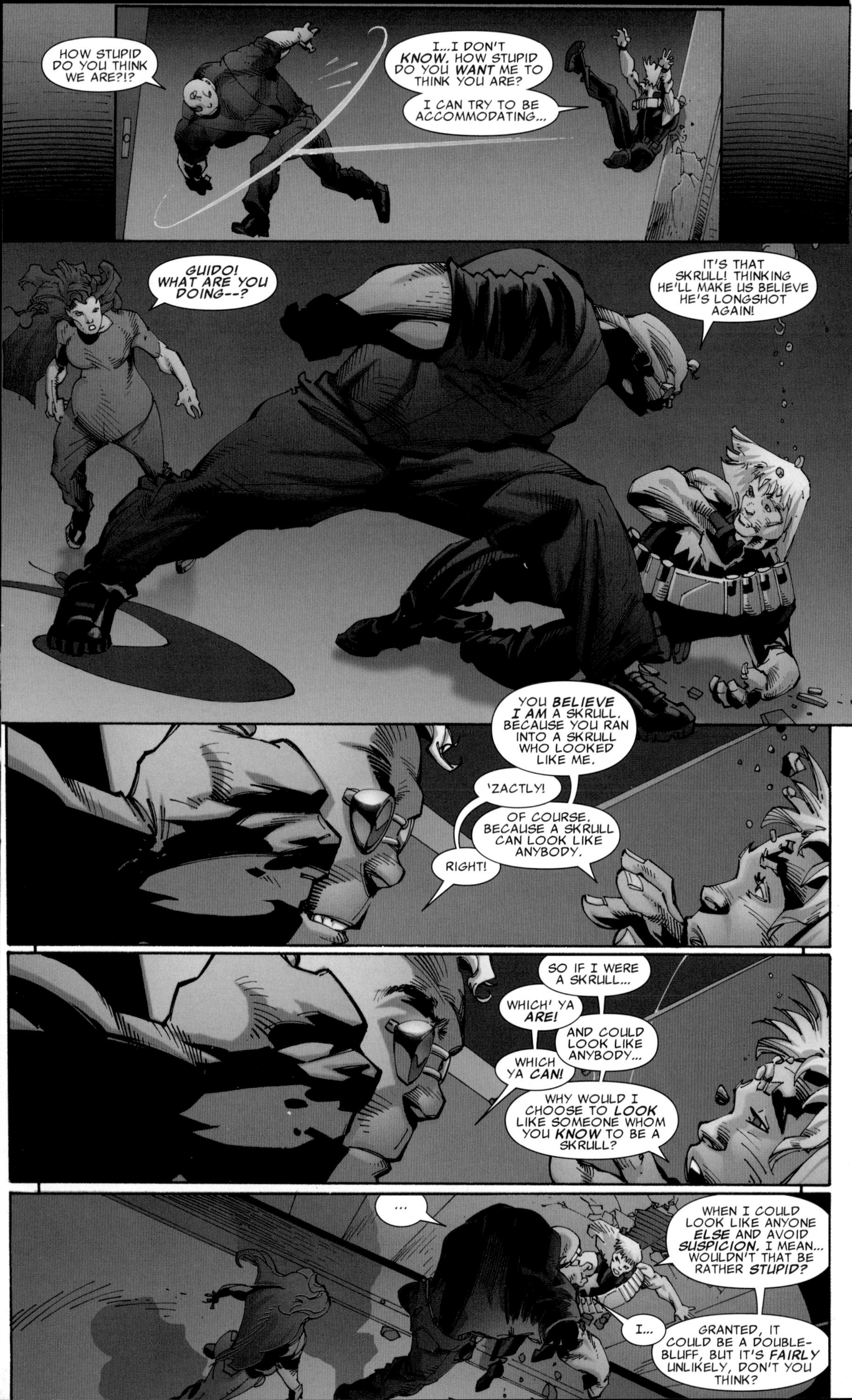
HOW STUPID DO YOU THINK WE ARE?!?
I...I DON'T KNOW. HOW STUPID DO YOU WANT ME TO THINK YOU ARE?
I CAN TRY TO BE ACCOMMODATING...
GUIDO! WHAT ARE YOU DOING--?
IT'S THAT SKRULL! THINKING HE'LL MAKE US BELIEVE HE'S LONGSHOT AGAIN!
YOU BELIEVE I AM A SKRULL, BECAUSE YOU RAN INTO A SKRULL WHO LOOKED LIKE ME.
'ZACTLY!
OF COURSE. BECAUSE A SKRULL CAN LOOK LIKE ANYBODY.
RIGHT!
SO IF I WERE A SKRULL...
WHICH' YA ARE!
AND COULD LOOK LIKE ANYBODY...
WHICH YA CAN!
WHY WOULD I CHOOSE TO LOOK LIKE SOMEONE WHOM YOU KNOW TO BE A SKRULL?
...
WHEN I COULD LOOK LIKE ANYONE ELSE AND AVOID SUSPICION. I MEAN... WOULDN'T THAT BE RATHER STUPID?
I...
GRANTED, IT COULD BE A DOUBLE-BLUFF, BUT IT'S FAIRLY UNLIKELY, DON'T YOU THINK?

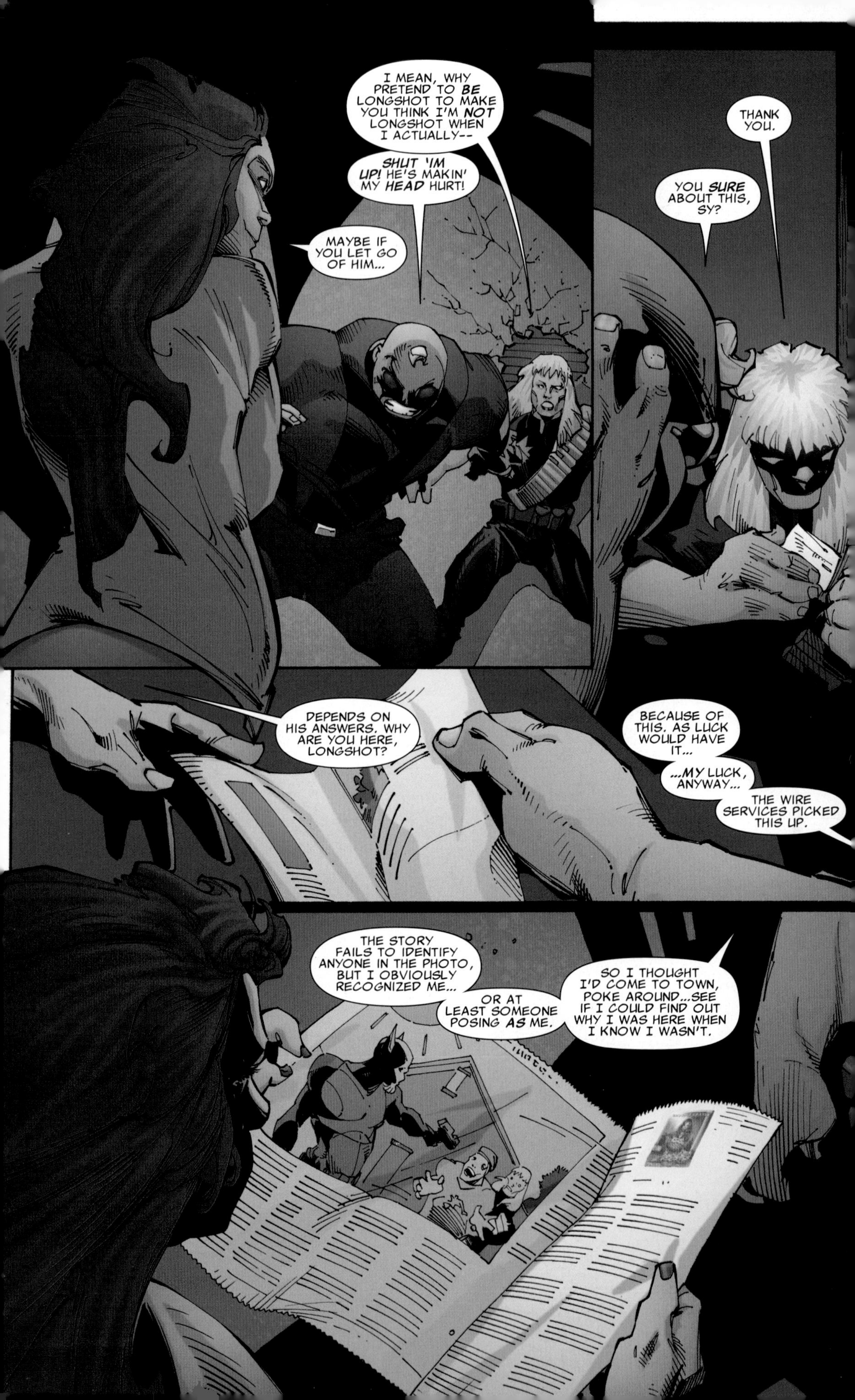
I MEAN, WHY PRETEND TO BE LONGSHOT TO MAKE YOU THINK I'M NOT LONGSHOT WHEN I ACTUALLY--
SHUT 'IM UP! HE'S MAKIN' MY HEAD HURT!
MAYBE IF YOU LET GO OF HIM...
THANK YOU.
YOU SURE ABOUT THIS, SY?
DEPENDS ON HIS ANSWERS. WHY ARE YOU HERE, LONGSHOT?
BECAUSE OF THIS. AS LUCK WOULD HAVE IT...
...MY LUCK, ANYWAY...
THE WIRE SERVICES PICKED THIS UP.
THE STORY FAILS TO IDENTIFY ANYONE IN THE PHOTO, BUT I OBVIOUSLY RECOGNIZED ME...
OR AT LEAST SOMEONE POSING AS ME.
SO I THOUGHT I'D COME TO TOWN, POKE AROUND...SEE IF I COULD FIND OUT WHY I WAS HERE WHEN I KNOW I WASN'T.

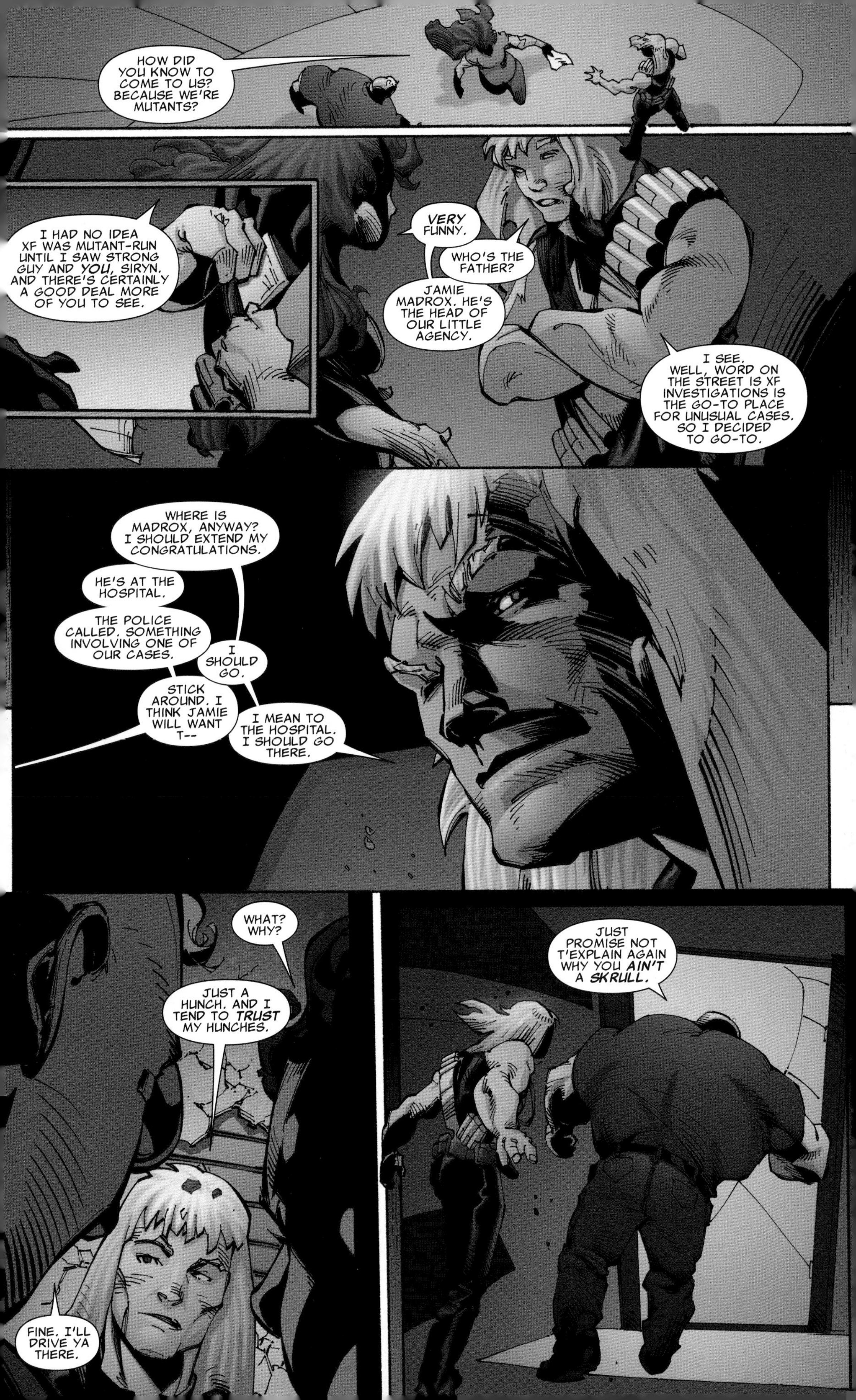

HOW DID YOU KNOW TO COME TO US? BECAUSE WE'RE MUTANTS?
I HAD NO IDEA XF WAS MUTANT-RUN UNTIL I SAW STRONG GUY AND *YOU*, SIRYN. AND THERE'S CERTAINLY A GOOD DEAL MORE OF YOU TO SEE.
VERY FUNNY.
WHO'S THE FATHER?
JAMIE MADROX. HE'S THE HEAD OF OUR LITTLE AGENCY.
I SEE. WELL, WORD ON THE STREET IS XF INVESTIGATIONS IS THE GO-TO PLACE FOR UNUSUAL CASES. SO I DECIDED TO GO-TO.
WHERE IS MADROX, ANYWAY? I SHOULD EXTEND MY CONGRATULATIONS.
HE'S AT THE HOSPITAL.
THE POLICE CALLED. SOMETHING INVOLVING ONE OF OUR CASES.
I SHOULD GO.
STICK AROUND. I THINK JAMIE WILL WANT T--
I MEAN TO THE HOSPITAL. I SHOULD GO THERE.
WHAT? WHY?
JUST A HUNCH. AND I TEND TO *TRUST* MY HUNCHES.
FINE. I'LL DRIVE YA THERE.
JUST PROMISE NOT T'EXPLAIN AGAIN WHY YOU *AIN'T* A *SKRULL*.

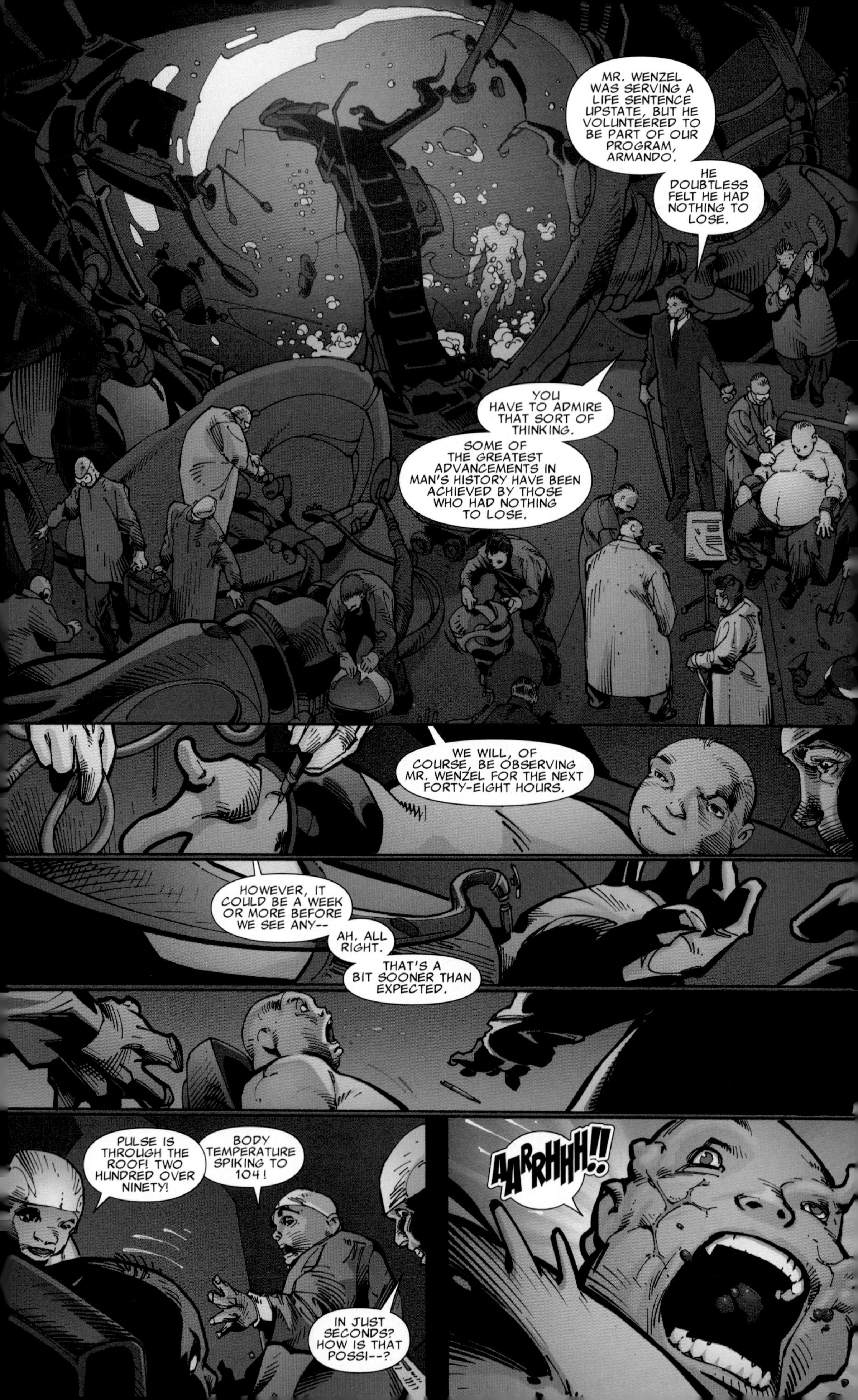
MR. WENZEL WAS SERVING A LIFE SENTENCE UPSTATE, BUT HE VOLUNTEERED TO BE PART OF OUR PROGRAM, ARMANDO.
HE DOUBTLESS FELT HE HAD NOTHING TO LOSE.
YOU HAVE TO ADMIRE THAT SORT OF THINKING.
SOME OF THE GREATEST ADVANCEMENTS IN MAN'S HISTORY HAVE BEEN ACHIEVED BY THOSE WHO HAD NOTHING TO LOSE.
WE WILL, OF COURSE, BE OBSERVING MR. WENZEL FOR THE NEXT FORTY-EIGHT HOURS.
HOWEVER, IT COULD BE A WEEK OR MORE BEFORE WE SEE ANY--
AH. ALL RIGHT.
THAT'S A BIT SOONER THAN EXPECTED.
PULSE IS THROUGH THE ROOF! TWO HUNDRED OVER NINETY!
BODY TEMPERATURE SPIKING TO 104!
IN JUST SECONDS? HOW IS THAT POSSI--?
AARRHHH!!

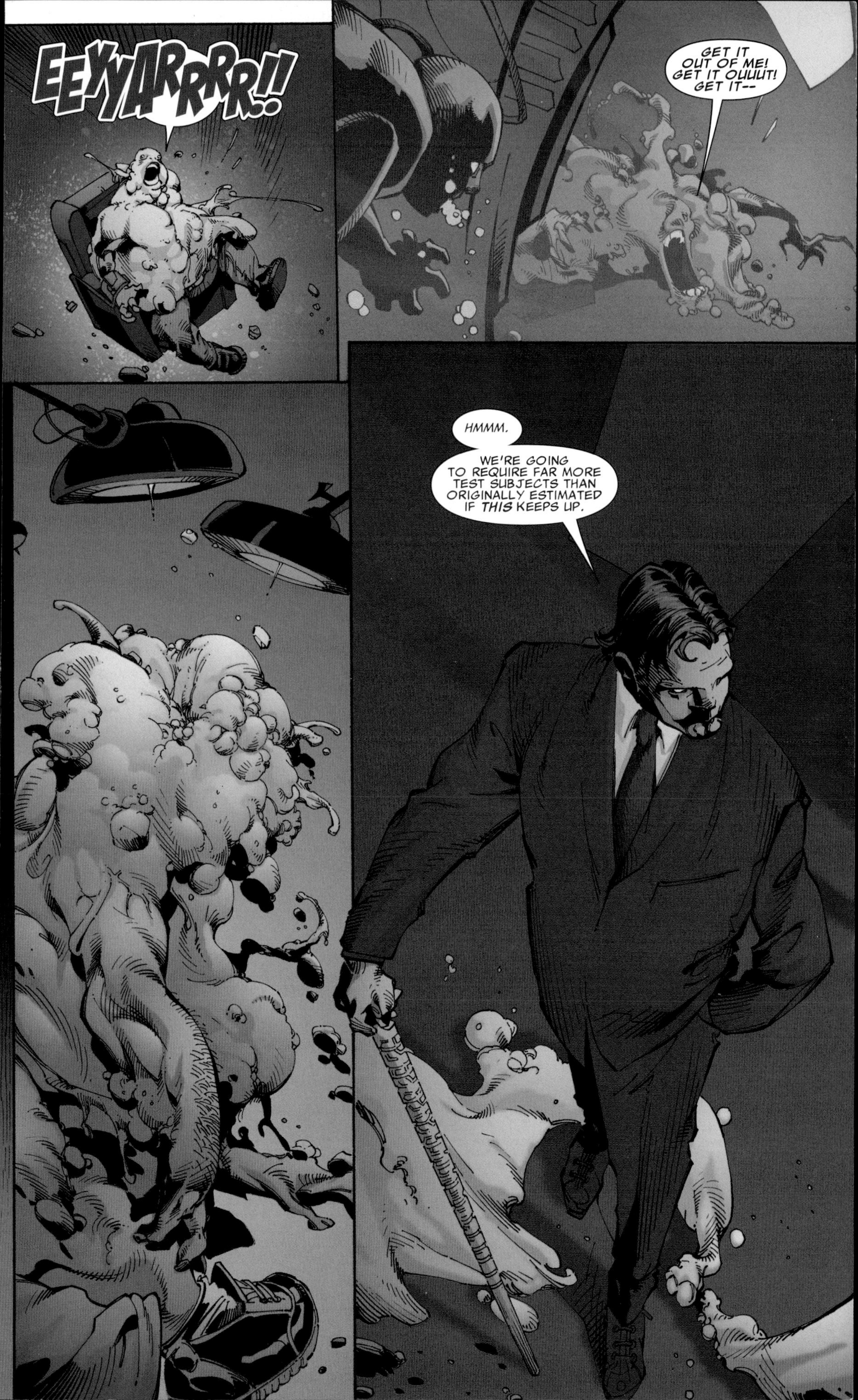
EEYYARRRR!!
GET IT OUT OF ME! GET IT OUUUT! GET IT--
HMMM.
WE'RE GOING TO REQUIRE FAR MORE TEST SUBJECTS THAN ORIGINALLY ESTIMATED IF *THIS* KEEPS UP.

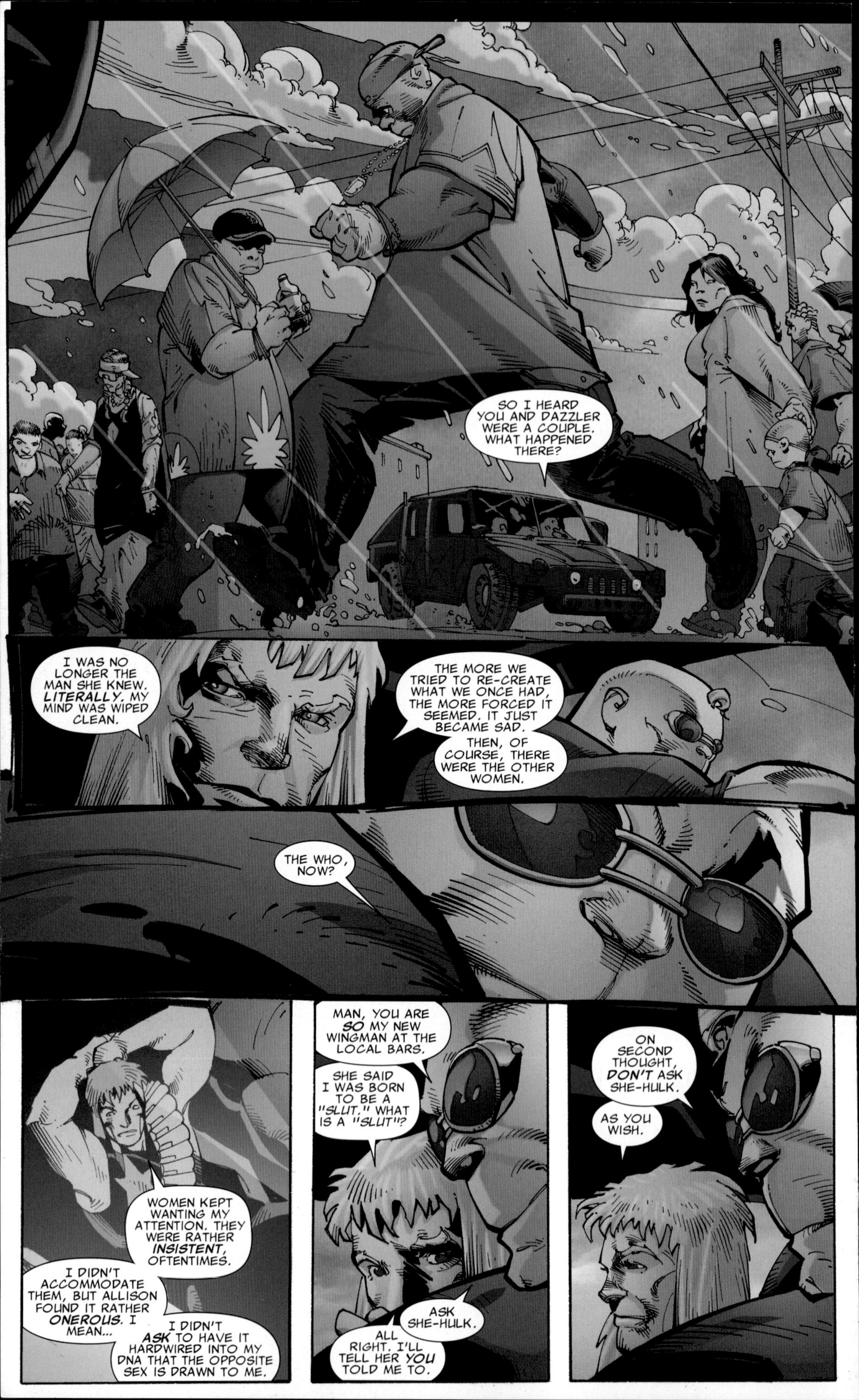
SO I HEARD YOU AND DAZZLER WERE A COUPLE. WHAT HAPPENED THERE?
I WAS NO LONGER THE MAN SHE KNEW. LITERALLY. MY MIND WAS WIPED CLEAN.
THE MORE WE TRIED TO RE-CREATE WHAT WE ONCE HAD, THE MORE FORCED IT SEEMED. IT JUST BECAME SAD.
THEN, OF COURSE, THERE WERE THE OTHER WOMEN.
THE WHO, NOW?
WOMEN KEPT WANTING MY ATTENTION. THEY WERE RATHER INSISTENT, OFTENTIMES.
I DIDN'T ACCOMMODATE THEM, BUT ALLISON FOUND IT RATHER ONEROUS. I MEAN...
I DIDN'T ASK TO HAVE IT HARDWIRED INTO MY DNA THAT THE OPPOSITE SEX IS DRAWN TO ME.
MAN, YOU ARE SO MY NEW WINGMAN AT THE LOCAL BARS.
SHE SAID I WAS BORN TO BE A "SLUT." WHAT IS A "SLUT"?
ASK SHE-HULK.
ALL RIGHT. I'LL TELL HER YOU TOLD ME TO.
ON SECOND THOUGHT, DON'T ASK SHE-HULK.
AS YOU WISH.

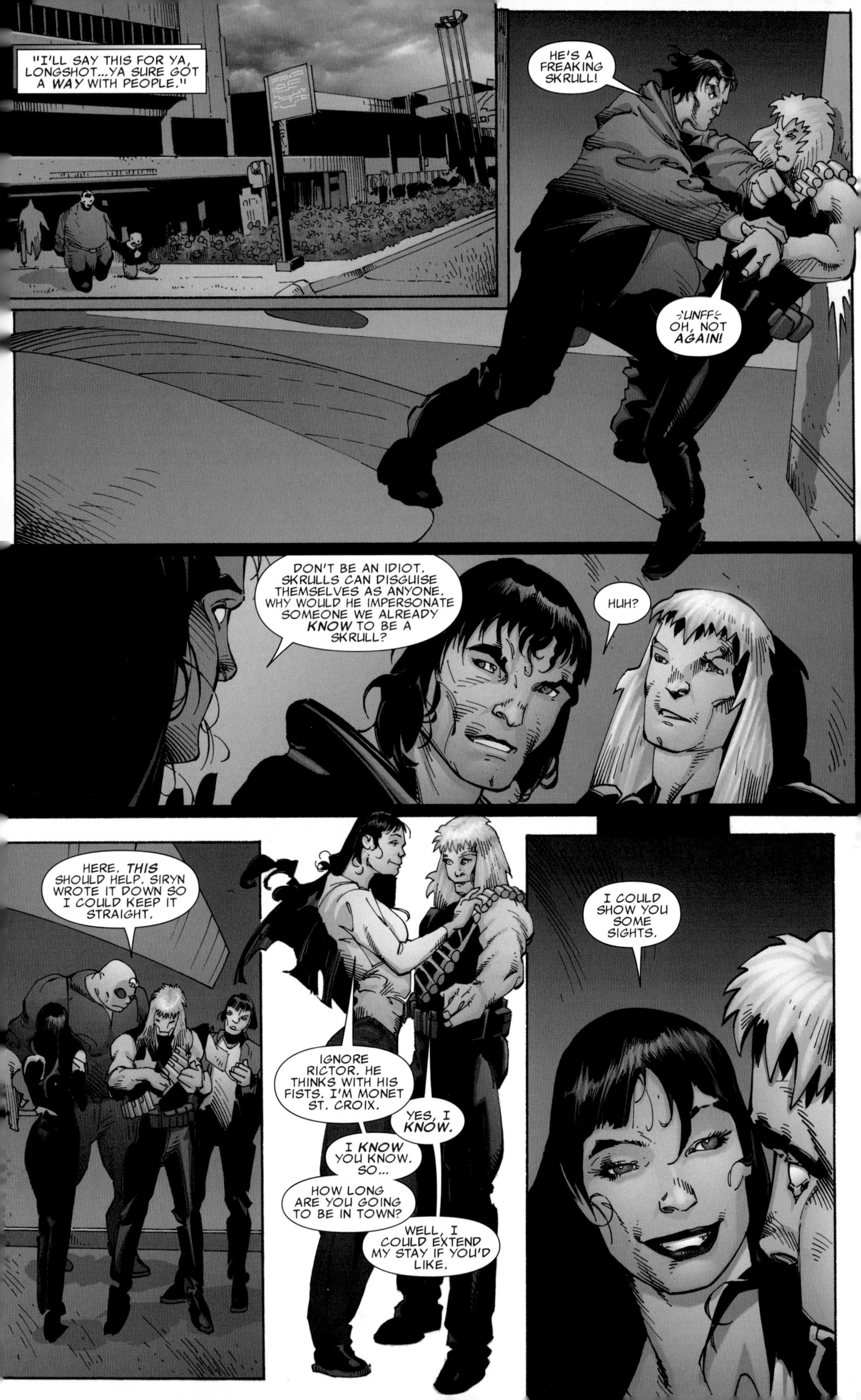

"I'LL SAY THIS FOR YA, LONGSHOT...YA SURE GOT A WAY WITH PEOPLE."
HE'S A FREAKING SKRULL!
UNFF OH, NOT AGAIN!
DON'T BE AN IDIOT. SKRULLS CAN DISGUISE THEMSELVES AS ANYONE. WHY WOULD HE IMPERSONATE SOMEONE WE ALREADY KNOW TO BE A SKRULL?
HUH?
HERE. THIS SHOULD HELP. SIRYN WROTE IT DOWN SO I COULD KEEP IT STRAIGHT.
IGNORE RICTOR. HE THINKS WITH HIS FISTS. I'M MONET ST. CROIX.
YES, I KNOW.
I KNOW YOU KNOW. SO...
HOW LONG ARE YOU GOING TO BE IN TOWN?
WELL, I COULD EXTEND MY STAY IF YOU'D LIKE.
I COULD SHOW YOU SOME SIGHTS.

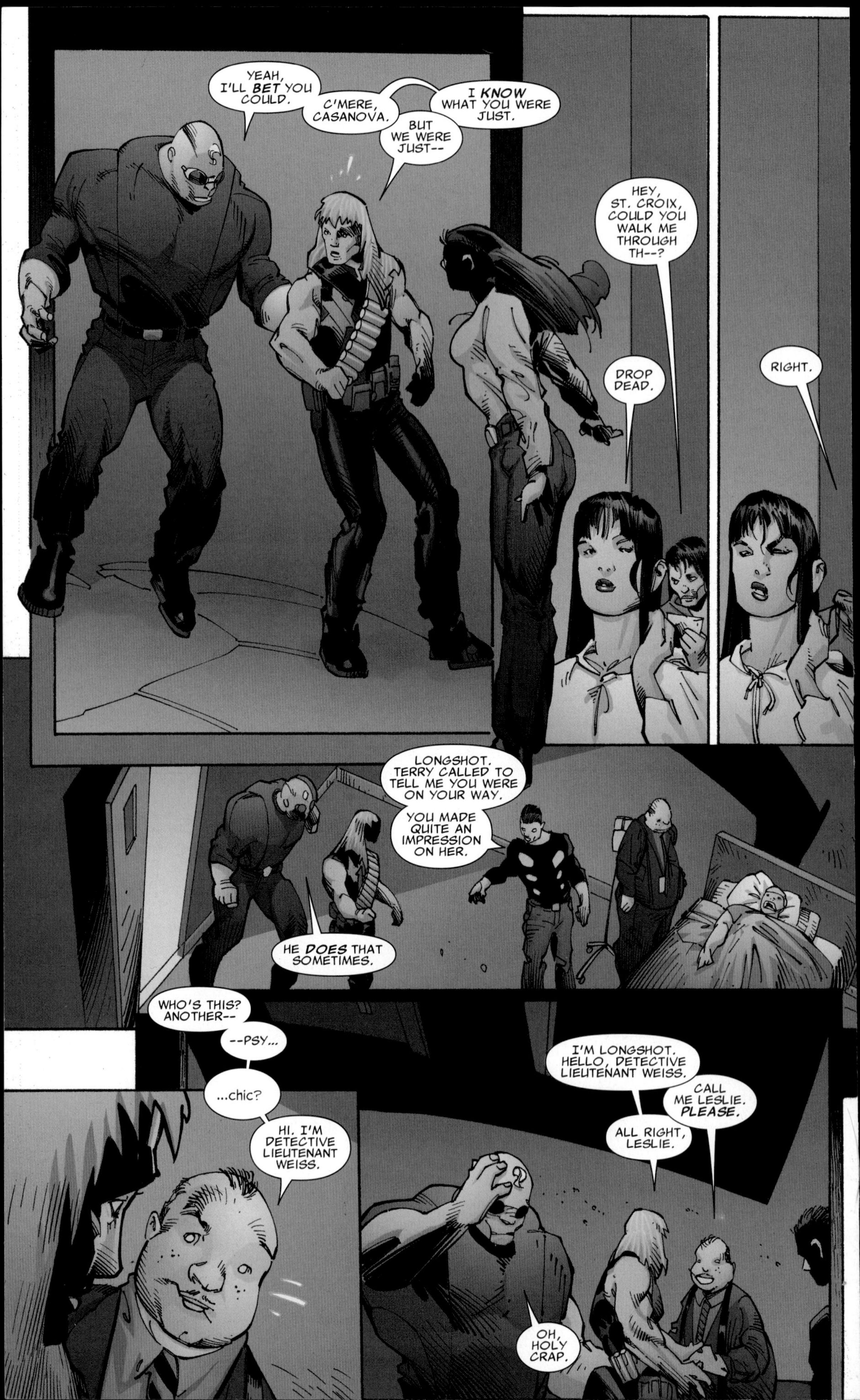
YEAH, I'LL BET YOU COULD.
C'MERE, CASANOVA.
I KNOW WHAT YOU WERE JUST.
BUT WE WERE JUST--
HEY, ST. CROIX, COULD YOU WALK ME THROUGH TH--?
DROP DEAD.
RIGHT.
LONGSHOT. TERRY CALLED TO TELL ME YOU WERE ON YOUR WAY.
YOU MADE QUITE AN IMPRESSION ON HER.
HE DOES THAT SOMETIMES.
WHO'S THIS? ANOTHER--
--PSY...
...chic?
HI. I'M DETECTIVE LIEUTENANT WEISS.
I'M LONGSHOT. HELLO, DETECTIVE LIEUTENANT WEISS.
CALL ME LESLIE. PLEASE.
ALL RIGHT, LESLIE.
OH, HOLY CRAP.

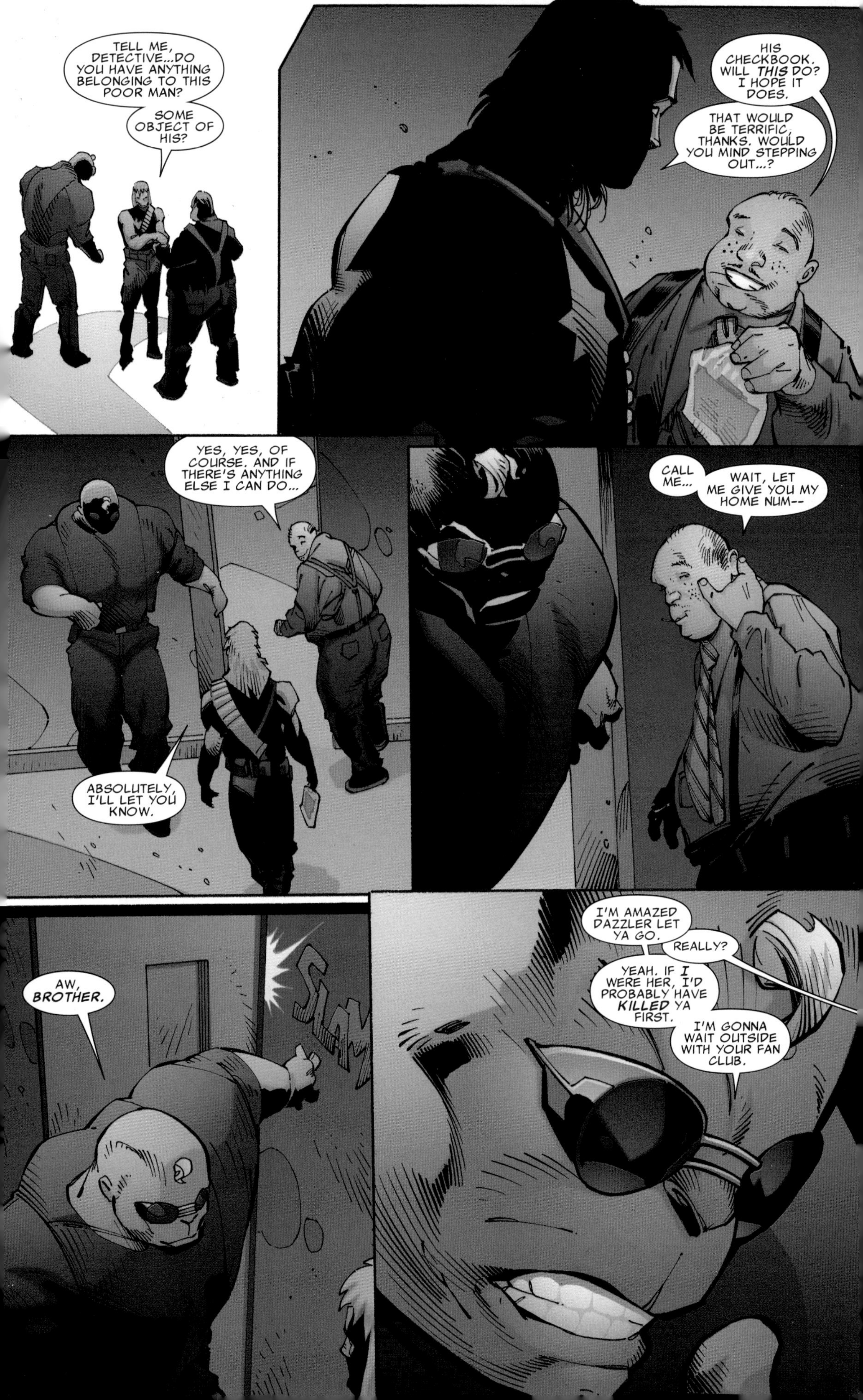
TELL ME, DETECTIVE...DO YOU HAVE ANYTHING BELONGING TO THIS POOR MAN?
SOME OBJECT OF HIS?
HIS CHECKBOOK. WILL THIS DO? I HOPE IT DOES.
THAT WOULD BE TERRIFIC, THANKS. WOULD YOU MIND STEPPING OUT...?
YES, YES, OF COURSE. AND IF THERE'S ANYTHING ELSE I CAN DO...
ABSOLUTELY, I'LL LET YOU KNOW.
CALL ME...
WAIT, LET ME GIVE YOU MY HOME NUM--
AW, BROTHER.
SLAM
I'M AMAZED DAZZLER LET YA GO.
REALLY?
YEAH. IF I WERE HER, I'D PROBABLY HAVE KILLED YA FIRST.
I'M GONNA WAIT OUTSIDE WITH YOUR FAN CLUB.

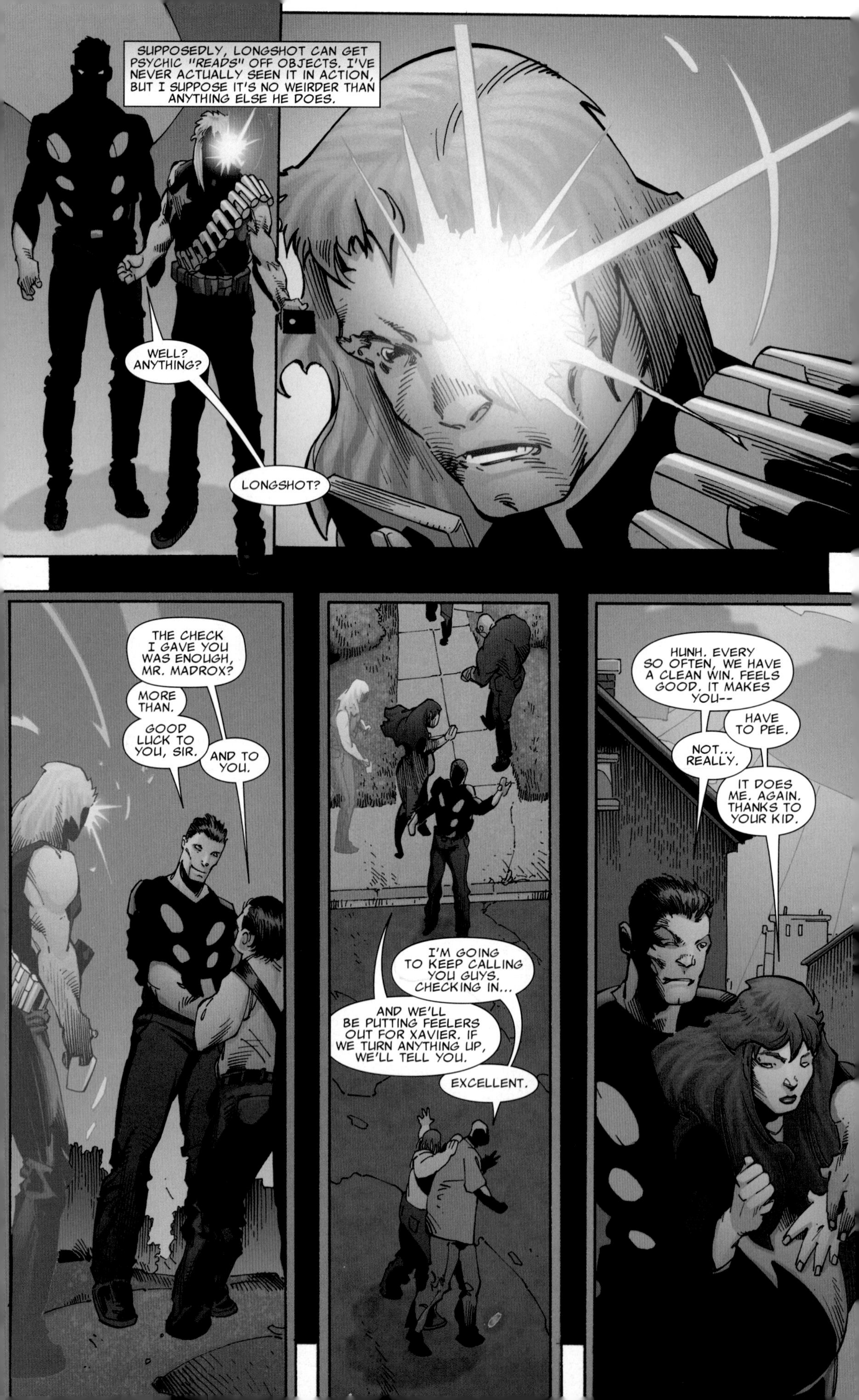
SUPPOSEDLY, LONGSHOT CAN GET PSYCHIC "READS" OFF OBJECTS. I'VE NEVER ACTUALLY SEEN IT IN ACTION, BUT I SUPPOSE IT'S NO WEIRDER THAN ANYTHING ELSE HE DOES.
WELL? ANYTHING?
LONGSHOT?
THE CHECK I GAVE YOU WAS ENOUGH, MR. MADROX?
MORE THAN.
GOOD LUCK TO YOU, SIR.
AND TO YOU.
I'M GOING TO KEEP CALLING YOU GUYS, CHECKING IN...
AND WE'LL BE PUTTING FEELERS OUT FOR XAVIER. IF WE TURN ANYTHING UP, WE'LL TELL YOU.
EXCELLENT.
HUNH. EVERY SO OFTEN, WE HAVE A CLEAN WIN. FEELS GOOD. IT MAKES YOU--
HAVE TO PEE.
NOT... REALLY.
IT DOES ME. AGAIN. THANKS TO YOUR KID.

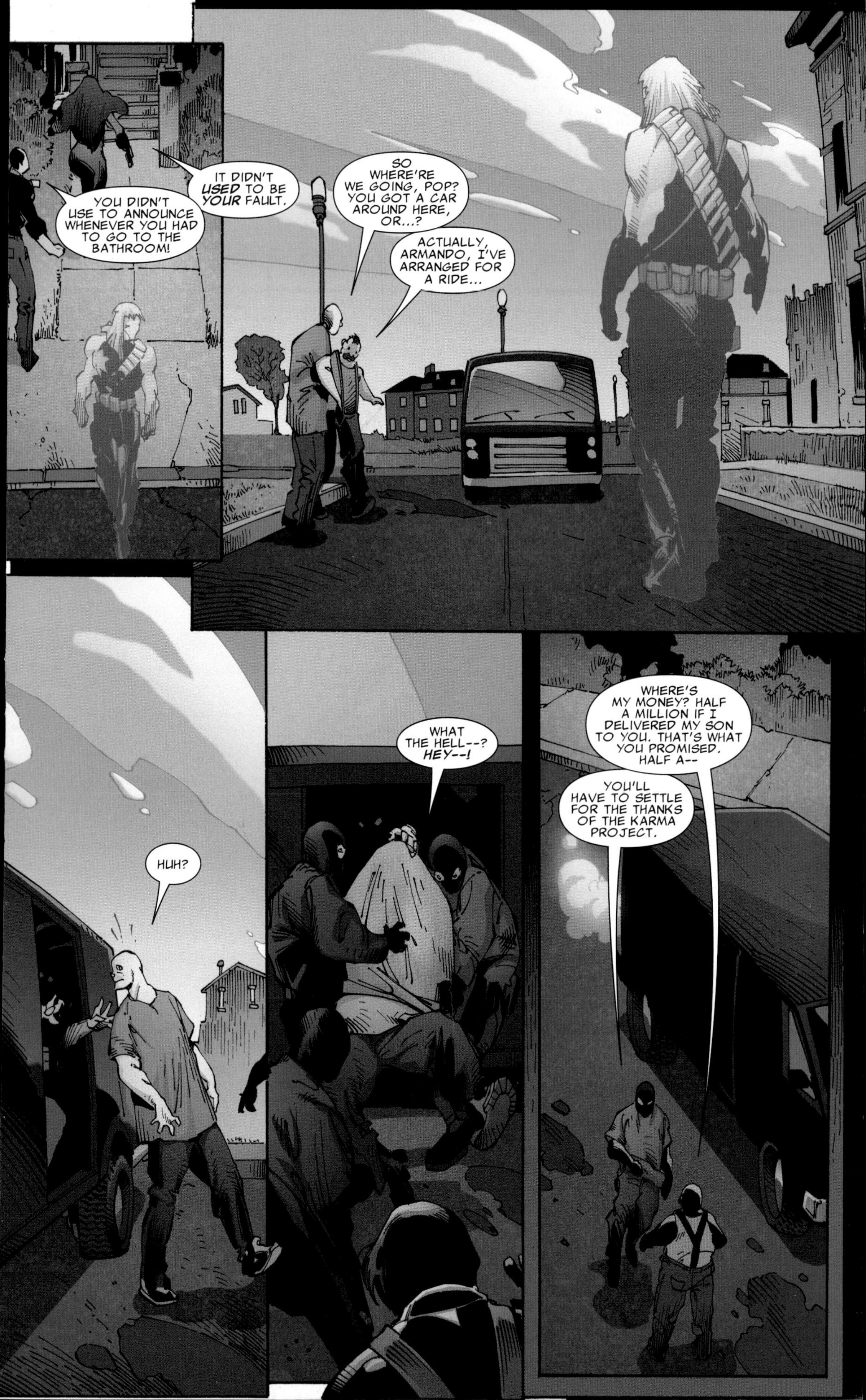
YOU DIDN'T USE TO ANNOUNCE WHENEVER YOU HAD TO GO TO THE BATHROOM!
IT DIDN'T USED TO BE YOUR FAULT.
SO WHERE'RE WE GOING, POP? YOU GOT A CAR AROUND HERE, OR...?
ACTUALLY, ARMANDO, I'VE ARRANGED FOR A RIDE...
HUH?
WHAT THE HELL--? HEY--!
WHERE'S MY MONEY? HALF A MILLION IF I DELIVERED MY SON TO YOU. THAT'S WHAT YOU PROMISED. HALF A--
YOU'LL HAVE TO SETTLE FOR THE THANKS OF THE KARMA PROJECT.

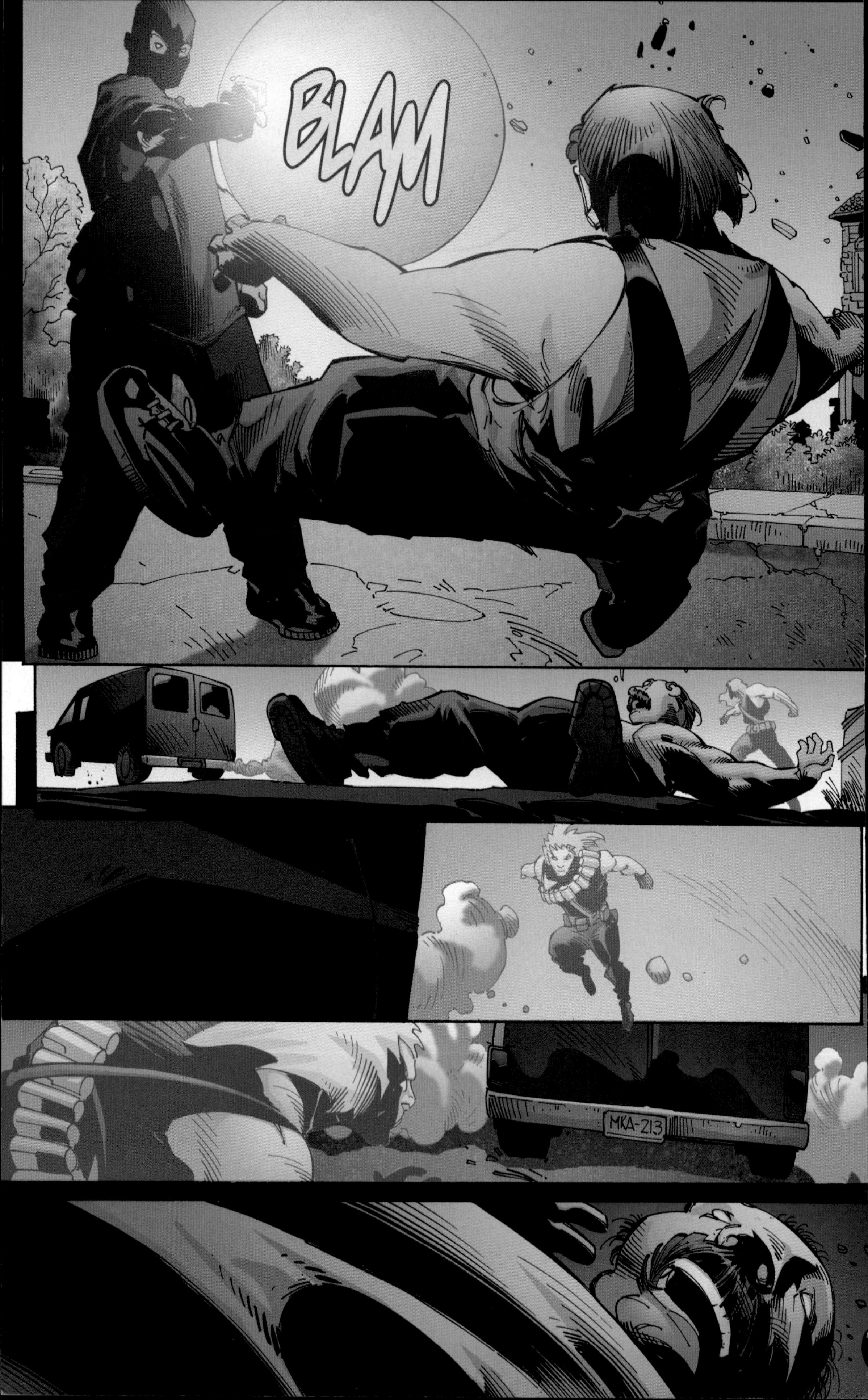
BLAM
MKA-213

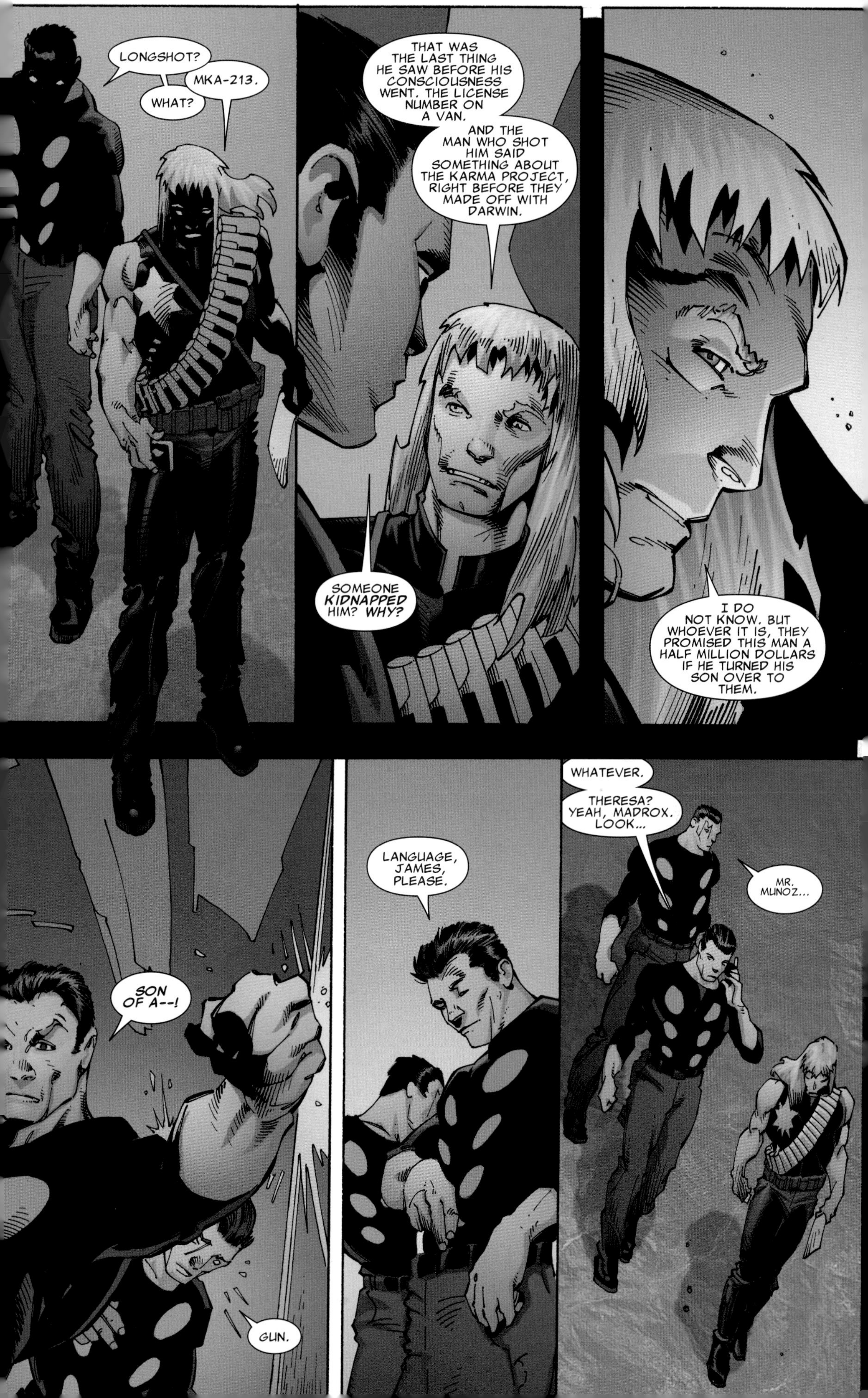
LONGSHOT?
MKA-213.
WHAT?
THAT WAS THE LAST THING HE SAW BEFORE HIS CONSCIOUSNESS WENT. THE LICENSE NUMBER ON A VAN.
AND THE MAN WHO SHOT HIM SAID SOMETHING ABOUT THE KARMA PROJECT, RIGHT BEFORE THEY MADE OFF WITH DARWIN.
SOMEONE ***KIDNAPPED*** HIM? ***WHY?***
I DO NOT KNOW. BUT WHOEVER IT IS, THEY PROMISED THIS MAN A HALF MILLION DOLLARS IF HE TURNED HIS SON OVER TO THEM.
SON OF A--!
GUN.
LANGUAGE, JAMES, PLEASE.
WHATEVER.
THERESA? YEAH, MADROX. LOOK...
MR. MUNOZ...

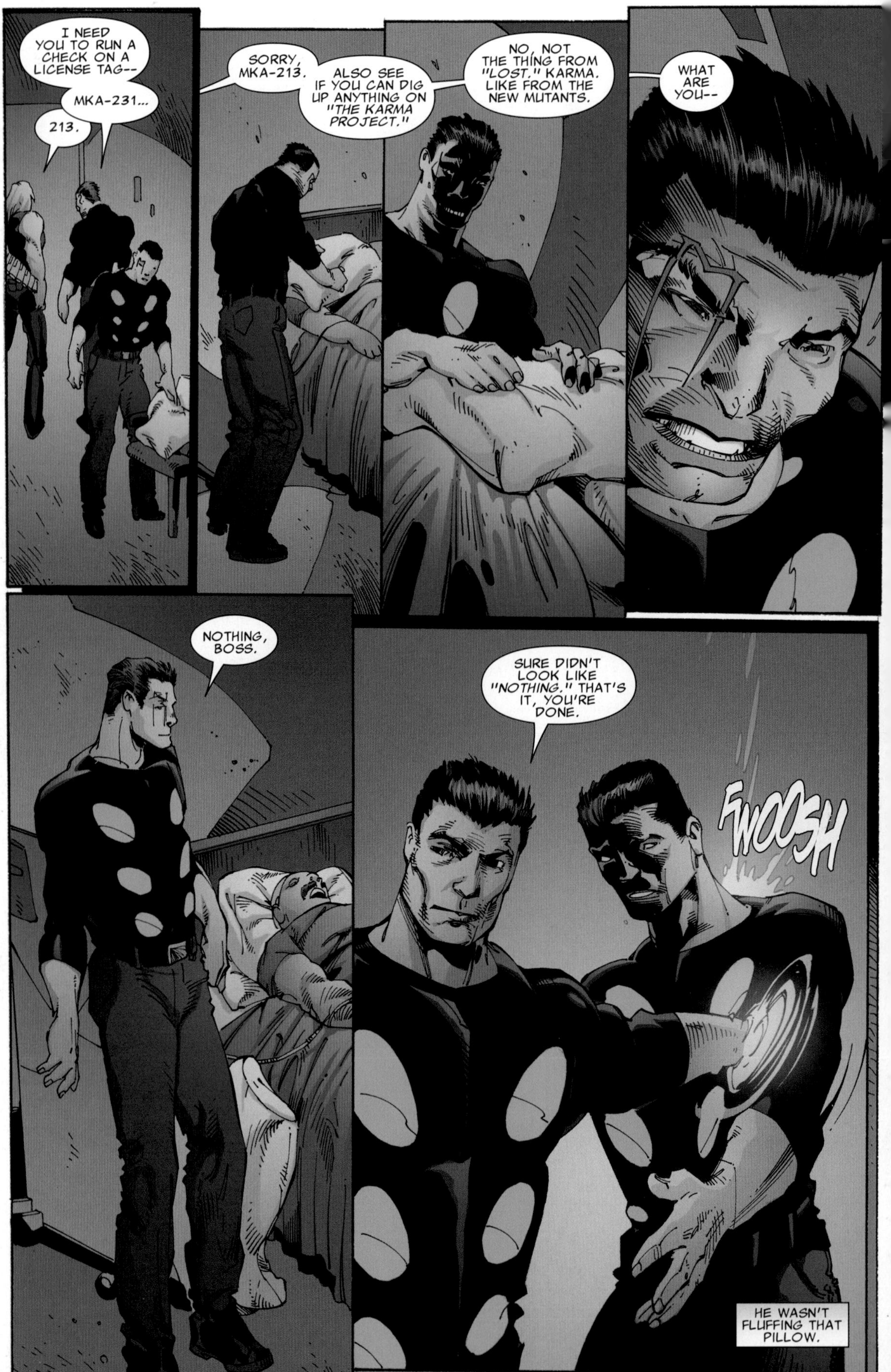
I NEED YOU TO RUN A CHECK ON A LICENSE TAG--
MKA-231...
213.
SORRY, MKA-213.
ALSO SEE IF YOU CAN DIG UP ANYTHING ON "THE KARMA PROJECT."
NO, NOT THE THING FROM "LOST." KARMA. LIKE FROM THE NEW MUTANTS.
WHAT ARE YOU--
NOTHING, BOSS.
SURE DIDN'T LOOK LIKE "NOTHING." THAT'S IT, YOU'RE DONE.
FWOOSH
HE WASN'T FLUFFING THAT PILLOW.

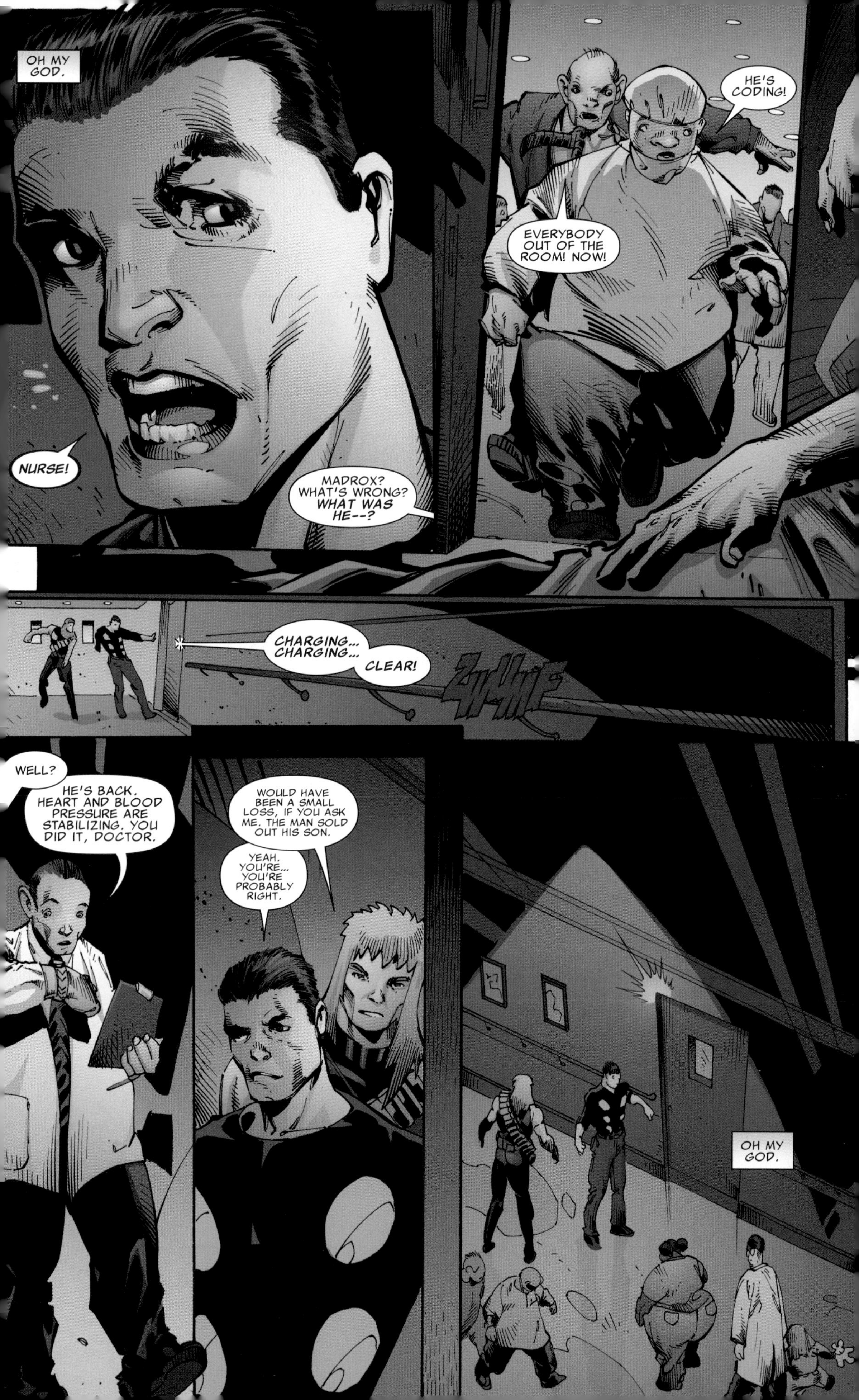
OH MY GOD.
NURSE!
MADROX? WHAT'S WRONG? WHAT WAS HE--?
HE'S CODING!
EVERYBODY OUT OF THE ROOM! NOW!
CHARGING... CHARGING...
CLEAR!
ZWUMF
WELL?
HE'S BACK. HEART AND BLOOD PRESSURE ARE STABILIZING. YOU DID IT, DOCTOR.
WOULD HAVE BEEN A SMALL LOSS, IF YOU ASK ME. THE MAN SOLD OUT HIS SON.
YEAH. YOU'RE... YOU'RE PROBABLY RIGHT.
OH MY GOD.

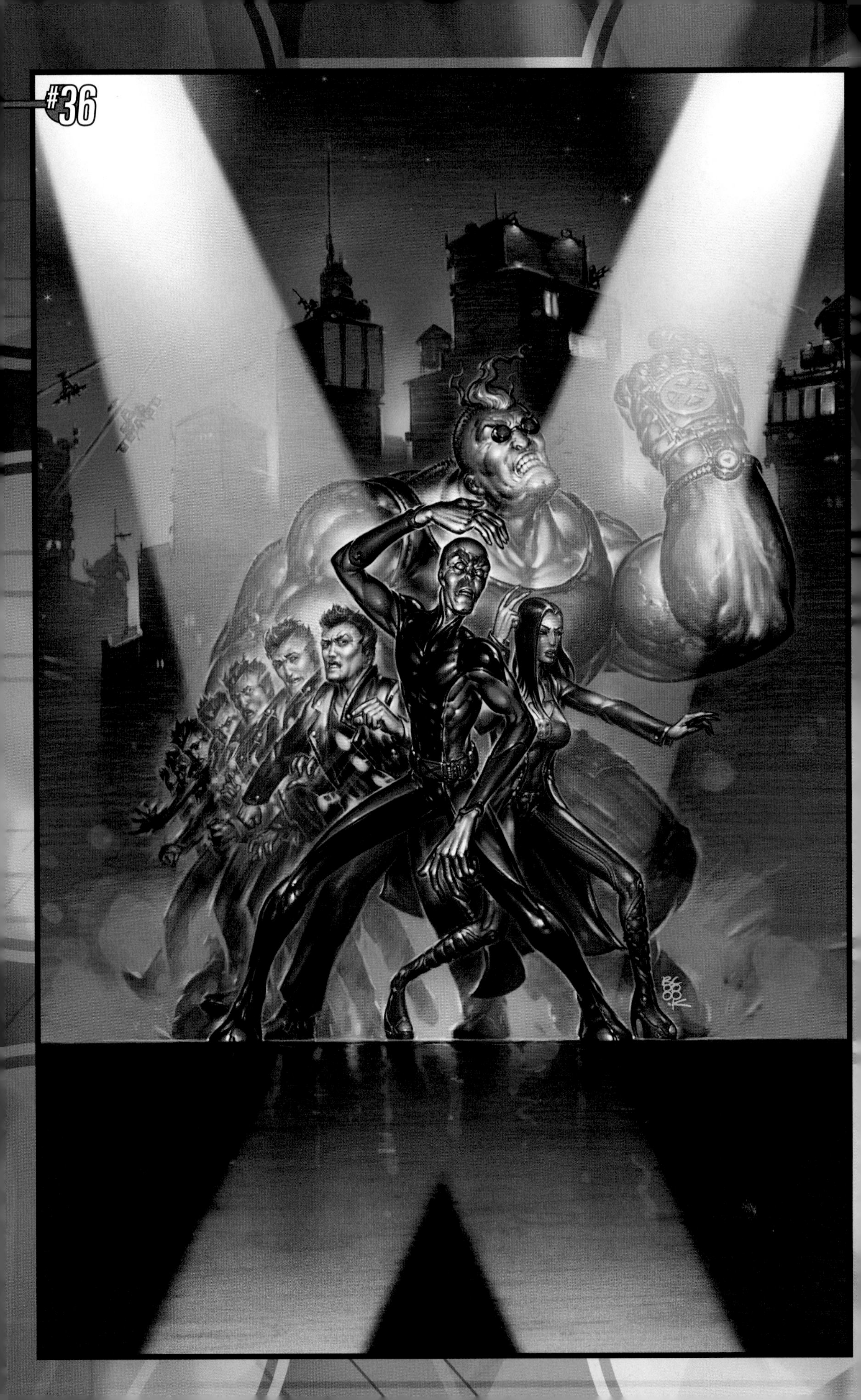
#36

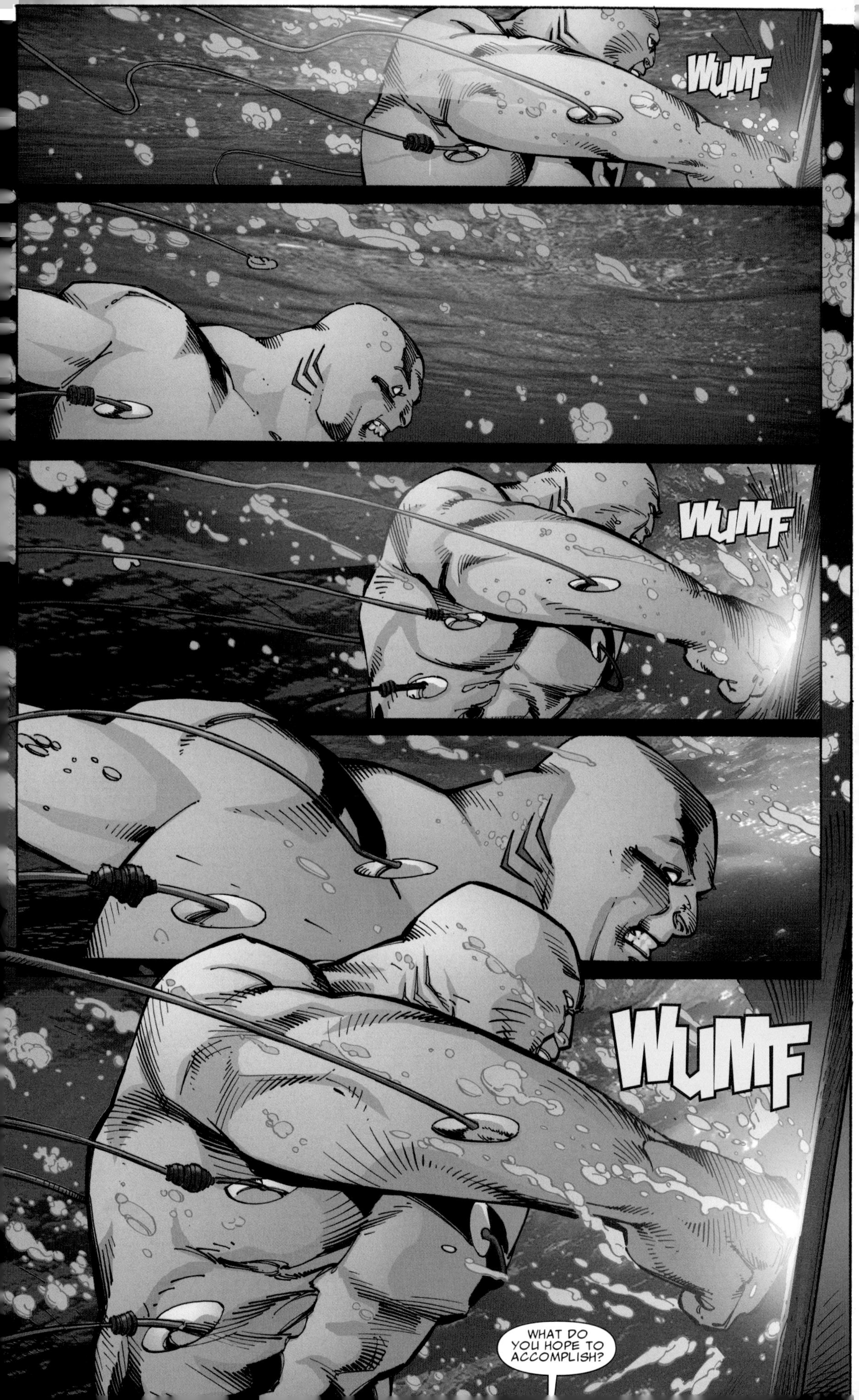
WUMF
WUMF
WUMF
WHAT DO YOU HOPE TO ACCOMPLISH?

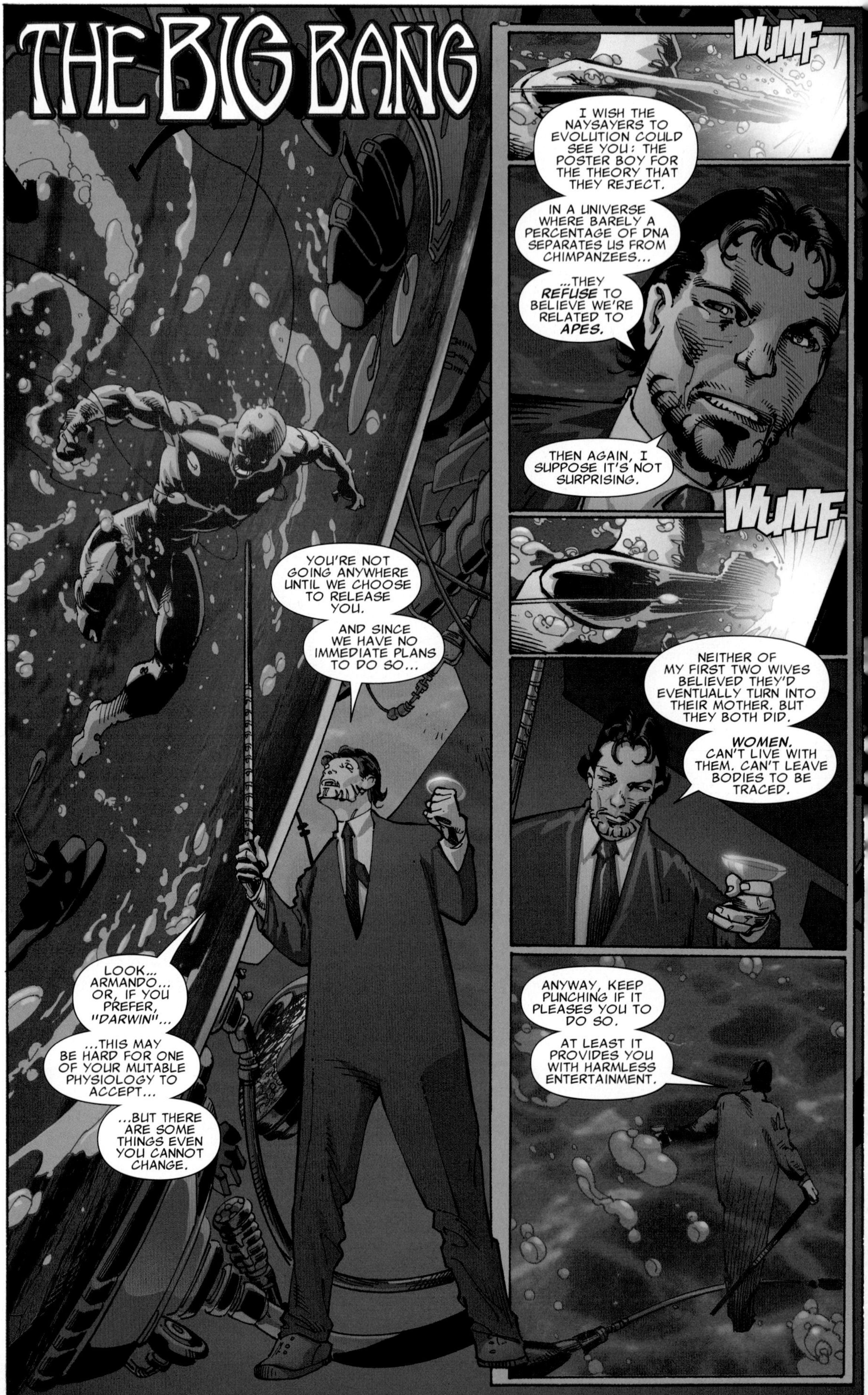
THE BIG BANG
WUMF
I WISH THE NAYSAYERS TO EVOLUTION COULD SEE YOU: THE POSTER BOY FOR THE THEORY THAT THEY REJECT.
IN A UNIVERSE WHERE BARELY A PERCENTAGE OF DNA SEPARATES US FROM CHIMPANZEES...
...THEY REFUSE TO BELIEVE WE'RE RELATED TO APES.
THEN AGAIN, I SUPPOSE IT'S NOT SURPRISING.
WUMF
YOU'RE NOT GOING ANYWHERE UNTIL WE CHOOSE TO RELEASE YOU.
AND SINCE WE HAVE NO IMMEDIATE PLANS TO DO SO...
NEITHER OF MY FIRST TWO WIVES BELIEVED THEY'D EVENTUALLY TURN INTO THEIR MOTHER. BUT THEY BOTH DID.
WOMEN. CAN'T LIVE WITH THEM. CAN'T LEAVE BODIES TO BE TRACED.
LOOK... ARMANDO... OR, IF YOU PREFER, "DARWIN"...
...THIS MAY BE HARD FOR ONE OF YOUR MUTABLE PHYSIOLOGY TO ACCEPT...
...BUT THERE ARE SOME THINGS EVEN YOU CANNOT CHANGE.
ANYWAY, KEEP PUNCHING IF IT PLEASES YOU TO DO SO.
AT LEAST IT PROVIDES YOU WITH HARMLESS ENTERTAINMENT.

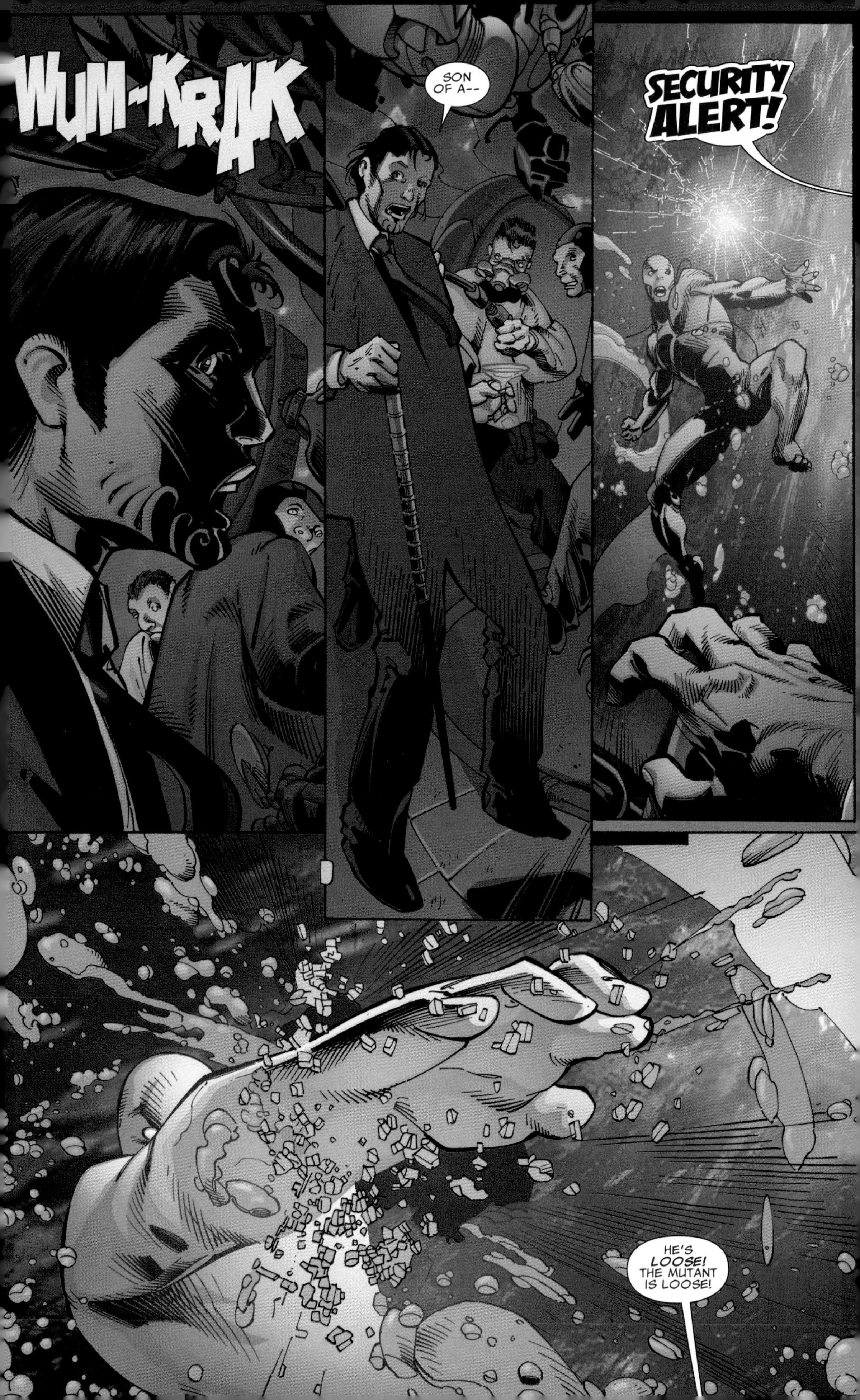
WUM-KRAK
SON OF A--
SECURITY ALERT!
HE'S LOOSE! THE MUTANT IS LOOSE!

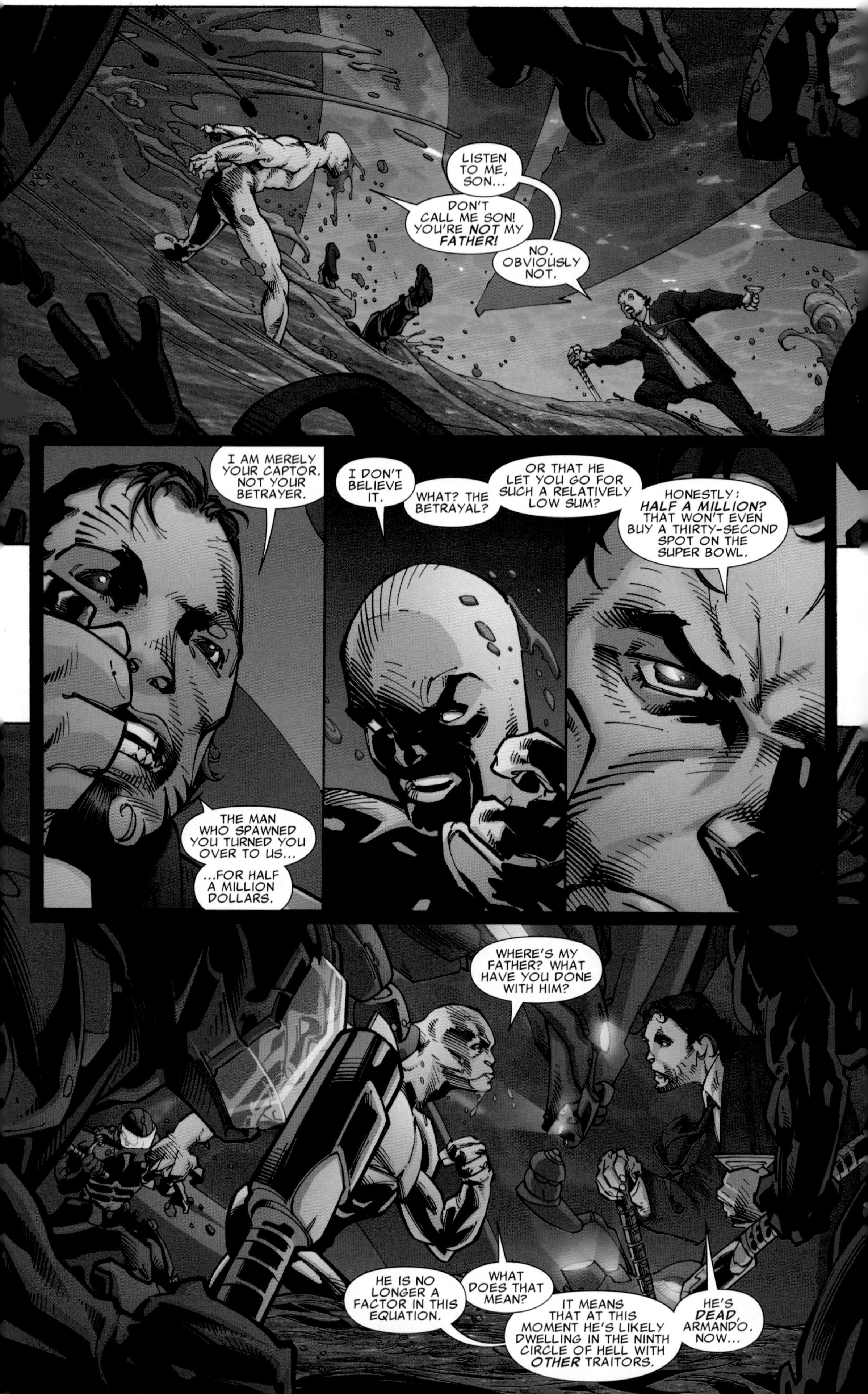
LISTEN TO ME, SON...
DON'T CALL ME SON! YOU'RE NOT MY FATHER!
NO. OBVIOUSLY NOT.
I AM MERELY YOUR CAPTOR. NOT YOUR BETRAYER.
THE MAN WHO SPAWNED YOU TURNED YOU OVER TO US...
...FOR HALF A MILLION DOLLARS.
I DON'T BELIEVE IT.
WHAT? THE BETRAYAL?
OR THAT HE LET YOU GO FOR SUCH A RELATIVELY LOW SUM?
HONESTLY: HALF A MILLION? THAT WON'T EVEN BUY A THIRTY-SECOND SPOT ON THE SUPER BOWL.
WHERE'S MY FATHER? WHAT HAVE YOU DONE WITH HIM?
HE IS NO LONGER A FACTOR IN THIS EQUATION.
WHAT DOES THAT MEAN?
IT MEANS THAT AT THIS MOMENT HE'S LIKELY DWELLING IN THE NINTH CIRCLE OF HELL WITH OTHER TRAITORS.
HE'S DEAD, ARMANDO. NOW...

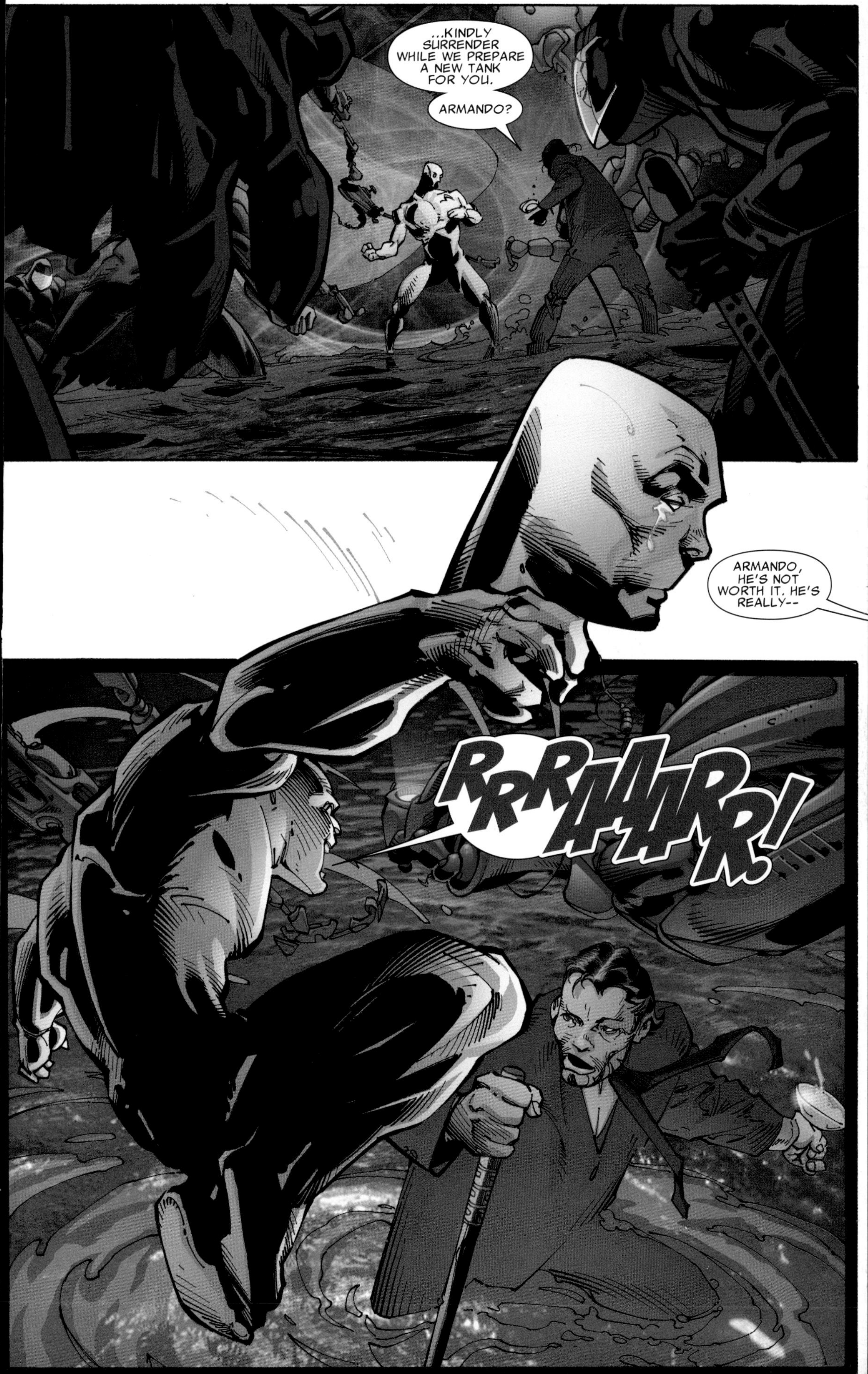
...KINDLY SURRENDER WHILE WE PREPARE A NEW TANK FOR YOU.
ARMANDO?
ARMANDO, HE'S NOT WORTH IT. HE'S REALLY--
RRRAAARR!

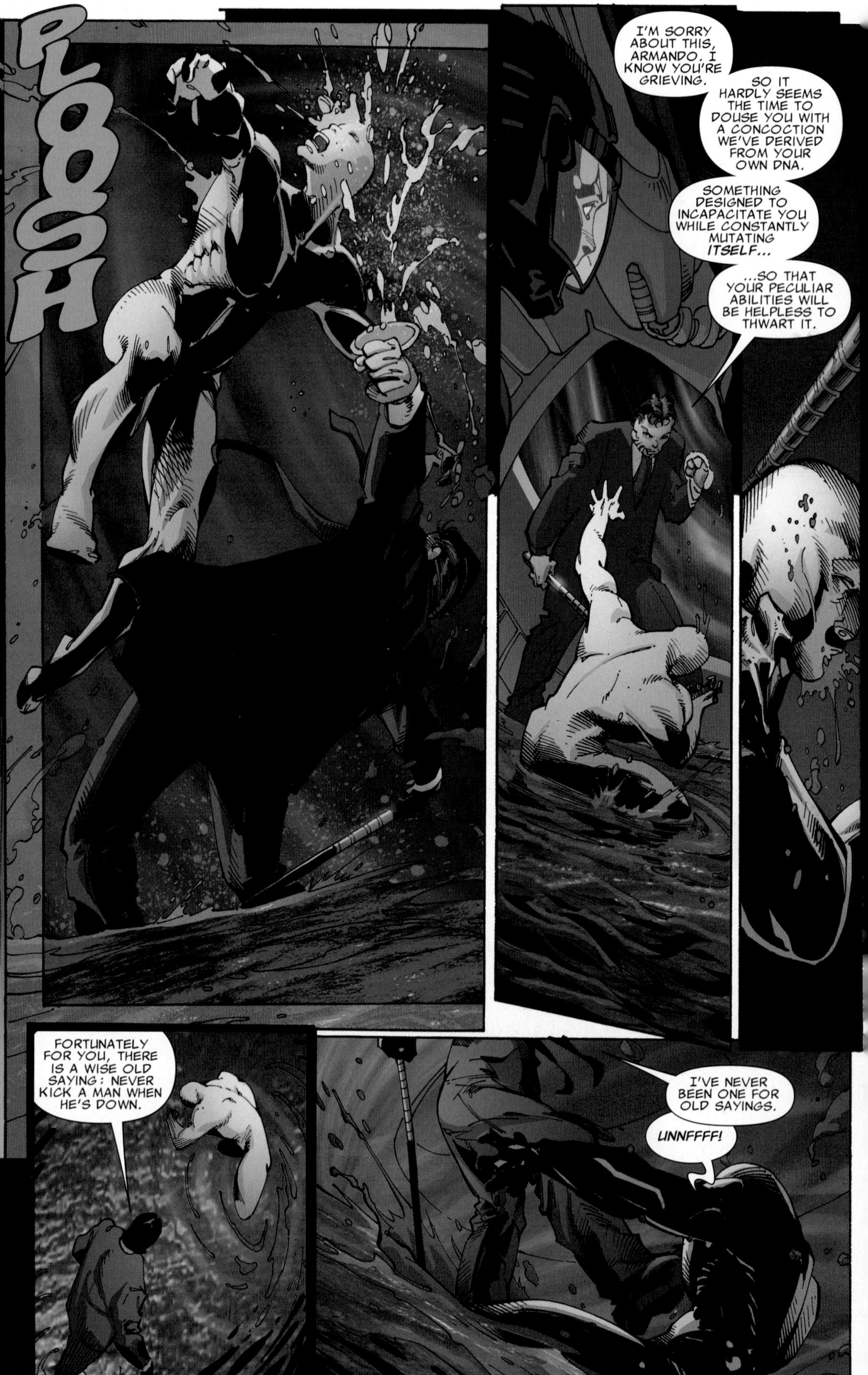
PLOOSH
I'M SORRY ABOUT THIS, ARMANDO. I KNOW YOU'RE GRIEVING.
SO IT HARDLY SEEMS THE TIME TO DOUSE YOU WITH A CONCOCTION WE'VE DERIVED FROM YOUR OWN DNA.
SOMETHING DESIGNED TO INCAPACITATE YOU WHILE CONSTANTLY MUTATING ITSELF...
...SO THAT YOUR PECULIAR ABILITIES WILL BE HELPLESS TO THWART IT.
FORTUNATELY FOR YOU, THERE IS A WISE OLD SAYING: NEVER KICK A MAN WHEN HE'S DOWN.
I'VE NEVER BEEN ONE FOR OLD SAYINGS.
UNNFFFF!

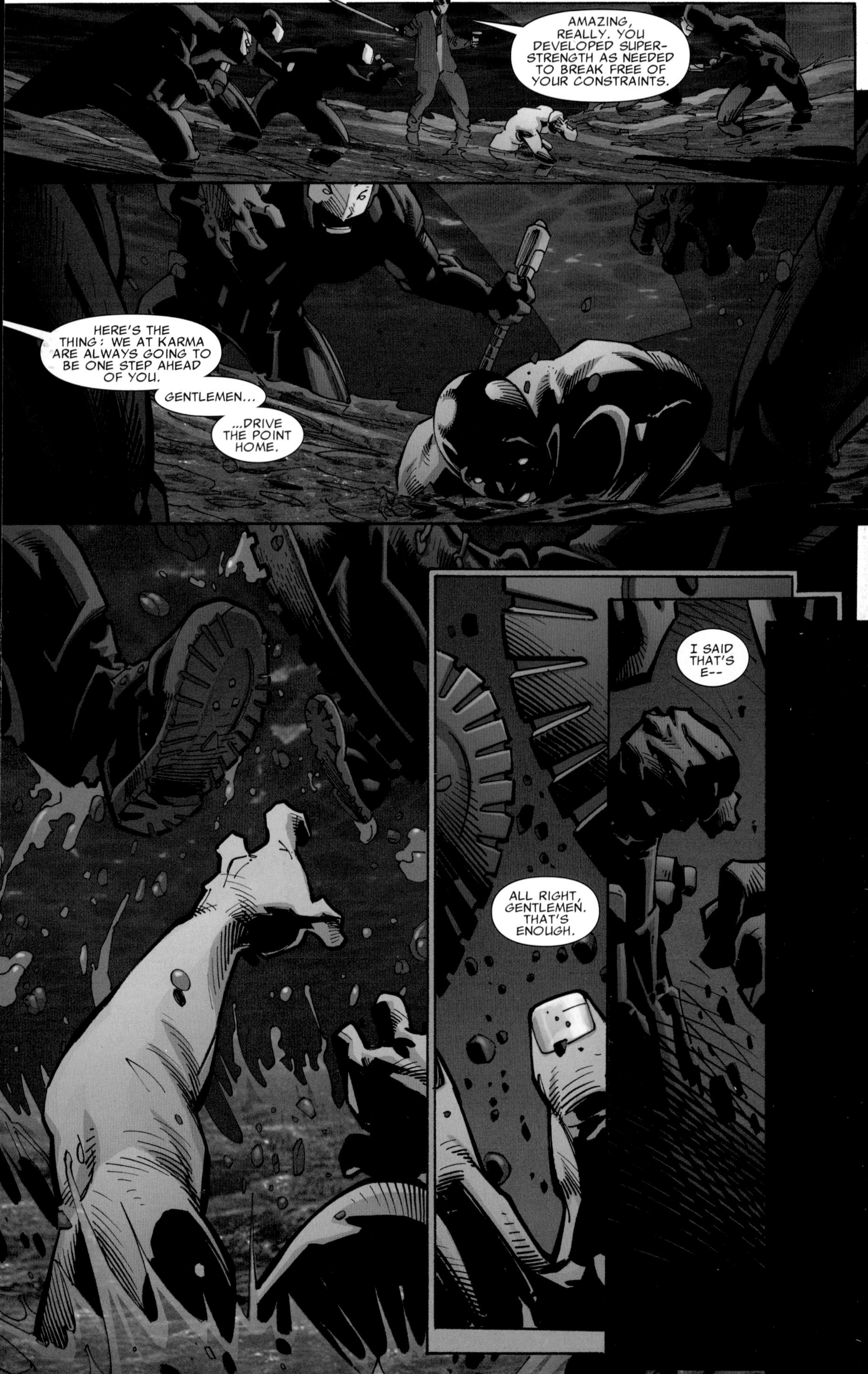
AMAZING, REALLY. YOU DEVELOPED SUPER-STRENGTH AS NEEDED TO BREAK FREE OF YOUR CONSTRAINTS.
HERE'S THE THING: WE AT KARMA ARE ALWAYS GOING TO BE ONE STEP AHEAD OF YOU.
GENTLEMEN...
...DRIVE THE POINT HOME.
ALL RIGHT, GENTLEMEN. THAT'S ENOUGH.
I SAID THAT'S E--

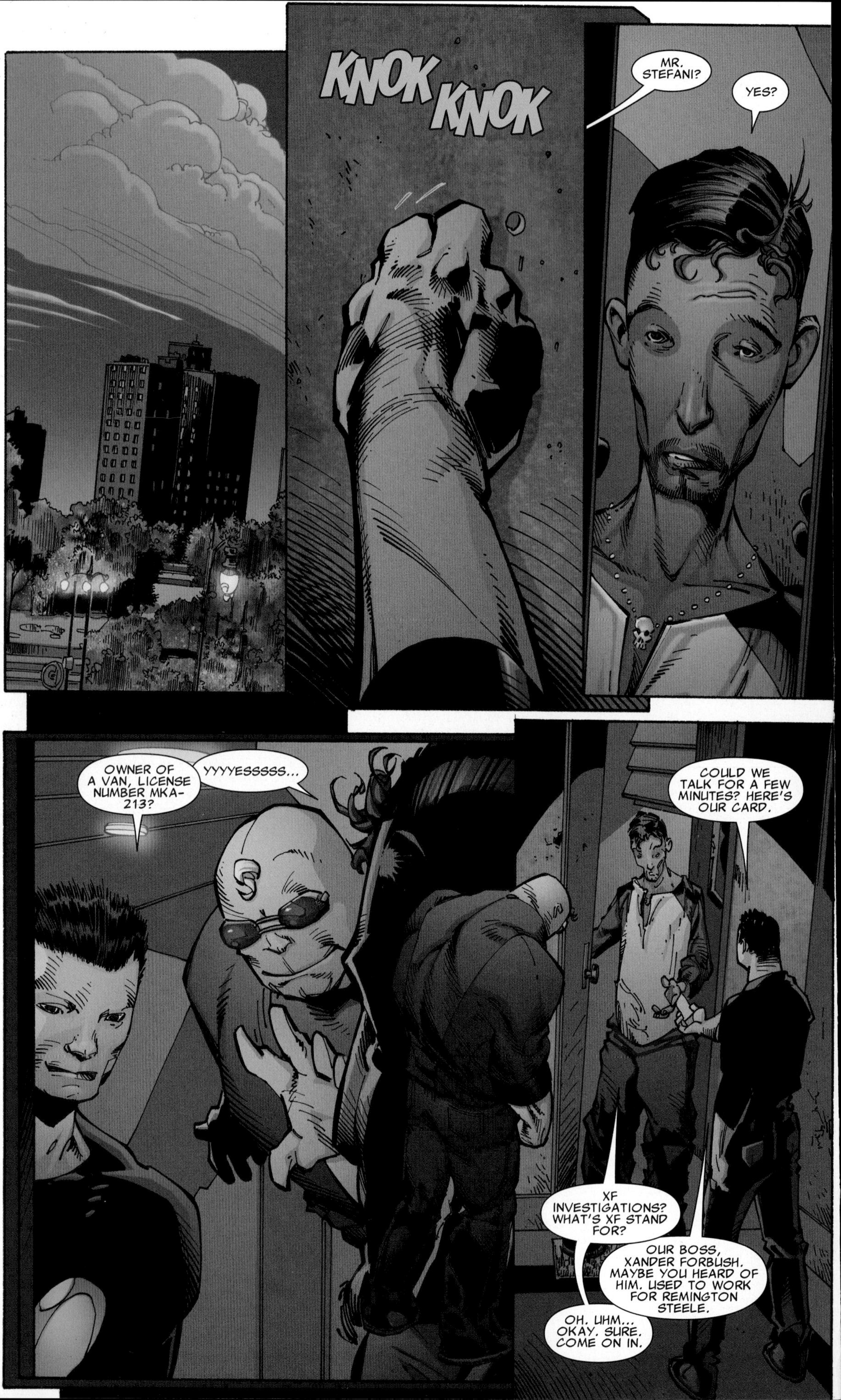
KNOK KNOK
MR. STEFANI?
YES?
OWNER OF A VAN, LICENSE NUMBER MKA-213?
YYYYESSSSS...
COULD WE TALK FOR A FEW MINUTES? HERE'S OUR CARD.
XF INVESTIGATIONS? WHAT'S XF STAND FOR?
OUR BOSS, XANDER FORBUSH. MAYBE YOU HEARD OF HIM. USED TO WORK FOR REMINGTON STEELE.
OH. UHM... OKAY. SURE. COME ON IN.

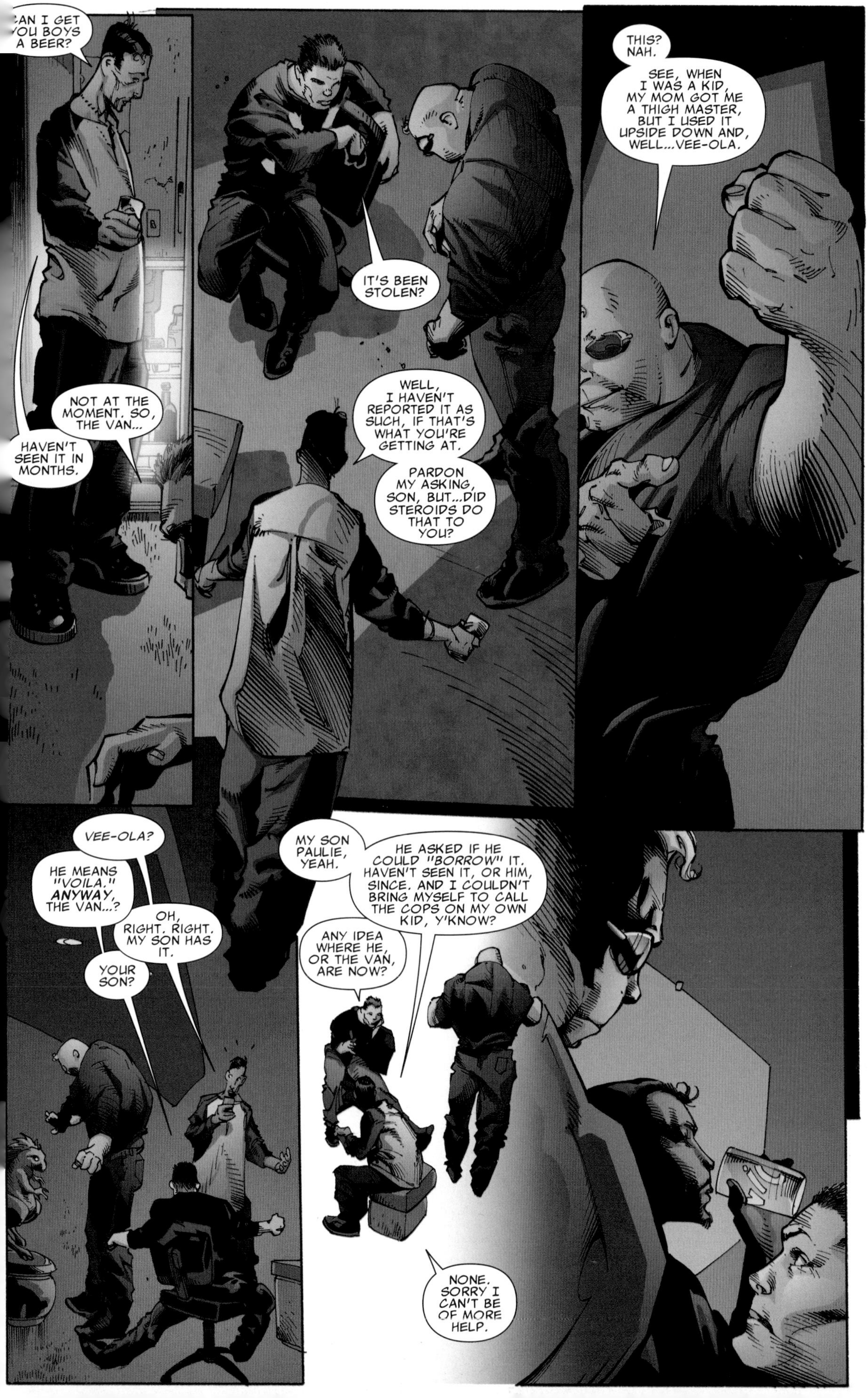
CAN I GET YOU BOYS A BEER?
NOT AT THE MOMENT. SO, THE VAN...
HAVEN'T SEEN IT IN MONTHS.
IT'S BEEN STOLEN?
WELL, I HAVEN'T REPORTED IT AS SUCH, IF THAT'S WHAT YOU'RE GETTING AT.
PARDON MY ASKING, SON, BUT...DID STEROIDS DO THAT TO YOU?
THIS? NAH.
SEE, WHEN I WAS A KID, MY MOM GOT ME A THIGH MASTER, BUT I USED IT UPSIDE DOWN AND, WELL...VEE-OLA.
VEE-OLA?
HE MEANS "VOILA." ANYWAY, THE VAN...?
OH, RIGHT. RIGHT. MY SON HAS IT.
YOUR SON?
MY SON PAULIE, YEAH.
HE ASKED IF HE COULD "BORROW" IT. HAVEN'T SEEN IT, OR HIM, SINCE. AND I COULDN'T BRING MYSELF TO CALL THE COPS ON MY OWN KID, Y'KNOW?
ANY IDEA WHERE HE, OR THE VAN, ARE NOW?
NONE. SORRY I CAN'T BE OF MORE HELP.

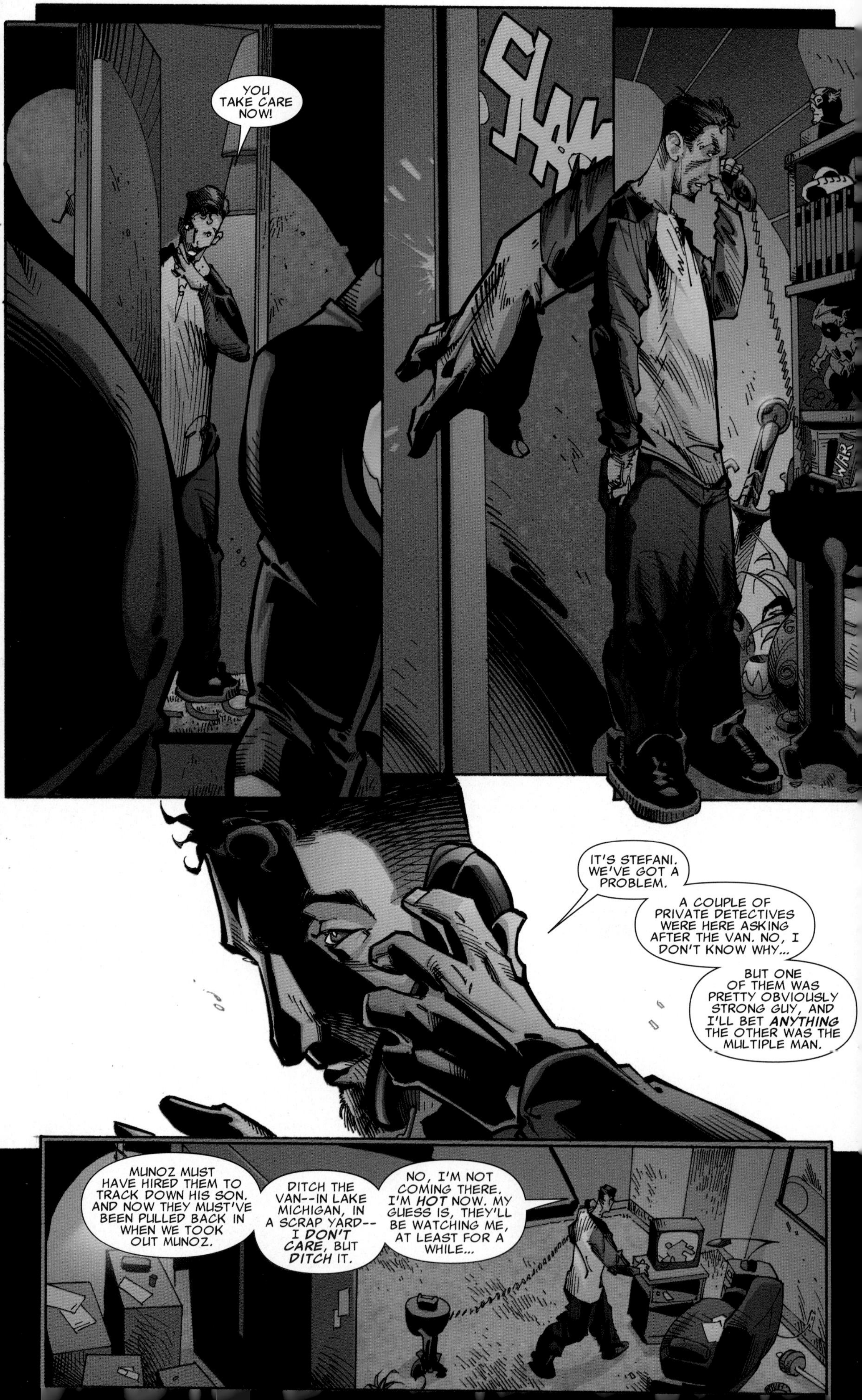
YOU TAKE CARE NOW!
SLAM
IT'S STEFANI. WE'VE GOT A PROBLEM.
A COUPLE OF PRIVATE DETECTIVES WERE HERE ASKING AFTER THE VAN. NO, I DON'T KNOW WHY...
BUT ONE OF THEM WAS PRETTY OBVIOUSLY STRONG GUY, AND I'LL BET ANYTHING THE OTHER WAS THE MULTIPLE MAN.
MUNOZ MUST HAVE HIRED THEM TO TRACK DOWN HIS SON, AND NOW THEY MUST'VE BEEN PULLED BACK IN WHEN WE TOOK OUT MUNOZ.
DITCH THE VAN--IN LAKE MICHIGAN, IN A SCRAP YARD--I DON'T CARE, BUT DITCH IT.
NO, I'M NOT COMING THERE. I'M HOT NOW. MY GUESS IS, THEY'LL BE WATCHING ME, AT LEAST FOR A WHILE...
WAR

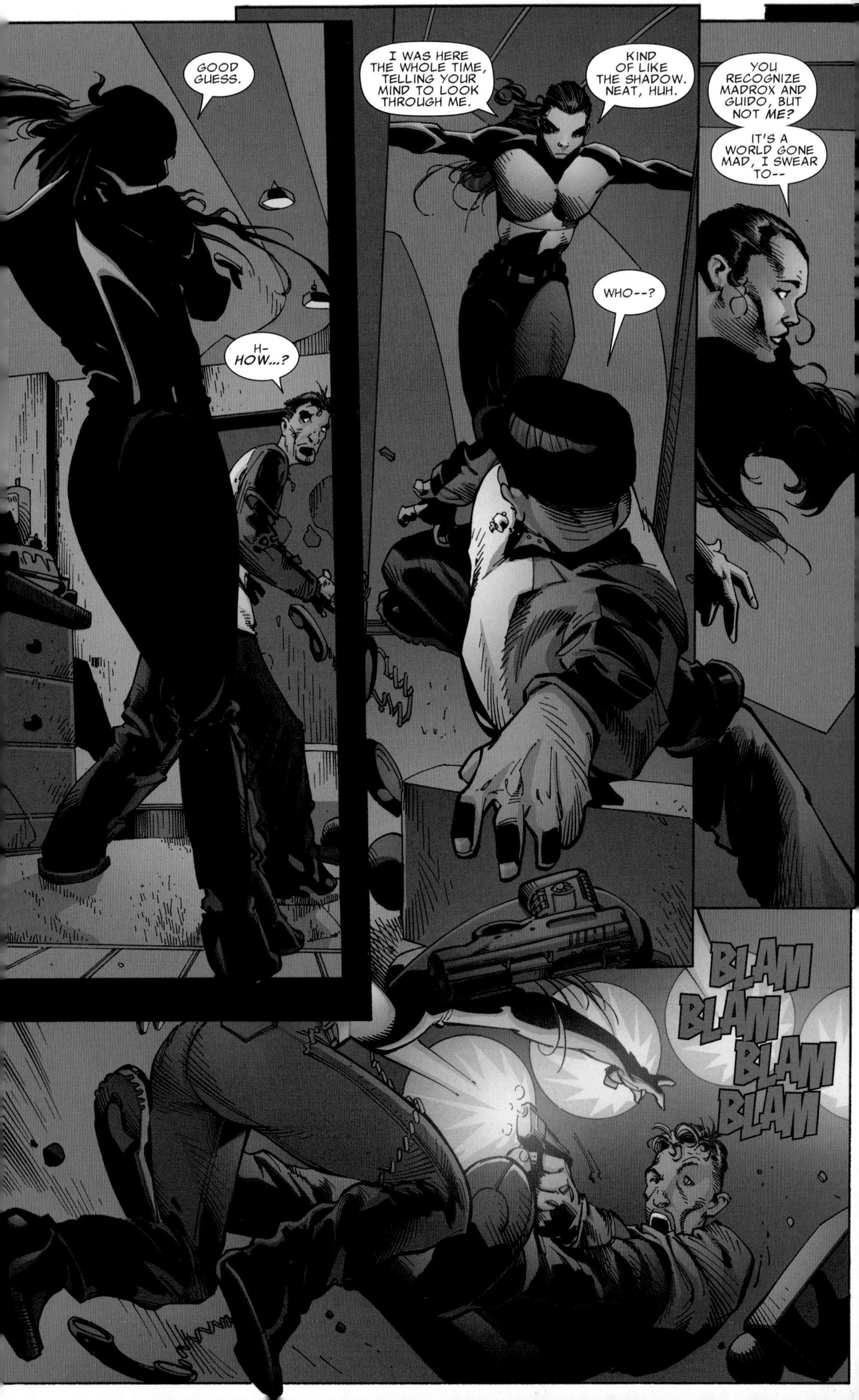
GOOD GUESS.
H- HOW...?
I WAS HERE THE WHOLE TIME, TELLING YOUR MIND TO LOOK THROUGH ME.
KIND OF LIKE THE SHADOW. NEAT, HUH.
WHO--?
YOU RECOGNIZE MADROX AND GUIDO, BUT NOT ME?
IT'S A WORLD GONE MAD, I SWEAR TO--
BLAM
BLAM
BLAM
BLAM

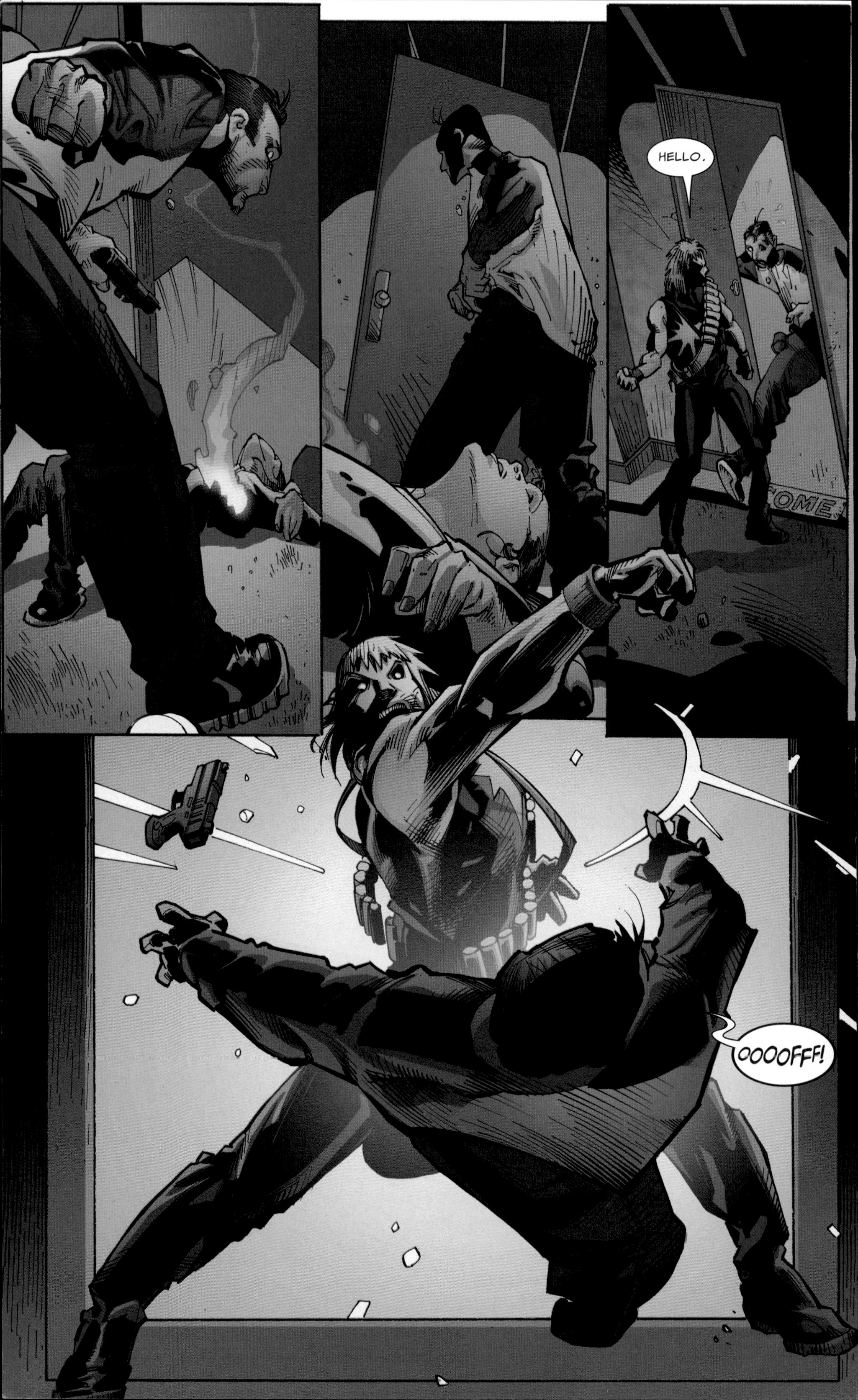
HELLO.
COME
OOOOFFF!

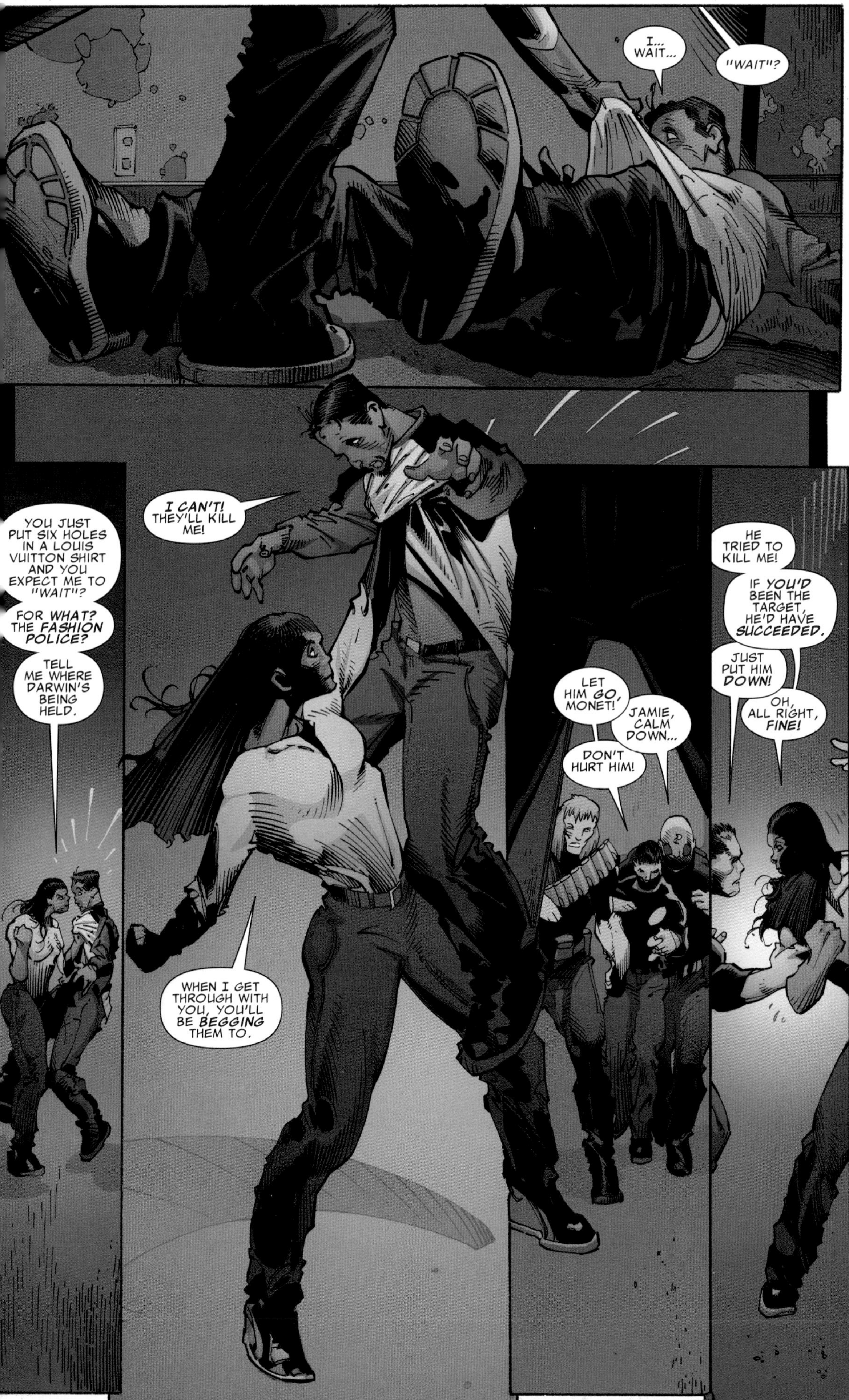
I... WAIT...
"WAIT"?
YOU JUST PUT SIX HOLES IN A LOUIS VUITTON SHIRT AND YOU EXPECT ME TO "WAIT"?
FOR **WHAT?** THE ***FASHION POLICE?***
TELL ME WHERE DARWIN'S BEING HELD.
I CAN'T! THEY'LL KILL ME!
WHEN I GET THROUGH WITH YOU, YOU'LL BE ***BEGGING*** THEM TO.
LET HIM ***GO,*** MONET!
JAMIE, CALM DOWN...
DON'T HURT HIM!
HE TRIED TO KILL ME!
IF ***YOU'D*** BEEN THE TARGET, HE'D HAVE ***SUCCEEDED.***
JUST PUT HIM ***DOWN!***
OH, ALL RIGHT, ***FINE!***

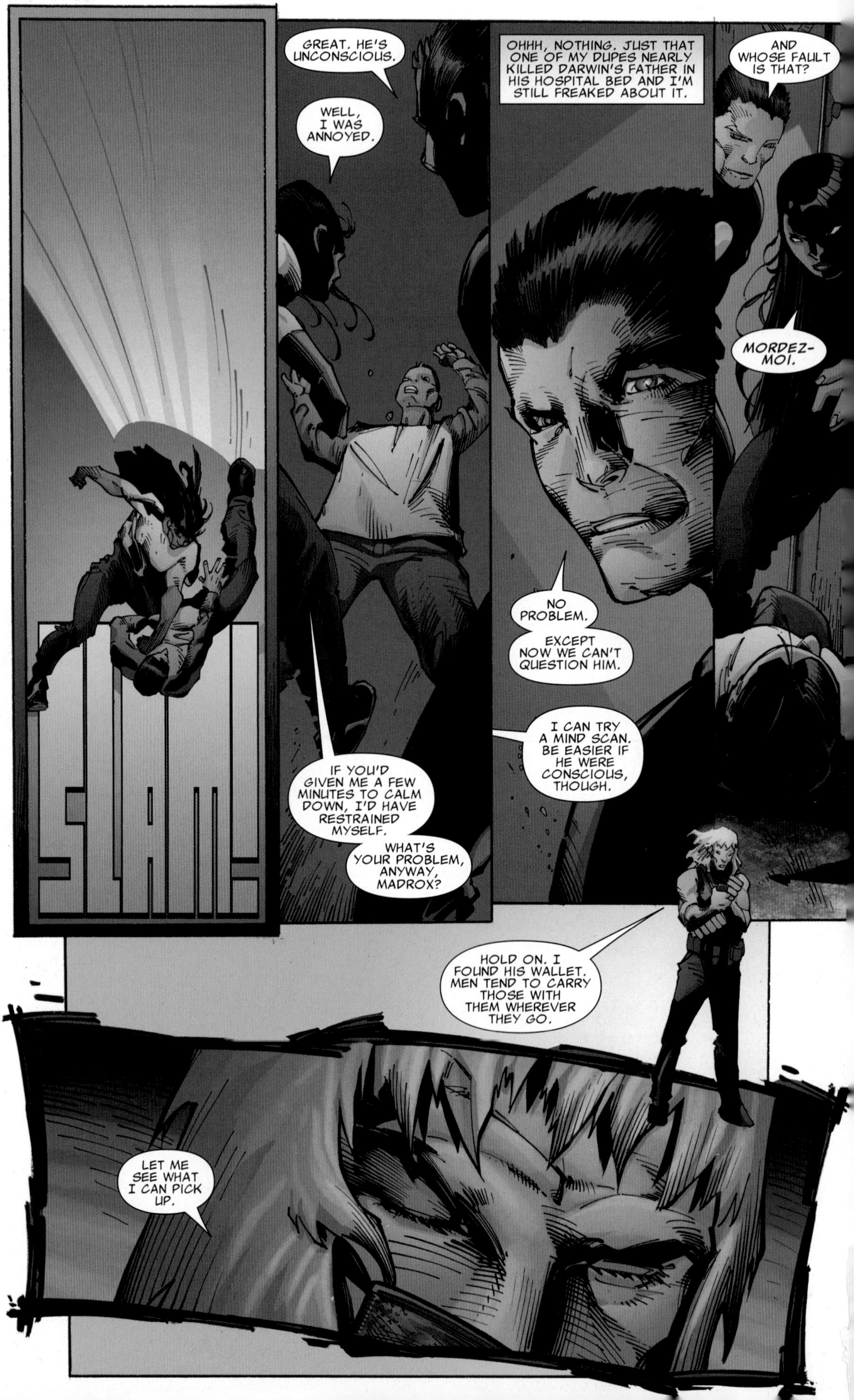
SLAM!
GREAT. HE'S UNCONSCIOUS.
WELL, I WAS ANNOYED.
IF YOU'D GIVEN ME A FEW MINUTES TO CALM DOWN, I'D HAVE RESTRAINED MYSELF.
WHAT'S YOUR PROBLEM, ANYWAY, MADROX?
OHHH, NOTHING. JUST THAT ONE OF MY DUPES NEARLY KILLED DARWIN'S FATHER IN HIS HOSPITAL BED AND I'M STILL FREAKED ABOUT IT.
NO PROBLEM.
EXCEPT NOW WE CAN'T QUESTION HIM.
I CAN TRY A MIND SCAN. BE EASIER IF HE WERE CONSCIOUS, THOUGH.
AND WHOSE FAULT IS THAT?
MORDEZ-MOI.
HOLD ON. I FOUND HIS WALLET. MEN TEND TO CARRY THOSE WITH THEM WHEREVER THEY GO.
LET ME SEE WHAT I CAN PICK UP.

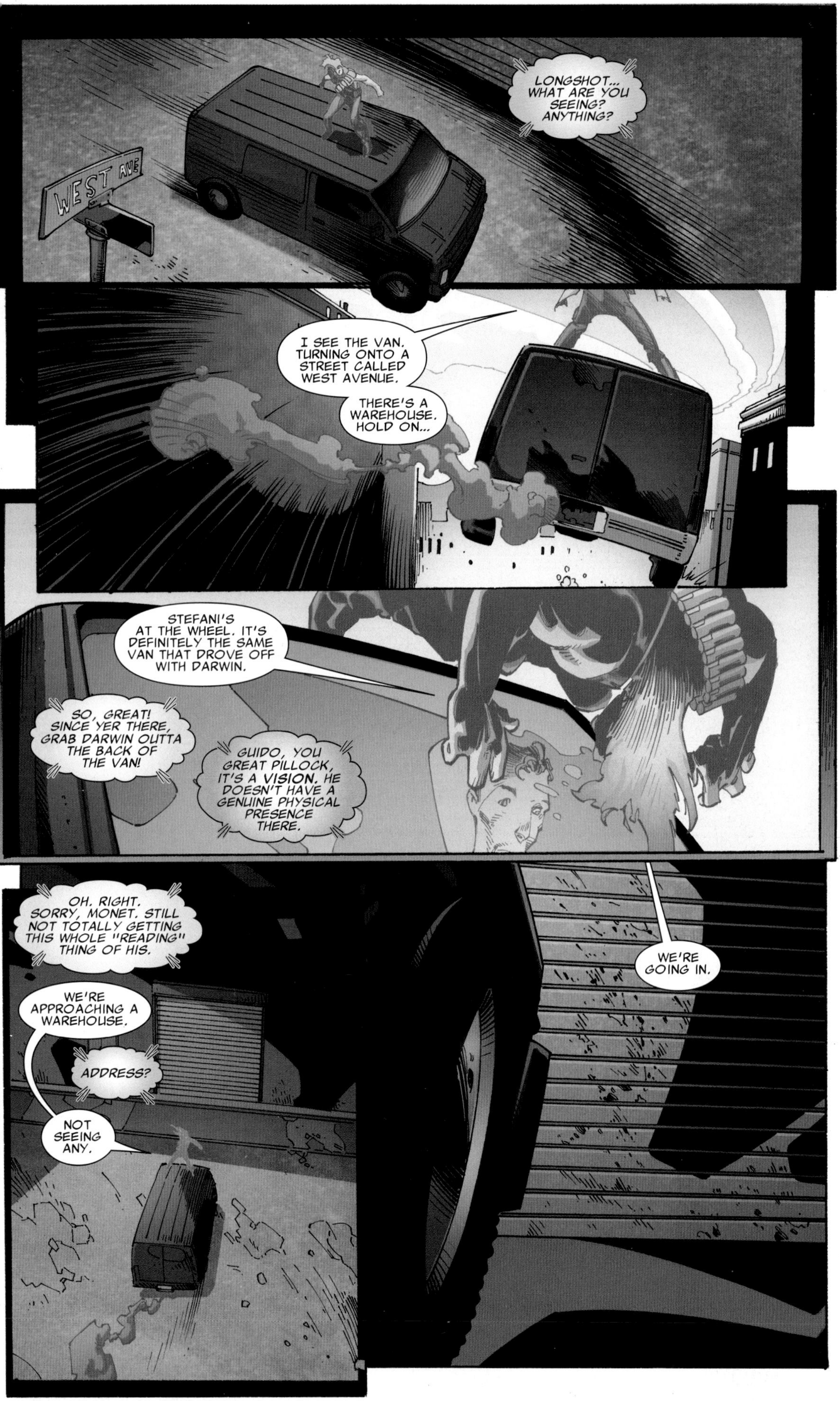
LONGSHOT... WHAT ARE YOU SEEING? ANYTHING?
WEST AVE
I SEE THE VAN, TURNING ONTO A STREET CALLED WEST AVENUE.
THERE'S A WAREHOUSE. HOLD ON...
STEFANI'S AT THE WHEEL. IT'S DEFINITELY THE SAME VAN THAT DROVE OFF WITH DARWIN.
SO, GREAT! SINCE YER THERE, GRAB DARWIN OUTTA THE BACK OF THE VAN!
GUIDO, YOU GREAT PILLOCK, IT'S A **VISION.** HE DOESN'T HAVE A GENUINE PHYSICAL PRESENCE THERE.
OH. RIGHT. SORRY, MONET. STILL NOT TOTALLY GETTING THIS WHOLE "READING" THING OF HIS.
WE'RE APPROACHING A WAREHOUSE.
ADDRESS?
NOT SEEING ANY.
WE'RE GOING IN.

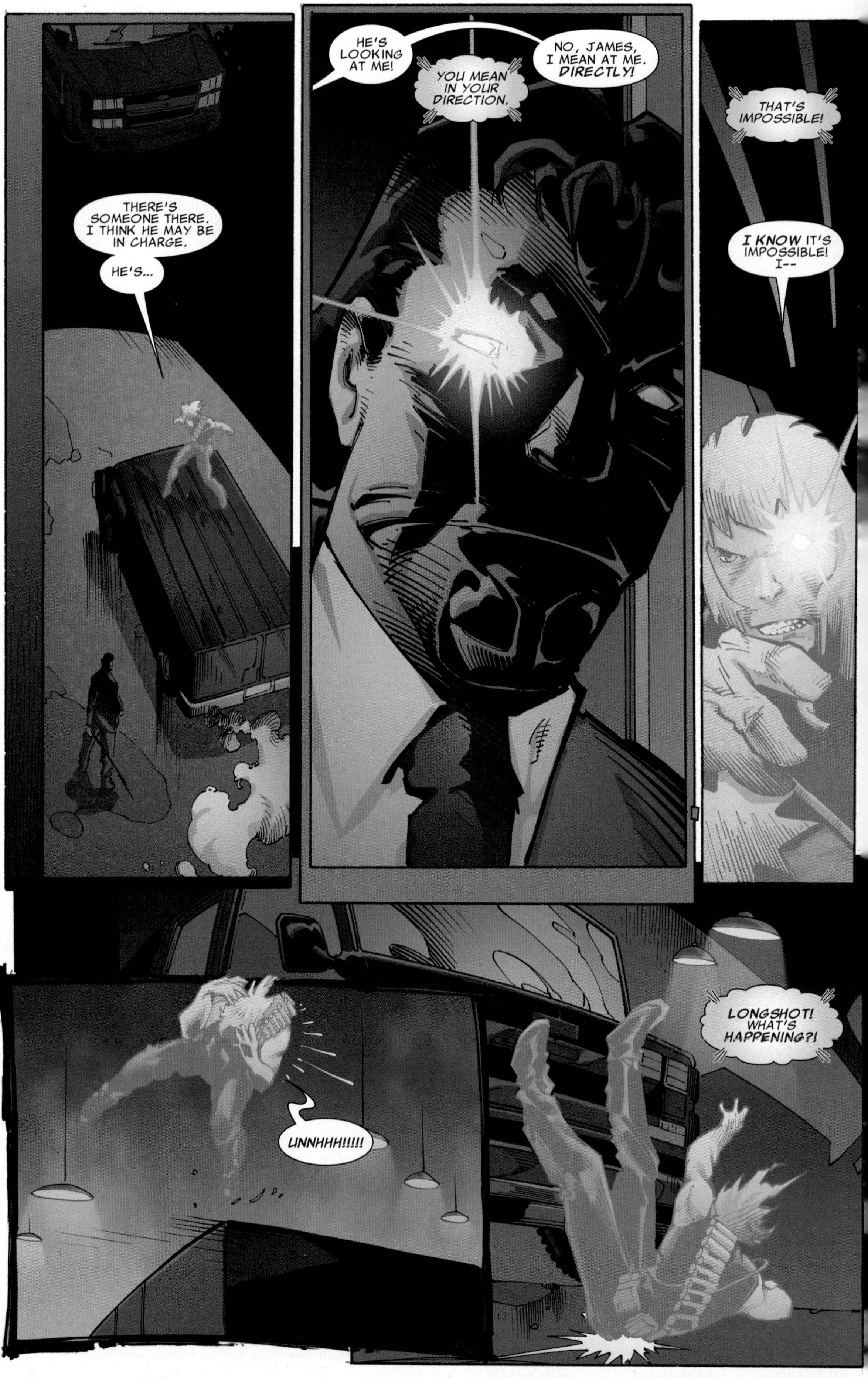
THERE'S SOMEONE THERE. I THINK HE MAY BE IN CHARGE.
HE'S...
HE'S LOOKING AT ME!
YOU MEAN IN YOUR DIRECTION.
NO, JAMES, I MEAN AT ME. DIRECTLY!
THAT'S IMPOSSIBLE!
I KNOW IT'S IMPOSSIBLE! I--
UNNHHH!!!!!
LONGSHOT! WHAT'S HAPPENING?!

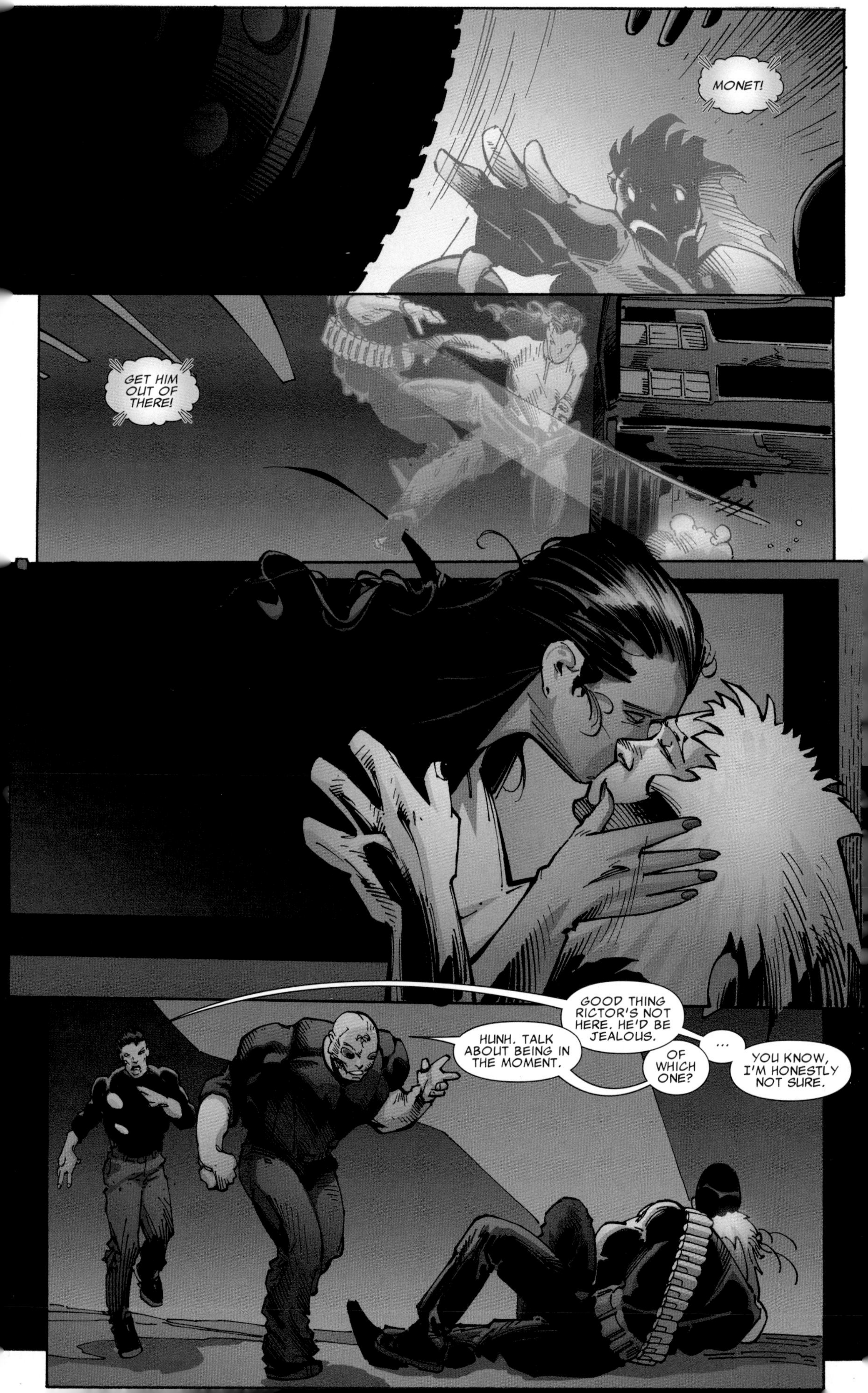
MONET!
GET HIM OUT OF THERE!
GOOD THING RICTOR'S NOT HERE. HE'D BE JEALOUS.
HUNH. TALK ABOUT BEING IN THE MOMENT.
OF WHICH ONE?
...
YOU KNOW, I'M HONESTLY NOT SURE.

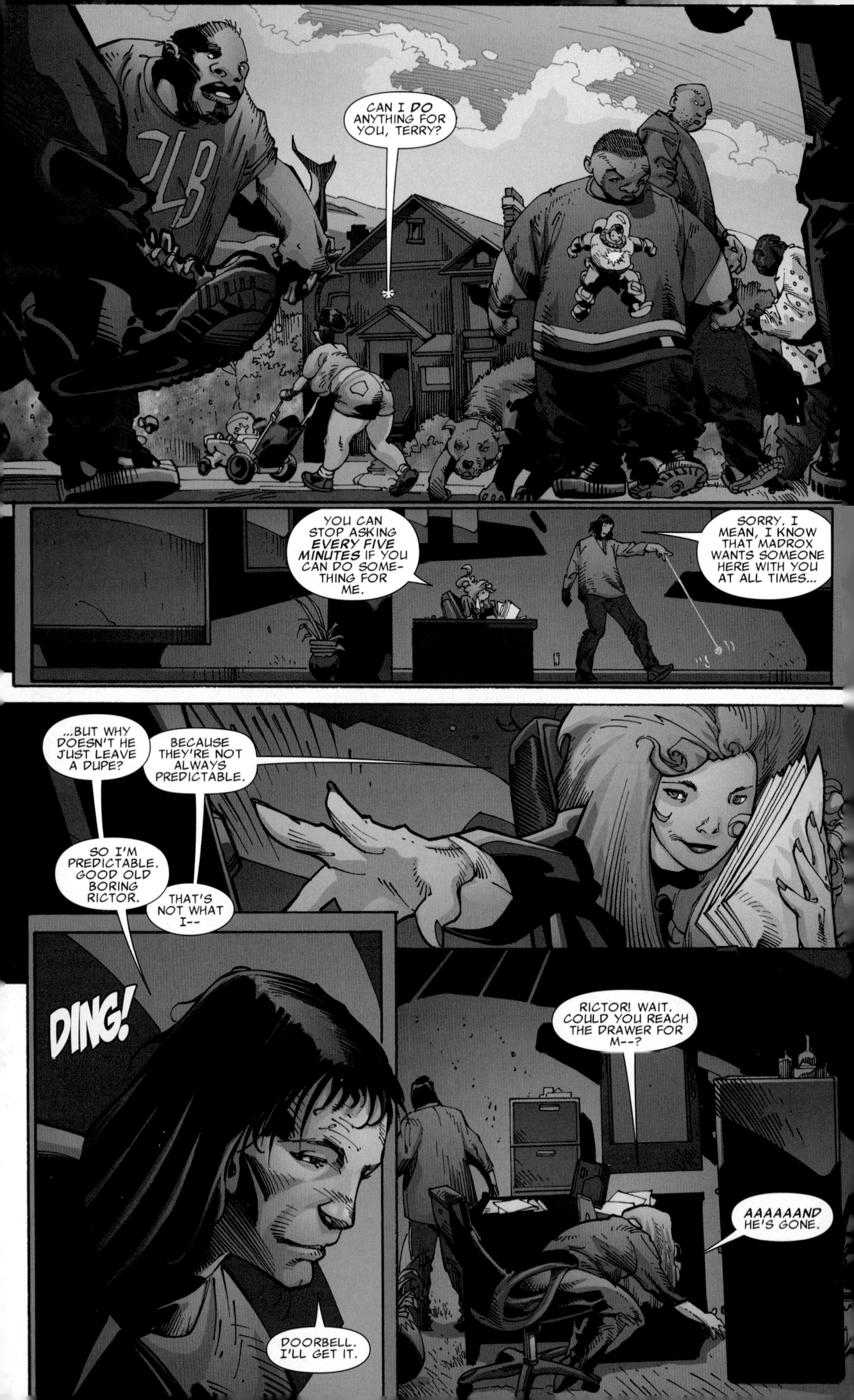
CAN I DO ANYTHING FOR YOU, TERRY?
YOU CAN STOP ASKING EVERY FIVE MINUTES IF YOU CAN DO SOMETHING FOR ME.
SORRY. I MEAN, I KNOW THAT MADROX WANTS SOMEONE HERE WITH YOU AT ALL TIMES...
...BUT WHY DOESN'T HE JUST LEAVE A DUPE?
BECAUSE THEY'RE NOT ALWAYS PREDICTABLE.
SO I'M PREDICTABLE. GOOD OLD BORING RICTOR.
THAT'S NOT WHAT I--
DING!
DOORBELL. I'LL GET IT.
RICTOR! WAIT. COULD YOU REACH THE DRAWER FOR M--?
AAAAAAND HE'S GONE.

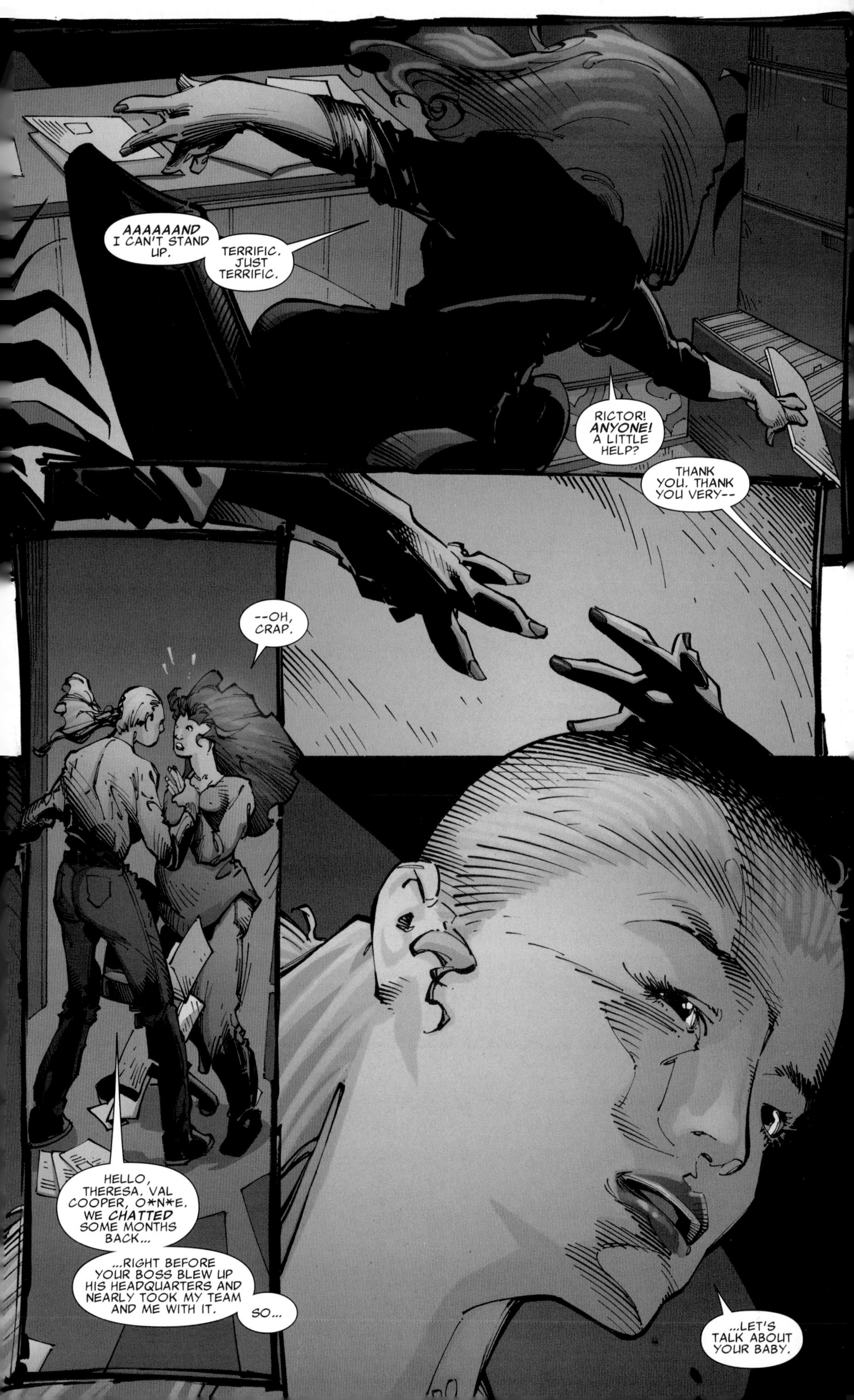
AAAAAAND I CAN'T STAND UP.
TERRIFIC. JUST TERRIFIC.
RICTOR! ANYONE! A LITTLE HELP?
THANK YOU. THANK YOU VERY--
--OH, CRAP.
HELLO, THERESA. VAL COOPER, O*N*E. WE CHATTED SOME MONTHS BACK...
...RIGHT BEFORE YOUR BOSS BLEW UP HIS HEADQUARTERS AND NEARLY TOOK MY TEAM AND ME WITH IT.
SO...
...LET'S TALK ABOUT YOUR BABY.

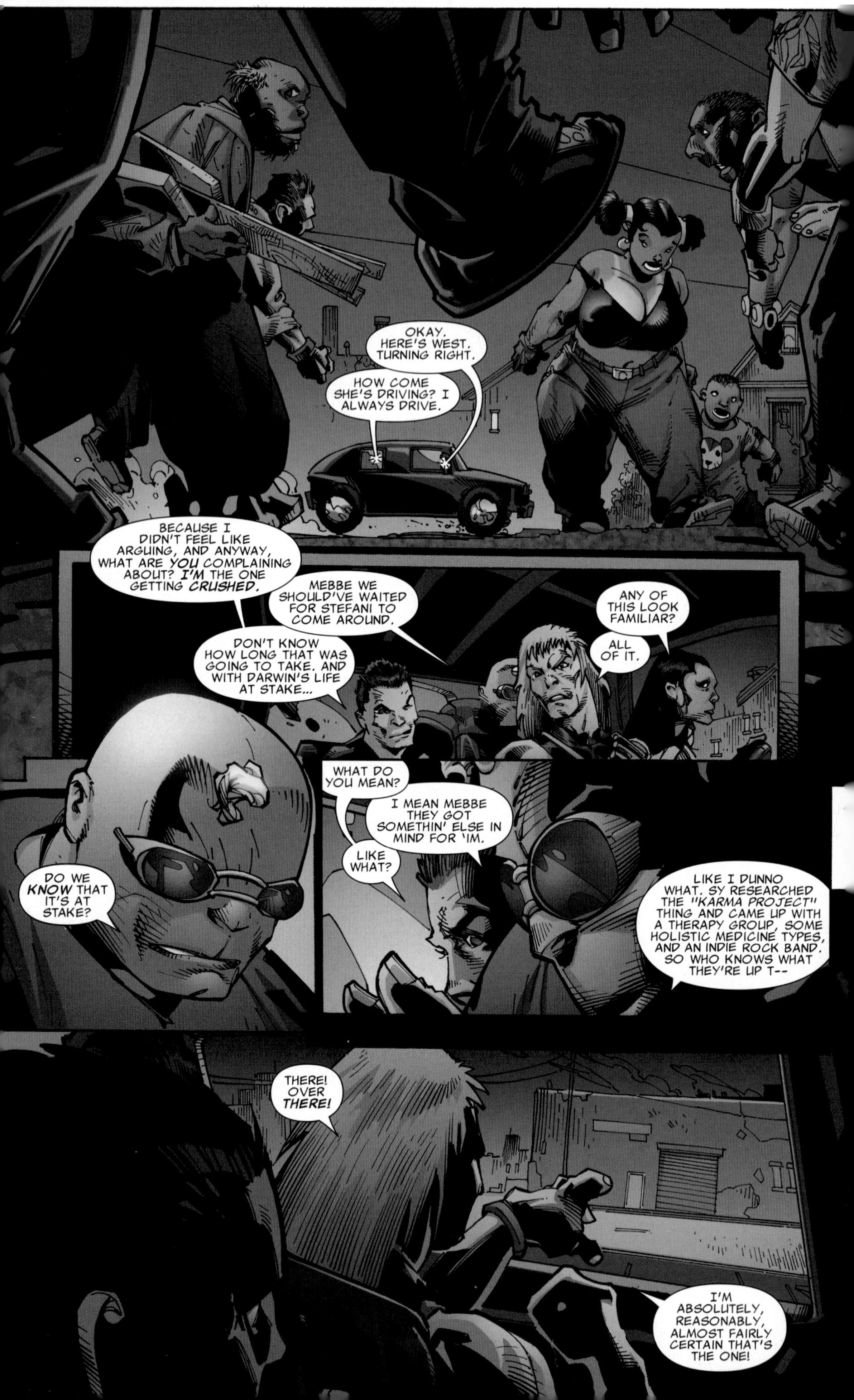

OKAY. HERE'S WEST. TURNING RIGHT.
HOW COME SHE'S DRIVING? I ALWAYS DRIVE.
BECAUSE I DIDN'T FEEL LIKE ARGUING, AND ANYWAY, WHAT ARE YOU COMPLAINING ABOUT? I'M THE ONE GETTING CRUSHED.
MEBBE WE SHOULD'VE WAITED FOR STEFANI TO COME AROUND.
DON'T KNOW HOW LONG THAT WAS GOING TO TAKE. AND WITH DARWIN'S LIFE AT STAKE...
ANY OF THIS LOOK FAMILIAR?
ALL OF IT.
DO WE KNOW THAT IT'S AT STAKE?
WHAT DO YOU MEAN?
I MEAN MEBBE THEY GOT SOMETHIN' ELSE IN MIND FOR 'IM.
LIKE WHAT?
LIKE I DUNNO WHAT. SY RESEARCHED THE "KARMA PROJECT" THING AND CAME UP WITH A THERAPY GROUP, SOME HOLISTIC MEDICINE TYPES, AND AN INDIE ROCK BAND. SO WHO KNOWS WHAT THEY'RE UP T--
THERE! OVER THERE!
I'M ABSOLUTELY, REASONABLY, ALMOST FAIRLY CERTAIN THAT'S THE ONE!

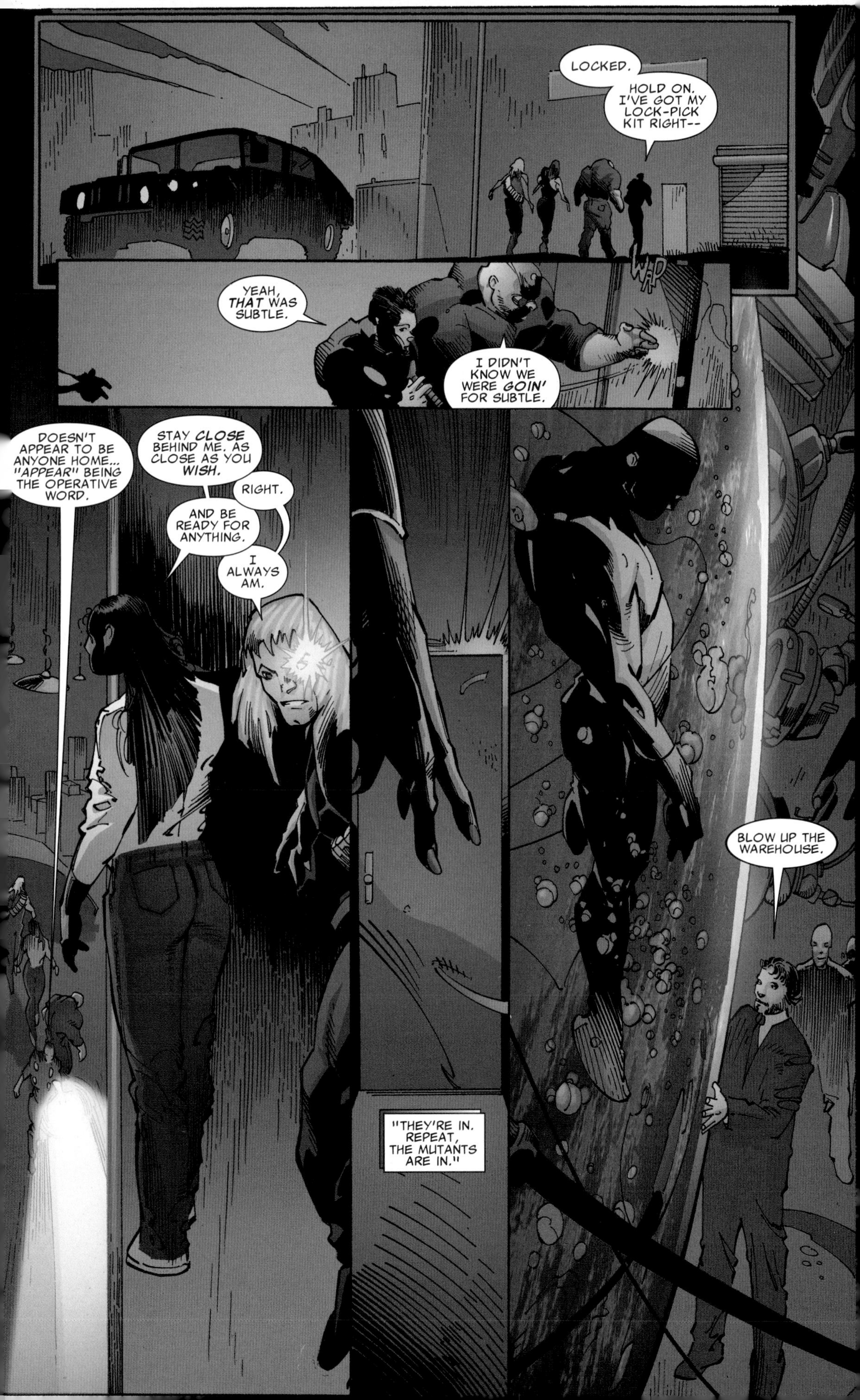
LOCKED.
HOLD ON. I'VE GOT MY LOCK-PICK KIT RIGHT--
WAP
YEAH, THAT WAS SUBTLE.
I DIDN'T KNOW WE WERE GOIN' FOR SUBTLE.
DOESN'T APPEAR TO BE ANYONE HOME... "APPEAR" BEING THE OPERATIVE WORD.
STAY CLOSE BEHIND ME. AS CLOSE AS YOU WISH.
RIGHT.
AND BE READY FOR ANYTHING.
I ALWAYS AM.
"THEY'RE IN. REPEAT, THE MUTANTS ARE IN."
BLOW UP THE WAREHOUSE.

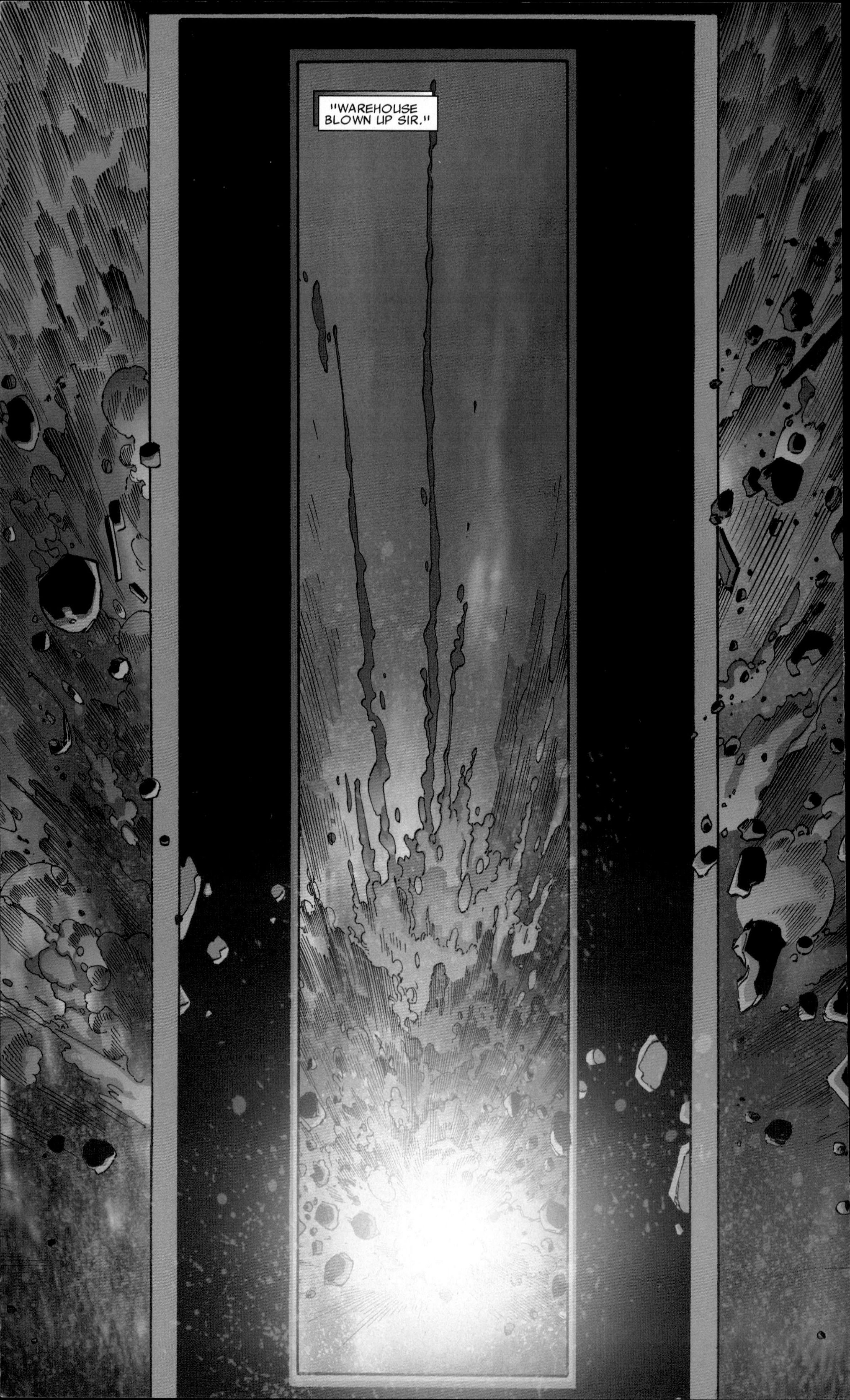
"WAREHOUSE BLOWN UP SIR."

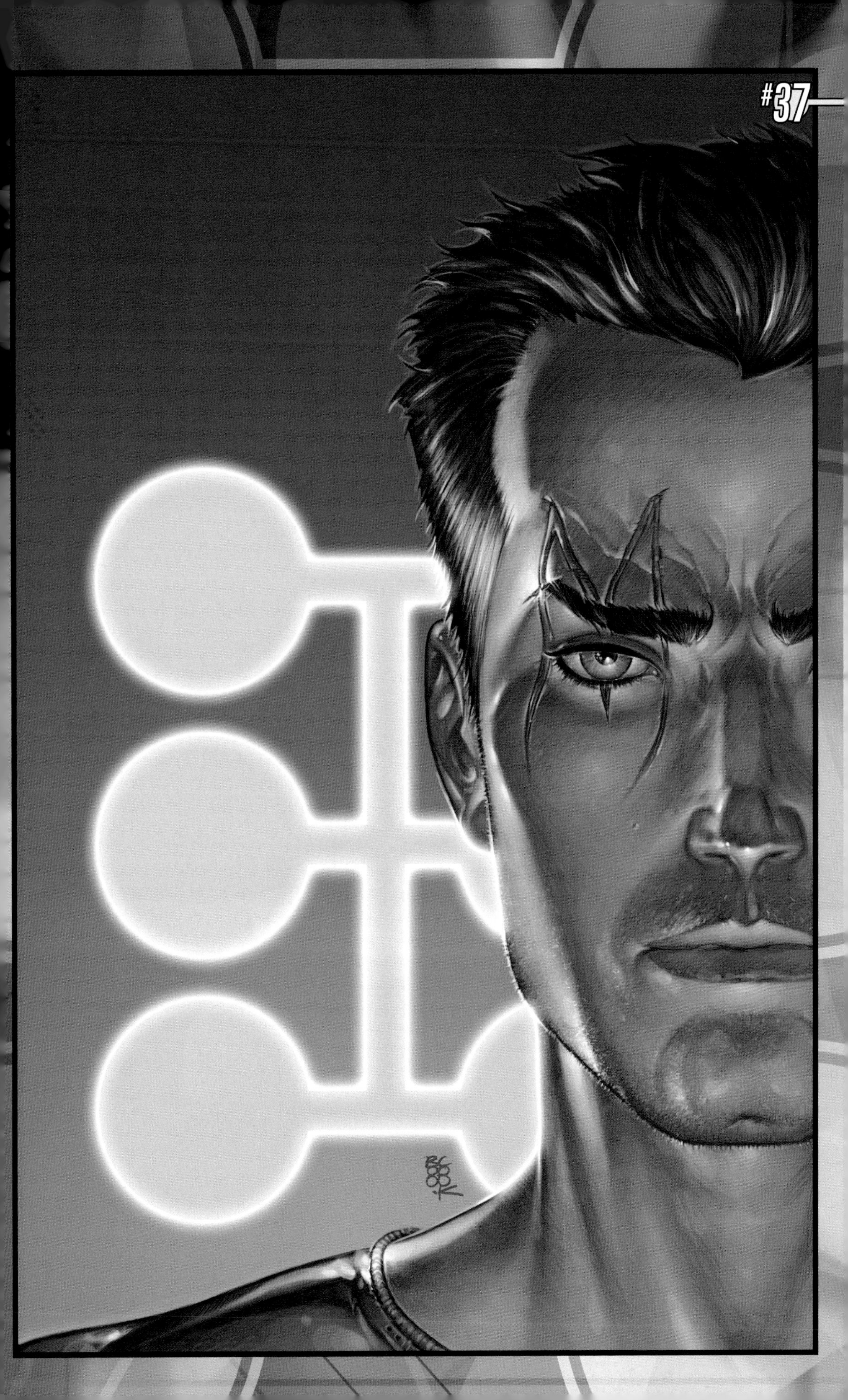
#37

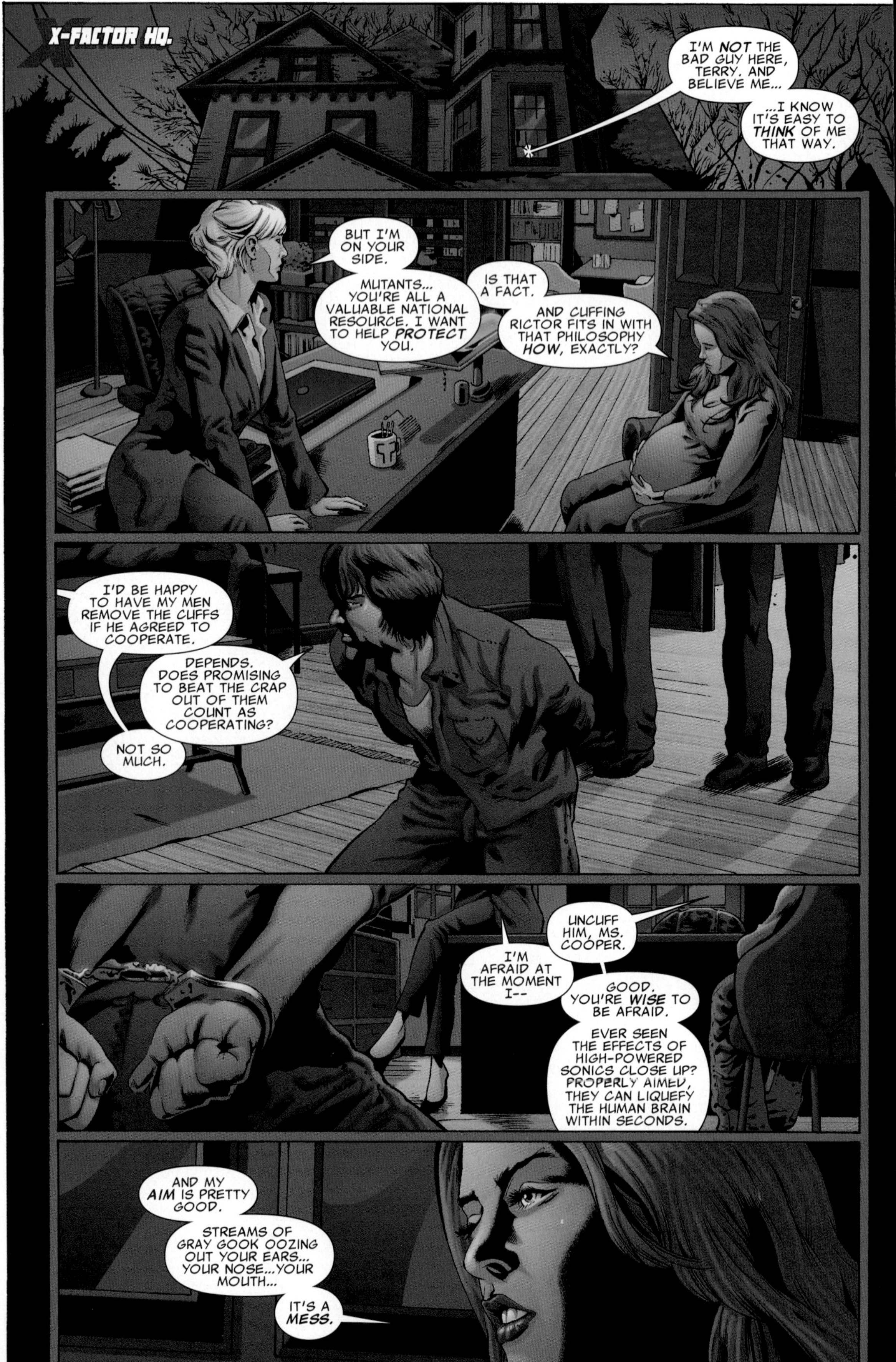
X-FACTOR HQ.
I'M NOT THE BAD GUY HERE, TERRY. AND BELIEVE ME...
...I KNOW IT'S EASY TO THINK OF ME THAT WAY.
BUT I'M ON YOUR SIDE.
MUTANTS... YOU'RE ALL A VALUABLE NATIONAL RESOURCE. I WANT TO HELP PROTECT YOU.
IS THAT A FACT.
AND CUFFING RICTOR FITS IN WITH THAT PHILOSOPHY HOW, EXACTLY?
I'D BE HAPPY TO HAVE MY MEN REMOVE THE CUFFS IF HE AGREED TO COOPERATE.
DEPENDS. DOES PROMISING TO BEAT THE CRAP OUT OF THEM COUNT AS COOPERATING?
NOT SO MUCH.
UNCUFF HIM, MS. COOPER.
I'M AFRAID AT THE MOMENT I--
GOOD. YOU'RE WISE TO BE AFRAID.
EVER SEEN THE EFFECTS OF HIGH-POWERED SONICS CLOSE UP? PROPERLY AIMED, THEY CAN LIQUEFY THE HUMAN BRAIN WITHIN SECONDS.
AND MY AIM IS PRETTY GOOD.
STREAMS OF GRAY GOOK OOZING OUT YOUR EARS... YOUR NOSE...YOUR MOUTH...
IT'S A MESS.

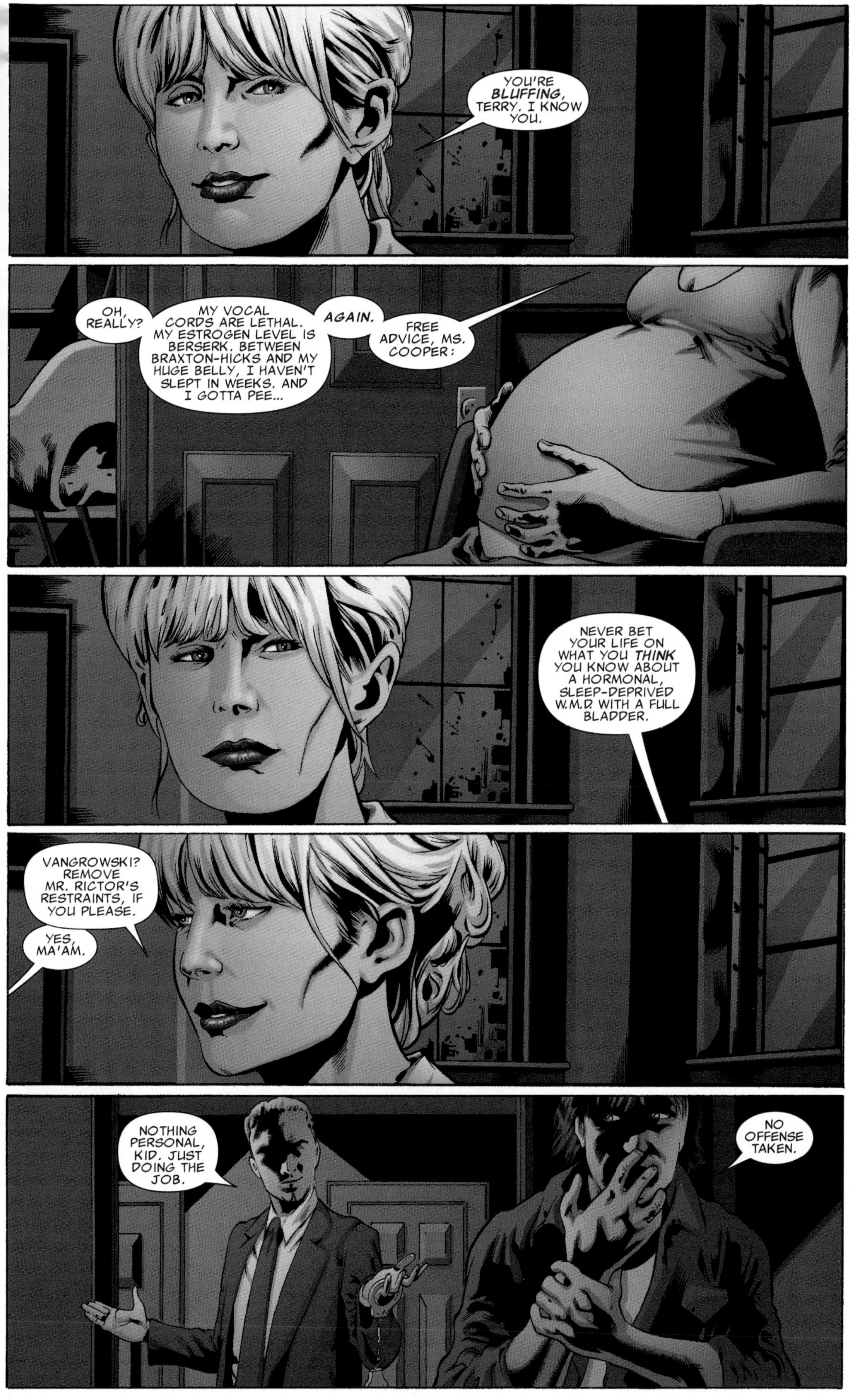

YOU'RE BLUFFING, TERRY. I KNOW YOU.
OH, REALLY?
MY VOCAL CORDS ARE LETHAL. MY ESTROGEN LEVEL IS BERSERK. BETWEEN BRAXTON-HICKS AND MY HUGE BELLY, I HAVEN'T SLEPT IN WEEKS. AND I GOTTA PEE...
AGAIN.
FREE ADVICE, MS. COOPER:
NEVER BET YOUR LIFE ON WHAT YOU THINK YOU KNOW ABOUT A HORMONAL, SLEEP-DEPRIVED W.M.D. WITH A FULL BLADDER.
VANGROWSKI? REMOVE MR. RICTOR'S RESTRAINTS, IF YOU PLEASE.
YES, MA'AM.
NOTHING PERSONAL, KID. JUST DOING THE JOB.
NO OFFENSE TAKEN.

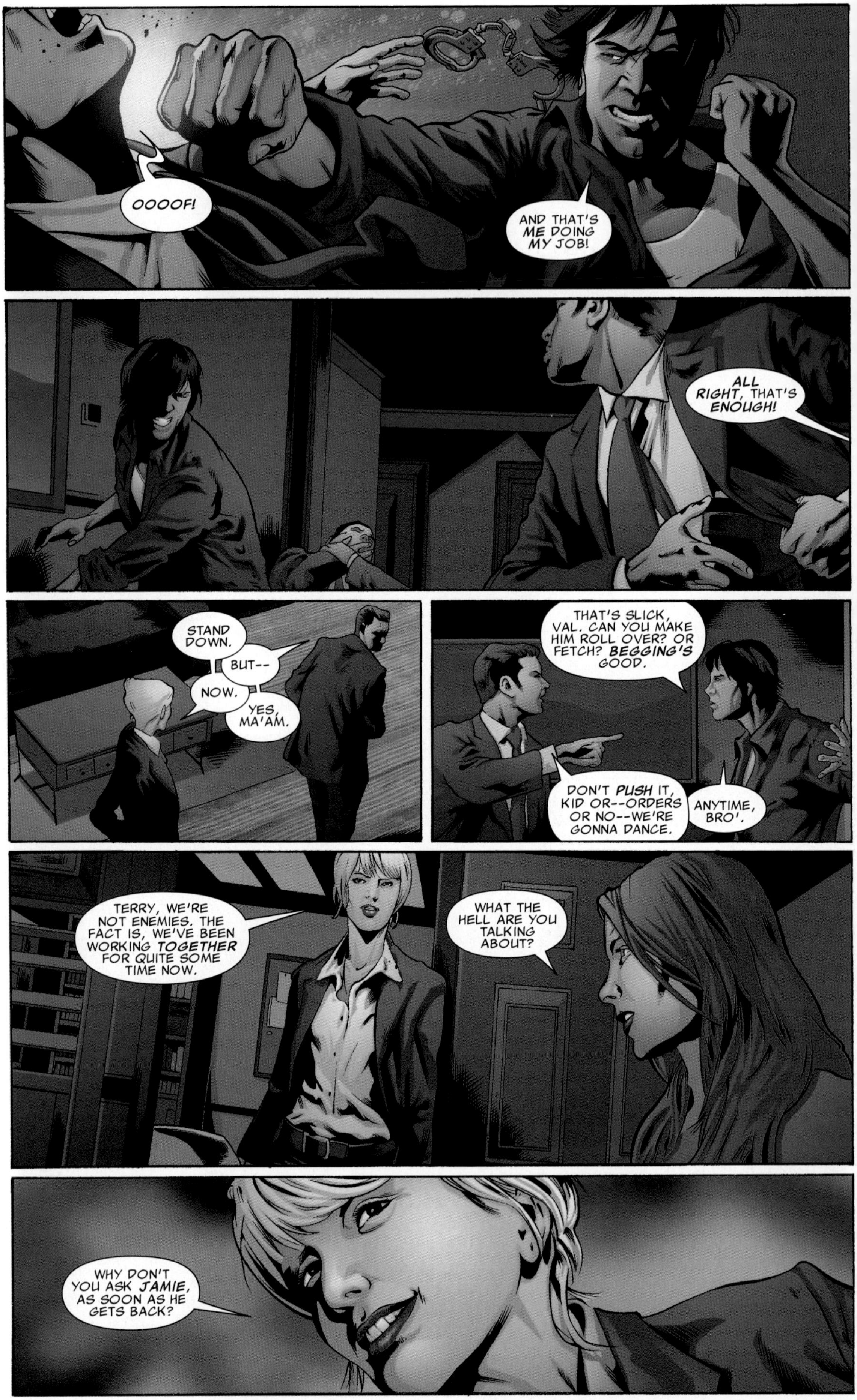
OOOOF!
AND THAT'S ME DOING MY JOB!
ALL RIGHT, THAT'S ENOUGH!
STAND DOWN.
BUT--
NOW.
YES, MA'AM.
THAT'S SLICK, VAL. CAN YOU MAKE HIM ROLL OVER? OR FETCH? BEGGING'S GOOD.
DON'T PUSH IT, KID OR--ORDERS OR NO--WE'RE GONNA DANCE.
ANYTIME, BRO'.
TERRY, WE'RE NOT ENEMIES. THE FACT IS, WE'VE BEEN WORKING TOGETHER FOR QUITE SOME TIME NOW.
WHAT THE HELL ARE YOU TALKING ABOUT?
WHY DON'T YOU ASK JAMIE, AS SOON AS HE GETS BACK?

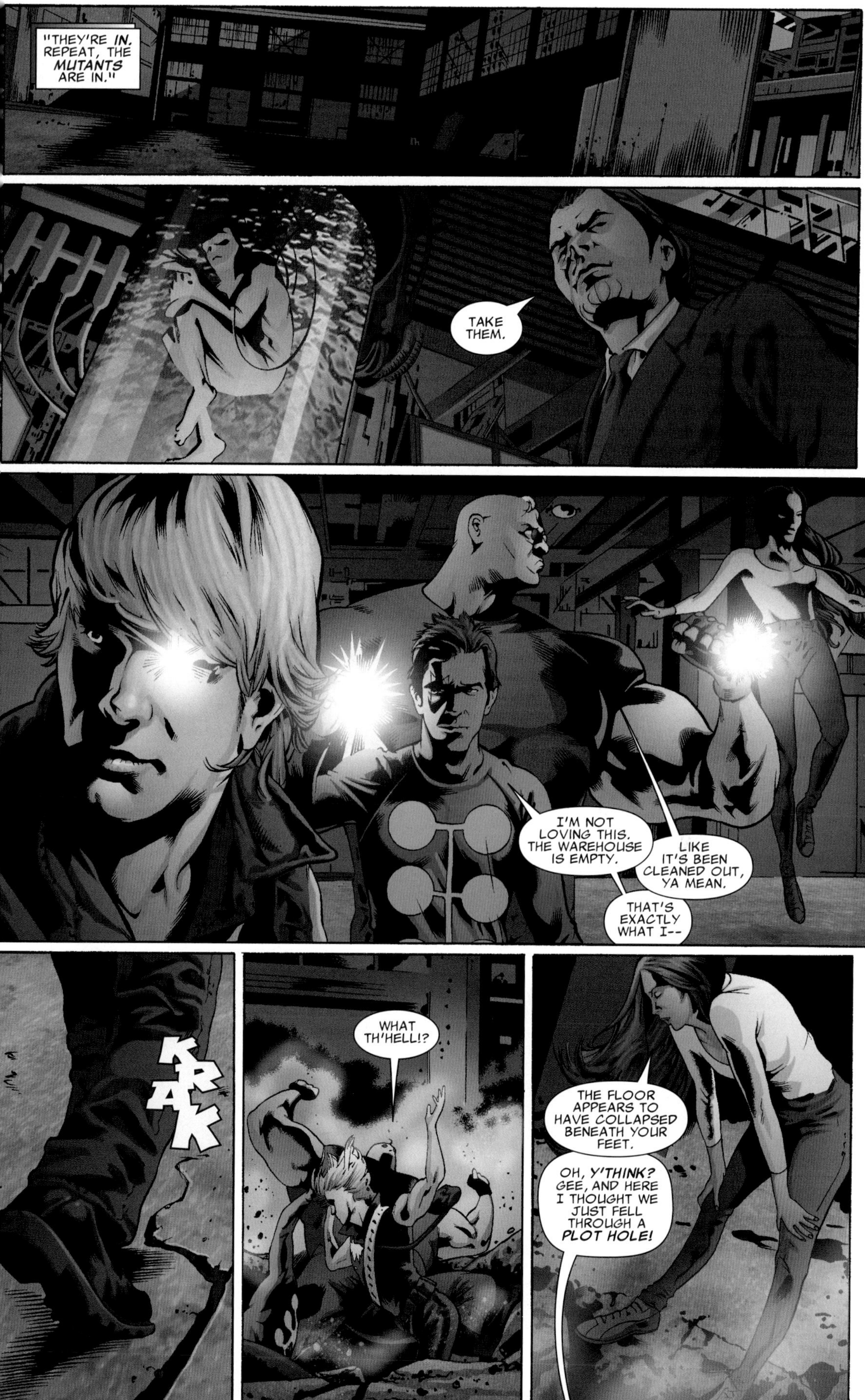
"THEY'RE IN. REPEAT, THE MUTANTS ARE IN."
TAKE THEM.
I'M NOT LOVING THIS. THE WAREHOUSE IS EMPTY.
LIKE IT'S BEEN CLEANED OUT, YA MEAN.
THAT'S EXACTLY WHAT I--
KRAK
WHAT TH'HELL!?
THE FLOOR APPEARS TO HAVE COLLAPSED BENEATH YOUR FEET.
OH, Y'THINK? GEE, AND HERE I THOUGHT WE JUST FELL THROUGH A PLOT HOLE!

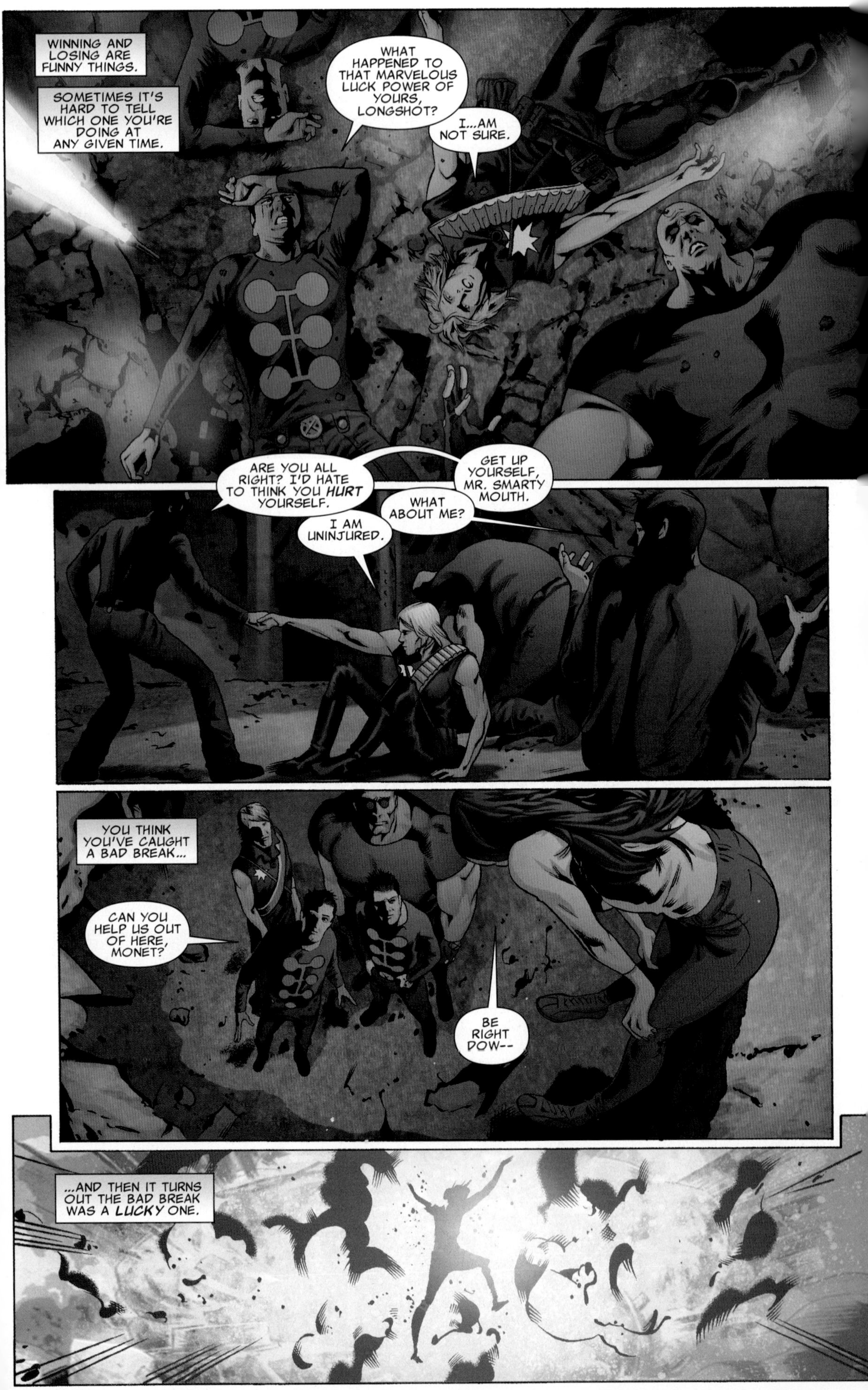
WINNING AND LOSING ARE FUNNY THINGS.
SOMETIMES IT'S HARD TO TELL WHICH ONE YOU'RE DOING AT ANY GIVEN TIME.
WHAT HAPPENED TO THAT MARVELOUS LUCK POWER OF YOURS, LONGSHOT?
I...AM NOT SURE.
ARE YOU ALL RIGHT? I'D HATE TO THINK YOU HURT YOURSELF.
GET UP YOURSELF, MR. SMARTY MOUTH.
WHAT ABOUT ME?
I AM UNINJURED.
YOU THINK YOU'VE CAUGHT A BAD BREAK...
CAN YOU HELP US OUT OF HERE, MONET?
BE RIGHT DOW--
...AND THEN IT TURNS OUT THE BAD BREAK WAS A LUCKY ONE.

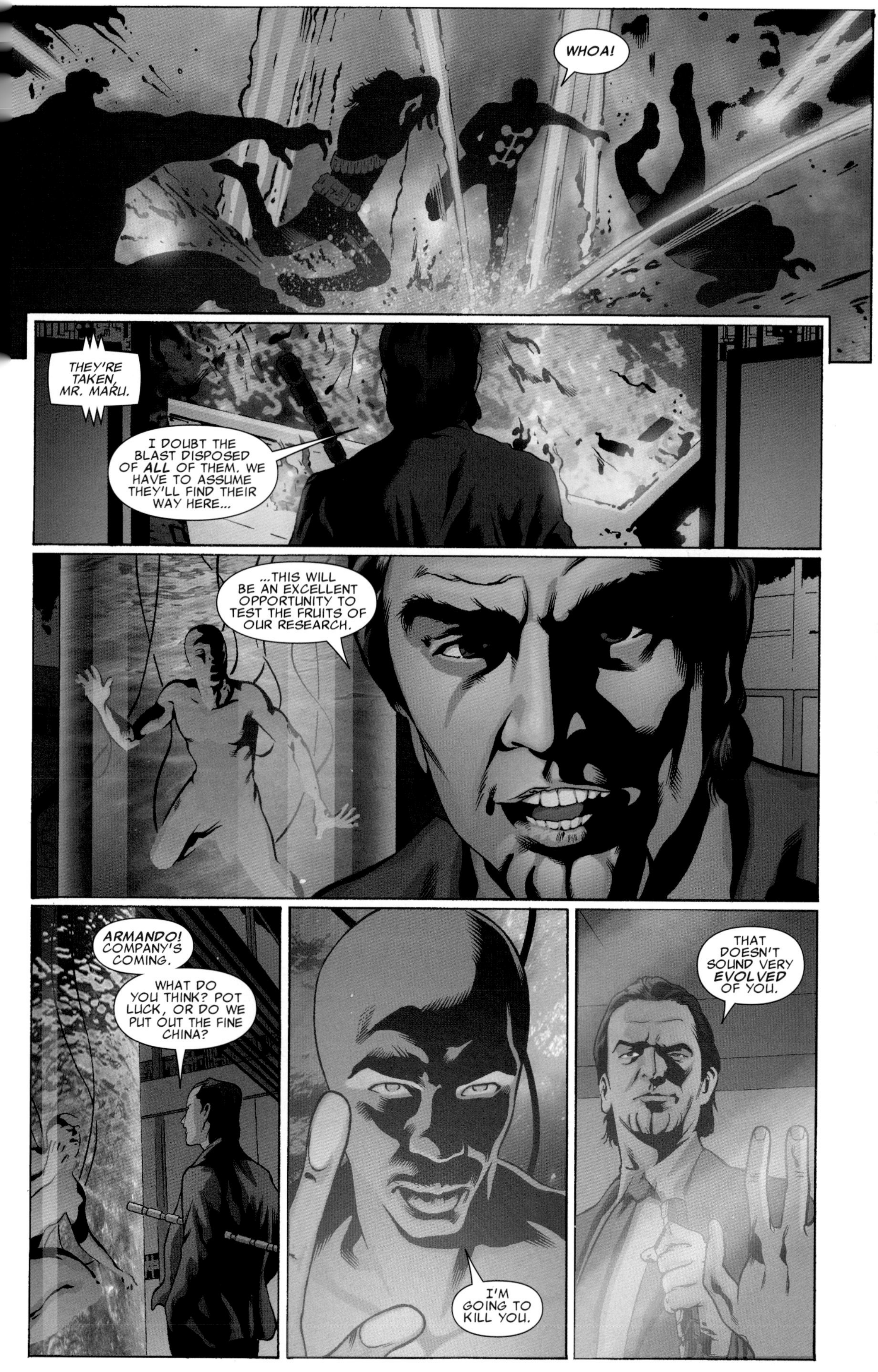
WHOA!
THEY'RE TAKEN, MR. MARU.
I DOUBT THE BLAST DISPOSED OF ALL OF THEM. WE HAVE TO ASSUME THEY'LL FIND THEIR WAY HERE...
...THIS WILL BE AN EXCELLENT OPPORTUNITY TO TEST THE FRUITS OF OUR RESEARCH.
ARMANDO! COMPANY'S COMING.
WHAT DO YOU THINK? POT LUCK, OR DO WE PUT OUT THE FINE CHINA?
I'M GOING TO KILL YOU.
THAT DOESN'T SOUND VERY EVOLVED OF YOU.

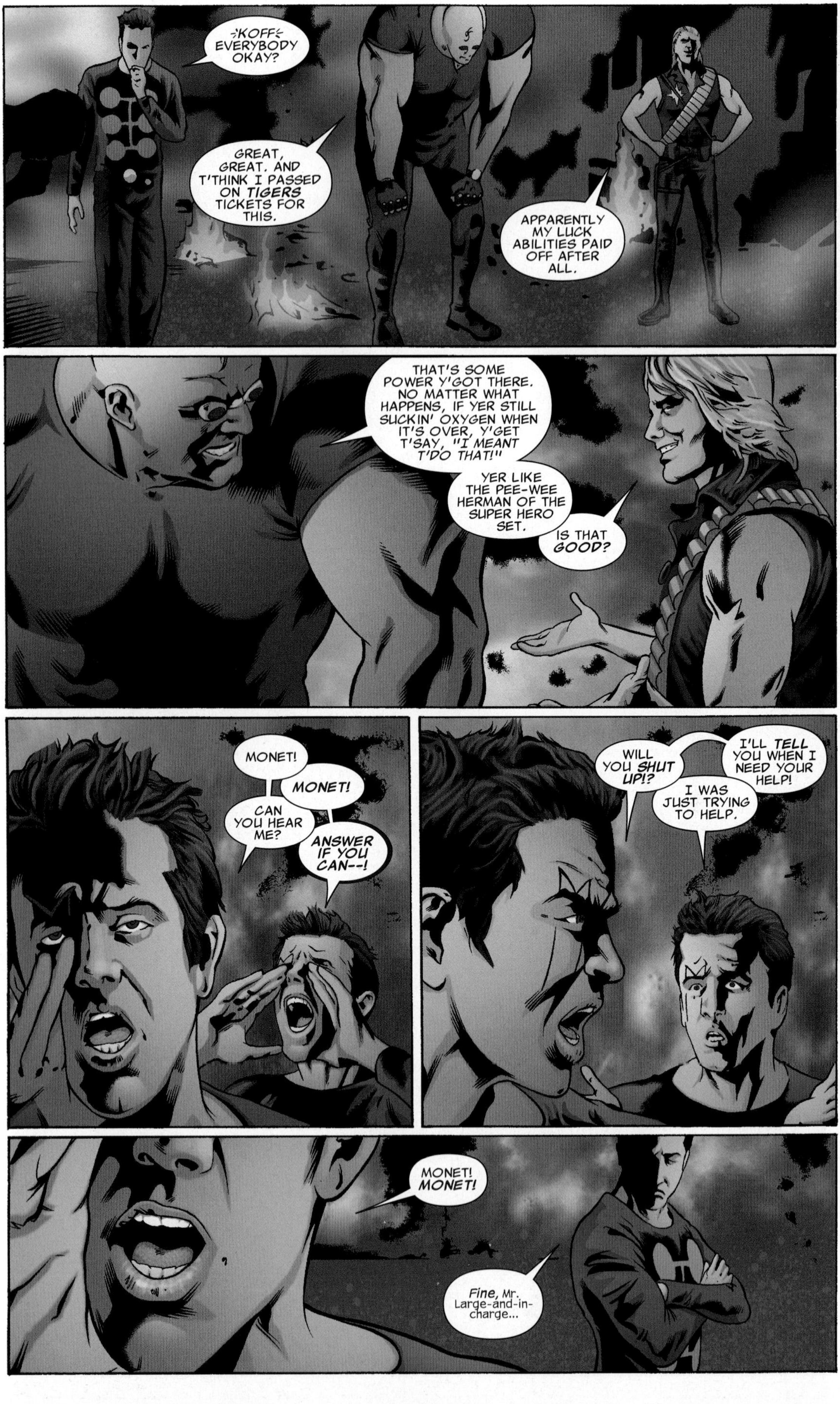

-KOFF- EVERYBODY OKAY?
GREAT, GREAT. AND T'THINK I PASSED ON TIGERS TICKETS FOR THIS.
APPARENTLY MY LUCK ABILITIES PAID OFF AFTER ALL.
THAT'S SOME POWER Y'GOT THERE. NO MATTER WHAT HAPPENS, IF YER STILL SUCKIN' OXYGEN WHEN IT'S OVER, Y'GET T'SAY, "I MEANT T'DO THAT!"
YER LIKE THE PEE-WEE HERMAN OF THE SUPER HERO SET.
IS THAT GOOD?
MONET!
MONET!
CAN YOU HEAR ME?
ANSWER IF YOU CAN--!
WILL YOU SHUT UP!?
I'LL TELL YOU WHEN I NEED YOUR HELP!
I WAS JUST TRYING TO HELP.
MONET! MONET!
Fine, Mr. Large-and-in-charge...

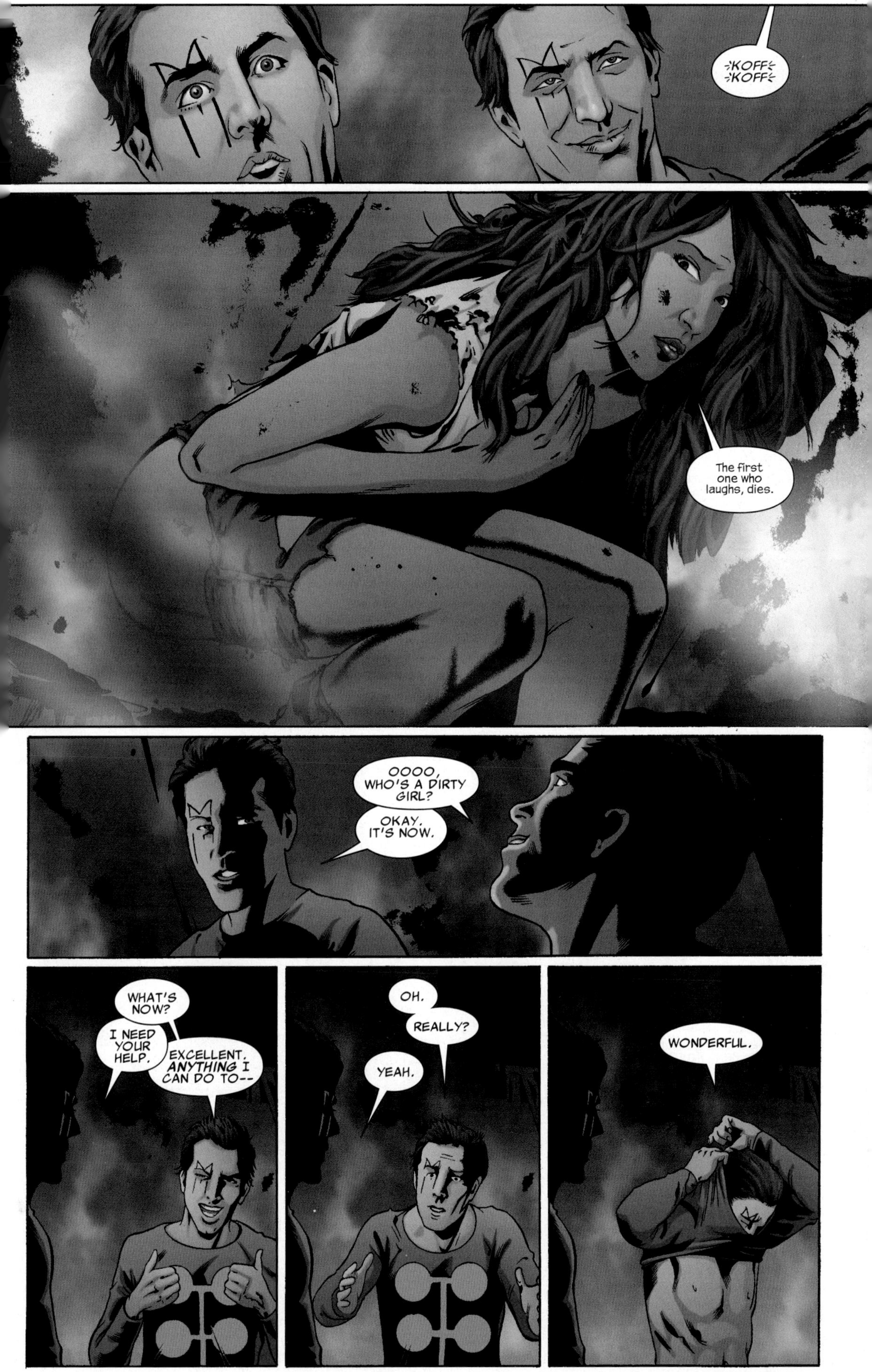
KOFF
KOFF
The first one who laughs, dies.
OOOO, WHO'S A DIRTY GIRL?
OKAY. IT'S NOW.
WHAT'S NOW?
I NEED YOUR HELP.
EXCELLENT. ANYTHING I CAN DO TO--
OH.
REALLY?
YEAH.
WONDERFUL.

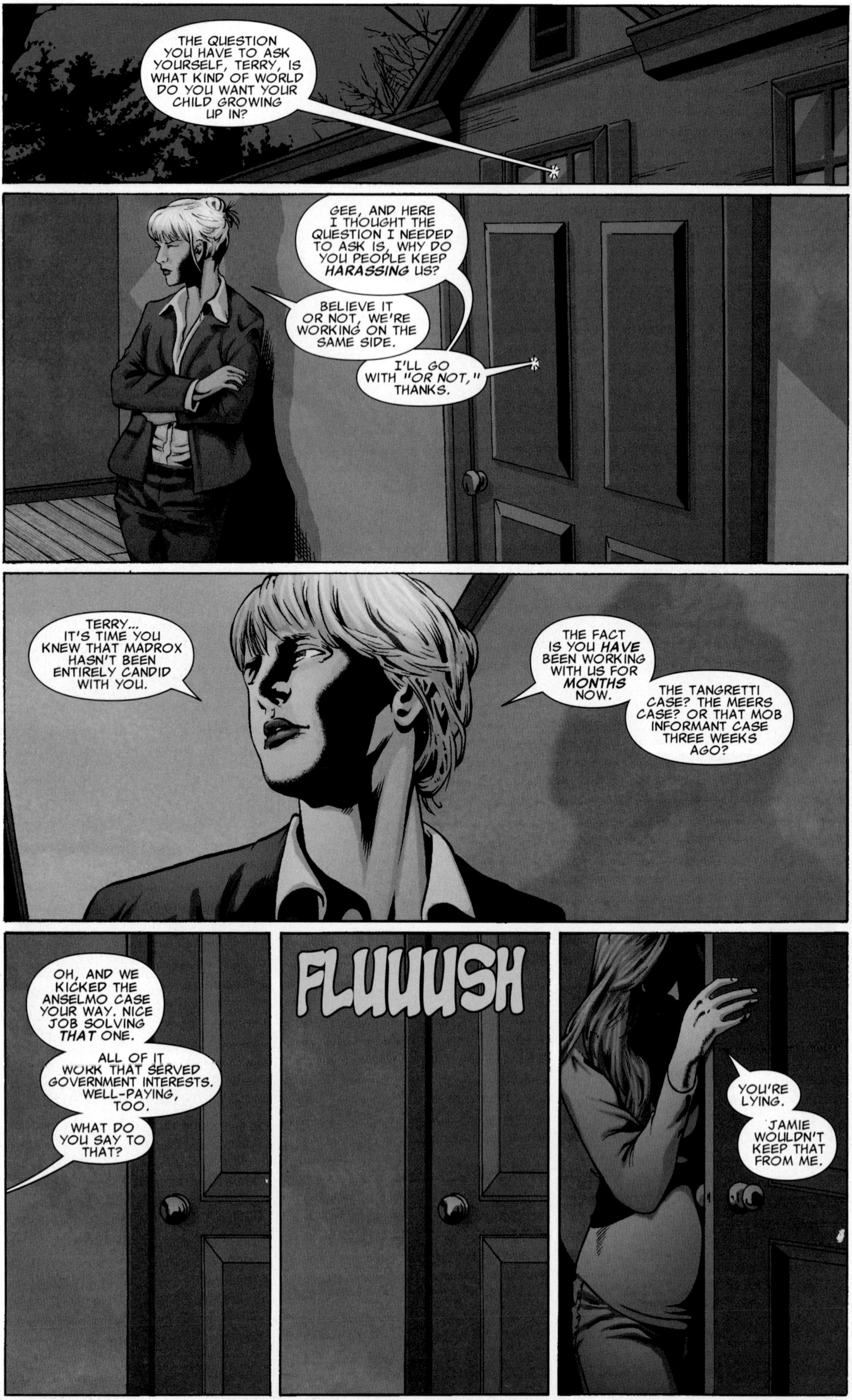
THE QUESTION YOU HAVE TO ASK YOURSELF, TERRY, IS WHAT KIND OF WORLD DO YOU WANT YOUR CHILD GROWING UP IN?
GEE, AND HERE I THOUGHT THE QUESTION I NEEDED TO ASK IS, WHY DO YOU PEOPLE KEEP HARASSING US?
BELIEVE IT OR NOT, WE'RE WORKING ON THE SAME SIDE.
I'LL GO WITH "OR NOT," THANKS.
TERRY... IT'S TIME YOU KNEW THAT MADROX HASN'T BEEN ENTIRELY CANDID WITH YOU.
THE FACT IS YOU HAVE BEEN WORKING WITH US FOR MONTHS NOW.
THE TANGRETTI CASE? THE MEERS CASE? OR THAT MOB INFORMANT CASE THREE WEEKS AGO?
OH, AND WE KICKED THE ANSELMO CASE YOUR WAY. NICE JOB SOLVING THAT ONE.
ALL OF IT WORK THAT SERVED GOVERNMENT INTERESTS. WELL-PAYING, TOO.
WHAT DO YOU SAY TO THAT?
FLUUUSH
YOU'RE LYING.
JAMIE WOULDN'T KEEP THAT FROM ME.

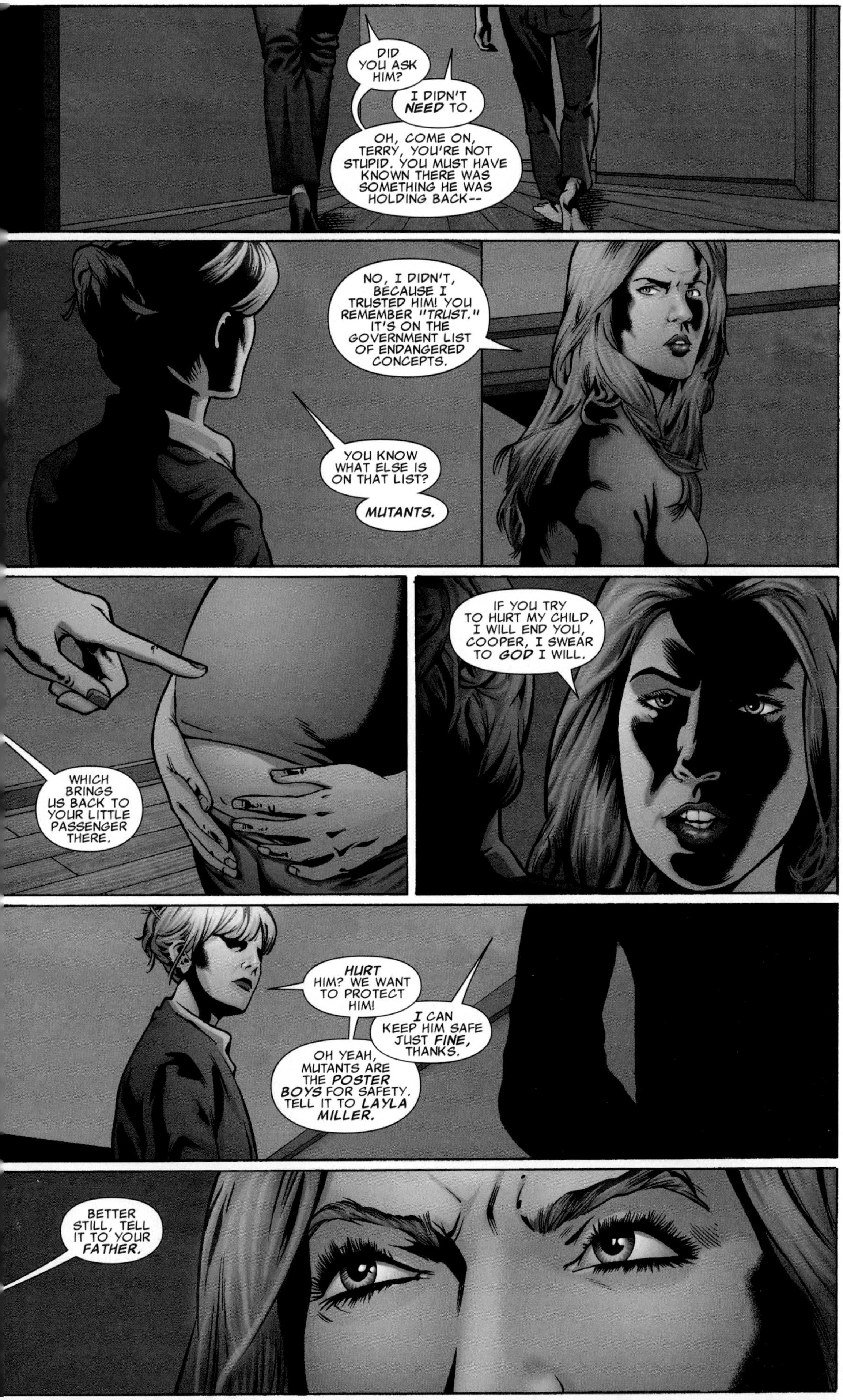
DID YOU ASK HIM?
I DIDN'T NEED TO.
OH, COME ON, TERRY, YOU'RE NOT STUPID. YOU MUST HAVE KNOWN THERE WAS SOMETHING HE WAS HOLDING BACK--
NO, I DIDN'T, BECAUSE I TRUSTED HIM! YOU REMEMBER "TRUST." IT'S ON THE GOVERNMENT LIST OF ENDANGERED CONCEPTS.
YOU KNOW WHAT ELSE IS ON THAT LIST?
MUTANTS.
WHICH BRINGS US BACK TO YOUR LITTLE PASSENGER THERE.
IF YOU TRY TO HURT MY CHILD, I WILL END YOU, COOPER, I SWEAR TO GOD I WILL.
HURT HIM? WE WANT TO PROTECT HIM!
I CAN KEEP HIM SAFE JUST FINE, THANKS.
OH YEAH, MUTANTS ARE THE POSTER BOYS FOR SAFETY. TELL IT TO LAYLA MILLER.
BETTER STILL, TELL IT TO YOUR FATHER.

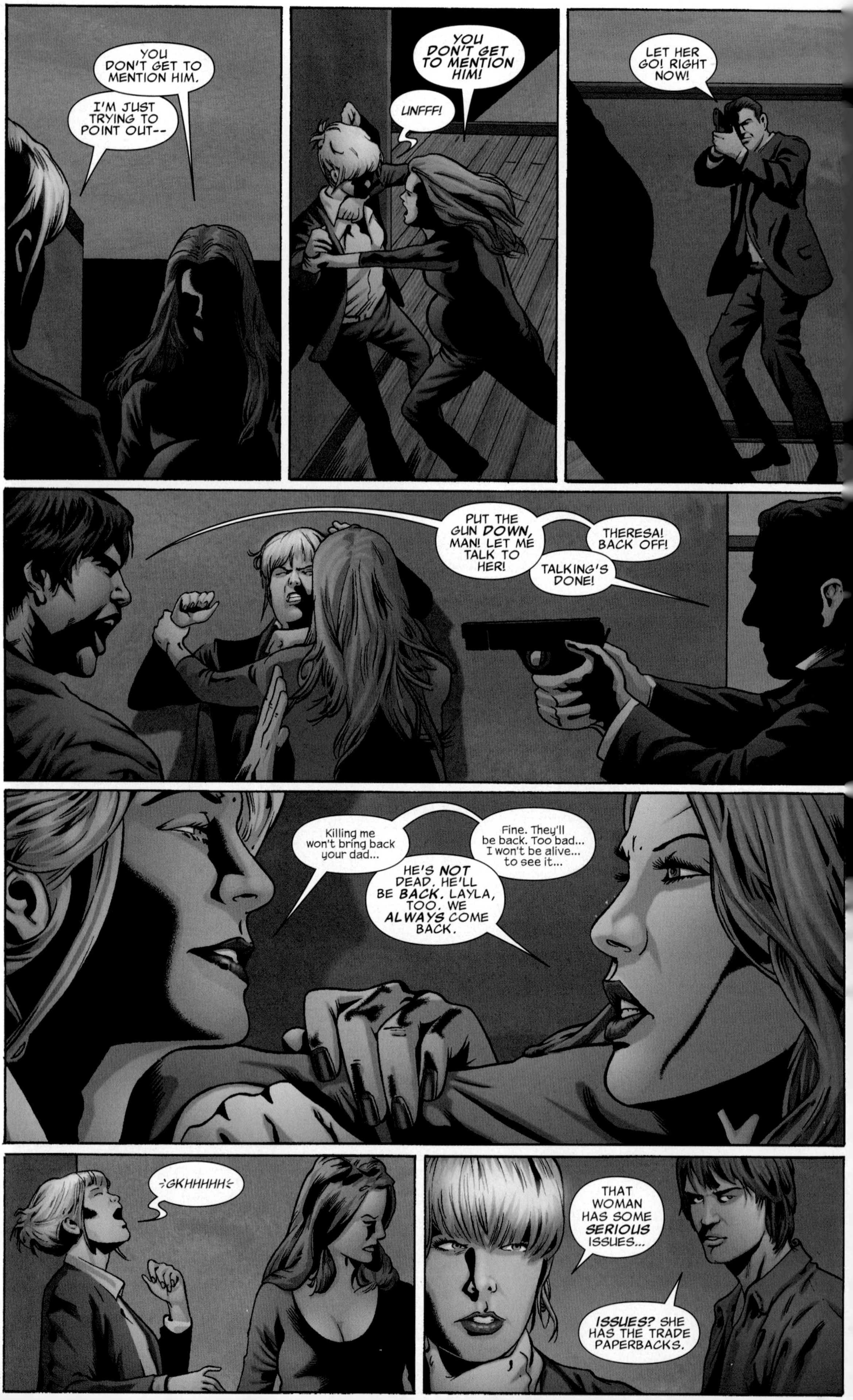
YOU DON'T GET TO MENTION HIM.
I'M JUST TRYING TO POINT OUT--
YOU DON'T GET TO MENTION HIM!
UNFFF!
LET HER GO! RIGHT NOW!
PUT THE GUN DOWN, MAN! LET ME TALK TO HER!
THERESA! BACK OFF!
TALKING'S DONE!
Killing me won't bring back your dad...
HE'S NOT DEAD. HE'LL BE BACK. LAYLA, TOO. WE ALWAYS COME BACK.
Fine. They'll be back. Too bad... I won't be alive... to see it...
GKHHHHH
THAT WOMAN HAS SOME SERIOUS ISSUES...
ISSUES? SHE HAS THE TRADE PAPERBACKS.

WHAT ARE *YOU* LOOKING AT?

HONESTLY? ADMIRING YER LEGS.

WELL, EYES *FRONT*, CAROSELLA.

HE'S RIGHT, THOUGH. THEY *ARE* QUITE LOVELY.

VERY TONED.

YOU THINK SO?

THANK YOU.

YOUR CALF MUSCLES ARE WELL-DEVELOPED. DO MUCH DANCING?

BALLET, GROWING UP. YOU'RE SWEET TO NOTICE.

I may barf.

I may *join* you.

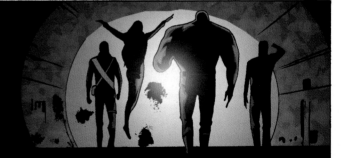

THE FORTUNES OF WAR CAN SEESAW FROM ONE MOMENT TO THE NEXT, SO MUCH SO THAT IT'S HARD TO FIND YOUR FOOTING.

AL CAPONE SAID IN "THE *UNTOUCHABLES*" THAT, AT THE END OF THE FIGHT, YOU SEE WHO'S LEFT STANDING, AND THAT'S HOW YOU KNOW WHO WON.

THEN AGAIN, GENERAL PYRRHUS SAID OTHERWISE.

THE TRUTH IS, YOU SOMETIMES DON'T KNOW FOR MONTHS OR EVEN *YEARS* WHO REALLY WON...

...OR IF THERE EVEN *WAS* A WINNER.

UH-OH.

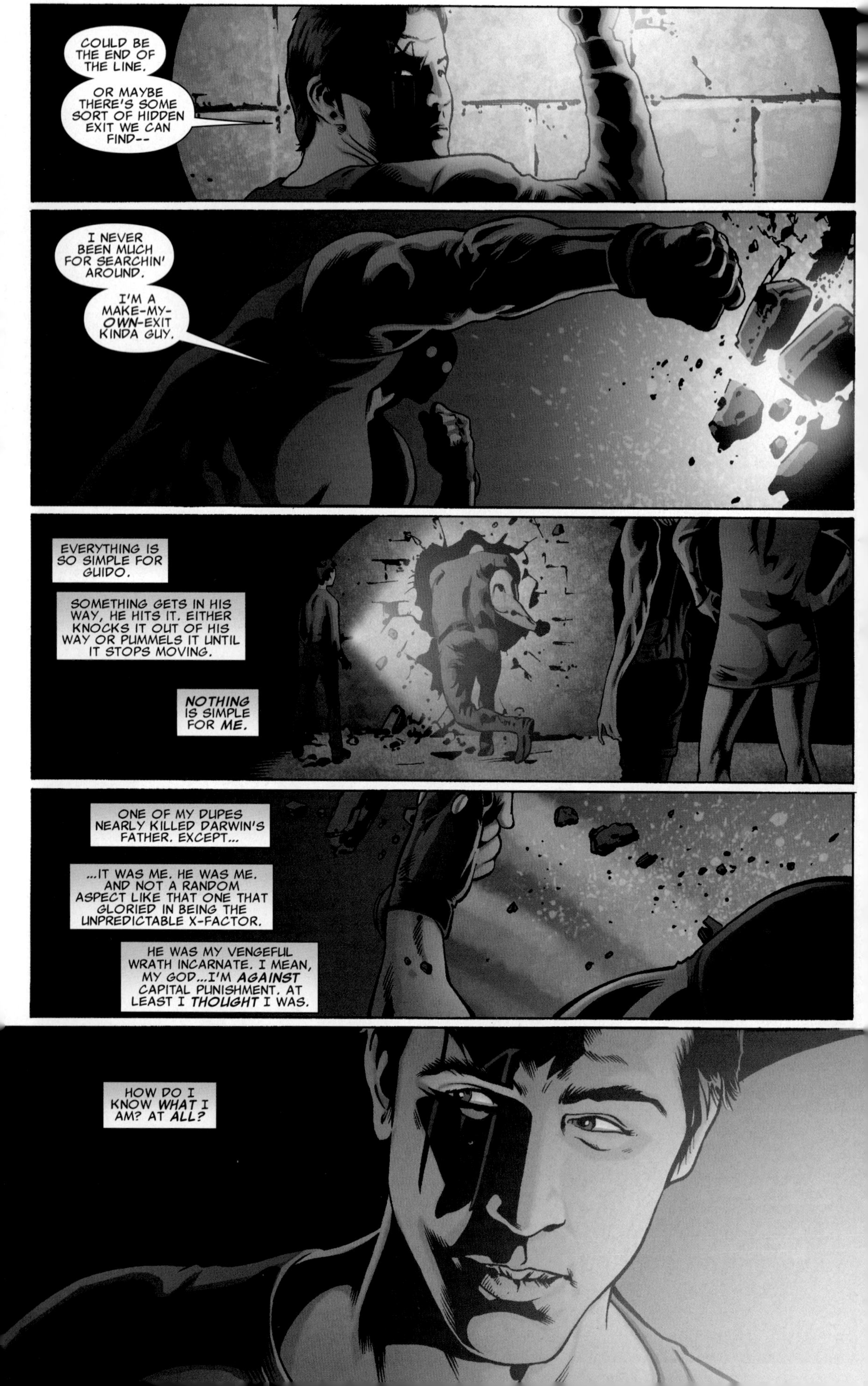
COULD BE THE END OF THE LINE.
OR MAYBE THERE'S SOME SORT OF HIDDEN EXIT WE CAN FIND--
I NEVER BEEN MUCH FOR SEARCHIN' AROUND.
I'M A MAKE-MY-OWN-EXIT KINDA GUY.
EVERYTHING IS SO SIMPLE FOR GUIDO.
SOMETHING GETS IN HIS WAY, HE HITS IT. EITHER KNOCKS IT OUT OF HIS WAY OR PUMMELS IT UNTIL IT STOPS MOVING.
NOTHING IS SIMPLE FOR ME.
ONE OF MY DUPES NEARLY KILLED DARWIN'S FATHER. EXCEPT...
...IT WAS ME. HE WAS ME. AND NOT A RANDOM ASPECT LIKE THAT ONE THAT GLORIED IN BEING THE UNPREDICTABLE X-FACTOR.
HE WAS MY VENGEFUL WRATH INCARNATE. I MEAN, MY GOD...I'M AGAINST CAPITAL PUNISHMENT. AT LEAST I THOUGHT I WAS.
HOW DO I KNOW WHAT I AM? AT ALL?

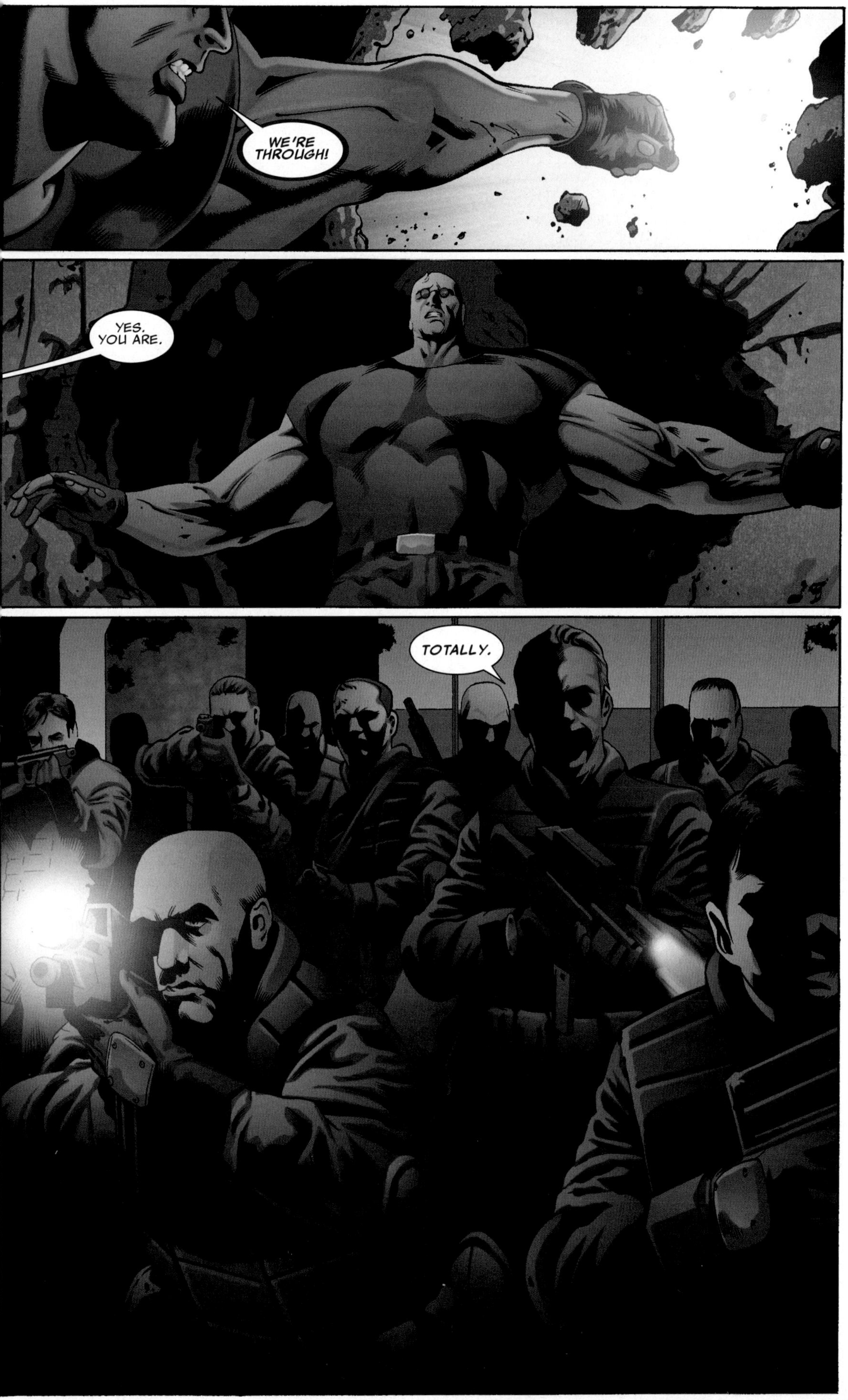
WE'RE THROUGH!
YES. YOU ARE.
TOTALLY.

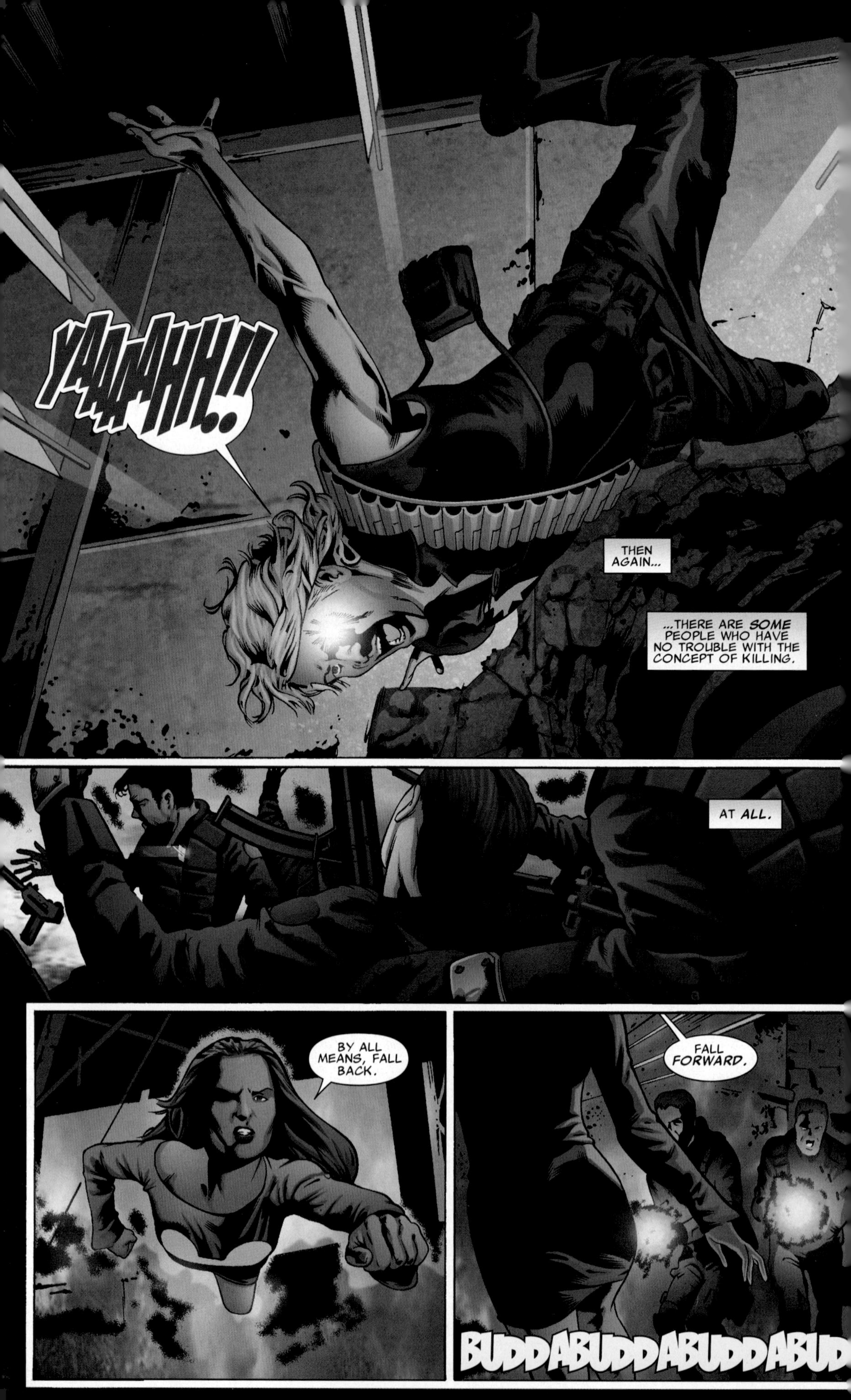
YAAAHH!!
THEN AGAIN...
...THERE ARE SOME PEOPLE WHO HAVE NO TROUBLE WITH THE CONCEPT OF KILLING.
AT ALL.
BY ALL MEANS, FALL BACK.
FALL FORWARD.
BUDDABUDDABUDDABUD

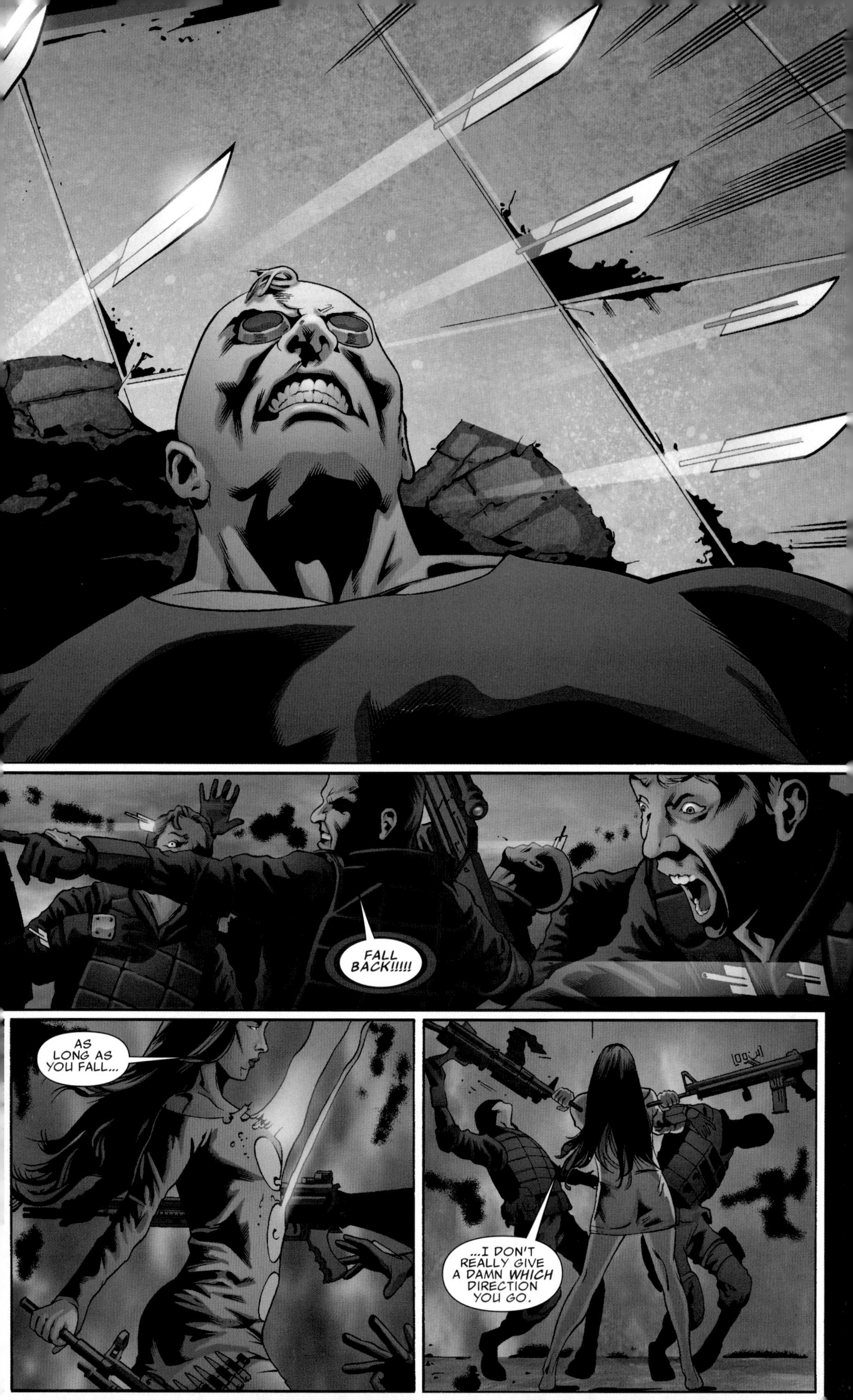
FALL BACK!!!!!
AS LONG AS YOU FALL...
...I DON'T REALLY GIVE A DAMN WHICH DIRECTION YOU GO.

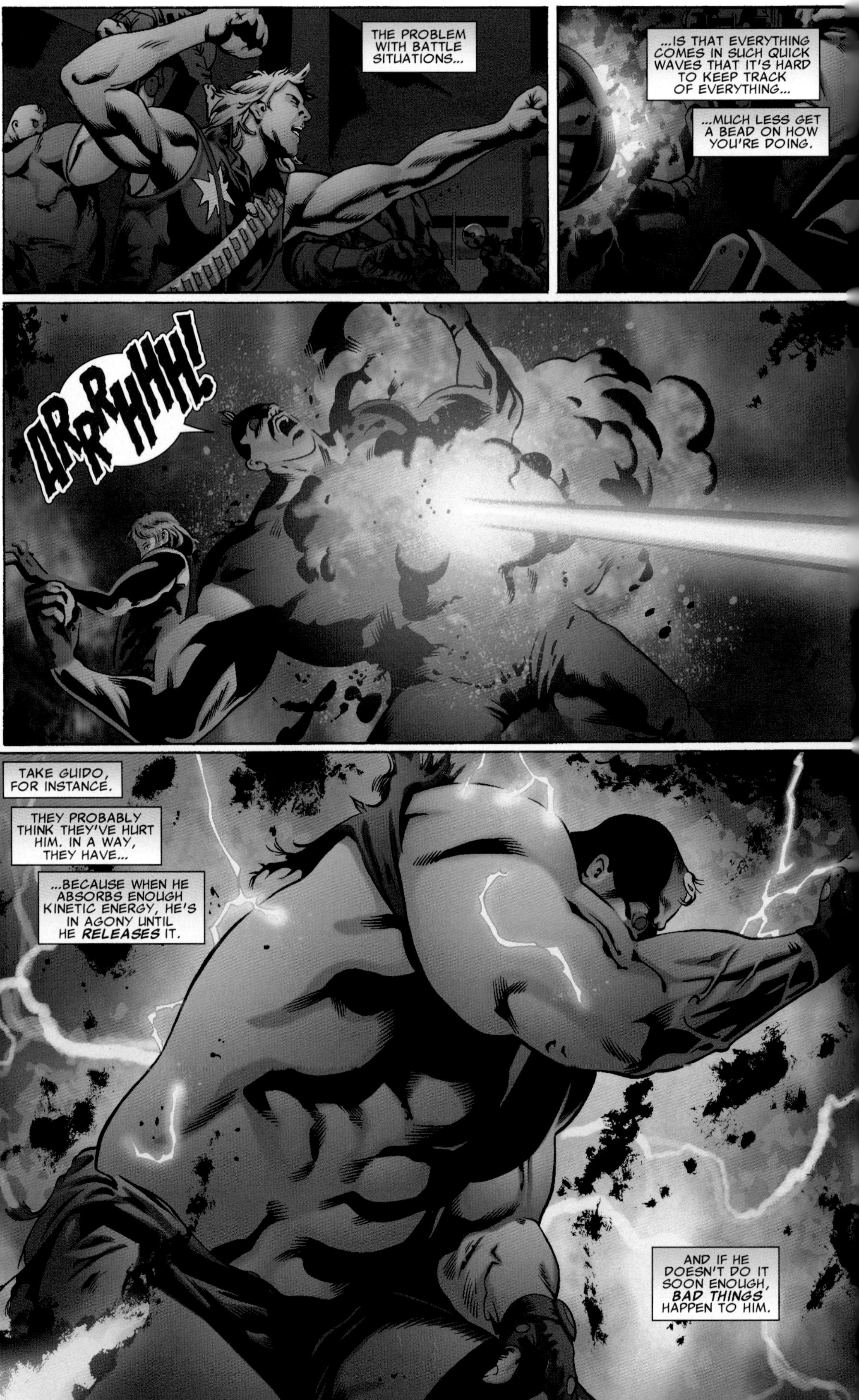
THE PROBLEM WITH BATTLE SITUATIONS...
...IS THAT EVERYTHING COMES IN SUCH QUICK WAVES THAT IT'S HARD TO KEEP TRACK OF EVERYTHING...
...MUCH LESS GET A BEAD ON HOW YOU'RE DOING.
ARRRHHH!
TAKE GUIDO, FOR INSTANCE.
THEY PROBABLY THINK THEY'VE HURT HIM. IN A WAY, THEY HAVE...
...BECAUSE WHEN HE ABSORBS ENOUGH KINETIC ENERGY, HE'S IN AGONY UNTIL HE *RELEASES* IT.
AND IF HE DOESN'T DO IT SOON ENOUGH, *BAD THINGS* HAPPEN TO HIM.

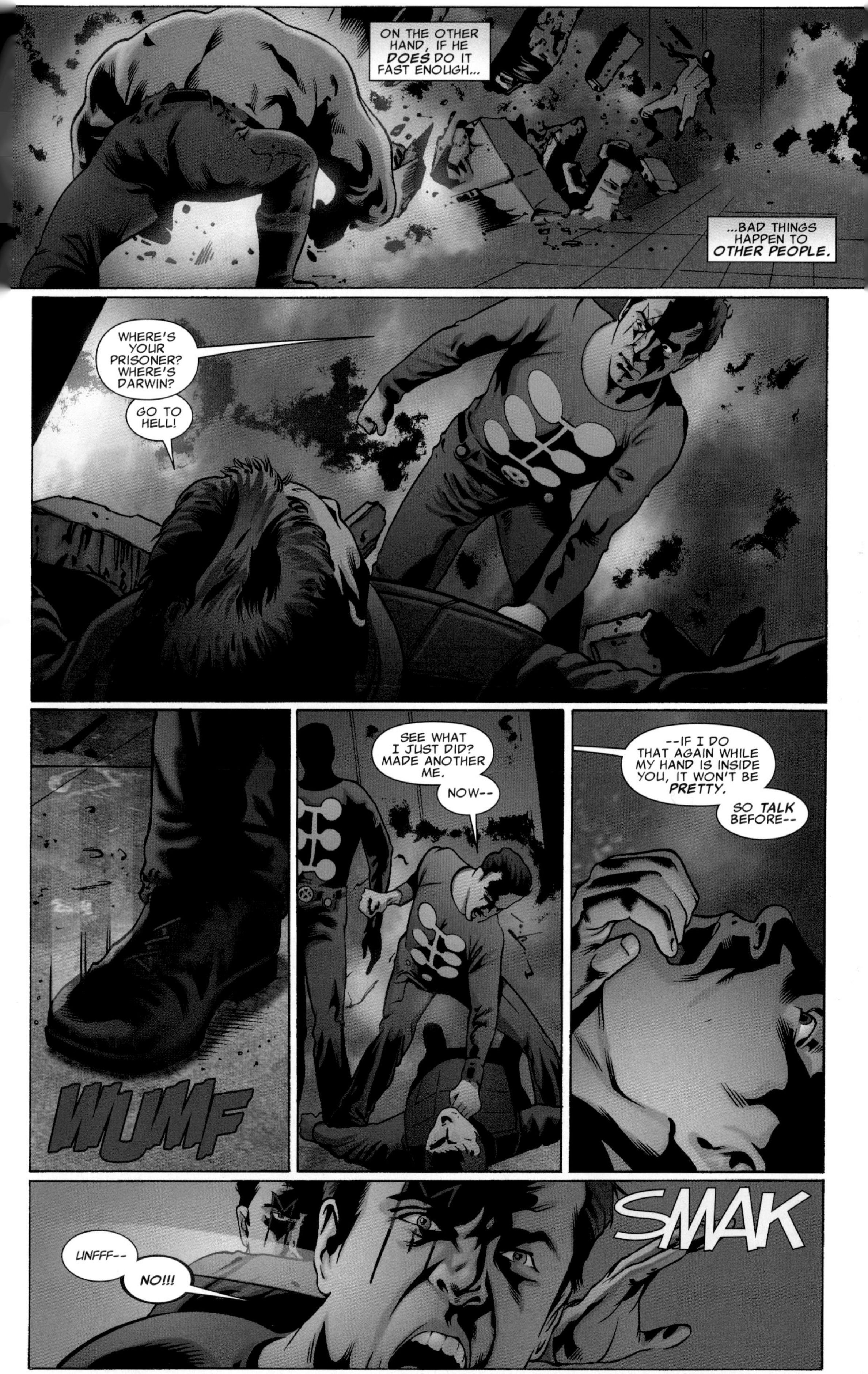
ON THE OTHER HAND, IF HE DOES DO IT FAST ENOUGH...
...BAD THINGS HAPPEN TO OTHER PEOPLE.
WHERE'S YOUR PRISONER? WHERE'S DARWIN?
GO TO HELL!
WUMF
SEE WHAT I JUST DID? MADE ANOTHER ME.
NOW--
--IF I DO THAT AGAIN WHILE MY HAND IS INSIDE YOU, IT WON'T BE PRETTY.
SO TALK BEFORE--
SMAK
UNFFF--
NO!!!

OH, YUCK.

WELL, *THAT* WAS EXCITING.

A little help...?

OH MY GOD... I'M OUT OF CONTROL...

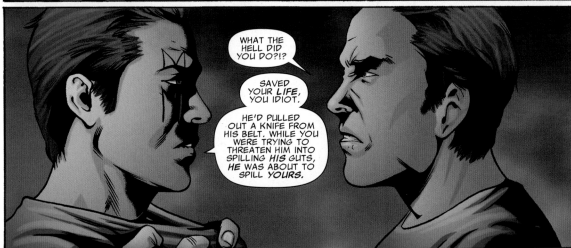

WHAT THE HELL DID YOU DO?!?

SAVED YOUR *LIFE,* YOU IDIOT.

HE'D PULLED OUT A KNIFE FROM HIS BELT. WHILE YOU WERE TRYING TO THREATEN HIM INTO SPILLING *HIS* GUTS, *HE* WAS ABOUT TO SPILL *YOURS.*

SEE, SEE THERE?

NOW KEEP YOUR HEAD IN THE GAME.

THIS *ISN'T* A GAME.

YEAH, IT *IS.* EXCEPT IT'S NOT ABOUT WINNING OR LOSING. IT'S ABOUT BEATING THE GAME ITSELF. DO *THAT,* AND NOTHING ELSE *MATTERS.*

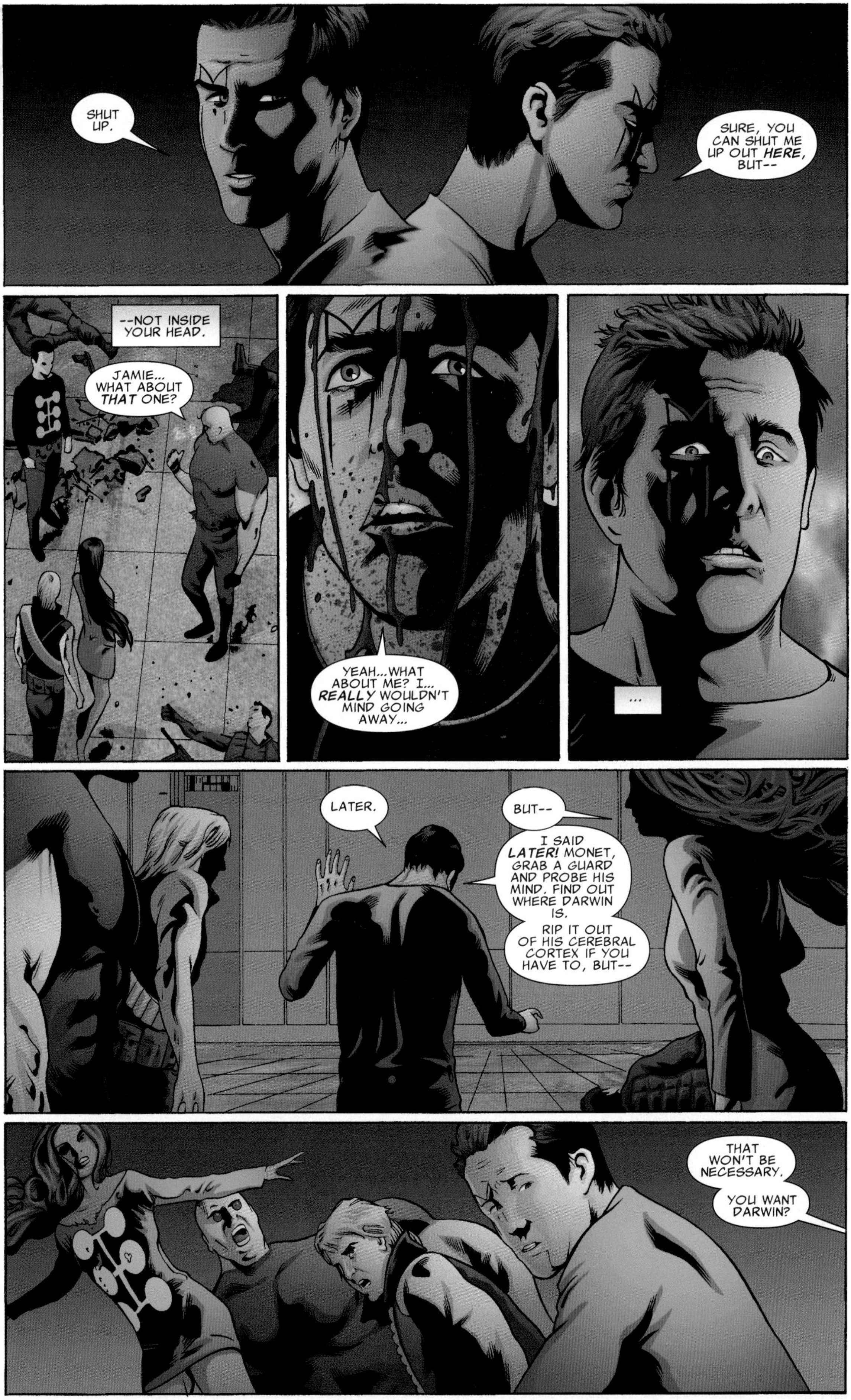
SHUT UP.
SURE, YOU CAN SHUT ME UP OUT HERE, BUT--
--NOT INSIDE YOUR HEAD.
JAMIE... WHAT ABOUT THAT ONE?
YEAH...WHAT ABOUT ME? I... REALLY WOULDN'T MIND GOING AWAY...
...
LATER.
BUT--
I SAID LATER! MONET, GRAB A GUARD AND PROBE HIS MIND. FIND OUT WHERE DARWIN IS.
RIP IT OUT OF HIS CEREBRAL CORTEX IF YOU HAVE TO, BUT--
THAT WON'T BE NECESSARY.
YOU WANT DARWIN?

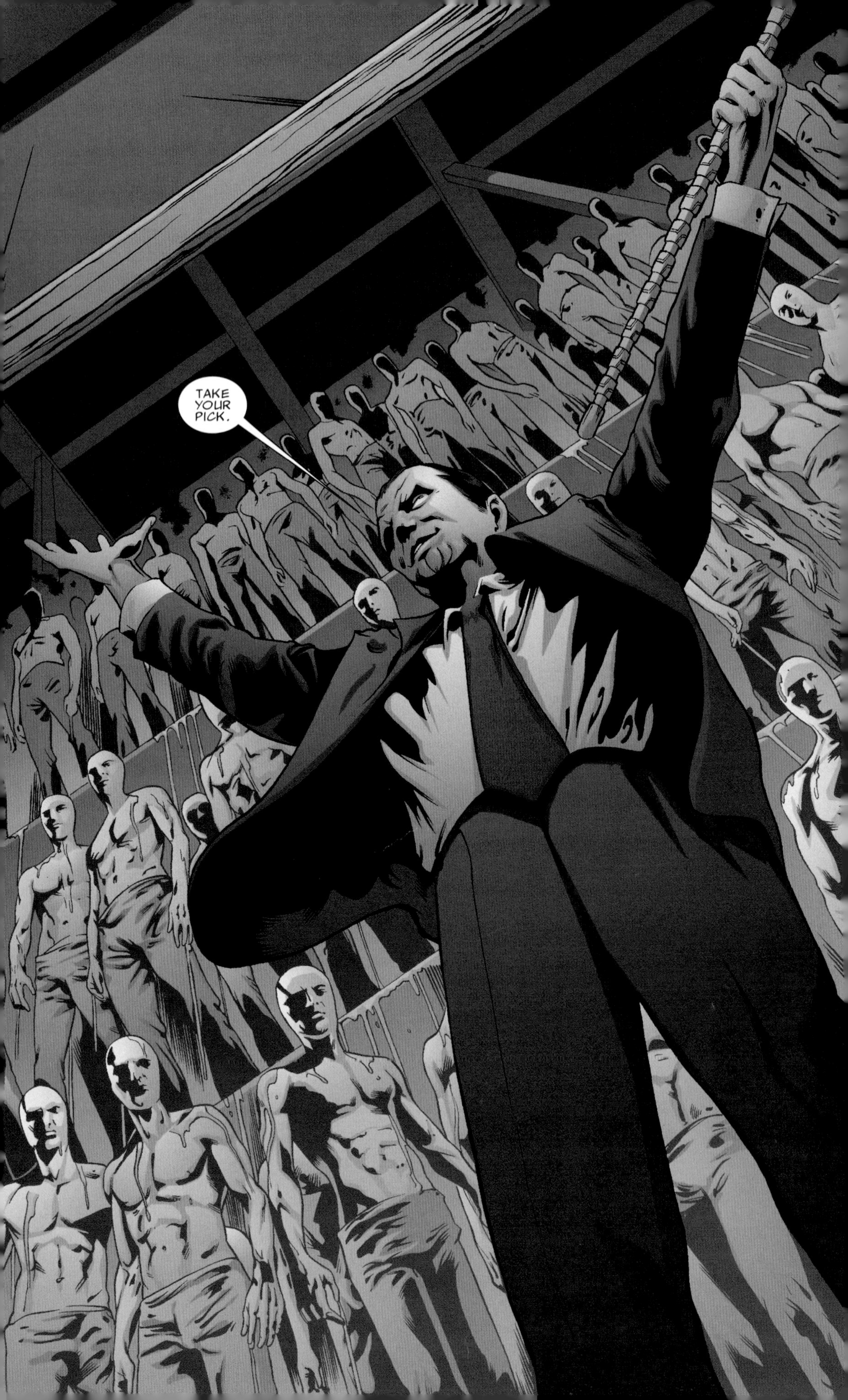
TAKE YOUR PICK.

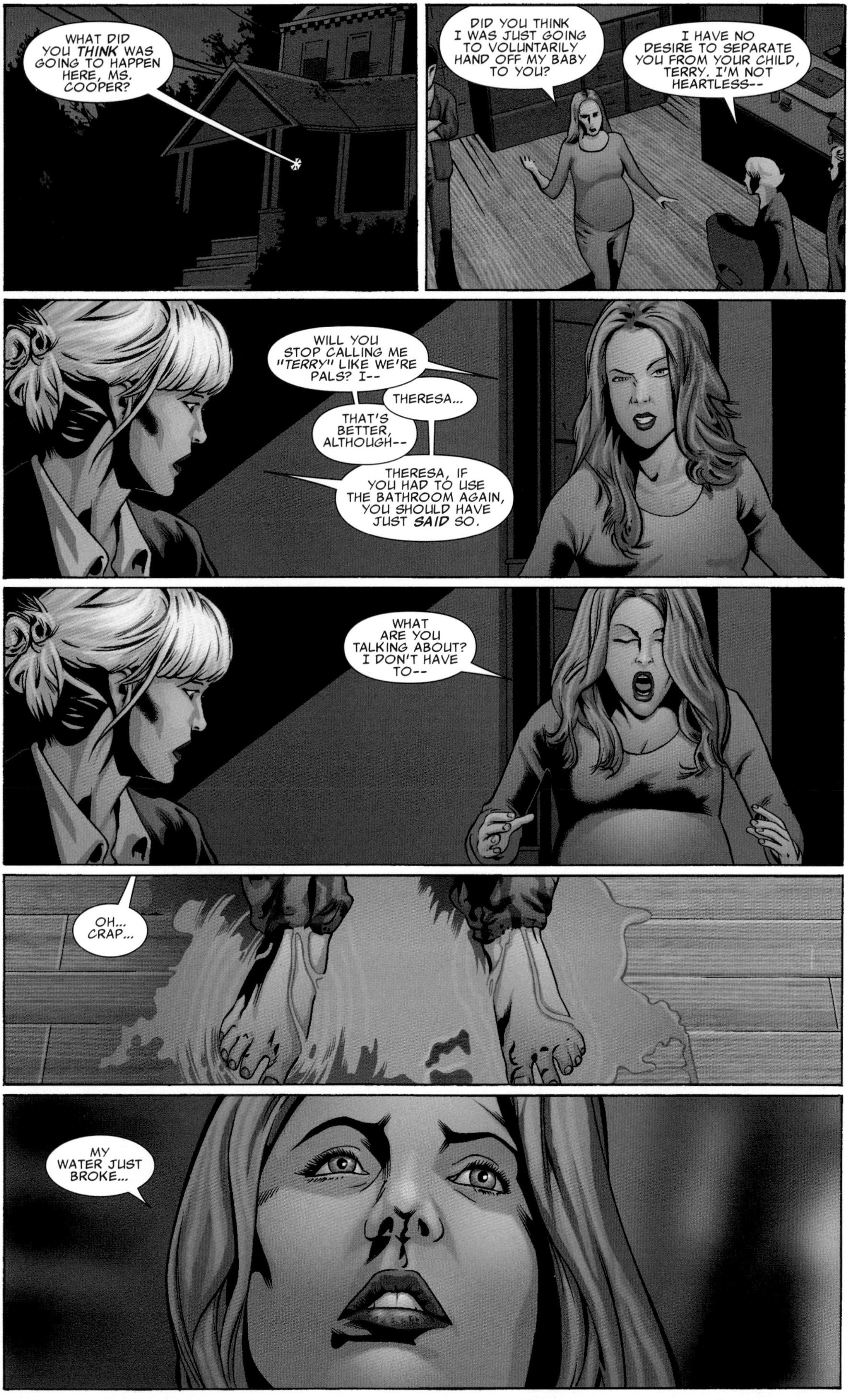
WHAT DID YOU *THINK* WAS GOING TO HAPPEN HERE, MS. COOPER?
DID YOU THINK I WAS JUST GOING TO VOLUNTARILY HAND OFF MY BABY TO YOU?
I HAVE NO DESIRE TO SEPARATE YOU FROM YOUR CHILD, TERRY. I'M NOT HEARTLESS--
WILL YOU STOP CALLING ME "*TERRY*" LIKE WE'RE PALS? I--
THERESA...
THAT'S BETTER, ALTHOUGH--
THERESA, IF YOU HAD TO USE THE BATHROOM AGAIN, YOU SHOULD HAVE JUST *SAID* SO.
WHAT ARE YOU TALKING ABOUT? I DON'T HAVE TO--
OH... CRAP...
MY WATER JUST BROKE...

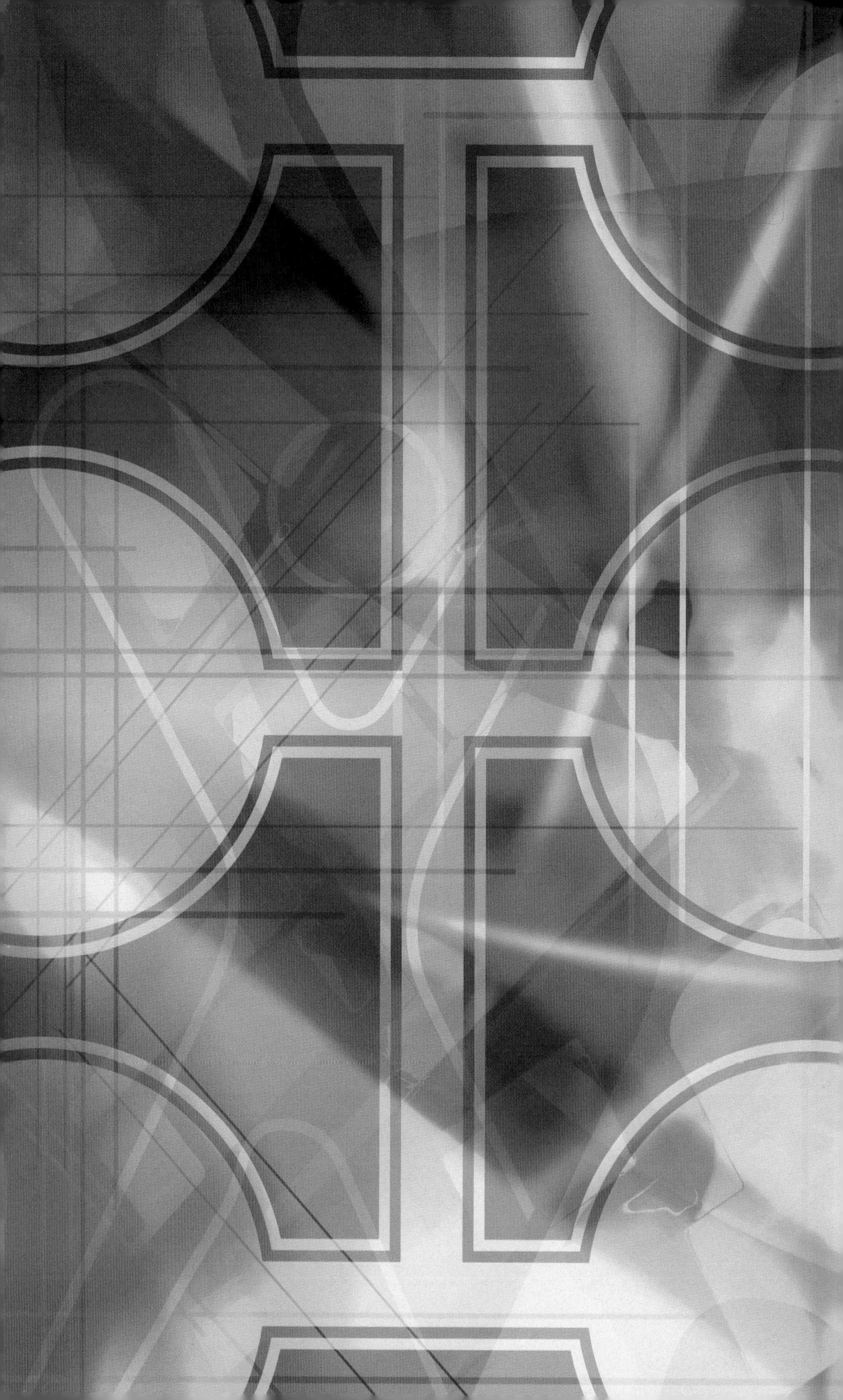

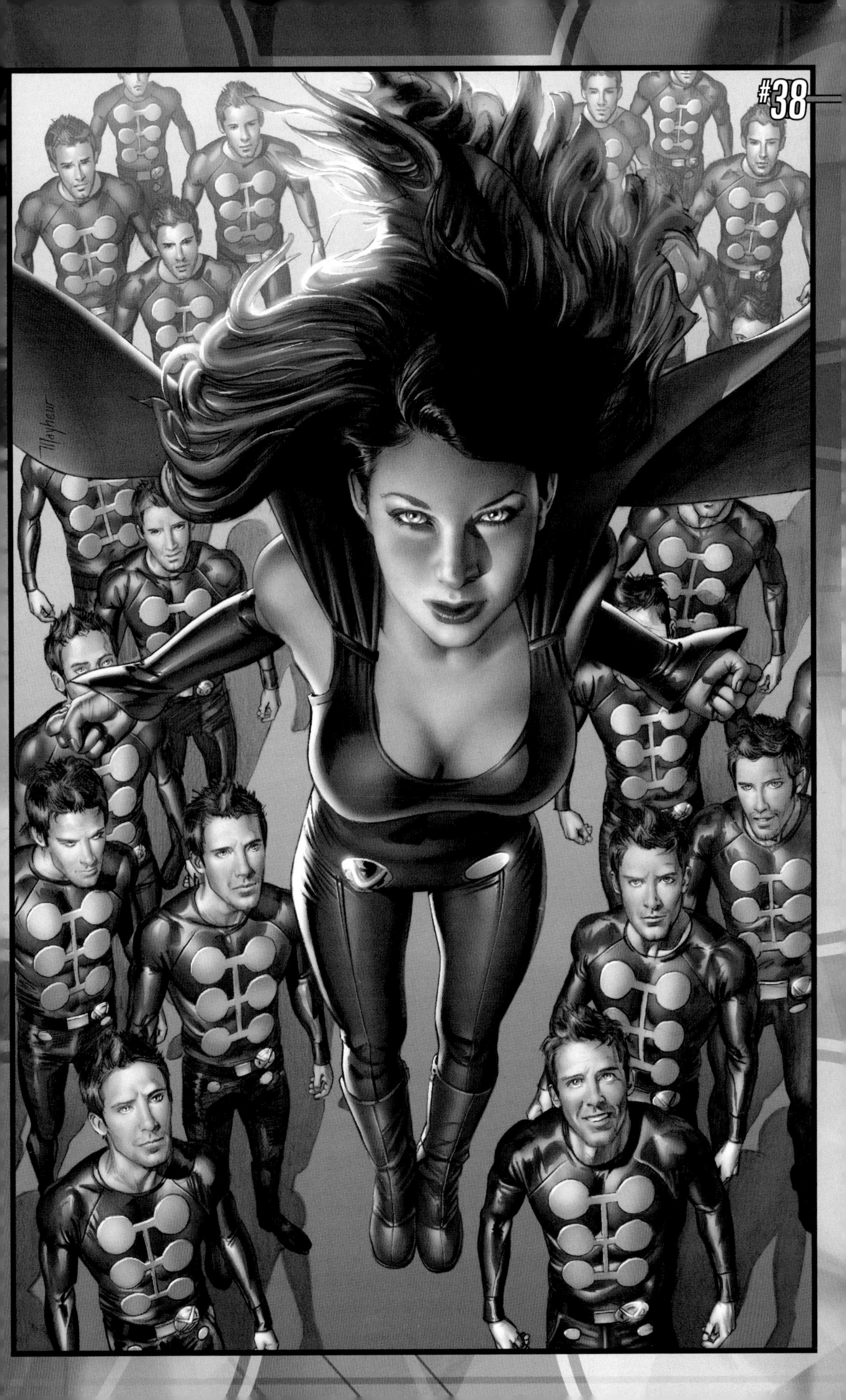
#38

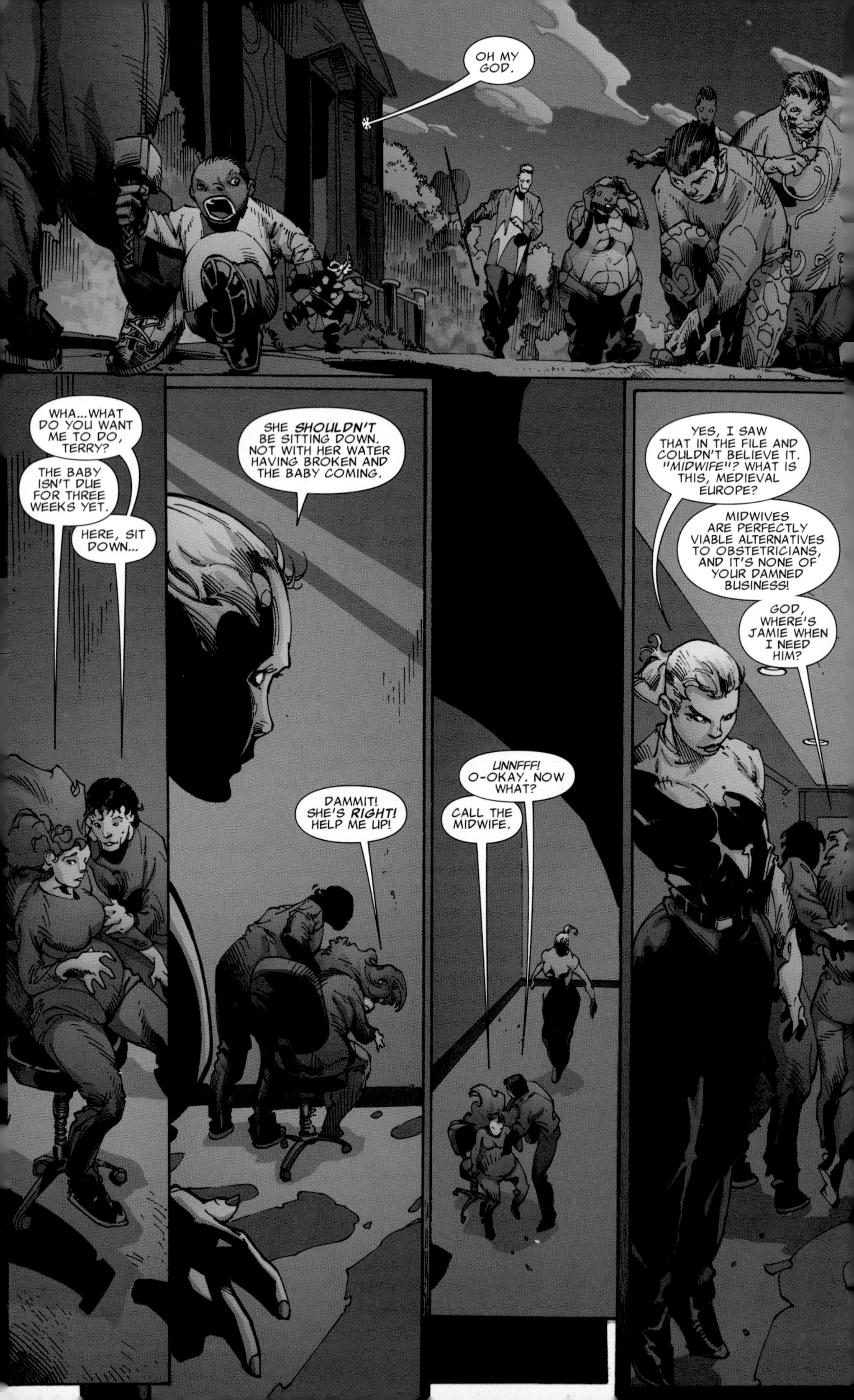
OH MY GOD.
WHA...WHAT DO YOU WANT ME TO DO, TERRY?
THE BABY ISN'T DUE FOR THREE WEEKS YET.
HERE, SIT DOWN...
SHE SHOULDN'T BE SITTING DOWN. NOT WITH HER WATER HAVING BROKEN AND THE BABY COMING.
DAMMIT! SHE'S RIGHT! HELP ME UP!
UNNFFF! O-OKAY. NOW WHAT?
CALL THE MIDWIFE.
YES, I SAW THAT IN THE FILE AND COULDN'T BELIEVE IT. "MIDWIFE"? WHAT IS THIS, MEDIEVAL EUROPE?
MIDWIVES ARE PERFECTLY VIABLE ALTERNATIVES TO OBSTETRICIANS, AND IT'S NONE OF YOUR DAMNED BUSINESS!
GOD, WHERE'S JAMIE WHEN I NEED HIM?

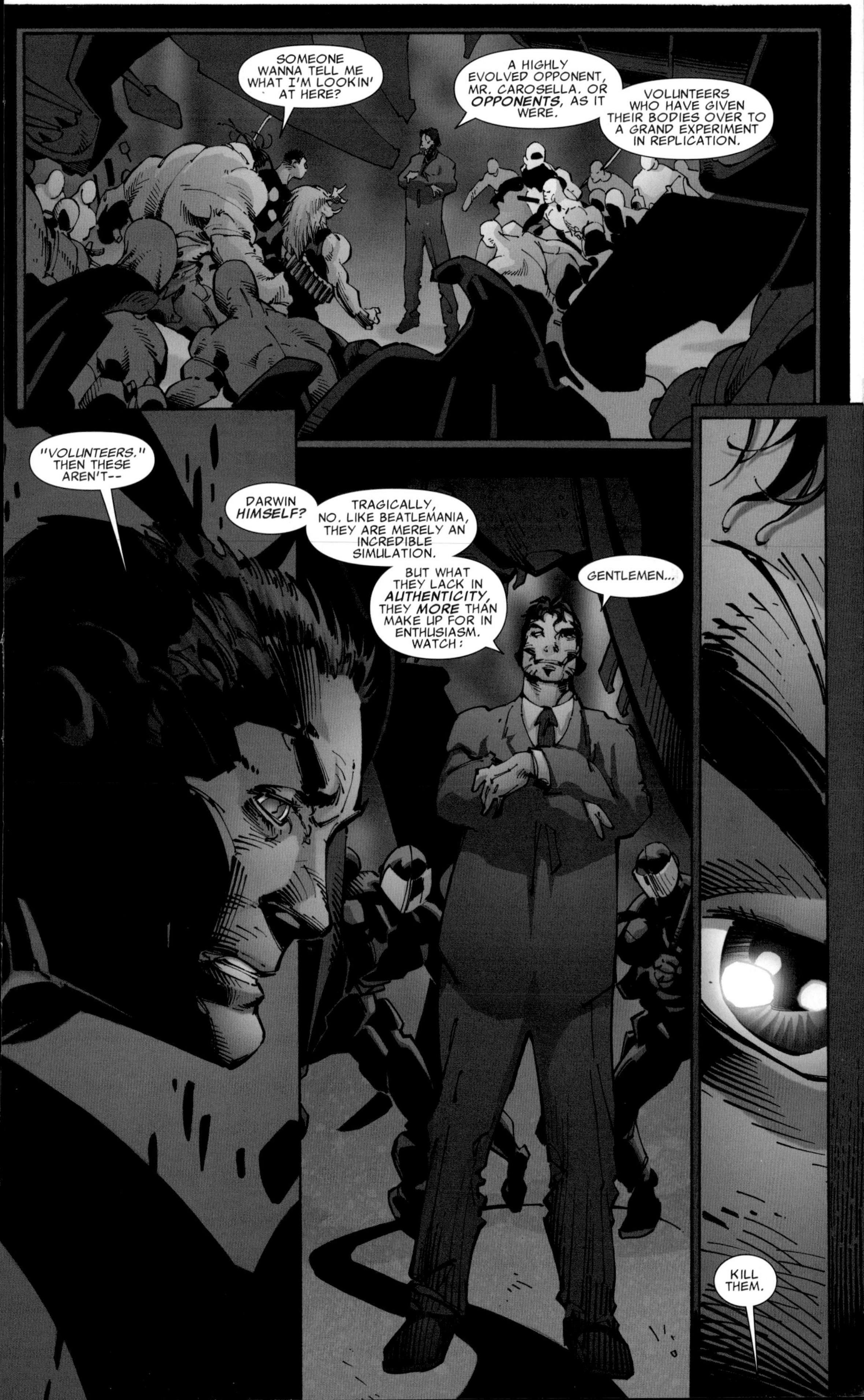
SOMEONE WANNA TELL ME WHAT I'M LOOKIN' AT HERE?
A HIGHLY EVOLVED OPPONENT, MR. CAROSELLA. OR OPPONENTS, AS IT WERE.
VOLUNTEERS WHO HAVE GIVEN THEIR BODIES OVER TO A GRAND EXPERIMENT IN REPLICATION.
"VOLUNTEERS." THEN THESE AREN'T--
DARWIN HIMSELF?
TRAGICALLY, NO. LIKE BEATLEMANIA, THEY ARE MERELY AN INCREDIBLE SIMULATION.
BUT WHAT THEY LACK IN AUTHENTICITY, THEY MORE THAN MAKE UP FOR IN ENTHUSIASM. WATCH:
GENTLEMEN...
KILL THEM.

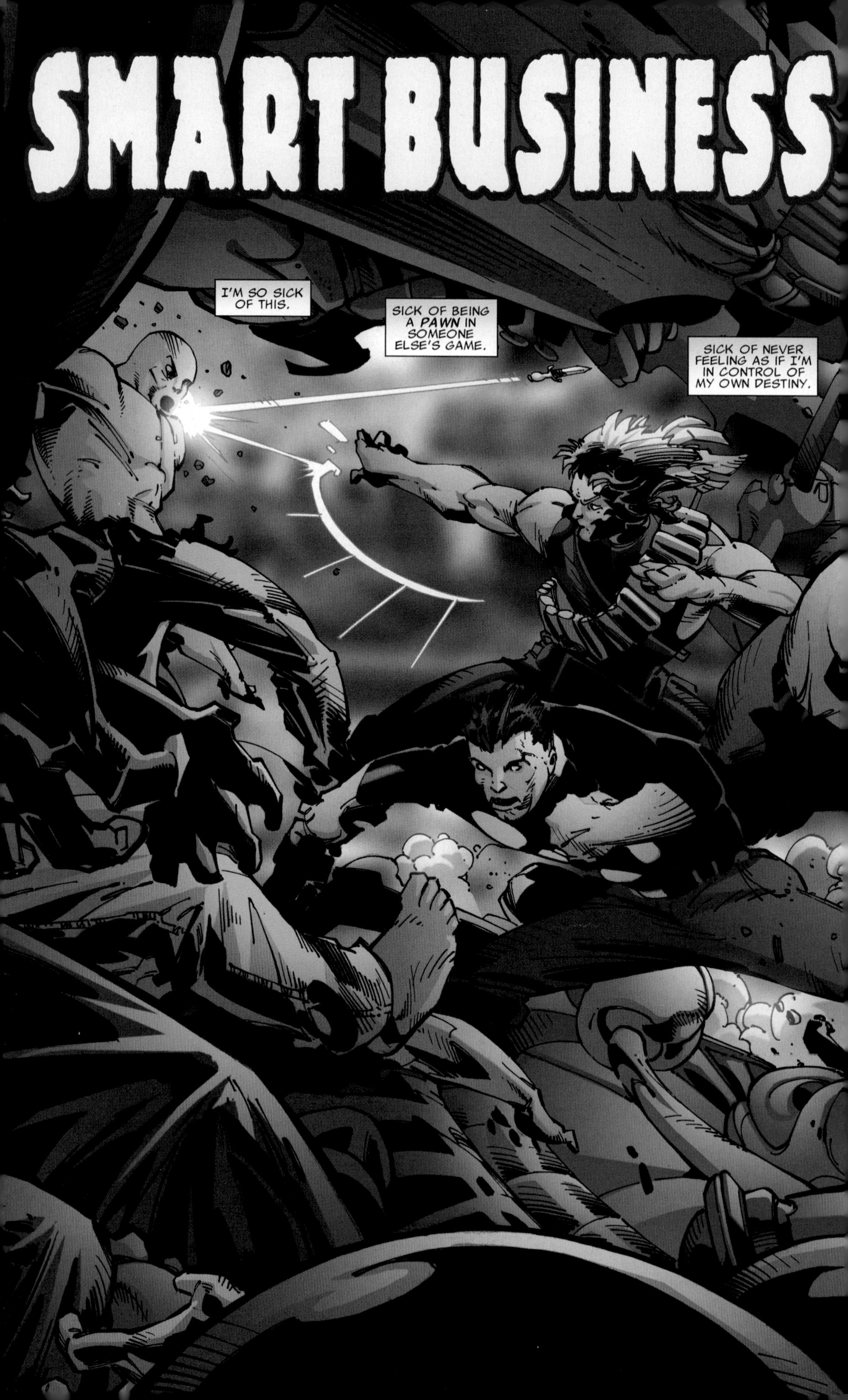
SMART BUSINESS
I'M SO SICK OF THIS.
SICK OF BEING A PAWN IN SOMEONE ELSE'S GAME.
SICK OF NEVER FEELING AS IF I'M IN CONTROL OF MY OWN DESTINY.

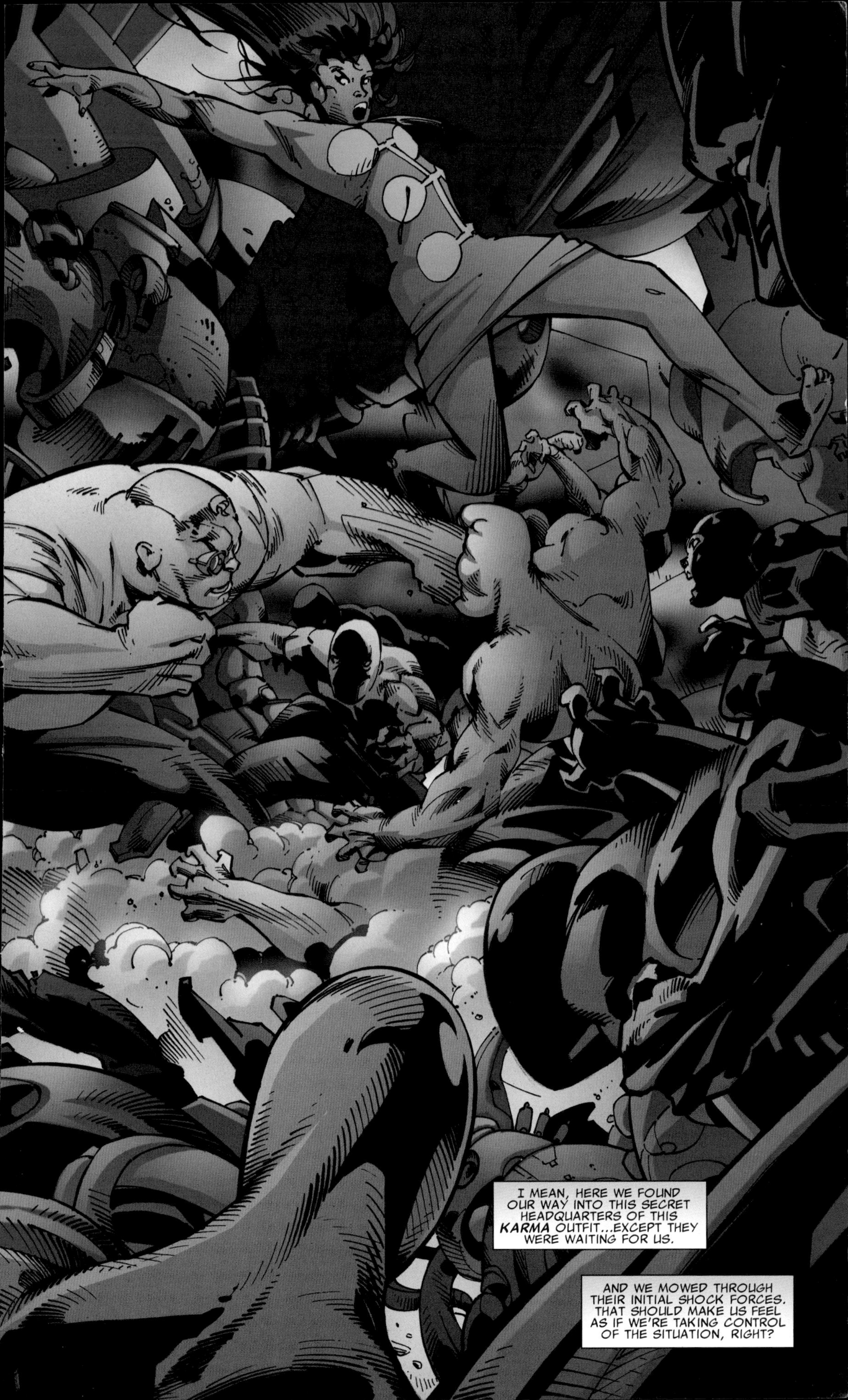
I MEAN, HERE WE FOUND OUR WAY INTO THIS SECRET HEADQUARTERS OF THIS KARMA OUTFIT...EXCEPT THEY WERE WAITING FOR US.
AND WE MOWED THROUGH THEIR INITIAL SHOCK FORCES. THAT SHOULD MAKE US FEEL AS IF WE'RE TAKING CONTROL OF THE SITUATION, RIGHT?

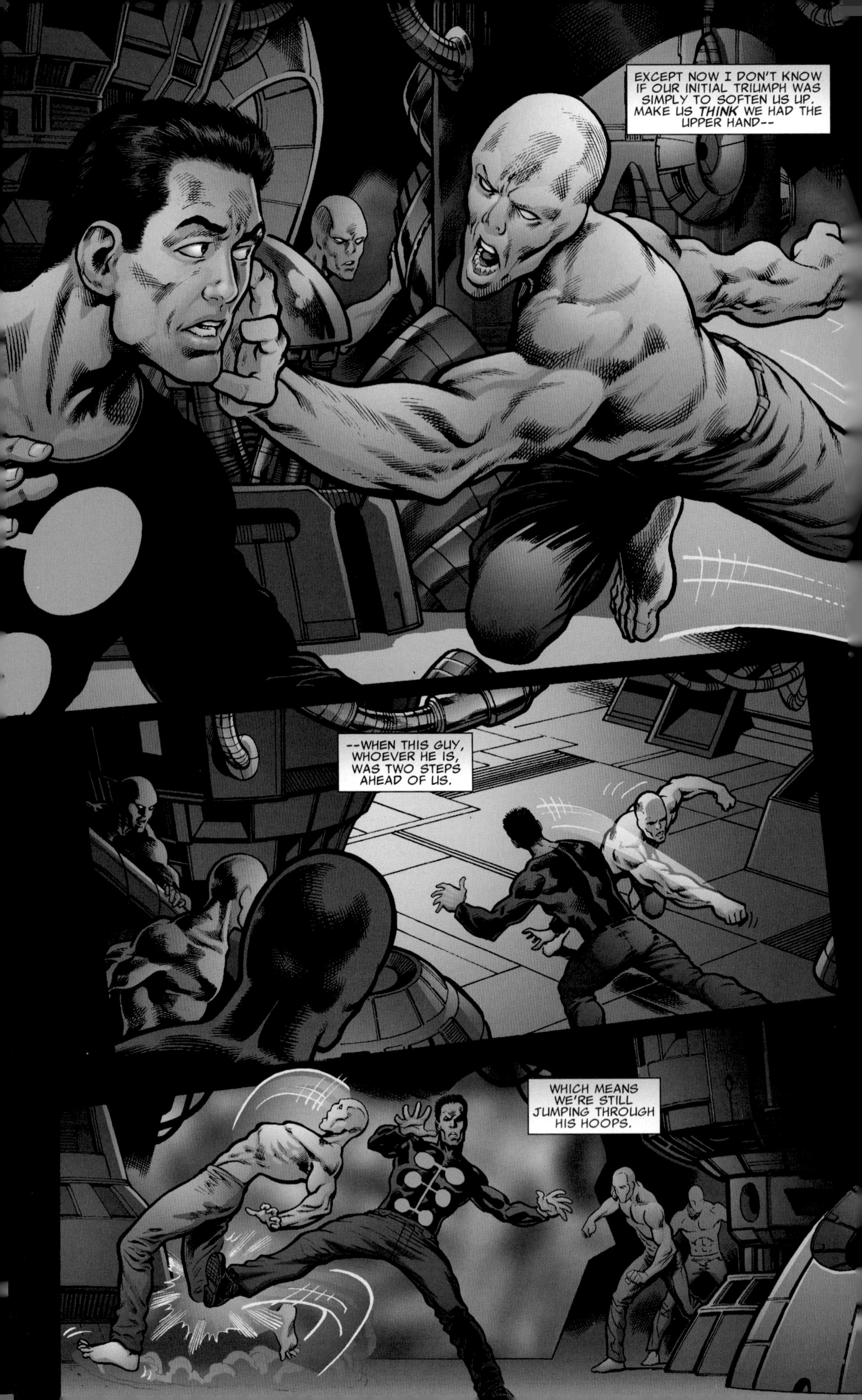
EXCEPT NOW I DON'T KNOW IF OUR INITIAL TRIUMPH WAS SIMPLY TO SOFTEN US UP. MAKE US *THINK* WE HAD THE UPPER HAND--
--WHEN THIS GUY, WHOEVER HE IS, WAS TWO STEPS AHEAD OF US.
WHICH MEANS WE'RE STILL JUMPING THROUGH HIS HOOPS.

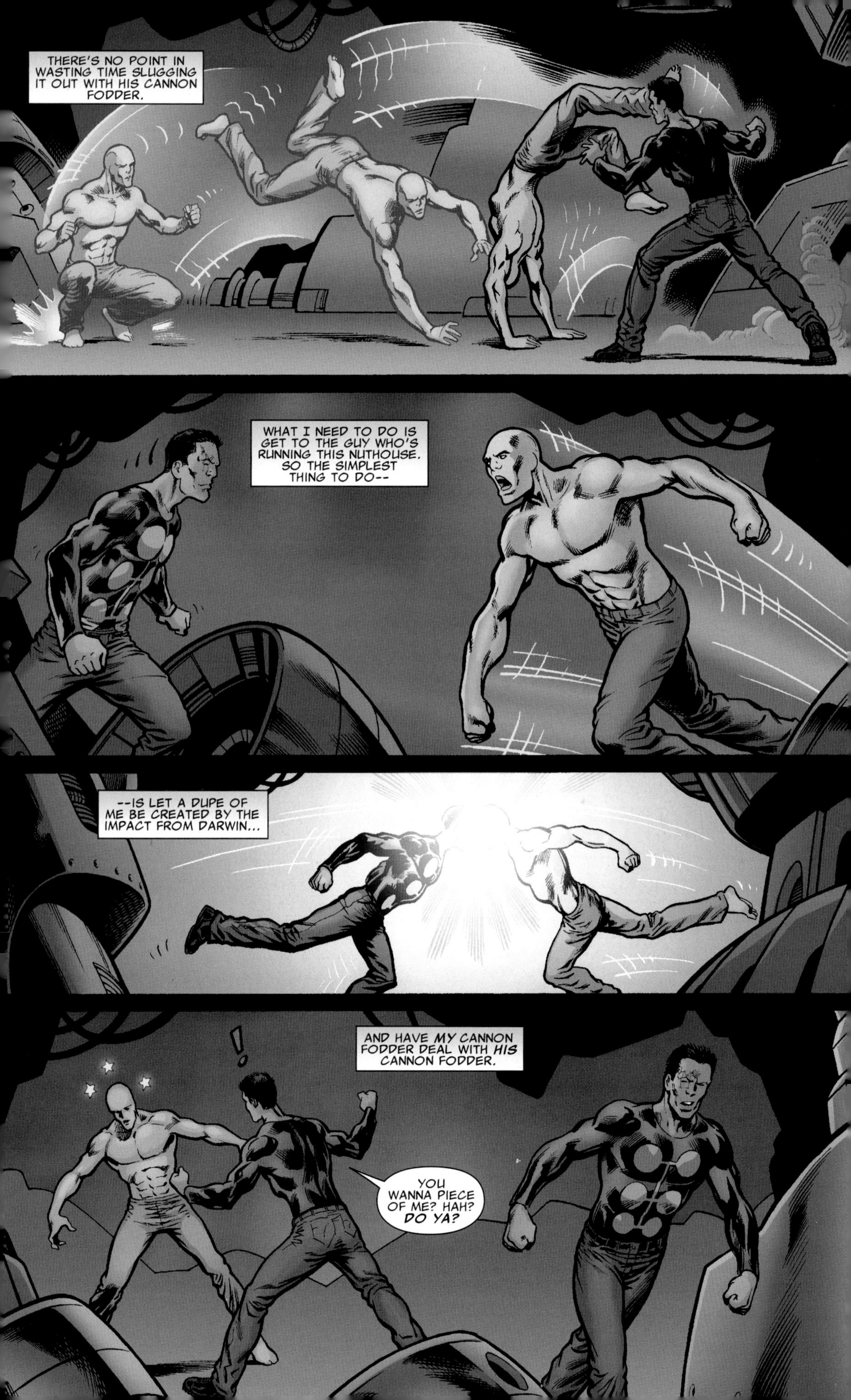
THERE'S NO POINT IN WASTING TIME SLUGGING IT OUT WITH HIS CANNON FODDER.
WHAT I NEED TO DO IS GET TO THE GUY WHO'S RUNNING THIS NUTHOUSE. SO THE SIMPLEST THING TO DO--
--IS LET A DUPE OF ME BE CREATED BY THE IMPACT FROM DARWIN...
AND HAVE MY CANNON FODDER DEAL WITH HIS CANNON FODDER.
!
YOU WANNA PIECE OF ME? HAH? DO YA?

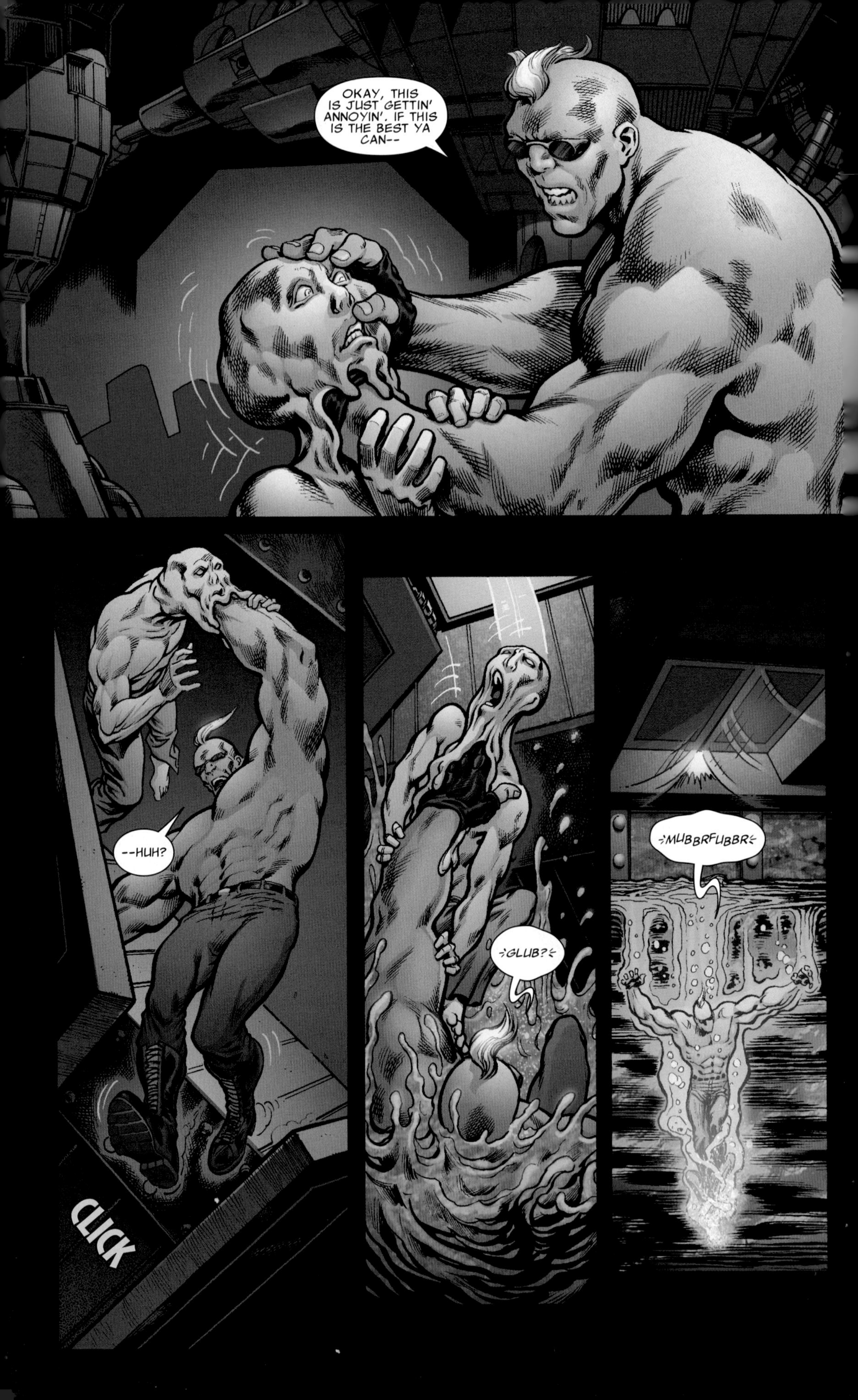
OKAY, THIS IS JUST GETTIN' ANNOYIN'. IF THIS IS THE BEST YA CAN--
--HUH?
CLICK
GLUB?
MUBBRFUBBR

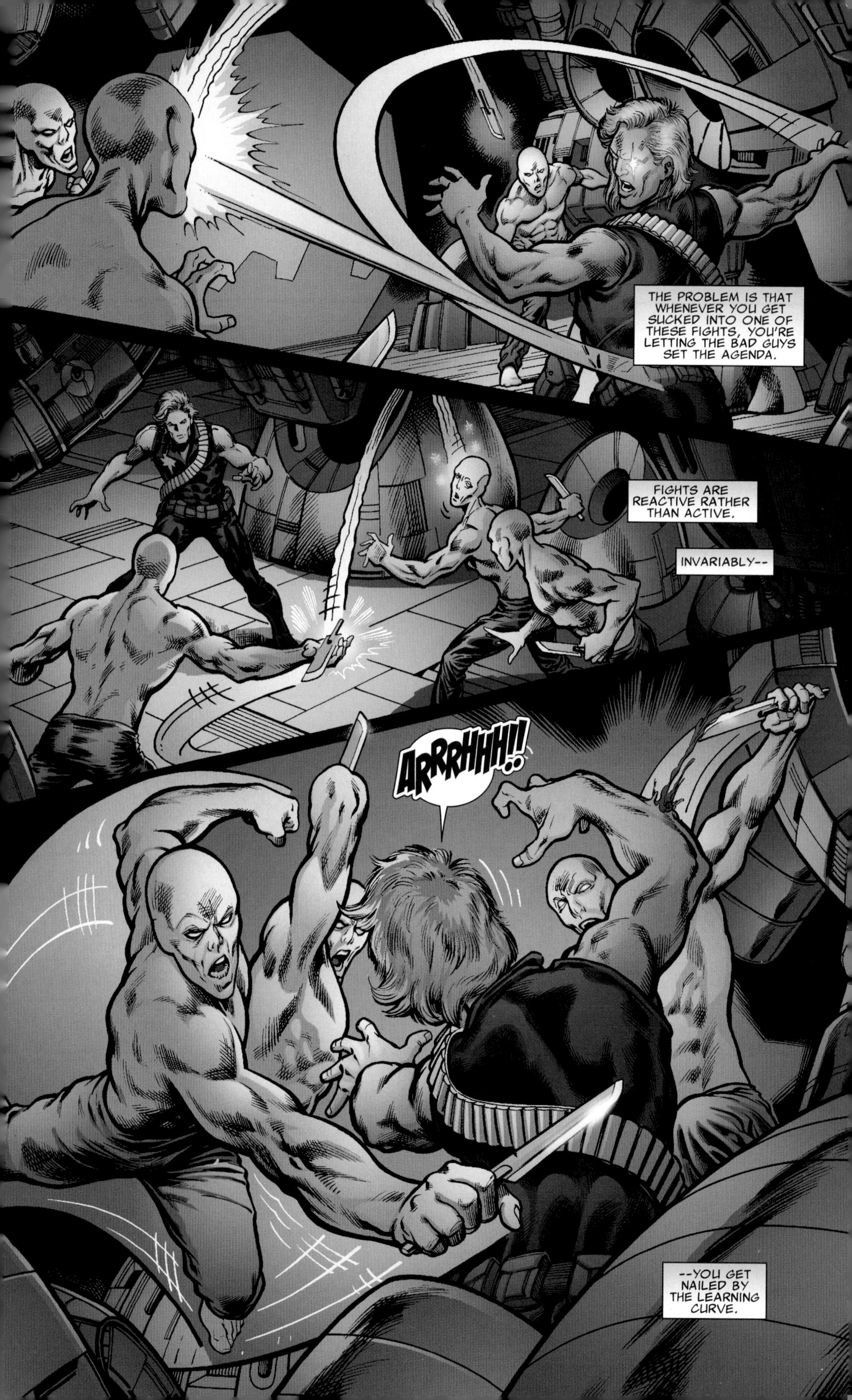
THE PROBLEM IS THAT WHENEVER YOU GET SUCKED INTO ONE OF THESE FIGHTS, YOU'RE LETTING THE BAD GUYS SET THE AGENDA.
FIGHTS ARE REACTIVE RATHER THAN ACTIVE.
INVARIABLY--
ARRRHHH!!
--YOU GET NAILED BY THE LEARNING CURVE.

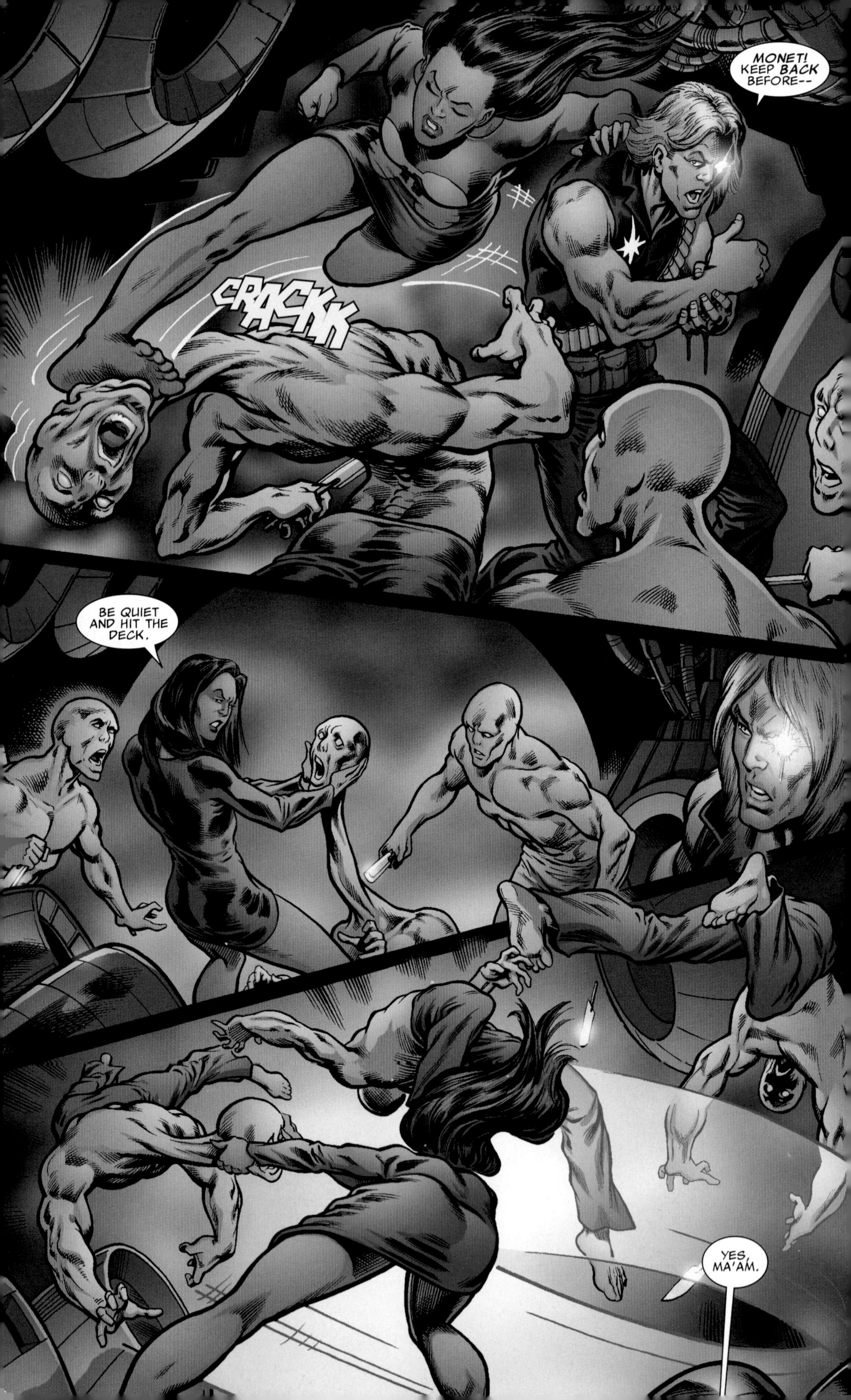
MONET! KEEP BACK BEFORE--
CRACKK
BE QUIET AND HIT THE DECK.
YES, MA'AM.

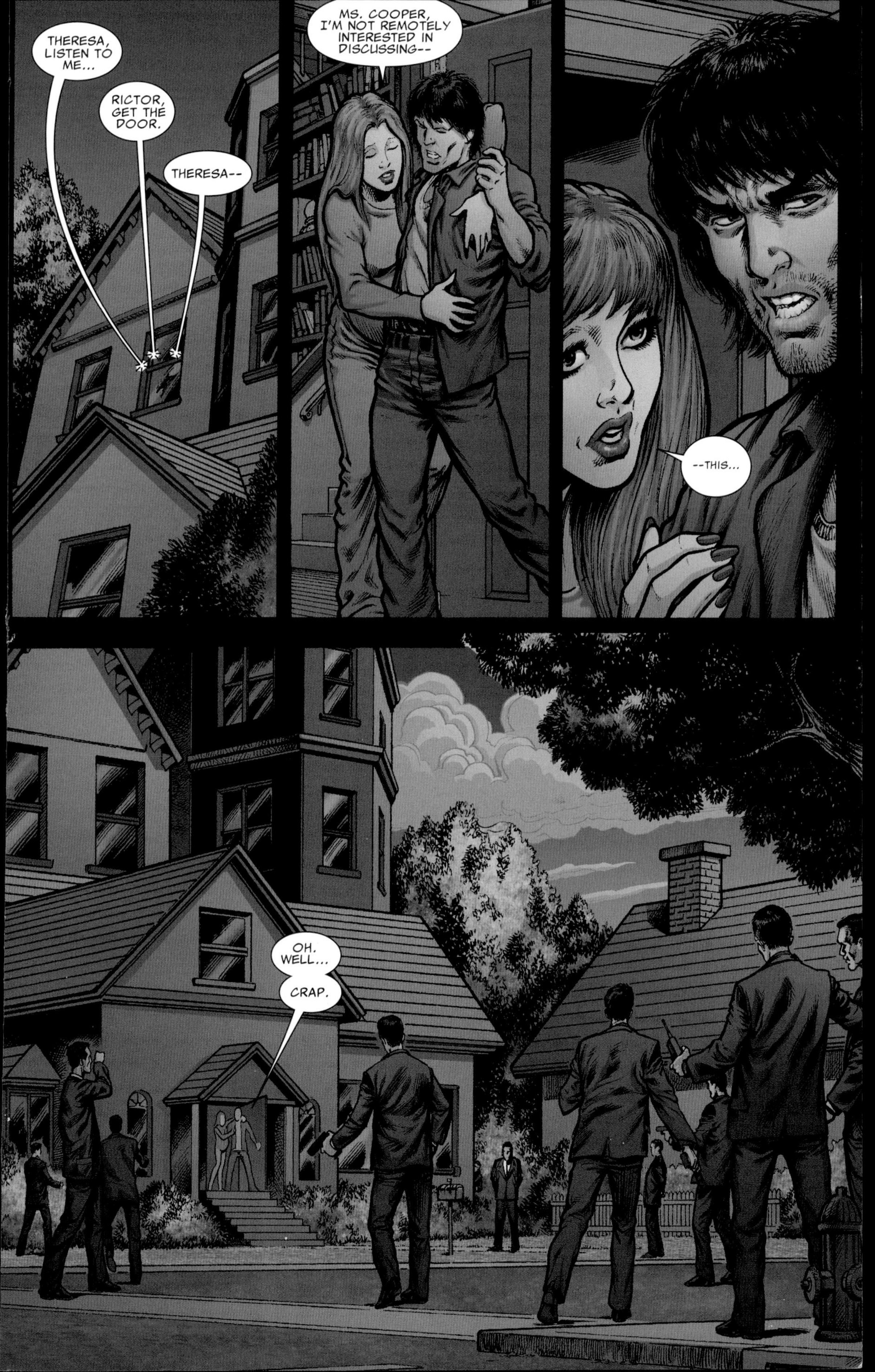
THERESA, LISTEN TO ME...
RICTOR, GET THE DOOR.
THERESA--
MS. COOPER, I'M NOT REMOTELY INTERESTED IN DISCUSSING--
--THIS...
OH. WELL...
CRAP.

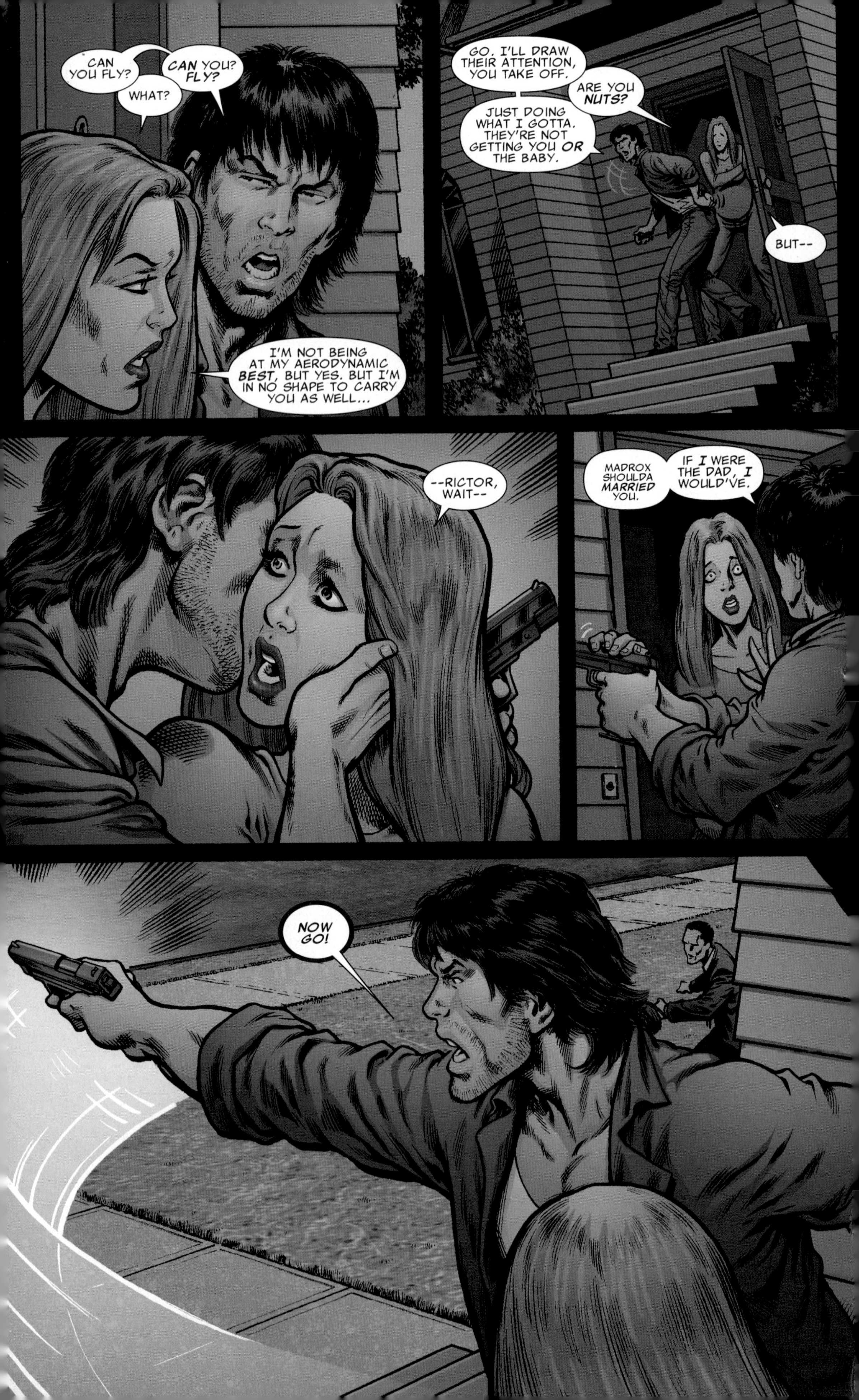
CAN YOU FLY?
WHAT?
CAN YOU? FLY?
I'M NOT BEING AT MY AERODYNAMIC BEST, BUT YES. BUT I'M IN NO SHAPE TO CARRY YOU AS WELL...
GO. I'LL DRAW THEIR ATTENTION, YOU TAKE OFF.
ARE YOU NUTS?
JUST DOING WHAT I GOTTA. THEY'RE NOT GETTING YOU OR THE BABY.
BUT--
--RICTOR, WAIT--
MADROX SHOULDA MARRIED YOU.
IF I WERE THE DAD, I WOULD'VE.
NOW GO!

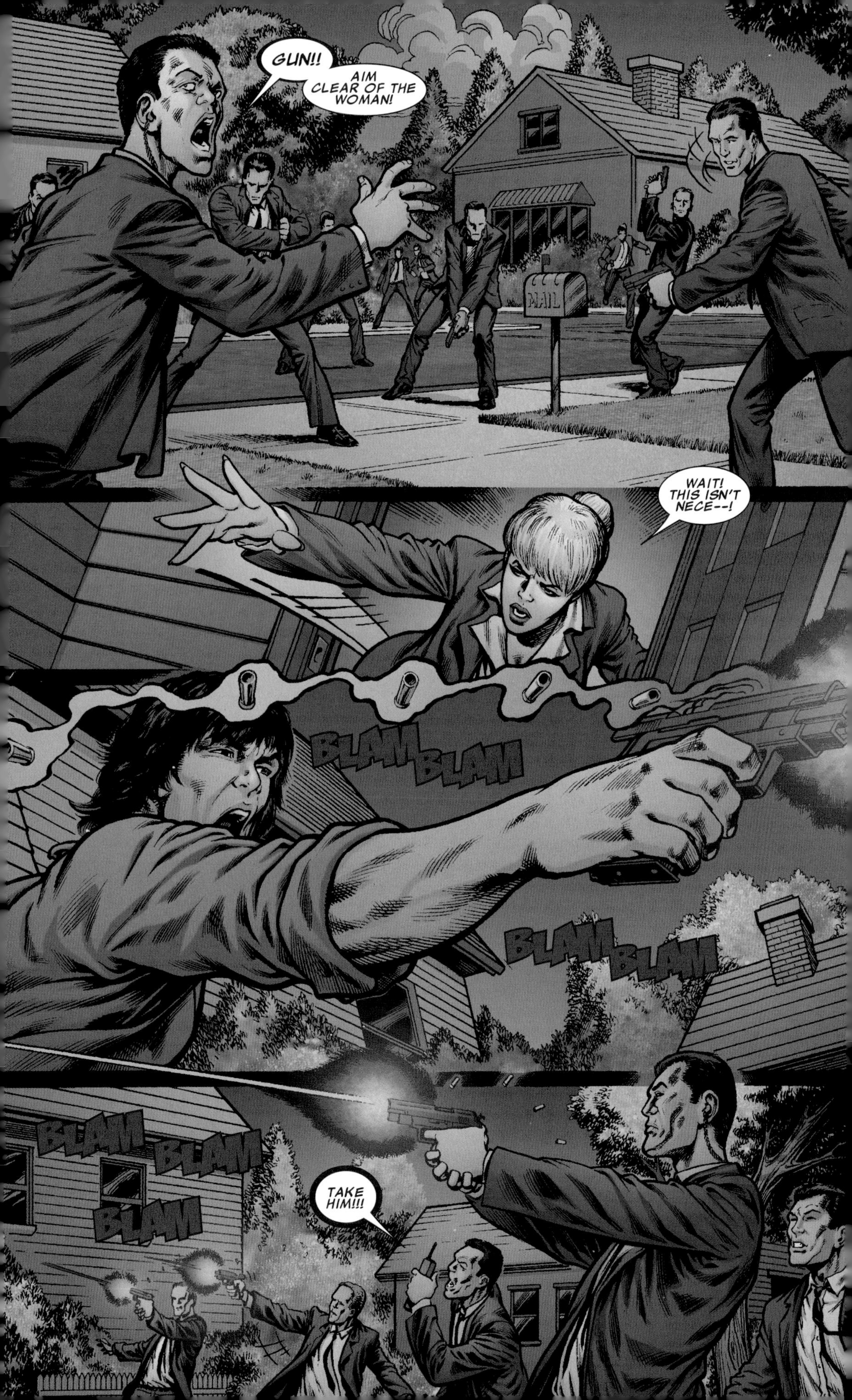
GUN!!
AIM CLEAR OF THE WOMAN!
WAIT! THIS ISN'T NECE--!
BLAM BLAM
BLAM BLAM
BLAM BLAM BLAM
TAKE HIM!!!

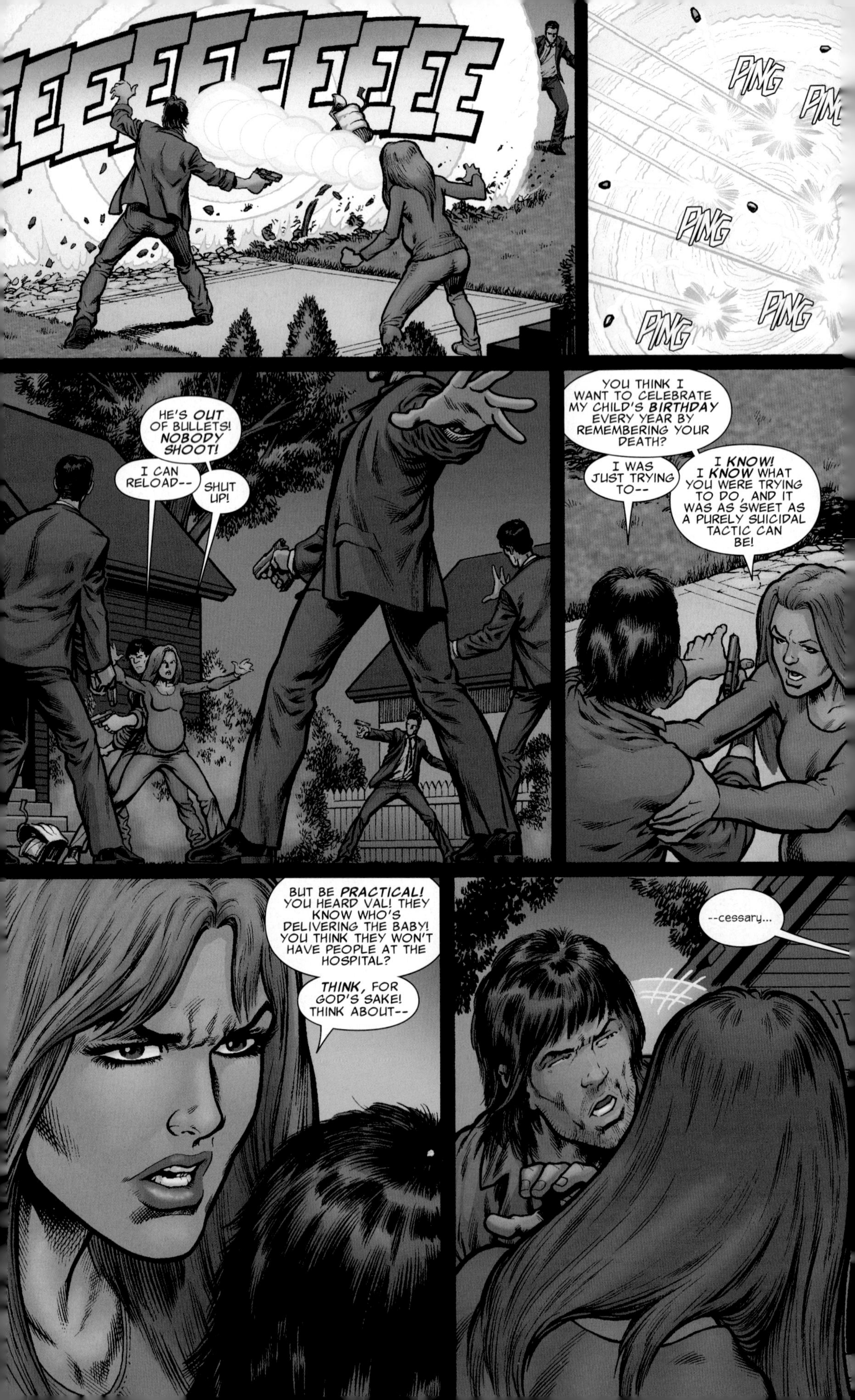
EEEEEEEEEEE
PING
PING
PING
PING
PING
HE'S OUT OF BULLETS! NOBODY SHOOT!
I CAN RELOAD--
SHUT UP!
YOU THINK I WANT TO CELEBRATE MY CHILD'S BIRTHDAY EVERY YEAR BY REMEMBERING YOUR DEATH?
I WAS JUST TRYING TO--
I KNOW! I KNOW WHAT YOU WERE TRYING TO DO, AND IT WAS AS SWEET AS A PURELY SUICIDAL TACTIC CAN BE!
BUT BE PRACTICAL! YOU HEARD VAL! THEY KNOW WHO'S DELIVERING THE BABY! YOU THINK THEY WON'T HAVE PEOPLE AT THE HOSPITAL?
THINK, FOR GOD'S SAKE! THINK ABOUT--
--cessary...

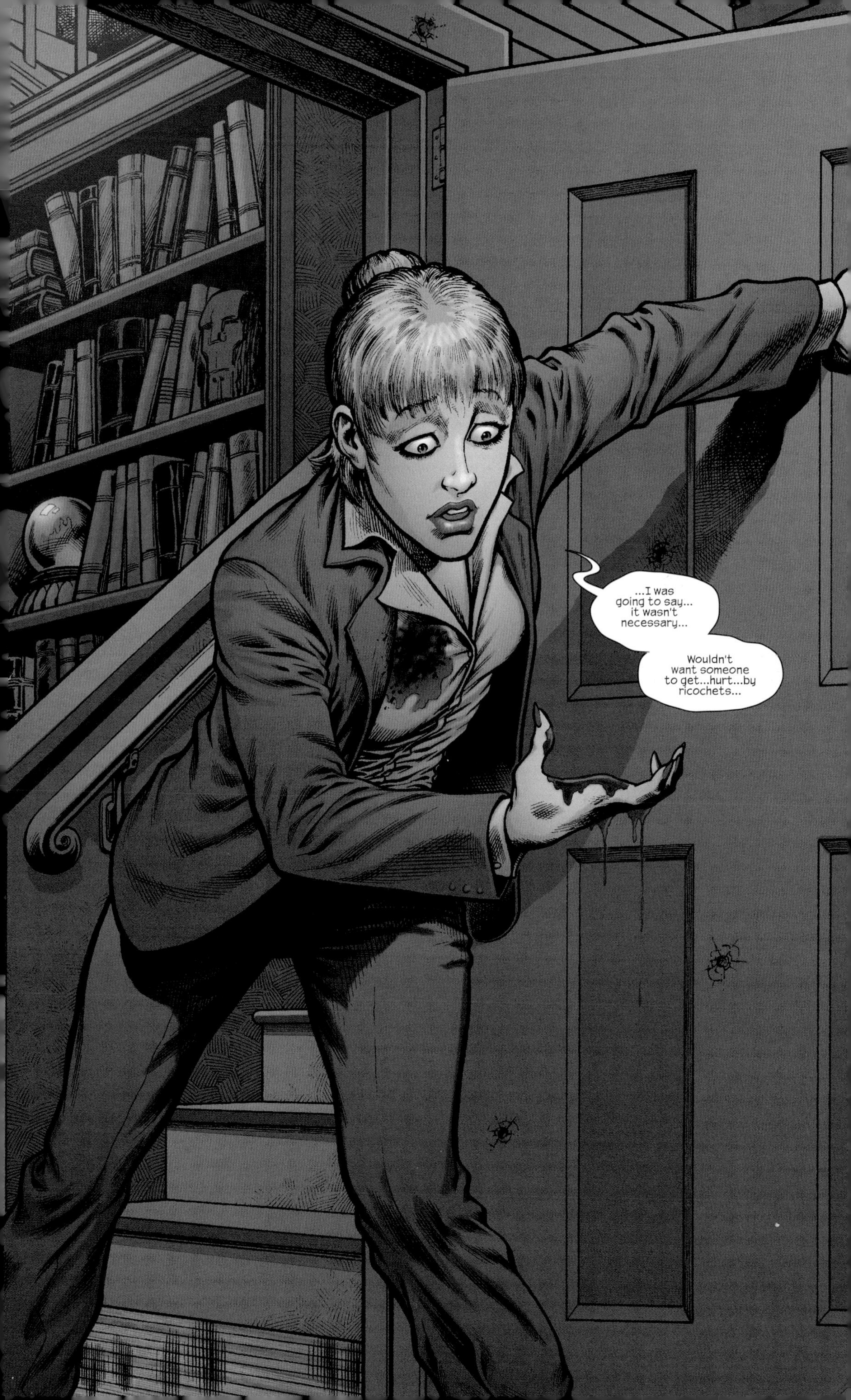
...I was going to say... it wasn't necessary...
Wouldn't want someone to get...hurt...by ricochets...

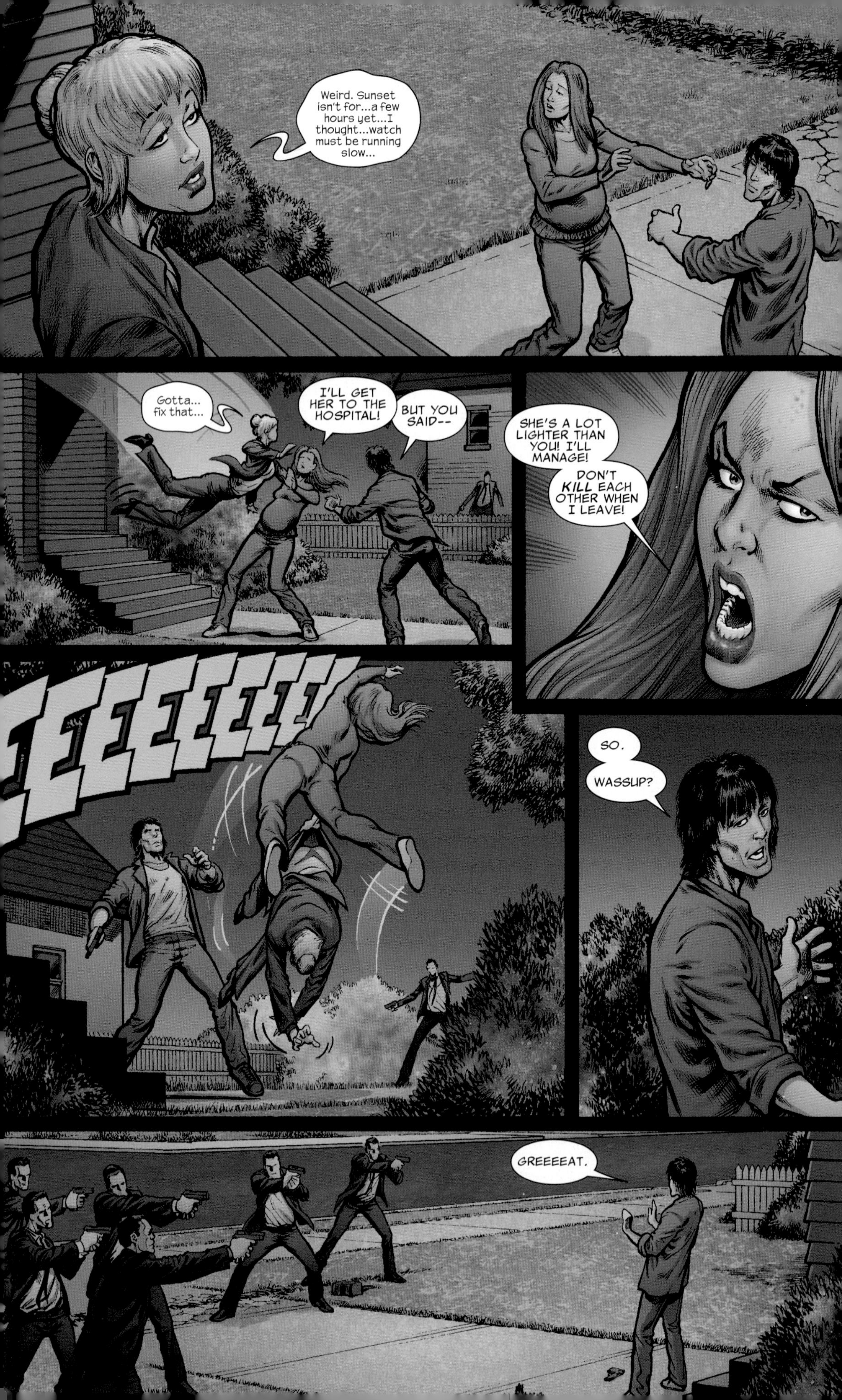
Weird. Sunset isn't for...a few hours yet...I thought...watch must be running slow...
Gotta... fix that...
I'LL GET HER TO THE HOSPITAL!
BUT YOU SAID--
SHE'S A LOT LIGHTER THAN YOU! I'LL MANAGE!
DON'T **KILL** EACH OTHER WHEN I LEAVE!
EEEEEEEE!
SO.
WASSUP?
GREEEEAT.

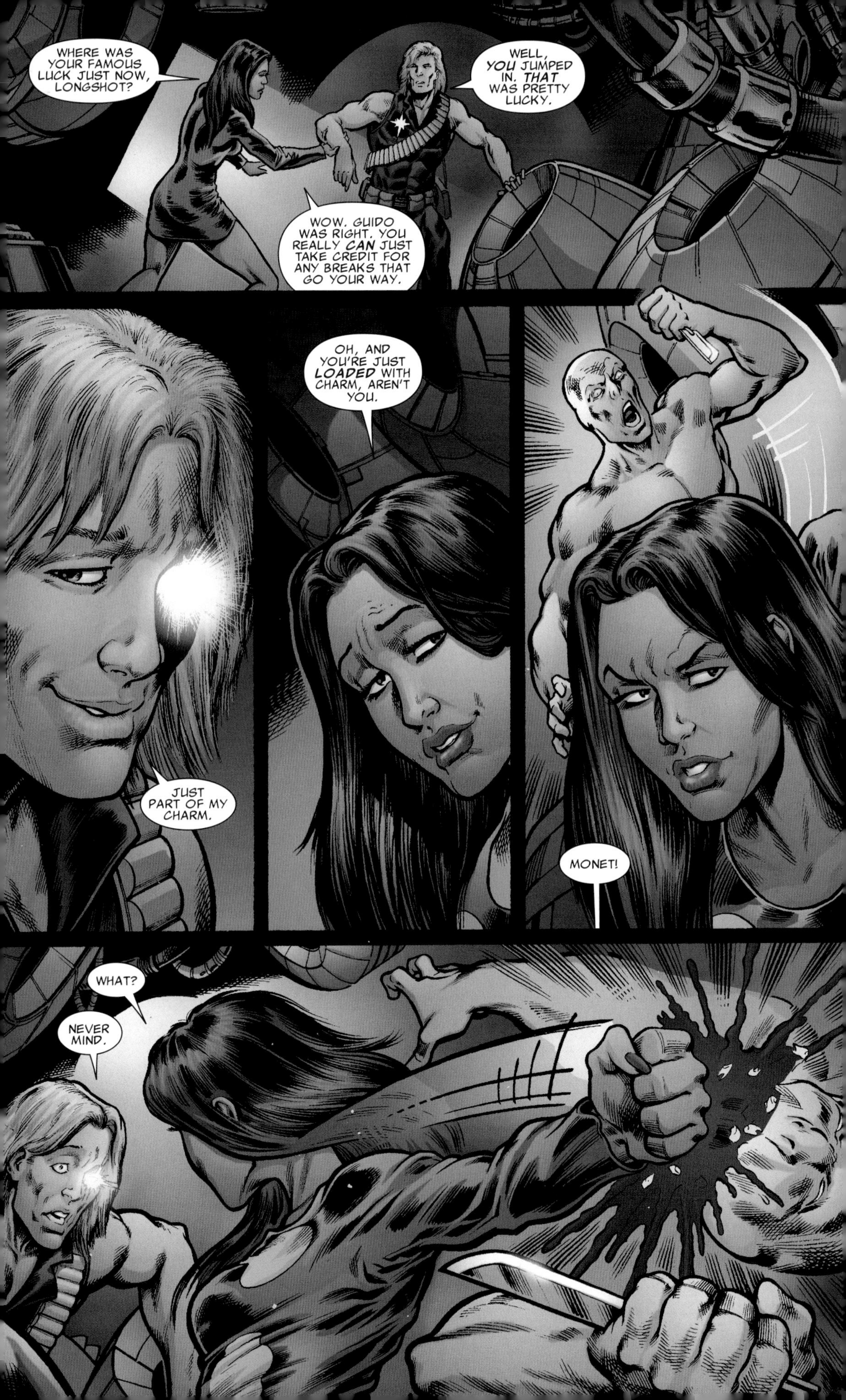
WHERE WAS YOUR FAMOUS LUCK JUST NOW, LONGSHOT?
WELL, YOU JUMPED IN. THAT WAS PRETTY LUCKY.
WOW. GUIDO WAS RIGHT. YOU REALLY CAN JUST TAKE CREDIT FOR ANY BREAKS THAT GO YOUR WAY.
JUST PART OF MY CHARM.
OH, AND YOU'RE JUST LOADED WITH CHARM, AREN'T YOU.
MONET!
WHAT?
NEVER MIND.

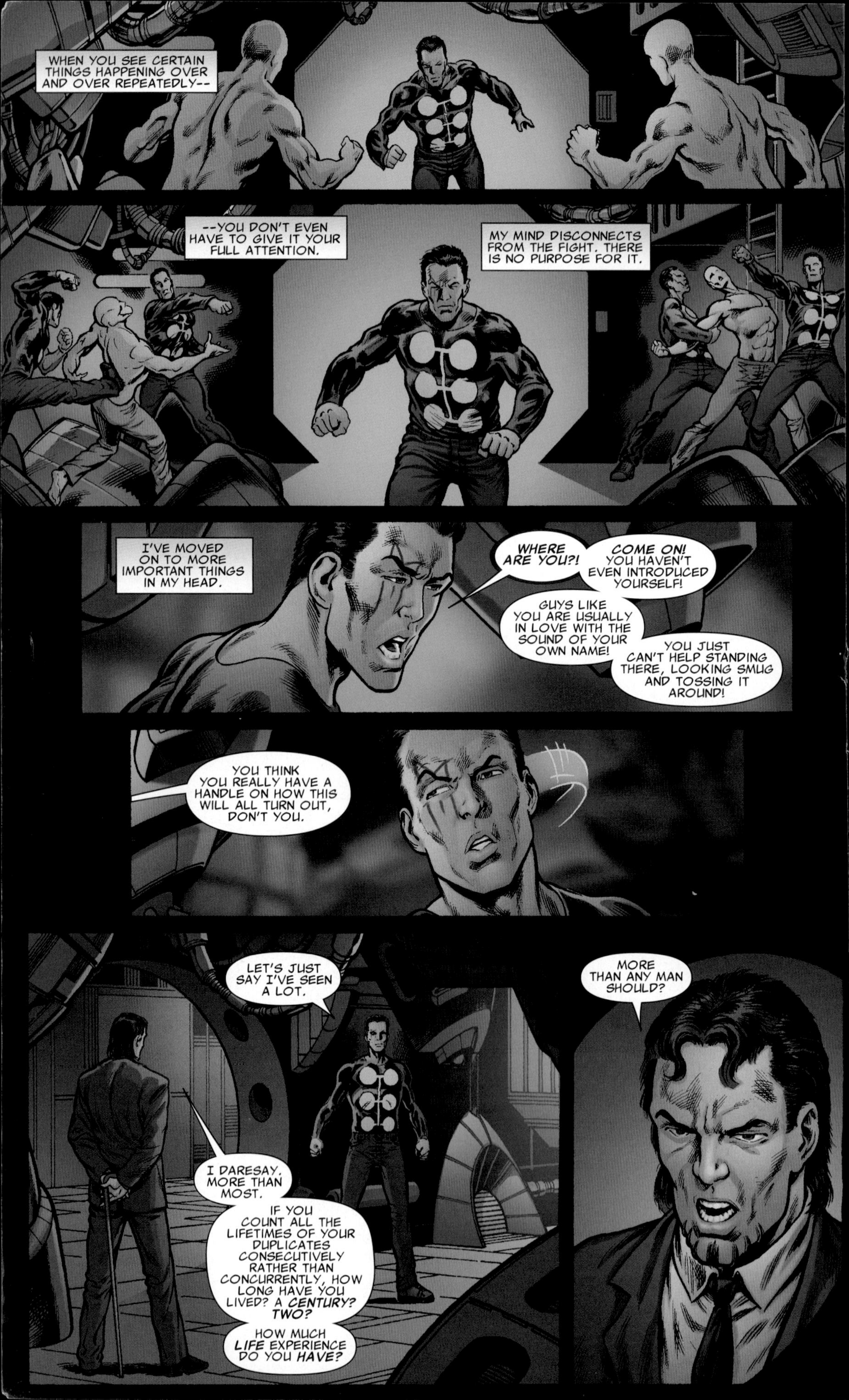
WHEN YOU SEE CERTAIN THINGS HAPPENING OVER AND OVER REPEATEDLY--
--YOU DON'T EVEN HAVE TO GIVE IT YOUR FULL ATTENTION.
MY MIND DISCONNECTS FROM THE FIGHT. THERE IS NO PURPOSE FOR IT.
I'VE MOVED ON TO MORE IMPORTANT THINGS IN MY HEAD.
WHERE ARE YOU?!
COME ON! YOU HAVEN'T EVEN INTRODUCED YOURSELF!
GUYS LIKE YOU ARE USUALLY IN LOVE WITH THE SOUND OF YOUR OWN NAME!
YOU JUST CAN'T HELP STANDING THERE, LOOKING SMUG AND TOSSING IT AROUND!
YOU THINK YOU REALLY HAVE A HANDLE ON HOW THIS WILL ALL TURN OUT, DON'T YOU.
LET'S JUST SAY I'VE SEEN A LOT.
I DARESAY. MORE THAN MOST.
IF YOU COUNT ALL THE LIFETIMES OF YOUR DUPLICATES CONSECUTIVELY RATHER THAN CONCURRENTLY, HOW LONG HAVE YOU LIVED? A CENTURY? TWO?
HOW MUCH LIFE EXPERIENCE DO YOU HAVE?
MORE THAN ANY MAN SHOULD?

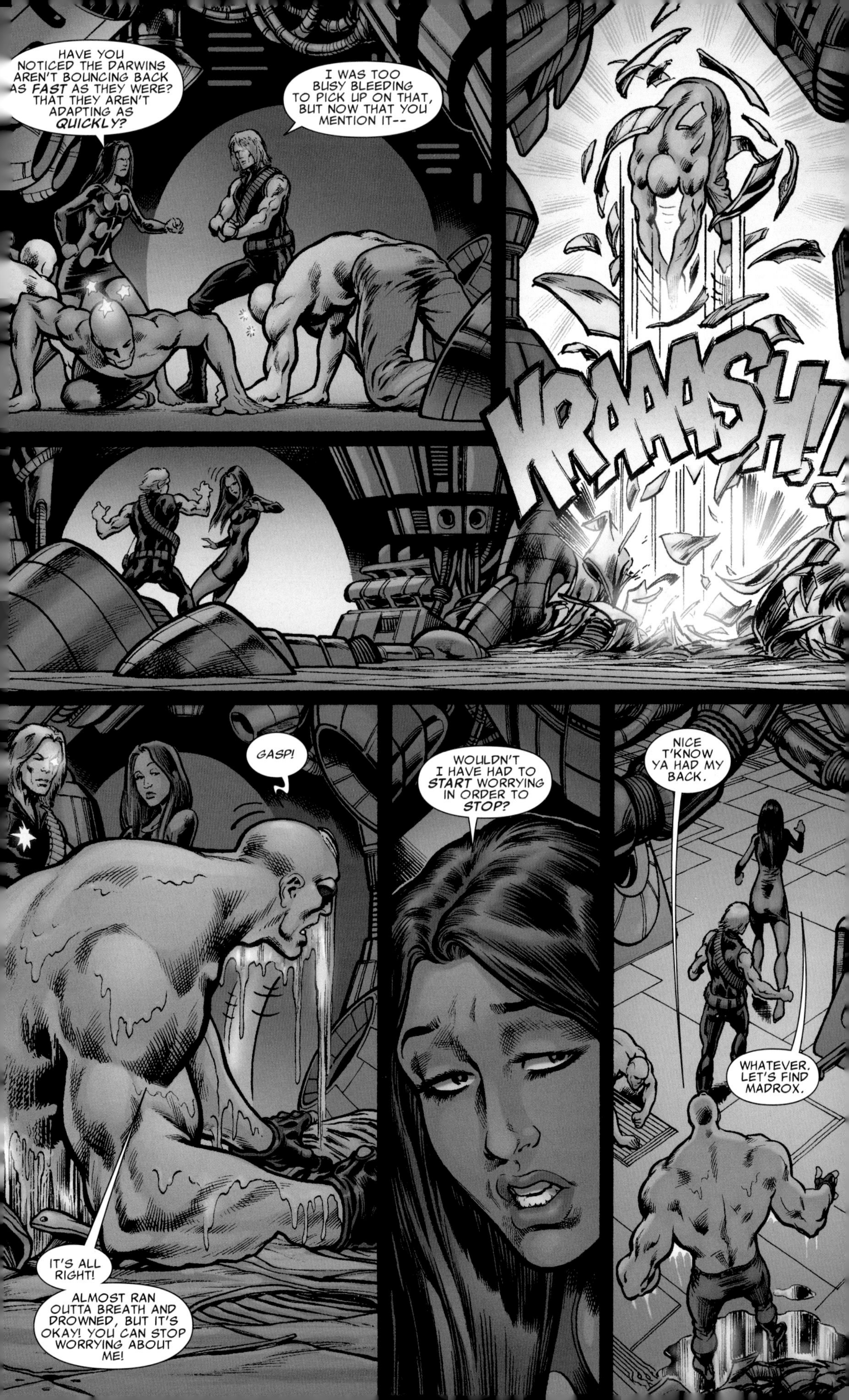

HAVE YOU NOTICED THE DARWINS AREN'T BOUNCING BACK AS FAST AS THEY WERE? THAT THEY AREN'T ADAPTING AS QUICKLY?
I WAS TOO BUSY BLEEDING TO PICK UP ON THAT, BUT NOW THAT YOU MENTION IT--
KRAAASH!!
GASP!
IT'S ALL RIGHT!
ALMOST RAN OUTTA BREATH AND DROWNED, BUT IT'S OKAY! YOU CAN STOP WORRYING ABOUT ME!
WOULDN'T I HAVE HAD TO START WORRYING IN ORDER TO STOP?
NICE T'KNOW YA HAD MY BACK.
WHATEVER. LET'S FIND MADROX.

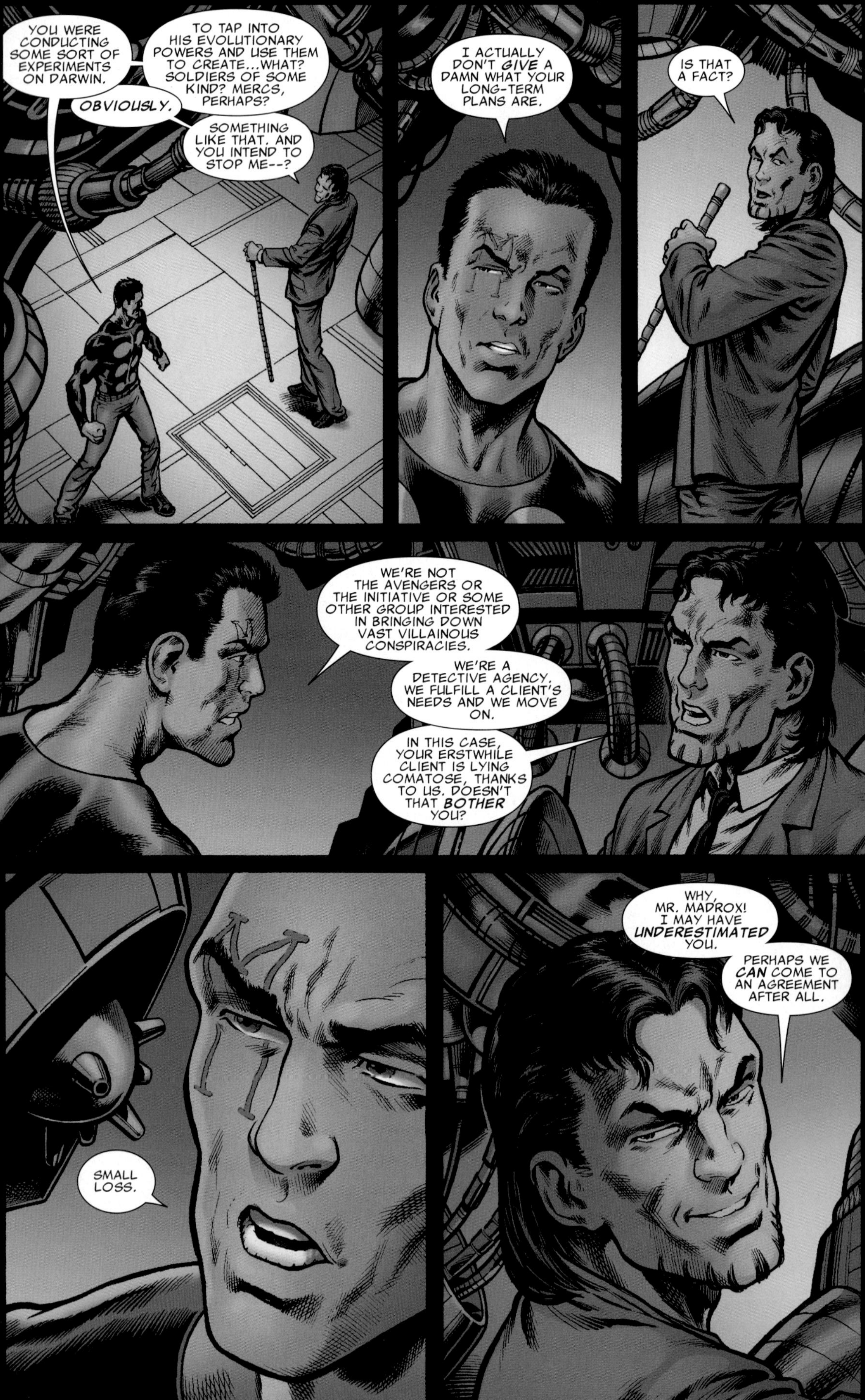
YOU WERE CONDUCTING SOME SORT OF EXPERIMENTS ON DARWIN.
TO TAP INTO HIS EVOLUTIONARY POWERS AND USE THEM TO CREATE...WHAT? SOLDIERS OF SOME KIND? MERCS, PERHAPS?
OBVIOUSLY.
SOMETHING LIKE THAT. AND YOU INTEND TO STOP ME--?
I ACTUALLY DON'T GIVE A DAMN WHAT YOUR LONG-TERM PLANS ARE.
IS THAT A FACT?
WE'RE NOT THE AVENGERS OR THE INITIATIVE OR SOME OTHER GROUP INTERESTED IN BRINGING DOWN VAST VILLAINOUS CONSPIRACIES.
WE'RE A DETECTIVE AGENCY. WE FULFILL A CLIENT'S NEEDS AND WE MOVE ON.
IN THIS CASE, YOUR ERSTWHILE CLIENT IS LYING COMATOSE, THANKS TO US. DOESN'T THAT BOTHER YOU?
SMALL LOSS.
WHY, MR. MADROX! I MAY HAVE UNDERESTIMATED YOU.
PERHAPS WE CAN COME TO AN AGREEMENT AFTER ALL.

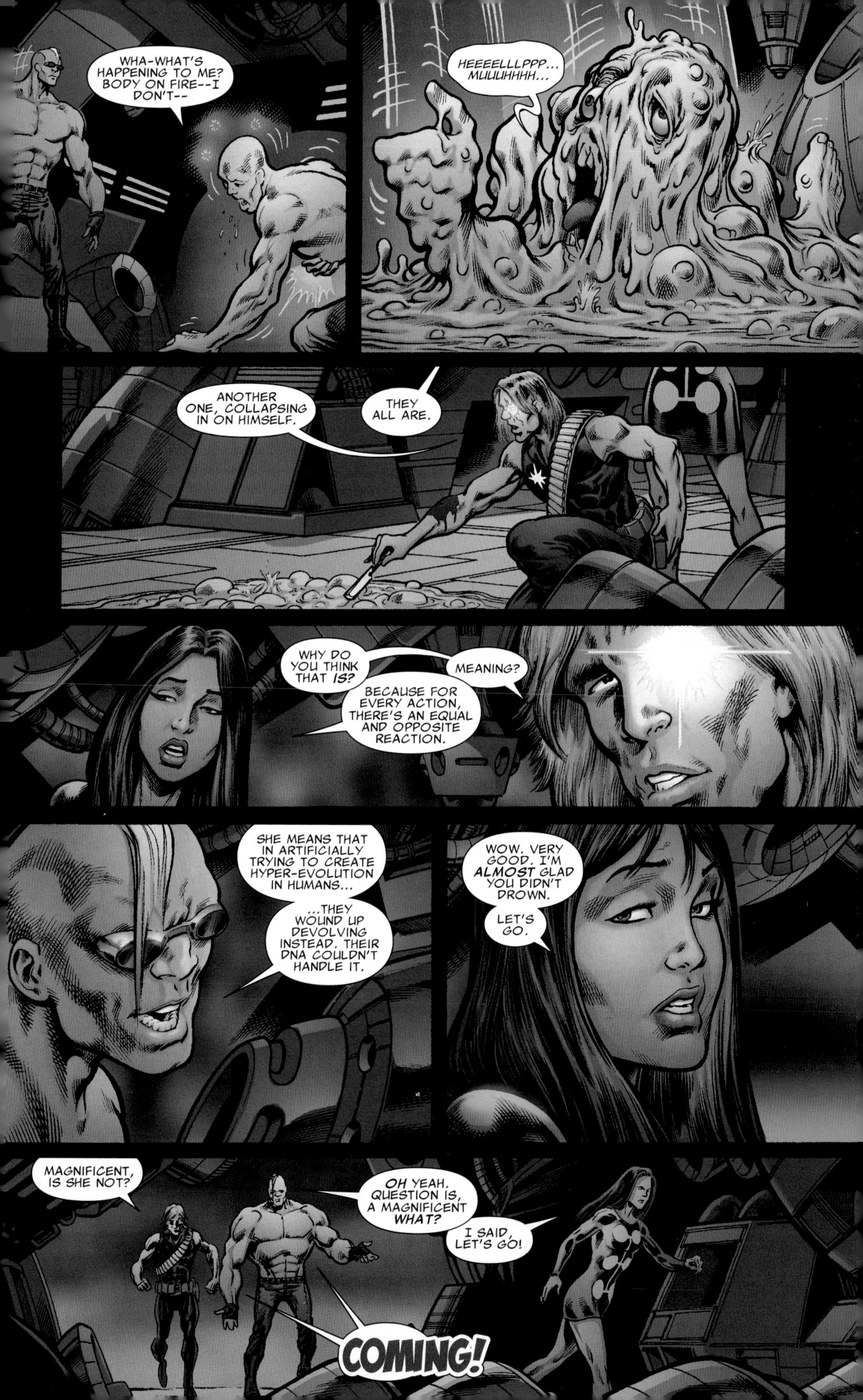
WHA-WHAT'S HAPPENING TO ME? BODY ON FIRE--I DON'T--
HEEEELLLPPP... MUUUHHHH...
ANOTHER ONE, COLLAPSING IN ON HIMSELF.
THEY ALL ARE.
WHY DO YOU THINK THAT IS?
MEANING?
BECAUSE FOR EVERY ACTION, THERE'S AN EQUAL AND OPPOSITE REACTION.
SHE MEANS THAT IN ARTIFICIALLY TRYING TO CREATE HYPER-EVOLUTION IN HUMANS...
...THEY WOUND UP DEVOLVING INSTEAD. THEIR DNA COULDN'T HANDLE IT.
WOW. VERY GOOD. I'M ALMOST GLAD YOU DIDN'T DROWN.
LET'S GO.
MAGNIFICENT, IS SHE NOT?
OH YEAH. QUESTION IS, A MAGNIFICENT WHAT?
I SAID, LET'S GO!
COMING!

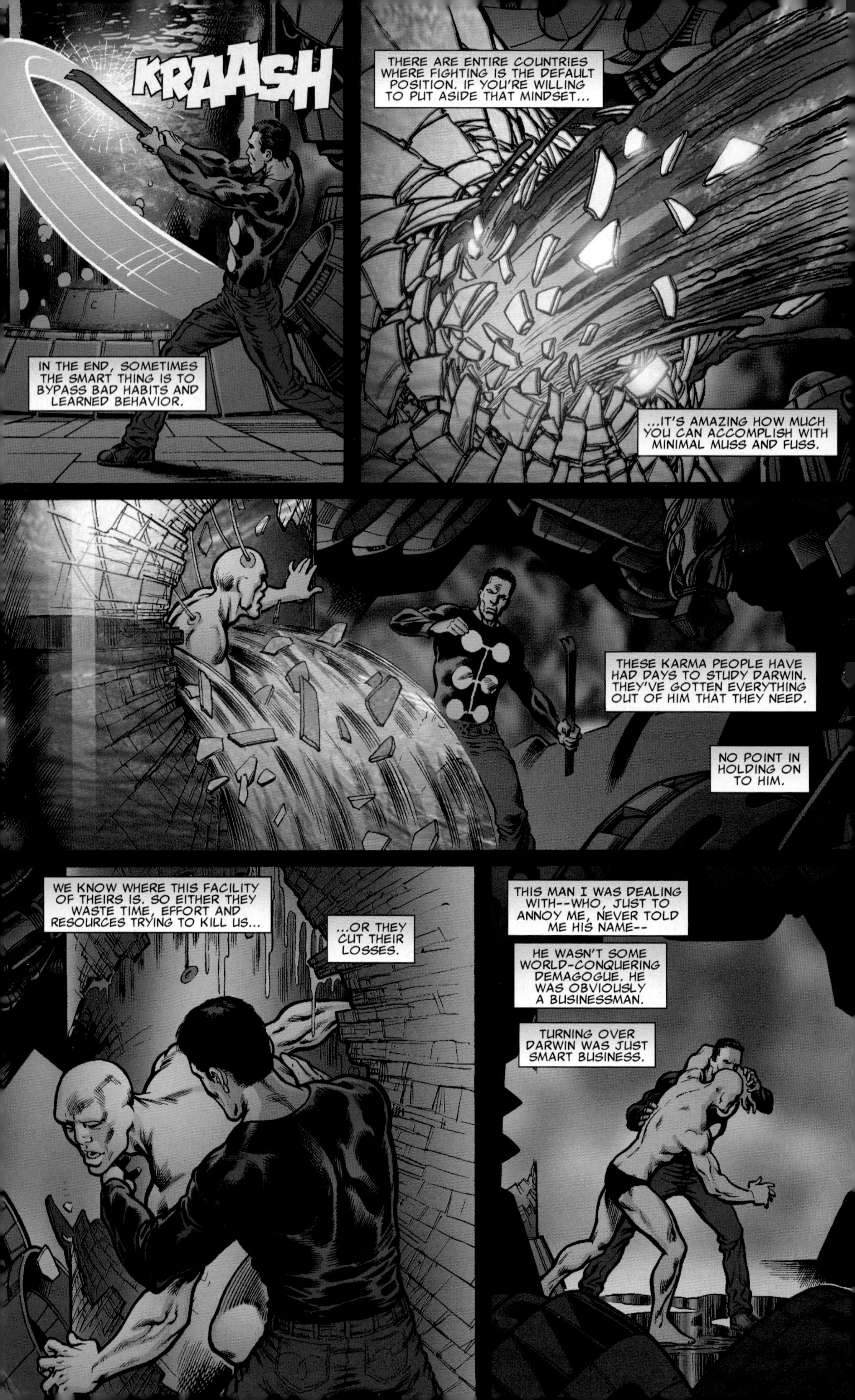
KRAASH
IN THE END, SOMETIMES THE SMART THING IS TO BYPASS BAD HABITS AND LEARNED BEHAVIOR.
THERE ARE ENTIRE COUNTRIES WHERE FIGHTING IS THE DEFAULT POSITION. IF YOU'RE WILLING TO PUT ASIDE THAT MINDSET...
...IT'S AMAZING HOW MUCH YOU CAN ACCOMPLISH WITH MINIMAL MUSS AND FUSS.
THESE KARMA PEOPLE HAVE HAD DAYS TO STUDY DARWIN. THEY'VE GOTTEN EVERYTHING OUT OF HIM THAT THEY NEED.
NO POINT IN HOLDING ON TO HIM.
WE KNOW WHERE THIS FACILITY OF THEIRS IS. SO EITHER THEY WASTE TIME, EFFORT AND RESOURCES TRYING TO KILL US...
...OR THEY CUT THEIR LOSSES.
THIS MAN I WAS DEALING WITH--WHO, JUST TO ANNOY ME, NEVER TOLD ME HIS NAME--
HE WASN'T SOME WORLD-CONQUERING DEMAGOGUE. HE WAS OBVIOUSLY A BUSINESSMAN.
TURNING OVER DARWIN WAS JUST SMART BUSINESS.

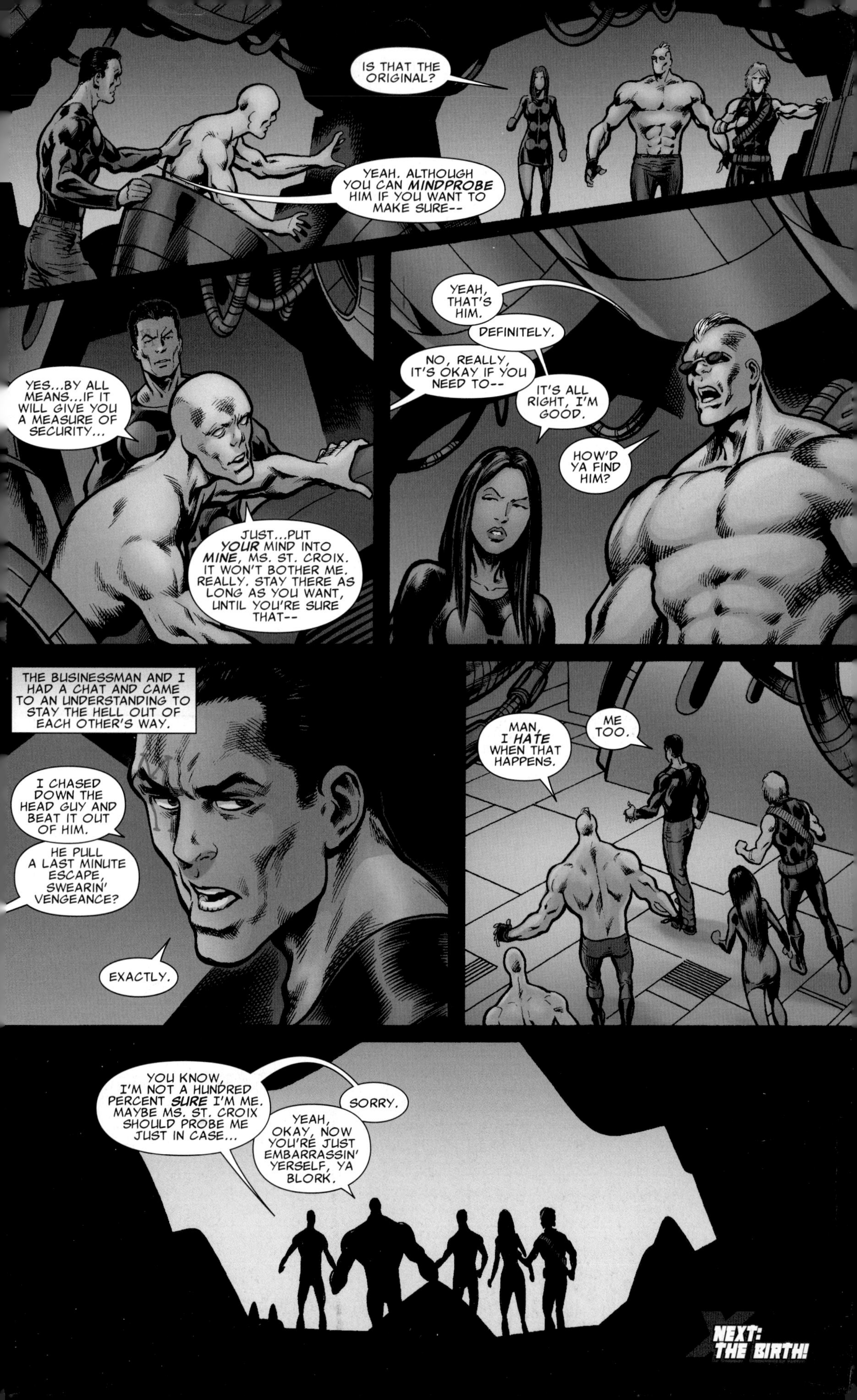
IS THAT THE ORIGINAL?
YEAH. ALTHOUGH YOU CAN MINDPROBE HIM IF YOU WANT TO MAKE SURE--
YES...BY ALL MEANS...IF IT WILL GIVE YOU A MEASURE OF SECURITY...
JUST...PUT YOUR MIND INTO MINE, MS. ST. CROIX. IT WON'T BOTHER ME. REALLY. STAY THERE AS LONG AS YOU WANT, UNTIL YOU'RE SURE THAT--
YEAH, THAT'S HIM.
DEFINITELY.
NO, REALLY, IT'S OKAY IF YOU NEED TO--
IT'S ALL RIGHT, I'M GOOD.
HOW'D YA FIND HIM?
THE BUSINESSMAN AND I HAD A CHAT AND CAME TO AN UNDERSTANDING TO STAY THE HELL OUT OF EACH OTHER'S WAY.
I CHASED DOWN THE HEAD GUY AND BEAT IT OUT OF HIM.
HE PULL A LAST MINUTE ESCAPE, SWEARIN' VENGEANCE?
EXACTLY.
MAN, I HATE WHEN THAT HAPPENS.
ME TOO.
YOU KNOW, I'M NOT A HUNDRED PERCENT SURE I'M ME. MAYBE MS. ST. CROIX SHOULD PROBE ME JUST IN CASE...
SORRY.
YEAH, OKAY, NOW YOU'RE JUST EMBARRASSIN' YERSELF, YA BLORK.
NEXT: THE BIRTH!

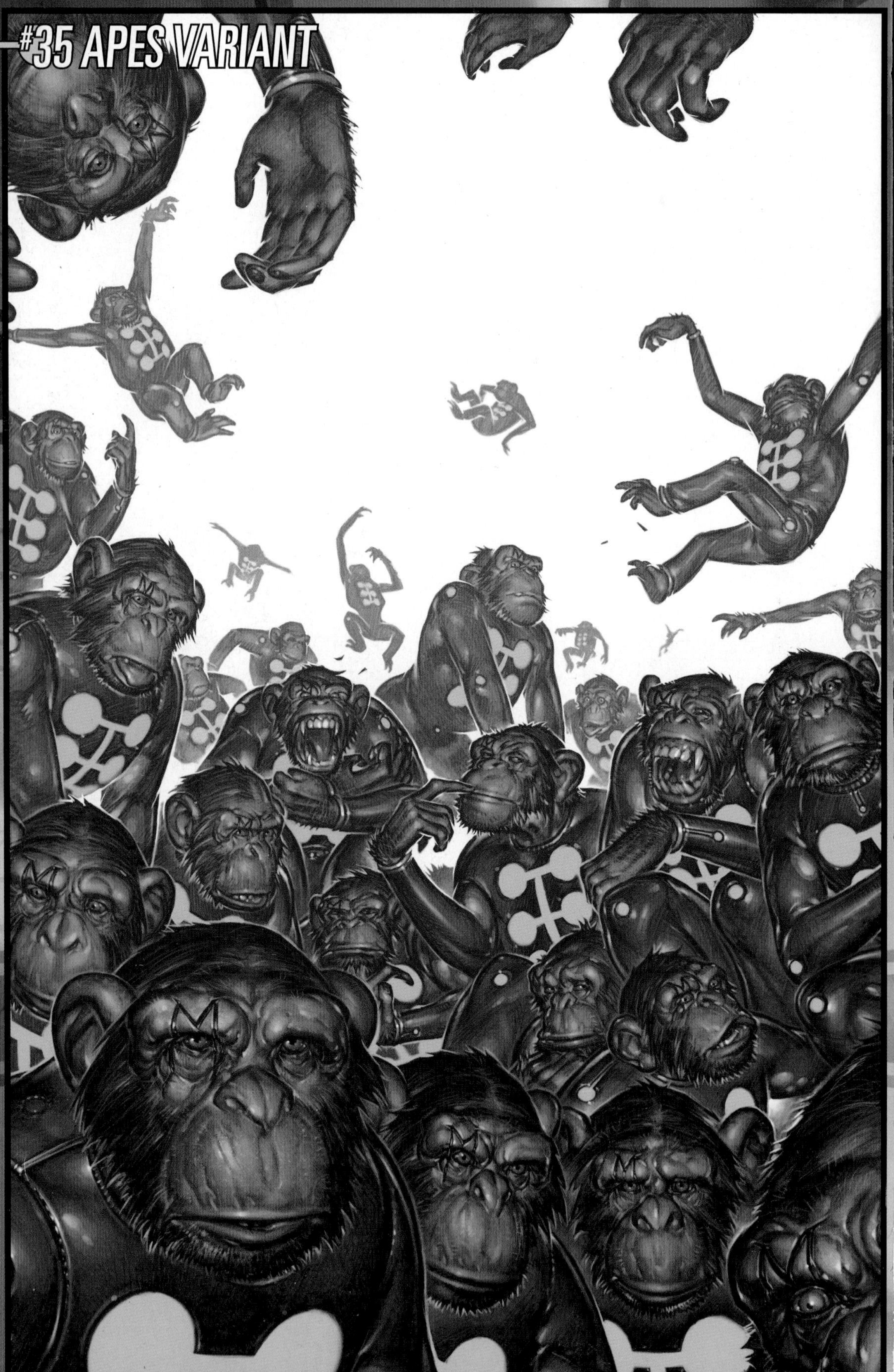

#35 APES VARIANT